British History

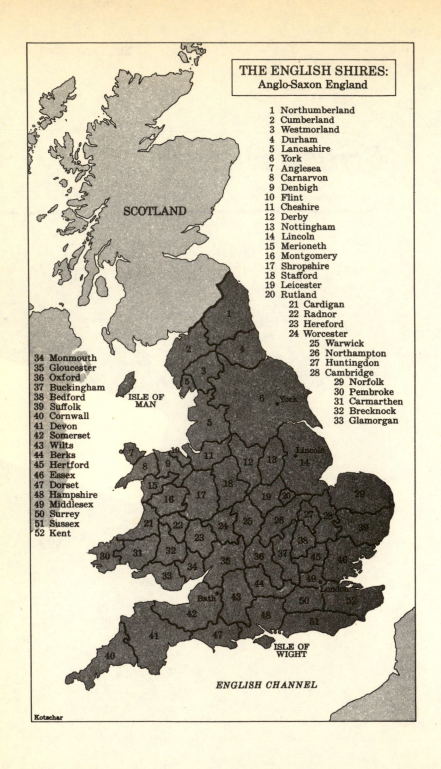

THE ENGLISH SHIRES:
Anglo-Saxon England

1 Northumberland
2 Cumberland
3 Westmorland
4 Durham
5 Lancashire
6 York
7 Anglesea
8 Carnarvon
9 Denbigh
10 Flint
11 Cheshire
12 Derby
13 Nottingham
14 Lincoln
15 Merioneth
16 Montgomery
17 Shropshire
18 Stafford
19 Leicester
20 Rutland
21 Cardigan
22 Radnor
23 Hereford
24 Worcester
25 Warwick
26 Northampton
27 Huntingdon
28 Cambridge
29 Norfolk
30 Pembroke
31 Carmarthen
32 Brecknock
33 Glamorgan

34 Monmouth
35 Gloucester
36 Oxford
37 Buckingham
38 Bedford
39 Suffolk
40 Cornwall
41 Devon
42 Somerset
43 Wilts
44 Berks
45 Hertford
46 Essex
47 Dorset
48 Hampshire
49 Middlesex
50 Surrey
51 Sussex
52 Kent

SCOTLAND

ISLE OF MAN

York

Lincoln

Bath

London

ISLE OF WIGHT

ENGLISH CHANNEL

Kotschar

HARPERCOLLINS COLLEGE OUTLINE

British History

4th Edition

Harold J. Schultz, Ph.D.
Bethel College, Kansas

HarperPerennial
A Division of HarperCollinsPublishers

To students in my history courses whose interest and questions have made the teaching and writing of British history a continuing delight.

An American BookWorks Corporation Production

Project Manager: Jonathon E. Brodman
Editor: Robert A. Weinstein

LIBRARY OF CONGRESS CATALOG CARD NUMBER 91-55399
ISBN: 0-06-467110-0

92 93 94 95 96 ABW/RRD 10 9 8 7 6 5 4 3 2 1

Contents

Preface

History is a Greek word which means, literally, "investigation." This volume of *British History* seeks to be an investigation into human history and accomplishments in that pivotal and historical island kingdom of Great Britain. Its function is to bring history to life and to offer in abbreviated form some coherence to the complexity and confusion that make up the human and historical record.

In this particular HarperCollins College Outline volume there are actually two goals: (1) to serve as a supplemental outline and condensed summary to assist students in grasping the more extensive study of British history and culture—a digest of the salient points of British history; and (2) an interpretation of the British heritage and achievements so that the book can stand on its own merits as a slim-line basic text.

British history, and hopefully this volume, can properly serve as a vehicle to understanding many of the institutions and ideas of the large English-speaking world. The inhabitants of this small island kingdom have left a legacy that extends far beyond the shores of the British Isles. Such varied achievements as the parliamentary system; common law; Shakespearean drama; the games of tennis, football, and golf; the writ of habeas corpus; the Industrial Revolution; the Anglican, Methodist, Presbyterian, and Congregational churches; and the Commonwealth of Nations that now includes fifty former territories of the British empire are all part of this legacy.

Many of the millions of British emigrants transplanted their institutions, traditions, and ideas of a fee society to the colonies. The United States was the largest of these transplantations. In fact, almost one-half of the span of American history (1607–1783) is essentially British colonial history. A. L. Rowse, the noted Elizabethan historian, in observing that the United States has picked up Britain's mantle of leadership in the Western world, argues that "America is, after all, the greatest achievement of the English people."

From pre-Roman Britain to post–World War II and the decline from greatness, this volume seeks to reveal the elements of order—of continuity and change—that mark the checkered history of Britain. Beyond the "what" and "when" and "how" of the historical narrative, a concerted effort is also made to ask "why" in order that the account may provide understanding, as well as information.

Many colleagues have contributed, either in their teaching or in their counsel, to the focus and features of this book. To Jonathon E. Brodman and Fred N. Grayson of American BookWorks Corporation, I am particularly indebted. Their encouragement and suggestions spurred my efforts in this project. Robert A. Weinstein's careful criticisms as project editor and reviewer helped immeasurably to sharpen the focus of the writing. Also, without the efficiency and word-processing skills of two very special assistants, Ilene Schmidt and Cynthia Goerzen, I would not have been able to complete this volume anywhere near the scheduled deadline.

HAROLD J. SCHULTZ

1

Celtic and Roman Britain

ca. 6000 B.C. North Sea floods the land joining Britain and the Continent

ca. 2500 B.C. Invasion of Britain by the Beaker Folk

Last Century B.C. The final migration of Celts to Britain

55 B.C. Julius Caesar invades Britain; recorded history begins

122 A.D. Emperor Hadrian orders the building of the wall dividing Scotland from England

407 A.D. Last Roman soldiers withdraw from Britain

Central to the history and character of the British people is their geographical location. Being situated twenty-one miles from the Continent makes Britain part of Europe, but with a separate and insular identity. The relation of Britain to the sea and her separation from the Continent are the keys to her history.

The early history of Britain is essentially a chronicle of invasions and migrations. Wave after wave of Continental tribes landed on British shores. After the last of these migrant settlers, the Celts, had subdued the tribes of southeast Britain, the Roman legions, in turn, subdued the Celts.

In contrast to the earlier invaders, the Romans came to Britain to rule and exploit the island, not to settle permanently. Roman rule was urban and efficient, but remained alien, and therefore only temporary in its effects.

AN ISLAND PEOPLE

Britain is an island and its history is uniquely shaped by that fact and its location just off the coast of Continental Europe. In early times the relation of Britain to the sea was largely passive, permitting wave after wave of invaders; in modern times the sea was a highway to profit and power. As an insular people Britain could oppose a standing army and the militaristic traditions linked to it. Britain was defended by the sea and its navy and became a maritime power. At first the sea isolated Britain from the more advanced civilizations around the Mediterranean. Then, as the Atlantic replaced the Mediterranean as the center of commerce and culture, Britain moved from the periphery to the center of power and world events.

The Land and Its Resources

The physical formation, climate and minerals of the country tempted the early invaders to settle and determined the paths of settlement they followed. Not having mastered nature, the successive invaders claimed the rich and accessible lowlands of southern and eastern Britain and drove the earlier inhabitants to the north and west. The physical map will show why it was so accessible from the Continent, for the land slopes downward from the highlands to the north and from the craggy coast of the Atlantic to the low, flat plains of the southeast. Because of the general slope of land from north to southeast most English rivers have their outlets on the south and the east coasts. Invaders moved inland by following the Trent, the Welland, the Nen, and the Thames rivers to the midlands. Later, these rivers doubled as main arteries of trade. In the southwest the Severn River served the same dual function for the area of the Welsh border. As the invaders reached the highlands of the north and west, they halted, and these inhospitable regions became havens for the displaced older cultures. Consequently, the Scottish Highlands, Wales, and Cornwall were inhabited by the older stocks; and to this day they are commonly called the "Celtic fringe."

The Islands

The five thousand British Isles, dominated by the two major islands of Britain (labeled *Britannia* by Julius Caesar) and Ireland, cover approximately 120,000 square miles, with the area of England totaling less than half this amount (50,331 square miles). The first human beings came to Britain in the Old Stone Age when the land was still joined to the Continent. With the closing of the Great Ice Age, the receding glaciations transformed the physical surface of the land and left it an island.

CLIMATE

Around 3500 B.C. in the Neolithic or Late Stone Age, the first agriculturalists crossed the Channel and revolutionized the existing society of cave-dwelling hunters by introducing a new way of life; they bred cattle, sowed grain, and later developed a flint-mining industry. The more temperate climate of Brittain after the Ice Ages was well suited to the growing of crops, and the southwest winds following the Gulf Stream kept England at a warmer and more equable temperature than its latitude would ordinarily permit. Although the rainfall was moderate, the oceanic climate produced fog, mist, and haze so that visitors, from Tacitus to modern tourists, have written about the wretched weather.

NATURAL RESOURCES

The temperate climate, coupled with a fairly rich soil, promoted the growing of wheat and barley. Good harbors and the long, irregular coastline encouraged fishing and ocean trade. Copper and tin were found in abundance. By smelting the two metals together, the inhabitants manufactured bronze, and so marked the close of the lengthy Stone Age. Much later, conveniently located deposits of coal and iron would support England's industrial revolution.

Prehistory of Britain

In Britain, as elsewhere, the story of early peoples can be traced through the various stone and metal ages. The migrant tribes moved westward in Europe and arrived in Britain during the Paleolithic (Old Stone) Age. Since each succeeding period or "age" was largely a transplanting from the Continent, Britain became a recipient of the migration of these peoples and the diffusion of their cultural practices in the period of prehistory.

The Stone Ages

From stone and bone tools and skeletal remains it has been calculated that humans (Homo sapiens) first appeared in Britain by way of a land bridge between 200,000 and 300,000 years ago. In the New Stone Age a more civilized race of long-headed agriculturalists (frequently designated as the Windmill Hill people) crossed the Channel and set up primitive farming communities in southern England side by side with the older hunting communities. Around 2500 B.C. these peaceful and mild-mannered settlers were attacked in turn by tall, powerful, warlike invaders from the mountainous areas of Europe. They brought with them metal implements and thereby introduced a new age of bronze.

The Beaker Folk

These latest invaders were designated as the Beaker Folk after the shape of their drinking vessels. These newcomers possessed a mastery of metal workmanship that was reflected in the variety of weapons and tools they produced. They wore woolen and linen clothes, greatly admired jewelry, but had little interest in farming. Where the earlier immigrants had worshipped Mother Earth, the Beaker Folk worshipped the Sun in temples open to the sky. Stonehenge, a circular grouping of massive stones, remains to this day a fascinating and impressive monument to their religious practices and to the engineering skill and organization of the peoples who built it.

Other immigrations followed and by 1500 B.C. the blending of these immigrant traditions established the distinctive Wessex culture in Britain: an age of bronze, an organized religion and priesthood, and a tribal aristocracy centered around a kinglike chief and a slowly evolving aristocracy.

The Celtic Invaders

The last of the early invaders were the Celts, the first conquerors of Britain about whom the Romans wrote. They transformed cultural life in the south of Britain, bringing with them the higher civilization of the Iron Age and the use of money. Once settled they founded kingdoms, instituted the priesthood, and created new art forms.

Celtic Origins

The word "Celt," in terms of British identity, is more a matter of civilization and language than race. Threatened by rival groups, the Celtic-speaking tribes of France and western Germany migrated to the British Isles to obtain relief from Continental conflicts. During the millennium before Christ, bands of Celtic invaders, armed with battle-axes and double-edged swords, landed on the south and east coasts and moved inland and as far north as Scotland.

Celtic Society

The invaders wove cloth, shaved their bodies, and made agriculture and grazing important industries. Communities of farmers lived in either hut villages or protected homesteads, and the clan—a group of families claiming descent from a common ancestor—became the center of their social organization. The two classes within Celtic society that counted most were the warriors and the priests. Over the years Celtic culture advanced as the tribes became expert in working tin, bronze, and iron; their pottery and their metal helmets indicated a growing interest and ability in the abstract decorative arts and in ornamentation. The south Britons had a gold coinage similar to that of Macedon, and their tribal leaders led a revelrous life, enriched with imported wines and luxury goods. Clearly the Celts were not primitive savages, painted with blue dye, and beyond the pale of civilization, as was once thought.

CELTIC RELIGION

Druidism originated in England and spread to Gaul (modern-day France and Belgium) and Ireland. The druids were an organized caste of priests who exercised great powers. They preached a religion of fear and immortality, worshipped various nature gods in sacred groves, and offered human sacrifices. Druid priests commanded prestige and served as judges and leaders of tribal opinion.

CELTIC BRITAIN AND GAUL

Druidism, trade, and racial affinity were three of the ties between Britain and Gaul, across the Channel. The link became even more direct in 75 B.C. when the Belgic tribes of Gaul claimed southeast Britain (modern-day Kent, Middlesex and Hertfordshire) as their kingdoms. These Gallic Celts dispersed the native Celts from the best lands of the southeast and were the first tribes to face the next invader, Caesar.

ROMAN BRITAIN

In contrast to the earlier Celt or later Saxon invaders, the Romans came to Britain to rule and exploit the island as part of a world empire, not to push back the inhabitants to the fringes of the region and settle in their place. The Roman objectives in this new method of conquest produced quite different results. Roman rule became urban and efficient. The atmosphere of the Mediterranean world with its Latin tongue, its country villas, and its new faith, Christianity, were introduced. Nevertheless their rule remained alien, and therefore only temporary in its effects.

The Roman Conquests

The annexation of Britain was scarcely a primary objective of Roman expansion, for the British Isles marked the fringe of civilization to those who ruled in imperial Rome. However, when the Romans decided to conquer and colonize Britain, their superior military and political organization was decisive.

The Invasions of Julius Caesar, 55-54 B.C.

Two attacks on Britain were made by Julius Caesar during his conquest of Gaul. Certainly one of his reasons was to punish the southern Britons who were providing aid to their kinsmen in northern Gaul. No doubt, too, Caesar's popularity and position would be enhanced by another victory that would provide tribute and slaves for his supporters in Rome and booty for his soldiers. His first expedition (55 B.C.) was a military failure, but he returned the next year with five legions. This time Caesar won several battles against Celtic armies and penetrated inland approximately to where London now stands. The Britons sued for peace, and Caesar granted a treaty on easy terms because, with renewed disturbances in Gaul, he was content with hostages and a promise of yearly tribute. The Romans then departed from Britain, and Caesar, lured on by larger stakes in Rome, crossed the Rubicon to his final triumph and tragedy.

RESULTS OF CAESAR'S INVASIONS

Caesar described his conquest graphically in his commentaries *On the Gallic Wars*, but his sorties into Britain had few permanent results except to increase trade between Britain and the Latinized province of Gaul and to permit Roman traders and settlers to enter Britain peacefully. Caesar's invasions also proved that the Romans could conquer Britain at their convenience if they were ready to devote time and men to that purpose. Almost a hundred years passed before it was convenient to do so.

Later Roman Conquests

Following Caesar's invasions Rome was preoccupied with more immediate matters and Britain received only perfunctory attention from the rulers in Rome. Under Emperor Claudius Rome renewed its interest, and this time Roman military and administrative control lasted nearly four centuries. Roman Britain was divided administratively into two units: a civil district in the southeast and a zone of military occupation in the highlands.

THE COMING OF CLAUDIUS

In 43 A.D. Emperor Claudius ordered Aulus Plautius to invade Britain. The decision was made because the emperor was anxious for glory and irritated by a revolt in Gaul instigated by the druids; and also because his Gallic origins increased his interest in conquering Britain. The British defenders, who were led by Caractacus, a son of Cunobelinus (Shakespeare's "Cymbeline"), displayed a vigorous but disunited resistance. The Roman historian Tacitus later commented upon this fact: "Our greatest advantage in coping with tribes so powerful is that they do not act in concert. Seldom is it that two or three states meet together to ward off a common danger. Thus, while they fight singly, they all are conquered."[*] Claudius himself came for a brief period to command the legions. Within three years Plautius reduced the divided Britons to guerrilla reprisals and brought southeast Britain under Roman rule.

QUEEN BOUDICCA'S REVOLT

During the governorships of Scapula (47–54) and Suetonius (59–61) the Roman occupation extended northward and westward. While Suetonius was suppressing the druids at their sacred center of worship in Anglesey, the Iceni under Queen Boudicca revolted (61). The Iceni and their neighboring tribes attacked the Romans and the Britons who fraternized with them in the towns of Colchester, London, and Verulamium (St. Albans), in retaliation for the Roman confiscation of their property and the public outrages com-

---

[*] *The Complete Works of Tacitus.* (New York: Random House, 1942), p. 684.

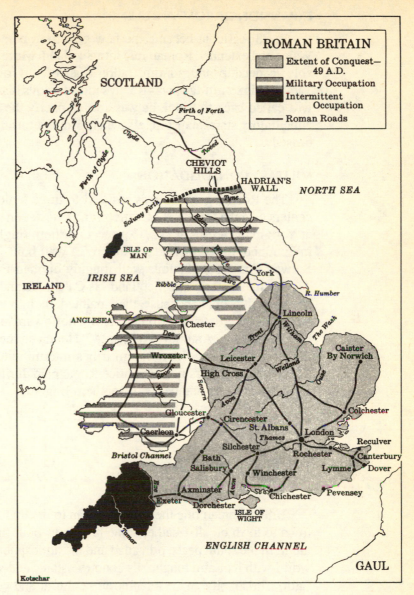

Fig. 1.1

mitted against their queen and her daughters. Tens of thousands were massacred in the uprising. Governor Suetonius returned with his legion and crushed the revolt in a crucial battle; Boudicca committed suicide, and Roman vengeance was inflicted upon the rebellious Britons.

EXPANSION OF ROMAN RULE

In 78 Agricola became the new governor, completed the conquest of Wales and extended Roman rule into Scotland. More is known of Agricola's able leadership and administration than of any other governor because Tacitus, his son-in-law, was Rome's most famous historian. Before Agricola was called back to Rome he was able to pacify the south of Britain by his conciliatory statesmanship; elsewhere Roman military expansion virtually ceased.

MILITARY CONSOLIDATION

The Roman garrison was reduced to three legions located at strategic centers near the frontiers—Caerleon and Chester on the border of Wales and at York in the north. In 122, to protect northern England from hostile tribes in Scotland, Emperor Hadrian ordered a wall built from the Tyne River to Solway Firth. This famous wall roughly divided England from Scotland. The Romans referred to "Scotland" as Caledonia and called its people Picts, or painted people, because they painted their bodies. A later emperor, Antonius Pius, extended Roman control northward and constructed a second fortification, the Antonine Wall, in 143. However, the Romans overextended their resources and the northern tribes intermittently overran both walls. These northern wars were the price Rome paid during these three centuries for the protection and peace of southern England.

PAX ROMANA

Under Roman rule the Britons began to live in towns and traveled from town to town on all-weather stone highways built for rapid military movement. In the south peace prevailed and the atmosphere of the Mediterranean world with its Latin tongue, its country estates and villas, and its dominant faith, Christianity, made a temporary cultural and commercial impact. But the Romans did not teach the Britons how to govern or how to defend themselves. They were dependent upon Roman rule for their peace as well as for their commerce and industry.

Roman Institutions

The Roman conquerors imposed on the Britons their imperial administrative structure which included racial and religious toleration and respect for local chiefs and customs as long as no political opposition was involved. Since Romans were convinced that civilization was based on urban life, the first thing they did was to build cities and the country village around which more efficient farming and cattle-raising developed.

ROMAN ADMINISTRATION

Between the reigns of Claudius (43) and Severus (211) the province of Britain was administered by Roman governors whose duties included maintaining peace, collecting taxes, and providing justice. For local government the Romans, like the British later in India and Africa, employed "indirect rule" by permitting loyal Celtic chiefs to continue to exercise authority over their tribesmen. On the frontiers the army administered the surrounding area, but in the Romano-British south, several privileged cities enjoyed self-government. In the cantons (tribal areas) the magistrates in Roman togas were usually local chiefs. This policy served both to Romanize Celtic leadership and to minimize friction between ruler and ruled. In the later years of Roman rule, after several ambitious generals had used their legions in Britain to defy the emperor, and after increasing raids from the Scots and the Picts had jeopardized Roman defenses, Britain was divided into two, and then four, provinces.

Roman Withdrawal

By the fourth century, the declining power of the Roman Empire encouraged the Picts, the Scots, and raiders from northern Europe to harass Roman outposts and to force the Romans to draw in their defensive borders. As the empire became more threatened by political factionalism and barbarian attacks from the east, Roman legions evacuated Britain to fight elsewhere and never returned. The last Roman soldier left the island in 407, and Britain, which had been defended by Rome for over three hundred years, had to fend helplessly for itself. Invaders now entered the country with ease and killed or displaced the Romanized Britons of the south and east.

Roman Achievements

Roman contributions to Britain were largely material. They built towns and established such features of urban life as forums, public baths, indoor plumbing, and amphitheaters. Joining these Romanized towns were a network of splendid stone highways that permitted the rapid movement of troops and commerce. The new city of London at the hub of this road system became the chief port of entry for commerce with the rest of the empire. The tradition of town houses and country estates (or villas) was another innovation. The urbanized Britons probably lived more comfortably under the Romans than at any other time until the nineteenth century, but some two-thirds of the Britons lived neither in town nor villas and Latin civilization made little impact on them. When Roman rule ended only the roads continued in use to remind the invading Saxons of Rome; in Wales a Celtic version of the Christian faith prospered, and Christianity was the only institution to survive the departure of the Romans. Perhaps, therefore, the greatest fact in the Roman occupation is a noteworthy negative fact—that the Roman conquerors did not succeed in permanently Latinizing Britain as they Latinized France (Gaul).

The early history of Britain is one of invasion with each wave of invaders establishing a more advanced cultural and political pattern in southeast Britain, but having only a marginal impact in either their government or presence in present-day Wales or Scotland.

The Romans transported their urban life and Roman government to Britain and brought a superior system of roads as well as Christianity to Celtic Britain. But they failed to teach the Britons how to sustain Roman administration or how to defend themselves; thus when the legions withdrew from the island the Britons were once again easy prey for the next invaders.

Selected Readings

Frere, Sheppard S. *Britannia: A History of Roman Britain* (1978)

Hawkins, Gerald S. *Stonehenge Decoded* (1965)

Laing, Lloyd. *Celtic Britain* (1979)

Myres, J. N. L. *The English Settlements* (1986)

Richmond, I. A. *Roman Britain* (1964)

Rivet, A. L. G. *Town and Country in Roman Britain* (1964)

Salway, Peter. *Roman Britain* (1981)

Tacitus, *On Britain and Germany* (1960)

2

Anglo-Saxon Supremacy and Conversion to Christianity

The Anglo-Saxon settlement that followed Roman rule established the fundamental character of Britain more than any other influx of immigrants. From the Anglo-Saxons England received its name, its language, its largest ethnic group, its shires, and, for the first time, political unity as a single kingdom, even though it lacked the necessary machinery for making the king powerful enough to govern his kingdom effectively.

When the Roman legions left the British Isles, Christianity did not leave with them. The Celtic Christian faith, from its center of Iona in the Irish Sea, and Latinized Christianity, with its ecclesiastical headquarters at Canterbury, blossomed in both moral leadership and scholarly achievement.

THE ANGLO-SAXON CONQUEST

The British Isles were so situated that they were equally accessible to the civilizations of northern and southern Europe. Taking advantage of the Roman retreat from the island, the war-like tribes of northwestern Germany initially terrorized and eventually settled in Britain. These Nordic invaders came in small bands under several chieftains and lacked any kind of unified command; but the cumulative effect was to erase a superior Roman civilization and replace it with a less advanced culture that was illiterate and largely untouched by Latin Christianity or the Mediterranean world.

The Northern Invaders

The Anglo-Saxons conquered the Britons in a fashion quite different from that of the Roman legions. Instead of a disciplined army of occupation the Nordic warriors crossed the Channel in shallow boats on sporadic forays and were followed years later by migrant clans of settlers. The conquest was never carried out systematically, and the invaders found it much easier to fight the Britons than to live peacefully together.

ANGLO-SAXON ORIGINS

The three dominant Nordic tribes that made these successful sorties into Britain were the Angles, the Saxons, and the Jutes. Hailing from the Jutland peninsula and northern Germany, they shared a common love of the sea and traced the descent of their kings from the god Woden. Unlike their neighboring Germanic tribes, they had rarely traded or fought with the Romans nor had they come under the influence of Roman civilization or Christianity. They brought with them their Germanic culture with its rugged code of justice and loyalty to a chief or military leader. Although these tribesmen were usually farmers, they were more widely known as sailors of great skill whose zest for piracy and warfare made them the terror of more civilized neighbors. When the southward invasion of the crumbling Roman Empire was preempted by their neighboring Germanic groups, these tribes took to the sea in their longboats and made Britain their prize.

Nature of the Invasion

The Anglo-Saxon conquest continued intermittently for two centuries; however, written records of the invasions are fragmentary at best and biased against the invaders. The Venerable Bede supports the traditional claim that the invasions began in the middle of the fifth century when two Jutish leaders, Hengist and Horsa, were invited to help the Britons defend themselves against repeated attacks by the Picts and the Scots from the north. Other details are provided by the Welsh monk Gildas in a tract, written in the first part of the sixth century, in which he bemoans the suffering and massacre of his countrymen at the hands of the Saxon invaders. However, we do know that the invaders first came for plunder; later they moved inland and decided to settle. About 500 A.D. the Britons temporarily halted the invasion with a victory at Mount Badon—perhaps under the British general Arthur (the legendary King Arthur of the Round Table and Camelot).

OUTCOME OF THE INVASION

For the most part, the gradual Saxon infiltration of the Romano-British southeast encountered no great resistance. The disunited Britons lacked spirit and strategy in facing both the invaders from the south and the Scots and Picts from the north. The outcome was the gradual replacement of the Roman-Celtic culture of central England with the more primitive culture of the Anglo-Saxons; the Britons were either killed or enslaved, or fled to the isles. However, the new invaders, like their Roman predecessors, did not triumph in the Celtic fringe. Particularly in central England, Roman cities were reduced to ruins since the Anglo-Saxons continued their style of living in the open countryside. Once settled, the Anglo-Saxons broke yet another Roman pattern—the involvement with Continental affairs.

The Heptarchy

Lacking a tradition of national unity or a single leader to unify their conquests, the marauding tribes carved out separate kingdoms in England. Gradually seven kingdoms, known as the heptarchy, emerged from the welter of rival claimants. Kent was occupied by the Jutes; the three kingdoms of Essex, Sussex and Wessex were settled by the Saxons; and the Angles claimed East Anglia, Mercia, and Northumbria. At times a common *Bretwalda* (Britain-ruler) imposed temporary unity over these kingdoms. Kent was the first dominant kingdom, especially during the reign of King Ethelbert (ca. 552–616). Northumbria succeeded Kent as the leading state in the early seventh century and was superseded by Mercia and Wales in 632.

OFFA II

The last of the Mercian overlords, Offa II, ruled from 757 to 796. During these years he extended his kingdom north and west, codified laws, and won recognition from the pope and Charlemagne. Offa conquered Wessex and established supremacy over all England south of the Humber; he is often considered the first overlord to be recognized as "king of the whole of the land of the English." With his death the Mercian supremacy of two hundred years passed in 802 to Wessex under King Egbert (775–839). Egbert defeated the Mercians, and his son Ethelwulf continued the consolidation of Wessex; but even before Egbert's death the Danes were making their first raids along the English coast.

THE RETURN OF CHRISTIANITY

Christianity did not desert the British Isles with the Roman legions. The Celtic Christian faith, although detached from Rome, remained vital in Wales through the years of Saxon encroachments. In 597 Latinized Christianity returned to Britain and eventually triumphed over both the Celtic church and the pagan religion of the Saxons. With the Roman Church reestablished, England once again made contact with the language, law, and administrative organization of Mediterranean civilization.

The Christian Faith

The new message from Rome and from the Celtic island of Iona was undoubtedly foreign to the Nordic tradition. Instead of a warrior's religion that reflected such traits of their culture as physical valor and feasts for martial heroes, Christianity spoke of love, repentance, and redemption. It suggested great hope, yet, at the same time, great fear of the afterlife. It also, in the organization of the Roman Catholic Church, retained the character and forms of the civil administration of the Western Roman Empire. The medieval Church, more than any other political or cultural organization, was an institutional legacy of the Roman Empire.

Celtic Christianity

For two hundred years Christianity in Britain was almost severed from Roman influence. During this time the Celtic (Welsh and Irish) church prospered in adversity; Christianity frequently was the badge of distinction separating the Celts from their pagan attackers. The new faith with its ascetic idealism and consummate dedication grew rapidly in the fifth and sixth centuries. From 432 to 461 Saint Patrick of Britain converted Ireland and founded a church more famous for the high degree of learning and autonomy of its monasteries than for its episcopal organization (church government administered through bishops). An Irish monk, Saint Columba, brought the faith to western Scotland in the next century. Missionaries set out from his monastery on the island of Iona in the Irish Sea to convert the Picts in Scotland, and later won converts in England and on the Continent. In 617 Oswald of Northumbria became a Christian during his exile in Iona and,

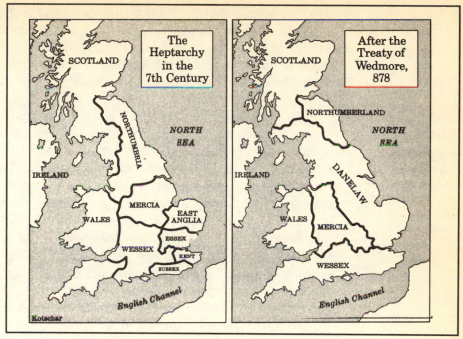

Fig. 2.1 Anglo-Saxon England

after becoming king in 634, assisted Celtic missionaries in introducing the Christian faith to all Northumbria.

Roman Christianity

In 597 Pope Gregory I, as part of his effort to convert the conquerors of the Roman Empire, sent the Benedictine monk Augustine, to Britain with forty missionaries. King Ethelbert of Kent cordially received the missionary party since his Frankish wife was already a Christian. Within a year the monks converted Ethelbert and made his capital, Canterbury, the seat of the archbishopric—a position it still holds today. In the seventh century Christianity gradually enlarged its influence in the heptarchy. When a king became a Christian, he would usually decree that Christianity was the official religion of his kingdom. Thus by the middle of the seventh century most of Britain had been converted to either Celtic or Roman Christianity, and the conflict between paganism and Christianity was replaced by a rivalry between two forms of Christianity.

SYNOD OF WHITBY, 664

Because the Celtic church survived and prospered outside the jurisdiction of Roman Catholicism, it developed differences on several matters of polity and theology. It preferred, for example, a decentralized or autonomous church organization, a simpler liturgy, and a different date for Easter; the Celtic clergy even shaved their heads in a different manner. When the rivalry could not be reconciled and the conflict left King Oswy of Northumbria with a divided church (and citizenry) in his kingdom, an ecclesiastical conference was summoned to settle the matter. Impressed by the political and cultural advantages of identifying his faith with the Latin world, Oswy decided in favor of the Roman communion. The Celtic churchmen gradually withdrew to Iona, leaving the Roman Church to organize England.

The Roman Church in England

Five years after the Synod of Whitby, Theodore of Tarsus became the new Archbishop. His organizing and administrative abilities were manifested in the precedents and reforms that shaped the organization of the English church. He set up regular church councils and laid the groundwork for the modern parish system. By providing counsel to rulers and offering the one basis for unity among feuding kingdoms, the power of the clergy increased. Under Theodore's successors the Church flourished both in missionary enterprise and in the dissemination of culture. It sent missionaries to the Continent and established schools in England whose graduates provided moral leadership and scholarly achievement. The outstanding caliber of this scholarship is exemplified by the "father of English history," the Venerable Bede (673–735), whose broad historical vision in his *Ecclesiastical History of the English People* caught for the first time the unity of the English as a people and, also, as part of a greater unity—the Church Universal. In Northumbria, in particular, the new learning and new art forms flourished. By the eighth century English scholarship was at least the equivalent of that in western Europe, and Christianity had again brought Britain back into the mainstream of western civilization.

ALFRED THE GREAT AND THE DANISH THREAT

Often considered the greatest of the Anglo-Saxon kings, Alfred well deserved the compliment. Scholar, educator, and military hero, he saved southern England from another submersion by Nordic invaders. His successful defense against the Danes preserved the identity of Anglo-Saxon Wessex and strengthened the Christian faith while his achievements as a scholar, translator, and educator gave his people a valuable literature in their own tongue.

The Danish Conquest

At the beginning of the ninth century the Anglo-Saxons experienced pirateering and pillage similar to that which they had inflicted on the Britons three hundred years earlier. The invaders were Norsemen (or Vikings) who hailed from Scandinavia. Their attacks on the British Isles were part of the great Viking expansion reaching from Russia to Greenland; the terror of their raids scourged European coasts for over two hundred years. In Britain, Viking attacks shifted in the middle of the ninth century from plundering expeditions to settlement as a large army of conquest landed and moved inland in 865. These invaders systematically pillaged and then seized the land and settled among the English population. The kings of Wessex repulsed the invaders on several occasions; but soon the kingdoms of Northumbria and East Anglia were destroyed and Mercia bought temporary peace with ransom money. By 870 only Wessex remained free of Danish control.

Alfred of Wessex

In 871, Alfred, the youngest son of King Ethelwulf, succeeded his brother, Ethelred, as king of Wessex. Already a military veteran at the age of twenty-two, Alfred halted the Danish advance that year, and a temporary truce was concluded while the Danes organized the rest of England. After repeated attacks in 876 and 878 Wessex was finally overrun by the Danes, and Alfred escaped only by hiding in the swamps of Somerset.

PEACE OF CHIPPENHAM, 878, AND GUTHRUM'S PEACE, 886

Rallying his scattered supporters, Alfred decisively defeated the Danes and their leader, Guthrum, at Edington—the turning point in the war. The peace treaty made at Chippenham imposed two demands on the Danes: Guthrum must accept baptism as a Christian, and the Danes must leave Wessex. Additional battles followed as more Danish invaders arrived and joined their kinsmen against Alfred. It was during these years that Alfred built England's first navy, erected strategic fortifications as places of refuge for his subjects, and remodeled the local militia (or *fyrd*) into active and reserve units. After seizing London in 886, Alfred was recognized as not only king of Wessex, but king of all England. That same year he concluded the Treaty of Wedmore with Guthrum which defined the boundary between Danish and English authority, with the Danish north and east identified as the Danelaw.

PEACETIME LEADERSHIP

Alfred's achievements do not end with his outstanding generalship. Danish raids had undermined law and order and had destroyed monasteries and churches; schooling and Christianity were in decline. The King showed his many talents beyond military generalship by leading a religious and literary revival. He hired the few scholars available to teach in his court school and expected royal officials to follow suit by educating themselves and, then, those around them. Alfred also translated important books from Latin into English, adding prefaces that revealed artistry and scholarship. His conception of an English nation also stimulated the writing of the

Anglo-Saxon Chronicle which recorded the narrative of England to his time. Alfred also kept in constant contact with Rome and with leaders on the Continent. He was Saxon England's greatest lawgiver, and toward the end of his reign he issued a code of laws for the Anglo-Saxon kingdoms. More than any previous king, he won the affection of his subjects and is the only ruler in British history who is known as "the Great."

ANGLO-SAXON INSTITUTIONS AND SOCIETY

The Anglo-Saxon tribes transplanted their Germanic institutions to Britain, but these practices did not unify the English people as much as did the monarchy and the Church. Whatever political unity was realized before Alfred was the consequence of the individual abilities of the monarch, for the king was the government. In contrast, the Church provided an ongoing parish organization and a common faith. Socially, inequality was recognized as a fact of life; each freeman had his rights, but these rights differed markedly from class to class.

Political Organization

The gradual appearance of some semblance of "national" unity was the most striking feature of the later Anglo-Saxon period. From dozens of tribal kings there emerged a single kingdom depending largely for survival on the personal power of the king. However, this movement toward unity and centralization failed to produce an adequate administrative structure; only substantial remodeling (by the Normans) would insure its survival. In contrast, local government introduced in Saxon England became an integral part of English constitutional practice.

KINGSHIP

At the center of government stood the king, who wielded full, but by no means absolute, power; treason against him was the most serious of all crimes. Royal power and prestige grew as the kingdom enlarged its boundaries and as the Church found it prudent to support the monarchy. The trend toward centralization was kept in check by limited revenue, a small staff of administrators, and the jealous guarding of local patriotism and practices. Aside from the *Danegeld* (a direct land tax on the whole kingdom), the king had few rights to tax. He derived his revenue from rents on his estates or from fees and fines, and, in addition, he had the right to exact personal work or services from his subjects.

THE WITAN

A weakness in Anglo-Saxon government was the lack of any fixed principle of royal succession. The Crown was usually inherited, but in practice the leading noblemen selected the new king from any member of the royal family. Most of these nobles, along with influential bishops and court officials, were members of the witan, which was an advisory council selected by the king. The witan served as the highest court in the land and assisted the king in framing decrees. Since only a royal summons could call the witan into session, it could not serve as a regular restraint on the power of the king. However, the king's consultation with this body helped set a precedent for the demands of consultative bodies in later centuries.

LOCAL GOVERNMENT

In the later Anglo-Saxon period most of England was divided into administrative districts known as shires. These began first in the kingdom of Wessex. As Wessex, under Alfred, expanded its authority into Mercia and the Danelaw, these districts were also established on the Wessex model. Four levels of local government evolved.

Shire. The shire (called "county" after the Norman Conquest) was the largest unit. Some shires marked the boundaries of early kingdoms, such as Kent; others took the name of the town which administered their areas, as Worcestershire. The chief official in the shire was the *ealderman*, who was originally the king's representative, but his office later became hereditary and more autonomous. A more direct agent of the king was the *shire reeve* (sheriff), who collected rents from the crown lands. When the king's powers grew under the Normans, so did the sheriff's, at the expense of the local earl (a nobleman of high rank). The bishop was the third important official of the shire.

Hundreds. Each shire was divided into several hundreds. Their boundaries may have been based originally on one hundred "hides" or men. One hide commonly consisted of an estate sufficient to support the family of an individual warrior. Each hundred, like the shire, had its own assembly or *moot*, and was presided over by the *hundred reeve*. Freemen elected the leaders of the hundred and participated in the sessions of the *hundred moot* which handled the bulk of local court cases.

Tun. The tun or agricultural village was the next level of local government. Urban life was not characteristic of the Anglo-Saxons, and the township was more of an agricultural community than a modern town. Village inhabitants met to draw lots for land tillage, but handled little legal or political business.

Borough. The last division was the borough. In the later Anglo-Saxon period the kings built fortresses in strategic or populous areas for security of the inhabitants and in these centers a market and a borough court of justice became common. The borough was created by a charter from the landlord, who was usually the king. The charter confirmed many privileges, one of the most valuable being the right of borough residents to collect their own taxes and pay the king a lump sum. The rise of the boroughs reflected both the increasing influence of the king and a revival of town life.

Law and Justice

The Saxon code of law was personal and elementary. The principle of "an eye for an eye" was in force, with the responsibility resting with the injured person, or his kinsmen, to exact private revenge on the offender. Over the centuries this code was modified by the influence of Christianity and the laws of the kings so that the injured party or his family accepted a cash payment or *bot* in lieu of physical retaliation on the offender; in the case of homicide *wergeld* was the fine paid to relatives of the deceased. An elaborate tariff or price list developed for various injuries (the price for the loss of the big toe was twenty shillings; five for the little toe) and for each social class. If a *churl* (a man who was in the lowest rank of freemen below an earl and a thane) killed an earl, the compensation was from three to ten times greater than if an earl killed a churl. The motive for the crime or the way the injury occurred was not considered important.

THE COURTS

Judicial procedures were an important feature of the shire moot and the hundred moot, although cases too important or controversial for the lesser courts were tried in the witan. The shire court usually met twice a year; the sheriff, earl, and bishop served as officials, and all the freemen were eligible to attend. Since laws were largely custom rather than statute, a defendant stated his case and the court decided what criminal charge, if any, applied and what penalty operated in that particular shire for such an offense. The hundred court met monthly and settled local civil and criminal cases with no provision for an appeal.

TRIALS

Each case opened with both plaintiff and defendant swearing their complaint or denial under oath. Trial was by compurgation or ordeal. In compurgation the defendant declared his innocence before man and God with a number of compurgators (character witnesses) swearing that his oath was true. In most criminal cases, or if the defendant lacked friends, the trial was by ordeal. This method operated on the premise that God would miraculously intervene to protect the innocent from injury or death. The three most common ordeals were by hot water, hot iron, and cold water. If the defendant was found guilty and lacked money to make a cash settlement, he was usually outlawed, mutilated or executed; jails were unknown.

Social Classes

The Anglo-Saxons arrived in England with a rather fluid social hierarchy based on the *comitatus* (a military band); in England the inequality between classes increased. The king and the earls, hereditary nobility, composed the aristocracy. Gradually a lesser class of free servants, known as *thanes* or *thegns*, emerged; they were frequently rewarded with land gifts in payment for their military service to the king. Beneath the thane was the churl (ceorl) who was a freeman and small landholder or artisan. Churls were liable for military service in the fyrd, but could move around freely. *Serfs* were personally free but bound to the land and the service of their lord. In time, many churls dropped to serf status because they lost their land or gave it to a lord in return for protection. The lowest class was the *thrall* or slave who most likely had lost his freedom by defeat in war or through legal punishment. Women were treated as perpetual minors under early Germanic law and custom. Gradually less restrictive traditions developed and by the tenth century women could hold property, and influential nunneries operated quite independently of secular male authority.

Economic Organization

Almost all these classes lived in small agricultural villages. Not until the rise of trade in the tenth and eleventh centuries did towns become important again. Farming villages generally consisted of the thatched huts of farm workers, the great house of the local lord, a mill, and a church. The villagers had a common pasture and meadows and cultivated their arable land by means of the two- or three-field open strip system. Economically, the communal village was virtually self-sufficient, and its daily routine was seldom unsettled except by war or pestilence. Land continued to be the basis of wealth although at the end of the Anglo-Saxon period commerce began to increase in the newly fortified centers, the boroughs. Some industry developed, particularly in the decorative arts, but the overwhelming majority of inhabitants continued to earn their living from the soil.

Anglo-Saxon Literature

Churchmen made a crucial contribution in nurturing and preserving the learning and literature of the age. Clerics copied and illuminated books with artistic designs and lettering, established and taught in the few schools, and made Latin literature available. The Venerable Bede was the outstanding scholar of the Old English period. His forty books covered a variety of theological and historical subjects; his most admired work, the *Ecclesiastical History of the English People*, provided the most inclusive and comprehensive account of the early history of England. His standard of scholarship was continued by Alcuin (735–804), who left York to head Charlemagne's palace-school, and by Alfred the Great. who wrote numerous translations from Latin into West Saxon. The epic poem *Beowulf* (composed ca. 750) tells the story of a pagan Saxon hero who valiantly defies men and dragons with equanimity. Aldhelm (ca. 640–709), the Bishop of Sherborne, was a noted Latin scholar and lover of English songs. His contemporary Caedmon, the first English poet known by name, was a Northumbrian monk who introduced Old Testament themes in his poems. In the eighth century Cynewulf's religious poems were admired as the most imaginative of the Old English verse.

After the Danish invasions the revival of prose was best represented in the vernacular sermons and discourses of Aelfric (ca. 955–ca. 1020). He also provided a readable English version of the first seven books of the Bible. *The Anglo-Saxon Chronicle*, which spans five centuries of English history, was the cumulative work of numerous monks in different monasteries. Alfred the Great is believed to have greatly stimulated the writing of this *Chronicle* and remains the towering figure of the Anglo-Saxon period who combined the best qualities of scholar, churchman and ruler.

FROM ALFRED TO EDWARD THE CONFESSOR

After Alfred's death in 899 the leadership of the House of Wessex continued strong under his son and grandson, only to decay and suffer eclipse under the second wave of Danish invaders. This time the Danes conquered all of England and restored political unity to the country. Following the death of Canute, Edward the Confessor, the last undisputed Anglo-Saxon king, ruled England in an undistinguished fashion that prepared the way for the Norman Conquest.

The Second Danish Invasion

The pattern of coexistence that emerged between the Dane and the Saxon under the aegis of the House of Wessex collapsed with the invasions of the tenth century. The defeated English ransomed themselves by the payment of the Danegeld in exorbitant sums. This payment of the Danegeld (a tax on land) established direct royal taxation in England and greatly hastened the decline of the freeholder into the serf.

The Rise and Fall of the House of Wessex

For seventy-five years the able successors of Alfred the Great extended the power and boundaries of Wessex. His son, Edward the Elder (899–924), assisted by his sister Ethelfleda, conquered all the lands south of the Humber River. Edward's son, Aethelstan (924–939), defeated the Scots and Picts, recovered the Danelaw, and claimed the title "Ruler of all Britain." Like his grandfather Alfred, Aethelstan was an outstanding ruler. Under King Edgar the Peaceful (959–975) Wessex reached its zenith of power and prosperity and was recognized as overlord by the Celtic kings of northern Britain; but decline was rapid after his death and further confounded by the return of the Danes.

ETHELRED THE UNREADY, 978–1016

The reign of Edgar's second son, Ethelred, was a total disaster. Erratic, cruel, and lazy, he was completely unprepared to defend England against the Danish invasion. He tried to buy off the Danes in 991 with an extravagant payment of the Danegeld. In 1003 he ordered a massacre of all Danes in his kingdom, which, in turn, brought bloody retribution by the Danish king, Swein, and forced Ethelred to flee to the safety of his in-laws in Normandy. In 1016 both Ethelred and his much abler son, Edmund Ironside, died and the English were left without a leader. Having little choice, the Saxon witan selected Canute, son of Swein, as King of England the following year.

KING CANUTE, 1016–1035

The young King, although a conqueror, soon adapted to English customs and stressed the continuity of his rule with the royal government of the past. He also converted to Christianity and won the support of the Church. When Canute added Norway to his English and Danish thrones, it looked as if a Scandinavian confederacy was in the making; however, his early death in 1035 cut short any such ambitions—for his empire died with him. His two sons, Harold and Harthacnut, wrangled for the English throne for the next seven years, but neither was able to win the allegiance of the English before they died. In 1042, with Canute's line having ended, the witan turned back to the royal family of Wessex and elected Edward, son of Ethelred the Unready, to the throne. With his reign Anglo-Saxon England shifted its centuries of association from the Germanic and Scandinavian world to the Normans on the French coast.

Edward the Confessor and the Normans

Half Norman by birth, Edward had spent most of his life in Normandy before attaining the English throne at the age of forty. A religious and retiring figure, he brought with him to England Norman ideas and friends; however, he gave more attention to the church than to the government. The favoritism of this kindly "French monk" toward Norman colleagues aroused the hostility of the Anglo-Saxon nobles, and his childless marriage meant that again there would be a disputed succession to the throne upon his death.

Godwin, earl of Wessex, led the protest and survived banishment to become the leading English heir to the throne. Upon his death in 1053 his four sons dominated royal politics as Edward became more of a recluse. The most powerful and capable of the sons, Harold, succeeded his father as Earl of Wessex and became increasingly popular in the country. King Edward reluctantly named Harold as his successor although he preferred William, duke of Normandy. The witan confirmed Harold as king upon the death of

Edward, but other aspirants disputed Harold's claim and prepared to challenge him for the crown. The foremost challenger was William of Normandy.

The Anglo-Saxon invaders, after their settlement was complete, carved out kingdoms and moved toward political unification under Alfred the Great. Contributing to that unification was the conversion of these invaders to Christianity since the Church provided an ecclesiastical organization common to all England and promoted learning.

The Anglo-Saxon settlement established the fundamental character of Britain and introduced units of local government that lasted, with adaptation, well into modern times. However, the power of royal authority still depended largely on the leadership of a personal monarchy to make it work effectively; it was not yet institutionalized.

With the reign of Edward the Confessor, Anglo-Saxon England shifted its centuries of association from the Scandinavian and Germanic world to the Normans on the French coast and ended its isolation from Continental affairs.

Selected Readings

Bede. *A History of the English Church and People* (1956)
Blair, Peter Hunter. *An Introduction to Anglo-Saxon England* (1977)
Brooke, Christopher. *The Saxon and Norman Kings* (1963)
Davies, Wendy. *Wales in the Early Middle Ages* (1982)
Duckett, Eleanor S. *Alfred the Great, the King and His England* (1956)
Loyn, Henry R. *The Vikings in Britain* (1977)
Sawyer, Peter H. *From Roman Britain to Norman England* (1978)
Stenton, F. M. *Anglo-Saxon England* (1971)
Wilson, David. *The Anglo-Saxons* (1981)

3

Norman England and the Expansion of Royal Government: 1066–1272

1066 William, duke of Normandy, defeats King Harold in the last successful invasion of Britain

1086 Domesday Survey of William the Conqueror

1100 Henry I recognized as king upon the death of childless William II

1153 Treaty of Wallingford provides for Matilda's son, Henry (II), to succeed Stephen as king

1154 Henry II, the first of eight Angevin or Plantagenet kings, is crowned

1162 Thomas Becket invested as Archbishop of Canterbury

1189 Richard I succeeds his father, Henry II, as king

1215 King John agrees to demands of his nobles and signs the Magna Charta at Runnymede

1258 Provisions of Oxford establish a baronial council and limit the power of Henry III

1264 Simon de Montfort defeats Henry III at Battle of Lewes

1272 Death of Henry III

The Anglo-Saxon kings gave England some sense of territorial and political unity and a tradition of monarchy over the centuries. The Norman kings introduced the necessary administrative machinery the Anglo-Saxons lacked to permit the king to govern effectively and to build the most tightly organized state in medieval Europe.

Under the Norman and Angevin rulers of Britain the ties with Scandinavia were broken and replaced by a new liaison with the Continent. In these years England was dominated by a French-speaking nobility and a Latin-speaking clergy. Paradoxically, under this foreign leadership, England developed distinctive political and judicial institutions which imitated no foreign models, but instead blended into a new synthesis the old Saxon traditions and the new Norman feudalism and administration. The outcome was the significant growth of royal power and the first effective restraints on its use.

Involvement with the Continent brought England a more effective political and military system; but it also meant that English kings became embroiled in French affairs, often at the expense of the country's interests. This Continental connection began with Edward the Confessor, but gained legitimacy and energy with William of Normandy's successful invasion of England in 1066.

THE NORMAN CONQUEST

William, duke of Normandy, did not accept the witan's choice of Harold Godwin to succeed Edward as king so he made careful preparations to make good his own claim to the throne. Aided by fortuitous circumstances, he defeated Harold and became king by conquest. The ruling Normans never displaced the Anglo-Saxons as the latter had done with the Britons, because the Normans were too few in number. Nevertheless, they destroyed the old English nobility and maintained their minority rule by a strong central government, the military technique of mounted knights and political feudalism, and the security of fortified castles.

Norman Rule   The Norman Conquest, unlike the easy yoke imposed on the English lords by Canute, proved to be severe in consequence. William confiscated Saxon estates and gave them to his followers. A monarchy based on political feudalism was transplanted from Normandy where the Duke had already established the most centralized and best administered state in Europe. This political feudalism rested on the allegiance (fealty) exacted from Norman nobles in England in return for land holdings granted by the king.

WILLIAM'S CLAIM TO THE THRONE

On the death of Edward the Confessor, William claimed the English throne on the grounds that Edward had promised to make him his heir, that Harold, when shipwrecked on the Normandy coast in 1064, had given him a sacred oath of support, and that by Viking descent he was related to the English royal family—he was the first cousin once removed of King Edward, although of illegitimate birth. Furthermore, Pope Alexander II had sanctioned William's aspirations. Strengthened by these claims, the Duke recruited an army of seven thousand and offered his recruits the blessing of the pope and the promise of English estates.

The Invasion of 1066

King Harold moved his troops to the south coast to meet the anticipated invasion of the Duke of Normandy on the Channel coast. While there Hardrada, king of Norway, another claimant to the throne, landed in Northumbria with the aid of Tostig, King Harold's bitterly hostile brother. Harold rushed north and, in the greatest military triumph of the century, repulsed the invaders at Stamford Bridge near York, killing both Harold Hardrada and Tostig. While King Harold was triumphing in the north, William landed unopposed at Pevensey on the south coast. With no respite Harold returned to the south without waiting for reinforcements and met William's army near Hastings on October 14.

In a pitched battle that lasted through the day, the disciplined Norman archers at last broke through the stubborn defense of the English *housecarls* or regulars. Victory became decisive when the King's two brothers were slain, and a random arrow struck down Harold. The Duke then cautiously moved on toward London, subduing Romney, Dover, and Canterbury en route. When no help was forthcoming from the northern earls, the people of London submitted, and William, the last successful foreign invader of England, was crowned in Westminster Abbey on Christmas Day.

William the Conqueror

For the next five years William crushed local resistance with a combination of kindness and cruelty and was merciless in punishing the northern rebellions. Fortified castles were built throughout the country, beginning with the Tower of London. Once again, the disunity of Anglo-Saxon England proved its undoing, since the revolts never won more than regional support and only succeeded in disinheriting and decimating the English nobility.

William was equally firm in repudiating the political claims of the Papacy. When Pope Gregory VII claimed England as a papal fief, William replied with the Triple Concordat which made royal permission necessary before any papal power could be exercised in England. As long as the Church's demands did not jeopardize his political authority, William permitted the establishment of ecclesiastical courts and helped Lanfranc, the new Archbishop of Canterbury, increase the administrative centralization of the church.

RESULTS OF THE CONQUEST

Although William retained Anglo-Saxon customs that did not conflict with his rule, he introduced many features into royal government that fundamentally altered English life, particularly its power structure. These influential changes included a reformed church which governed its affairs more fully under Continental leadership; a political feudal system based on landholding; a dramatic centralizing of royal power; an increase of commercial activity with the Latin world; and the adoption of the language and manners of the French court. Consequently, there began the five-century involvement of the kings of England with the French empire.

ANGLO-NORMAN FEUDALISM

William brought with him the political and economic practices of his native Normandy and fastened them on the more loosely structured English society. However, the system came too late to have the stifling effects on the English nation that it had on parts of the Continent. Norman feudalism saved England from the more immediate dangers of anarchy and civil war and gave the country the means of coping with its greatest flaw—a lack of national unity and administration.

A Pyramid of Power

William operated on the principle, never claimed by Anglo-Saxon kings, that all the land belonged to him. In theory this meant that no tenant or vassal could be more powerful than the king. In practice, though, they often were more powerful than the king, especially on the Continent. As a case in point, the Duke of Normandy was far more powerful than his lord, the King of France, and defied him with impunity. Therefore, in structuring political feudalism in England, William made sure that no vassal could treat him as he had treated his liege lord in France. He scattered the holdings of his vassals so they could not form consolidated fiefs, such as he held in Normandy, or as Earl Godwin had possessed under Edward the Confessor. He also retained the fyrd as an effective counterforce to the retinues of the lords. By this more centralized structure he overcame the great liability of Continental feudalism—that the parts were greater than the whole.

Origins of Feudalism

The roots of feudalism can be traced to the vast villas of Roman days and the half-free *coloni* who worked the land but were not free to leave it. In the early ninth century Charlemagne had granted tracts of land to select subjects and promised them immunity from royal administration. With Charlemagne's death and the collapse of his empire there grew up over the next two hundred years an improvised system of land tenure based on military service. The lord granted a parcel of land to his vassal and in return received homage and knightly military service. Such an arrangement provided local protection from the menace of Viking raids after the weakening royal power of the French kings could no longer guarantee the safety of their subjects. Rival rulers had little money with which to purchase allegiance, but they had much land at their disposal when the empire was divided after Charlemagne's death. This emerging feudal arrangement became, in essence, a political, military, and social relationship between the king (or lord) and his vassals in which one's relationship to the land was the determining factor of rank. The land granted by the lord to his vassal was known as a fief or *feudum* (from which the term *feudal* is derived).

Lord and Vassal

Feudalism under William in England quite quickly became formalized into a contractual relationship on a personal basis between lord (the donor of a parcel of land) and the vassal (the recipient). In England William kept for himself one-fourth of the estates he confiscated from his Anglo-Saxon subjects, gave one-fourth to the Church, and parceled out the remaining land to the barons of his conquering army on the conditions of feudal tenure. As their liege lord William guaranteed his vassals protection and justice. In return they swore their allegiance (homage and fealty) to him and promised to supply annually a specified number of knights for forty days of military service. They were further obligated to entertain the king (or the lord to whom they owed their fealty) on visits, to attend his court, and to pay certain fees, such as bearing the expense of knighting the lord's oldest son or paying the cost of his daughter's marriage.

To strengthen his hold over the barons, William permitted no castles to be built without royal consent, and in the Oath of Salisbury he demanded prime allegiance, not only from his tenants-in-chief, but from all their vassals. This centralization of power was likewise reflected in the continuation of the Danegeld and in an elaborate census of the ownership and wealth of the kingdom. On William's orders royal commissioners traveled to every hundred and village and asked detailed questions concerning every manor. The meticulous findings of this statistical survey were recorded in the famous Domesday Book of 1086.

WILLIAM AND LOCAL GOVERNMENT

Although William, as conqueror, remodeled and increased the powers of the central government, he retained many Anglo-Saxon institutions, rather than expose his new subjects unnecessarily to strange laws and customs. His Great Council preserved the function of the Saxon witan, and the fyrd was a useful check on the military strength of the barons. The machinery of local government continued to function in the shires where royal authority now penetrated effectively for the first time through the office of the sheriff. The sheriff replaced the earl as the official representative of the king. In this way royal power was no longer distant and indirect, but near at hand and visible in each community, since the king gave the sheriffs full administration of local government and control of the local militia. When William died in 1087, he left England its first powerful and well-defined system of government. Even if William was a stern ruler who imposed feudal centralization by force, he was not an absolute ruler, and he did provide more order and security than was customary in Europe at this time.

The Manor

The manor was the economic unit of feudalism. As an agricultural unit it was the part (or the whole) of the fief that the vassal retained for personal use. Like its Anglo-Saxon predecessor, it was practically self-sufficient, with a village, common fields, mill, and blacksmith shop. A major change from Anglo-Saxon days was the reduction of freemen; the Domesday survey classified 84 percent of the rural population as serfs. The manorial relationship between lord and serf was most unequal. In return for some meager protection and facilities, the serf spent most of the day tilling his lord's land or performing other obligations for him; even a percentage of a serf's produce was claimed by the lord. The serf was bound to the soil by law and could not leave the manor without the lord's consent. Any disputes between the serf and the lord were tried in the manorial court presided over by the lord's steward.

THE REIGNS OF WILLIAM II, HENRY I, AND STEPHEN

William entrusted to his sons and successors a monarchy whose controlling influence was exerted through feudal tenure and baronial service, central administration, and local government. These three pillars of sovereignty were tested in the reigns of the three monarchs that followed King William. During these turbulent years, the power of the barons was checked, public finances were systematized, and justice reformed—all attesting to the growing stability of the English monarchy.

Centralization and Disruption

At first, the efforts of William II and Henry I to increase royal authority were successful. Then under the weak and indecisive Stephen, the barons exploited the situation to break free from royal control, and for nineteen years England was convulsed by baronial rivalries and warring factions. It became clear by the end of Stephen's reign that a strong and effective government based on heredity rather than election was greatly to be preferred over its lack which often brought misery, war and anarchy.

William II, 1087–1100

King William had bequeathed Normandy to his eldest son, Robert; to his second son, William Rufus, he bequeathed the English Crown; to his youngest son, Henry, he left 5,000 marks. A series of minor wars was the outcome of the three brothers quarreling among themselves over their inheritance. William II was an excellent soldier and maintained the strong monarchy inherited from his father, but he was brutal, cruel and cynical in an age of public piety. During this era of the Crusades when Christian rulers sought to reclaim the Holy Land from Muslim control, he openly despised the clergy and disregarded conventional morality. He employed all the powers of the feudal monarchy and feudal courts to extract money from his subjects. He was equally greedy for Church lands and blocked new appointments to vacant bishoprics and abbeys, appropriating their revenues for himself. A bitter quarrel ensued with Archbishop Anselm over the respective authority of church and state, an argument that would plague future reigns as well. William's military exploits proved his inherited soldierly qualities as he suppressed two revolts in England and invaded the Welsh and Scottish borders. In this way he kept intact his father's conquests and made it possible for his brother to reunite England with Normandy.

Henry I, 1100–1135

When William II died without a son Henry moved swiftly to gain approval from the royal council before his elder brother, Robert, returned from the Crusades. To hold baronial support Henry promised in his coronation charter to abide by the laws of Edward the Confessor and William I and to halt all unreasonable methods of collecting money from the nobles and the Church. To further strengthen his position, he recalled Archbishop Anselm from exile and married Edith-Matilda, the nearest blood kin of the royal House of Wessex. The year after his coronation Henry repulsed an invasion attempt by Robert and then reciprocated by attacking Normandy and decisively defeating Robert at Tinchebray in 1106—a revenge, said the English, for Hastings. Normandy thereby came under Henry's rule and the rest of his reign was relatively tranquil.

CENTRAL GOVERNMENT UNDER HENRY I

After subduing Normandy, King Henry took advantage of his peaceful reign to reshape the central administration. His flair for organization produced law and order and filled the treasury as he greatly expanded the royal judicial system as well as royal administration through the issuance of hundreds of royal writs.

THE CURIA REGIS

From the Great Council of barons the King selected a small group of administrators, the *curia regis*, and gave them specialized roles. One councilor became *justiciar*, or chief minister, and was given authority to act in the name of the king. Second in importance was the *chancellor*, who was responsible for the legal and secretarial duties of the government. The office of *treasurer* increased in power, and an account was demanded of all receipts and expenditures.

THE EXCHEQUER

Disputes over tax cases were soon held in a special session of the curia regis called the exchequer, which took its name from the fact that royal accounting was first calculated on a checkered cloth. The staff of the exchequer drafted writs issued from the exchequer, and twice yearly required an audit from sheriffs and other officials who collected money for the king. The exchequer was the first modern accounting practice known in the West. Henry discovered that tight control of expenditures and efficient administration brought greater revenues. His reign is often seen as the "seedbed of the modern state" and the "coming of age of the royal administration."[*]

In time the Exchequer Court became a separate common law court. To raise more money Henry allowed the barons to make a money payment (*scutage*) in place of contributing knights as required by the feudal code. He also increased the business and revenue of royal courts by sending itinerant judges on circuit; he thus turned the local courts into royal courts and permitted royal justice and authority to reach into every local hamlet.

Stephen versus Matilda, 1135–1154

Henry's hopes for his dynasty were jeopardized when his only legitimate son, William, drowned in 1120 crossing the Channel. He made the barons swear allegiance to his daughter, Matilda, and then promptly had her married to fifteen-year old Geoffrey of Anjou without the barons' consent. On Henry's death the barons chose his nephew, Stephen of Blois, as king, and

---

[*] C. Warren Hollister. *The Making of England, 55 B.C. to 1399*. (Lexington: D. C. Heath, 1988), p. 135.

a disputed succession began. Stephen was mild and chivalrous, but utterly unable to rule his kingdom. In many respects he was just the opposite of his father. Only by increasing concessions to the barons and to the Church was he able to maintain his title. The country was racked by civil war and lawlessness for nineteen long years until the warring factions signed the Treaty of Wallingford (1153), providing for Matilda's son, Henry, to succeed Stephen. The next year Stephen died.

HENRY II AND THE COMMON LAW

When Henry II, the first of eight Angevin or Plantagenet kings, came to the throne in 1154 at the age of twenty-one, he also inherited an impressive empire on the Continent. The extent of his possessions meant that Henry was in England only thirteen of the thirty-five years of his reign. Very much like his grandfather, Henry I, the young king with energy, vision, and charisma extended the administrative and legal reforms of that earlier reign. His attention to England's legal system made his reign especially noteworthy in the development of the fundamental features of common law. Along with Alfred, Edward I, and Elizabeth I, he ranks as one of the greatest of Britain's monarchs.

Restoration of Royal Power

King Henry had inherited from his parents Normandy, Touraine, and Maine. At nineteen he had married Eleanor of Aquitaine, who had divorced King Louis VII of France to wed him. She brought as her dowry Aquitaine and Toulouse. To these possessions, totaling nearly half of France, Henry added the overlordship of Wales, Ireland and Scotland. Although Henry never conquered Scotland, Anglo-Norman institutions flooded the country in the twelfth century to replace the Celtic system of land tenure and administration. In Ireland, Henry's vassal Strongbow (the Welsh Richard of Clare, earl of Pembroke) plundered Ireland with abandon. By 1200 Anglo-Normans governed two-thirds of Ireland and imposed their feudal system upon the defeated Irish.

Within England Henry's first task was to restore order and authority where royal power had dangerously eroded during Stephen's reign. Henry regained Crown lands by revoking the royal grants of lands and offices that had been made during Stephen's reign and by ordering the demolition of hundreds of unlicensed castles. The return to the peace of a strong central government was helped by the object lesson that Stephen's misrule had made on his subjects.

ROYAL REVENUE

To maintain his vast holdings Henry II needed increased revenues. To secure more income he restored the exchequer to the position of prominence it held under Henry I, extended scutage to lay nobles and hired mercenaries with the money raised, and levied an income and personal property tax (the Saladin tax) on everyone not embarking on the Second Crusade.

Common Law

Between them Henry I and Henry II enormously expanded royal jurisdiction at the expense of feudal and local justice. Henry II picked up the old Roman concept of the king as legislator and brought new meaning and influence to the monarchy. Once Henry had consolidated his holdings, he turned his attention to administration and judicial reform. Here his passion for organization and efficiency resulted in better justice and a wider respect for royal authority. The outcome was a distinctive legal system known as English common law that became one of the great legal traditions of the world and the basis for the American legal system. Judges selected the best of local laws and customs and applied them to the whole realm. In time this provided uniform laws for England by which a disputed question of law was decided by legal precedent. This accent on judge-made law and trial by jury led to the position that the law was supreme, and even the king could not disregard it. On the Continent, in contrast, Roman law became the dominant legal concept.

The King's Justices

Henry II wished to make English justice more uniform and to minimize the overlap and confusion prevailing in various courts. Itinerant judges became trustworthy agents of the Crown as King Henry increased their jurisdiction and introduced courts into every county. The expansion of royal justice made access to the courts easier for the people and at the same time curtailed the power and jurisdiction of the local sheriff or baron. Judges sent on circuit had the sole right to hear murder charges. In the Assize (county court session) of Northampton (1176) the powers of the royal judges were increased to try all criminals.

With the expansion of royal jurisdiction, there arose a broader interpretation for royal decrees and ordinances (any offense on the "king's highway" was an offense against the Crown). In civil cases the extension of the royal writ increased the business of royal courts. In Norman times only exceptional suits which involved the king's friends could secure a royal writ which ordered the case to be tried in royal courts instead of local courts. Under Henry II new writs were introduced, and any freeman who had a suit which fit any of these judicial forms could pay a fee for a royal writ and secure a trial in a royal court with a better chance of justice being rendered. Royal writs became popular and royal courts expanded rapidly.

THE DEVELOPMENT OF THE JURY

Henry II did not introduce trial by jury but he made it an integral part of the royal judicial procedure. The jury evolved in Western Christendom from sworn inquests ordered by the kings whereby a group of men were placed under oath and ordered to provide truthful information. At the Assize of Clarendon (1166) King Henry expanded the practice and ordered that juries of twelve men in each hundred moot at county court sessions were to denounce criminals in their neighborhood; such groups were called present-ment or accusing juries (the origin of the grand jury). Trial by jury was also introduced in assizes to decide disputes over ownership of land. In time, trial by jury replaced all other types of trials and, by the thirteenth century, it was extended to criminal cases through the efforts of the Church. The jury was more likely to provide a rational and just decision than trial by ordeal or compurgation, and in later centuries it became an invaluable safeguard of civil liberties.

PROPERTY LAW

In civil cases King Henry introduced the writ of right which ordered a feudal lord to provide justice for the plaintiff or the king would step into the case through the sheriff. The writ of praecipe ignored the feudal court; it ordered the sheriff to command the restoration of land to the plaintiff or have the defendant appear in royal court to explain his failure to comply. Both of these laws were encroachments on the baronial courts.

CHURCH AND STATE

The Church's authority had grown greatly in the century preceding Henry II's reign. Powerful popes, the increasing stature of canon law, and a religious revival that resulted in the erection of thousands of churches in eleventh-century Europe had won for the Church wider spheres of influence. In England King Stephen had made major concessions to the Church to keep its backing. In his efforts to reform the legal system, Henry now ran into conflict with the Church over the jurisdiction of secular and ecclesiastical courts.

Constitutions of Clarendon, 1164. The Church courts had extended their jurisdiction to include the right to try all cases involving the clergy, whatever the offense. The privilege of "benefit of clergy" was often claimed by anyone who could read or speak Latin, since the penalties of the Church courts were usually very lenient. To define the respective powers of Church and government, Henry drew up a statement called the Constitutions of Clarendon. It decreed, among its sixteen articles, that accused clergy could continue to be tried in Church courts, but, if they were found guilty of criminal offenses, they would be turned over to the secular courts for punishment. Inspired by the opposition of Thomas Becket, the newly appointed Archbishop of Canterbury, the bishops were most reluctant to agree to the Constitutions; however, they yielded when it became obvious that Becket's case was futile.

Thomas Becket. Becket had served as chancellor with such distinction that Henry II nominated him for the vacant archbishopric in 1162. To Henry's angry amazement the investiture turned his former close ally into an adamant champion of the Church. Archbishop Becket's stubborn resistance to the Clarendon reforms resulted in his exile. After the pope threatened Henry with excommunication and a papal interdict on England that would have forbidden most Christian sacraments and burials in the country, a reconciliation was arranged between the two antagonists.

Again, the unbending archbishop provoked Henry's anger by refusing to absolve the bishops who had participated in the coronation ceremonies of the King's son. This time four overzealous knights, thinking they were doing King Henry a service, took the law into their own hands and murdered Becket on the altar steps of Canterbury. The murder canonized Becket and brought public humiliation to Henry. The King tried to make atonement by visiting Becket's tomb as a penitent and embarking on a crusade to conquer Ireland for the Church. Nevertheless, Henry could not pursue his reform of the Church courts and was obligated to withdraw some of the terms of the Constitutions. In the long run most of his demands were upheld and the expansion of the Church courts was halted.

Henry and His Sons

Henry II had far more success ruling his kingdom than his own family. His infidelities and his authoritarian manner contributed to his wife, Eleanor, and their four sons at one time or another all plotting with his enemies to unseat him. This ingratitude and treachery was all the more marked because of Henry's generosity and affection for his children. Two sons, Henry and Geoffrey, died before their father, but Richard and John continued plotting until King Henry's death. In 1188 Richard and King Philip Augustus of France attacked Henry and forced humiliating terms on him the following year. When his favorite son, John, also betrayed him, Henry died, a broken man.

The Angevin Empire

Efforts to hold together Henry II's dominions on both sides of the Channel demanded a skillful and powerful ruler. This Henry was, and his continuous travel permitted him to transplant effective governmental procedures from one region to another. Yet Henry was forced to spend most of his time outside England protecting his domains from rebellion and the schemes of the French king. Under his less skillful successors these landholdings in France became a liability, for they claimed too much attention and depleted the treasury. King Richard the Lion-Hearted spent most of his reign in France and died besieging a castle. John lost Normandy,

Poitou, and Anjou to the King of France. These defeats broke up the Angevin empire although Henry III made feeble efforts to recapture these legacies. In the Treaty of Paris (1259), Henry III finally renounced his right to Normandy, Anjou, Poitou, Touraine, and Maine. Not until the Hundred Years' War would English rule again become so involved in French territories.

MAGNA CHARTA

Henry II had provided the administrative and judicial machinery for a strong central government that had few restraints other than the feudal contract and the customary laws and practices of the realm to prevent the misuse of royal power. When King John abused his coronation and feudal oaths, the barons' only option was sullen acquiescence or insurrection. Eventually they took up arms and in 1215 they forced John to sign a written guarantee of customary and feudal obligations. In the short run the charter was looked upon largely as a feudal document that strengthened the position of the barons and reminded the king that there were certain limitations to his power. In time the charter became part of the common law and was enshrined as a symbol of the supremacy of law and the written guarantee of certain legal and political rights.

The Reign of Richard, 1189–1199

It was a tribute to the administrative structure which Henry II had set up that England survived intact the reign of King Richard, who, in fact, did little for England. Richard was only in the kingdom for six months of his ten-year reign, and then chiefly to raise money to continue his fighting abroad. A warrior-knight, who became a legendary symbol of romantic chivalry, Richard had little interest in routine administration, preferring to farm out his royal privileges to his brother, Prince John, and the wealthy barons in return for money. Richard's heroic military adventures on the Third Crusade and later in France against Philip Augustus won him glory but consumed his subjects' money. While the King was out of the country, the government was in the hands of Prince John, who took advantage of Richard's absence to win power for himself. However, John was thwarted by Richard's supporters, led by the two justiciars, William Longchamp and Hubert Walter, who were protecting Richard's interests. (These years form the period of time in which the tales of Robin Hood are based.) But the barons were no longer on the defensive as they were in the reign of Henry II, and emboldened by the lack of royal leadership, they challenged the encroachments of the central government.

Reign of John, 1199–1216

Richard's empty treasury, the restive barons and a war in France were the legacies John acquired when he won the throne he had so long coveted. Often called England's "worst king," John was a victim of his own character and of circumstances. Although he was courageous and clever, he had the knack of alienating nearly everyone by his cruelty, greed, and failure to honor his word. Above all, he was unsuccessful in every venture he handled, partly because he had the bad luck of being pitted against two of the most powerful figures of the Middle Ages: Philip Augustus of France and Pope Innocent III.

JOHN AND THE KING OF FRANCE

King John had secured the annulment of his childless marriage and was planning to wed a Portuguese princess, but he fell in love with a fourteen-year-old French girl, Isabella of Angoulème, who was betrothed to one of his vassals. Undaunted by the betrothal he married her, only to have Hugh the Brown, the jilted fiancé, appeal to King Philip II for justice. In order to resolve the situation the King of France, as John's suzerain (according to feudal custom, since John held Normandy, Anjou, and Aquitaine as fiefs, he was a vassal of the French King), summoned him to stand trial. When John refused to appear, Philip pronounced the forfeiture of all his French domains. John's reputation was sullied even more by his probably accomplice in the murder of his nephew, Arthur, a rival claimant to the throne. By 1204 John lost all the Plantagenet empire north of the Loire River; only Aquitaine remained unconquered. Repeated defeats had damaged the King's prestige. To obtain revenue to avenge these losses John extracted money from the barons by old and new taxes, feudal levies, and arbitrary impositions.

JOHN AND THE POPE

As his next antagonist King John unfortunately challenged the powerful Pope Innocent III. John and the monks of Canterbury had chosen rival candidates as archbishop of Canterbury upon the death of Hubert Walter (1205). Innocent rejected both candidates and picked a third, Stephen Langton. Enraged, John refused to accept Langton and confiscated the revenues of the seat of Canterbury; thereupon, Innocent placed England under an interdict (1208) halting all Church services. John retaliated by persecuting the clergy and seizing Church property; Innocent threatened to depose the King. Although the Pope's decrees did not hurt John immediately, they encouraged his enemies, particularly the disaffected barons and Philip Augustus of France. When Philip prepared to invade England with the Pope's blessing, John had no recourse but to submit to Innocent (1213). The King accepted Langton as archbishop, restored the confiscated Church properties, and relinquished England and English-ruled eastern Ireland to the Pope to receive them back as fiefs of Rome. Saved from invasion and with the Pope now on his side, John took the offensive against Philip but he had not yet won back the support of his barons.

JOHN AND THE BARONS

In 1214 after his plans to defeat Philip collapsed, King John asked for another scutage from his nobles; however, the barons refused to comply. Instead they referred to the charter of Henry I as precedent and demanded that John sign a new charter listing his and their feudal rights and obligations and that he abide by such contractual rights. The barons had felt their position threatened ever since the galloping centralization of Henry II. Confronted with an inept king who had misused royal powers and upset the feudal balance, about half of the barons were prepared, in their own self-interest, to challenge John.

Without doubt John had abused his feudal prerogatives by charging excessive fees for relief of feudal duties, forcing marriage on female wards, and imprisoning families of recalcitrant barons; but he was quite indifferent to the fact. In the negotiations that followed, Archbishop Langton served as mediator between the King and his subjects. John delayed and schemed, but could not win over either the barons, the churchmen, or the people of London. On June 15, 1215, at Runnymede he agreed to their demands and signed the Magna Charta.

Magna Charta

The sixty-three clauses of the charter lacked sweeping statements of political doctrine but dealt primarily with feudal grievances and legal protection. Specific abuses in John's use of warship, relief, and scutage were to end and no extraordinary taxes were to be levied without consent of the Great Council—the germ for later claims of no taxation without representation. Protection from arbitrary arrest was strengthened by clause thirty-nine, making it unlawful to arrest a freeman "except by the lawful judgment of his peers or by the law of the land." A committee of twenty-five barons was to make sure the agreement was honored by the King. If he did not, they were entitled to check the King by force of arms. Other clauses dealt with the ancient liberties of London, the rights of merchants, and weights and measures.

Importance of the Charter. This charter was a much broader confirmation of rights and privileges than the charter of Henry I. Nevertheless, its detailed provisions were essentially feudal and soon became dated. Certainly John had no intention of honoring it and within four months was preparing for war against the barons. Over the centuries, however, the charter became increasingly meaningful and a part of common law as attested by its confirmation forty times in later reigns. The written confirmation of mutual contractual rights and privileges proved that the king could be brought to terms and that dissident factions could join together and negotiate peacefully with the king. Later, commoners would use the same method and demand redress of grievances before passing laws desired by the king.

Underlying the charter were two principles upon which English constitutionalism and the modern concept of a limited monarchy grew. First, the king was not above all law, but was limited by the prescribed laws of his realm, and, second, if the king flaunted the contractual relationships by unilateral action, his subjects reserved the right to force him to observe the laws.

Civil War. Since King John signed the charter as a politically expedient move, he immediately repudiated it and marched against the insurgents in October 1215. Thereupon the barons of the north offered the Crown to Louis, son of King Philip. While John was attempting to quench this political rebellion, French invasion forces occupied London. Only John's sudden death a year later from over-indulgence in food and drink spared England a full-scale civil war.

HENRY III AND THE BARONS

King John's death the year after the signing of the Magna Charta initiated the long reign (1216–1272) of his nine-year old son, Henry III. Henry resembled Edward the Confessor in his piety and simplicity and is consigned, rather appropriately, by the Italian poet, Dante, to the purgatory of children and simpletons. Intimidated by both his French relatives and the papacy, Henry had the misfortune of being cast as an "un-English" King in an age of rising English patriotism. In the ensuing experiments in forms of government the parliamentary idea seemed to hold the widest appeal.

Foreign Influence on Henry's Reign

During King Henry's minority the nobles rallied around the Crown and eventually drove Prince Louis and the French out of England. First William Marshall and later Hubert de Burgh—the last of the great justiciars—served as regents for the young King. Five years after coming of age he dismissed the masterful de Burgh (1232) and revealed his own administrative incompetence when he became sole ruler. He quickly became dependent upon French advisors and Henry's reign became largely a feud between English and non-English factions. During these years Henry was lured into a foolish and costly foreign policy that won him nothing but heavy debts. He tried and failed to reconquer the Angevin empire. Even more expensive was the papal scheme to award the throne of the Two Sicilies to Henry's second son, Edmund, in return for substantial military and financial obligations. Nothing came of this farfetched project but yet another serious drain on the royal treasury.

FAMILY FAVORITES

King Henry alienated many of his subjects by replacing de Burgh with Peter des Roches of Poitou. The new justiciar's financial reforms and his dismissal of the sheriffs provoked the English barons. More foreign advisors came in the train of Henry's charming and clever bride, Eleanor of Provence. She found posts for eight uncles and many fortune-seeking relations. In 1220 the King's widowed mother remarried and provided Henry with four half-brothers to keep in royal style.

PAPAL POWER

The papacy exploited Henry's subserviency to the point that finally the English clergy united with the barons against the Pope and the King. Financial demands upon the English Church were so exorbitant that one-fifth of its income was earmarked for Rome. Next the Pope filled vacancies in the English Church with Italian clerics, many of whom never bothered to visit England, but nevertheless drew good incomes from their posts.

Law and Administration Under Henry III

Participation in the business of government broadened in the thirteenth century as rising affluence drew more and more knights, burghers, and landholders into the functions of the local and central government. Centralized government had come to stay. The question during the Angevin dynasty was: Who should control it? Royal administration and royal law grew incrementally and by the end of the century a rather comprehensive legal system was in place and the royal courts of King's Bench, Common Pleas, and Exchequer were staffed by professional judges for the first time. The great thirteenth-century jurist, Henry de Bracton provided a philosophical and systematic interpretation for these royal courts and common law in his legal treatise, *On the Laws and Customs of England.*

Constitutionally these years were a time when the country was seeking to find workable political institutions that would permit the exercise of royal authority but also obligate the monarch to live within the customary law of the realm and not above it. To be an effective and accepted ruler the king increasingly needed to listen to and be in cooperation with the politically conscious "community of the realm." As Henry's reign progressed, he more and more governed without baronial advice and counsel. In 1258 the barons moved from idle grumbling about Henry's foreign advisors and his arbitrary rule to open defiance and brought about a coup d'etat that transferred many of the powers of the king to a baronial oligarchy.

PROVISIONS OF OXFORD, 1258

At Oxford the disaffected baronial faction defied the King's efforts to increase taxes and forced upon him an ordinance which established a baronial council of fifteen to run the government in the king's name. Foreign favorites were to be dismissed and the Great Council—now also called a "parliament"—was to meet three times a year. These revolutionary proposals limited the powers of the king but failed to find any acceptable alternative to the royal administrative machinery that would win wide support. Soon the barons quarreled among themselves and Henry, learning nothing, reasserted his authority. When both the Pope and Louis IX of France backed Henry, civil war broke out in 1264.

Simon de Montfort

Leading the disaffected baronial party was Henry's French brother-in-law, Simon de Montfort, who as Earl of Leicester had championed the Provisions of Oxford successfully. He now demonstrated his military abilities and defeated King Henry and his son, Edward, at the battle of Lewes (1264). The next year, Montfort, as de facto ruler, summoned to London a parliament that he hoped would replace the monarchy with an enlightened oligarchy. To broaden his support he included all the elements of future parliaments by requesting two knights from each county and two citizens from each friendly borough to meet with the Lords, thereby making this parliament the most representative body convoked before Edward I's Parliament of 1295. However, Montfort's scheme fell through as the barons became suspicious of each other and the break from royal rule seemed too radical to digest. In 1265 the royal army led by Prince Edward, who had escaped from imprisonment, defeated the rebellious barons and killed Montfort at the battle of Evesham. The revolutionary idea of abolishing the monarchy had failed and with Montfort's demise vanished the last of the influential Frenchmen who shaped English policy.

DEATH OF HENRY III

In 1266 King Henry once again confirmed the Magna Charta. Now in his old age, gradually turned over control of the government to his son, Edward, who was astute enough to learn the lessons that Montfort's disaffection taught. Five years later the King died while his son was crusading. Henry III had been able to survive the barons' efforts to replace him, but, like his father, he had been forcibly brought to account for his misrule. Most of his heirs and his subjects never quite forgot that fact.

The North Sea, rather than the English Channel or the Atlantic, was the hub of British links with Europe for six centuries. In 1066 the Norman invasion and Continental Catholicism changed all this and thereafter deeply involved the Norman and Angevin kings in Continental politics, often at the expense of the country's interests.

The Norman Conquest was one of the turning points in English history. A series of strong Norman kings revolutionized England's power structure and molded English institutions with Norman feudalism to exalt the authority of the king and central administration of government.

Especially under Henry I and Henry II an effective royal judiciary and central administration flourished and the fundamental features of common law became institutionalized. The unfettered growth of royal authority was checked by the Magna Charta and other written guarantees of certain rights and restrictions of the king and his subjects. The supremacy of law, even over the king, began to take shape as an important part of the nation's constitutional history far ahead of any similar developments on the Continent.

Selected Readings

Appleby, John T. *John, King of England* (1960)

Barlow, Frank. *The Feudal Kingdom of England, 1042–1216* (1955)

Brown, R. Allen. *The Normans and the Norman Conquest* (1969)

Brundage, James A. *Richard Lion Heart: A Biography* (1974)

Douglas, David C. *William the Conqueror: The Norman Impact Upon England* (1964)

Duncan, Archibald A. M. *Scotland: The Making of the Kingdom* (1975)

Goldman, James. *The Lion in Winter* (1983)

Holt, James C. *Magna Carta* (1965)

Kelly, Amy. *Eleanor of Aquitaine and the Four Kings* (1950)

Poole, A. L. *From Domesday to Magna Carta, 1087–1216* (1955)

Sayles, George O., and Henry G. Richardson. *The Governance of Medieval England from the Conquest to Magna Carta* (1963)

Warren, W. L. *Henry II* (1973)

4

Medieval Society

During the twelfth and thirteenth centuries the Roman Catholic Church acquired its greatest authority and influence. Western Christendom still spoke a common language, Latin, taught a single faith, and brought together rival monarchs for the Crusades to the Holy Land. Only within the religious and cultural bonds of Christendom did Europe find the unity it so conspicuously lacked in political affairs.

The Norman Conquest had identified England more directly with medieval European civilization, and the country benefited greatly from the attachment. However, national stirrings made England one of the first countries to show the marks of a separate and unique identity.

During the central years of the Middle Ages (1000–1300) there occurred a visible awakening of Europe's intellectual and artistic energies. These years witnessed the rise of universities and the building of magnificent cathedrals. Distinguished theologians and philosophers of the age successfully reconciled faith and reason within an ordered structure of society that symbolized medieval civilization at its height.

THE CRUSADES

In Britain and in Europe the influence of the Crusades was profound and reflected the magnitude of religious fervor of this period. Although the original goals of converting the "Muslim infidels" and reconquering the Holy Land failed, several unanticipated consequences of these religious wars were of great importance.

Appeal of the Crusades

Among the various motives that stirred the Crusaders to action were: (1) the capture of the Holy Land by the Turks and the ensuing mistreatment of Christians on pilgrimages to Jerusalem; (2) the hope of the papacy to reunite the Eastern Church which had separated from the Roman Catholic Church in 1054; (3) the influence of powerful preachers, like Peter the Hermit, who could persuade the laity into believing that the Crusades were the will of God; and (4) the promise of material reward and foreign adventure for nobles and knights joining a crusade.

SCOPE OF THE CRUSADES

The Crusades began in 1096 and continued intermittently for two centuries. The First Crusade (1096–1099) wrested the Holy Land from the Turks and set up feudal Christian kingdoms; no later Crusade achieved any comparable military success. The Second Crusade (1147–1150) failed to recover ground lost to the Muslim reconquest. The Third Crusade (1189–1192), led by Richard I of England, Frederick Barbarossa (the Holy Roman Emperor), and Philip Augustus of France, hoped to retake Jerusalem from Saladin, Sultan of Egypt and Syria. Richard was successful in his siege of Acre, but returned to England when he found his forces insufficient to attack Jerusalem. Numerous other Crusades followed, although not all were fought against the Turks. Some were sidetracked into sacking Constantinople—as the Fourth in 1204—or fighting the Albigenses, the Christian heretics in

France. Gradually, the Crusades lost their appeal and momentum as the original spirit and fervor that motivated the Crusaders became vague or expired.

RESULTS OF THE CRUSADES

When the Turks recaptured Acre, the last stronghold of the Christians, in 1291, the hopes of reuniting Christendom or assuring Christian rule in the Holy Land were abandoned. Despite these failures the results of the Crusades were significant. The very failure of the Crusaders to break the Muslim barrier to overland trade with the East forced Europe to seek new sea routes to the Orient. When these were discovered, Britain's maritime location would put it in an excellent position for trade. Other indirect results included the increase in royal power in England because of the absence, and frequently the death, of recalcitrant barons on a crusade; a broadening of British cultural horizons by the fruitful contact with the learning, history, and inventions (gunpowder, paper) of the East; a remarkable growth in towns and commerce which had the effect of increasing the circulation of money and raising prices; and the adoption of new methods of warfare, especially the techniques of fortification and siege that were employed by the Muslims in the Near East. More important, the Crusades contributed a visible sense of national identity. For many Englishmen the expedition to the Holy Land was their first trip away from their local community. They forgot their parochialism in a foreign land and took pride in being identified as Englishmen.

MONKS AND FRIARS

The Christian Church probably had a greater hold upon the minds and actions of people in the Middle Ages than any time before or since. To the medieval world, the men and women who prayed and cared for body and soul were as indispensable a part of society as those who fought or tilled the soil. The twelfth century became the golden age of the monasteries, to be followed in the next century by the arrival of the mendicant orders.

English Monasticism	The Norman Conquest had produced few changes in monastic life, since the French abbots continued the ways of their Anglo-Saxon predecessors. Lanfranc (1069–1089) and Anselm (1093–1109), the two outstanding monks who became archbishops of Canterbury, had introduced the religious devotion and rigorous standards of Bec Abbey. In twelfth-century Britain monasticism achieved its greatest expansion and influence. There were eighty-eight religious houses in England in 1100; a century later, nearly four

hundred. In 1066 one-sixth of the land was owned by monasteries; by the death of King John (1216), between a quarter and a third. For the first time an order for women who wished to live communally was created in the twelfth century. By 1189 it had fourteen houses with 960 nuns. As original monastic ideals invariably became tarnished by excessive wealth and a laxity of spiritual devotion and discipline, reform movements arose to give new life to the orders.

THE CISTERCIAN ORDER

Most of the earlier monastic foundations in England were Benedictine houses. Among the new or reforming orders the Cistercians made the greatest impact on Britain. The Cistercian order was founded in 1098 at Citeaux by Robert of Molesme and Stephen Harding. The latter, an Englishman, wrote the famous Cistercian constitution, *Carta Caritatis* (Rule of Love). Early in the twelfth century Cistercian foundations appeared in Surrey and Yorkshire. Insisting on the simplicity and austerity envisioned by Saint Benedict, the monks built their foundations in isolated fields, cultivated crops, and reared prize-winning sheep.

THE MENDICANT ORDERS

In the thirteenth century more religious orders appeared. These hoped to avoid the pitfalls of previous communities that became preoccupied with the successful administration of their holdings. Rather than separating themselves in cloistered abbeys, the *frères* or friars lived in the world to convert sinners. They upheld their spiritual values by observance of a common rule and the rejection of worldly possessions, thus becoming known as the *mendicant*, or begging, orders. The Franciscans (founded by Saint Francis in 1210) emphasized a life of service to the poor and sick through good works and charity. The Dominicans (founded in 1216 by Saint Dominic, a Spanish scholar) set out to preach the Gospel and to combat heresy. The Dominicans reached England in 1221 and the Franciscans in 1224. Both orders gained popularity because of their zealous endeavor, their devotion, and the simplicity of their lives. Two other begging orders, the Augustinians and the Carmelites, followed. Then, like the monks before them, the four orders, in time, frequently neglected the rules which had made them great.

DECLINE OF THE RELIGIOUS ORDERS

The increase in power and possessions, which had caused laxity in the earlier monastic orders, also affected the begging friars who grew "too well fed" and disregarded their vows of poverty and obedience. Contemporary critics like Walter Map and Matthew Paris lamented the greed and immorality found in religious communities. Yet the monasteries continued to run schools, to offer hospitality to travelers, and to administer relief to the sick and poor. Eventually, the schools and hospitals which became dominant in the fields of education and social service were founded outside the pale of the monasteries. As a result, great scholars and Church leaders were no longer monks by necessity. Up to the year 1189 all archbishops of Canterbury, except Becket, had come from the monastic orders; after that date only three regular clergy became archbishops.

LEARNING, LITERATURE, AND ARCHITECTURE

Long before the intellectual renaissance of the twelfth century—with its establishment of new schools, deeper study of law, logic, and classical literature, and new spirit of inquiry—the English Church had promoted education. Until the thirteenth century the Church was for all practical purposes the exclusive patron of the liberal arts. Gradually new schools were opened independent of the monasteries, and instead of scholars moving to monasteries, churchmen now studied at Oxford and Cambridge. Norman and Gothic architecture expressed most visibly the creativity, the power, and the mystery of medieval Christianity.

The New Universities

A direct result of the intellectual revival was the rise of universities in Europe in the twelfth century. These schools at first consisted of teachers and students with few, if any, buildings. When either the teachers or students organized a guild for the purpose of administering their academic affairs, a university came into existence. These universities were characterized by a cosmopolitan student body, faculties of teachers who had master's degrees, and specialization in either law, medicine, or theology. Respected schools or guilds existed in Exeter, Lincoln, and Winchester. The first "university," however, was founded at Oxford when a quarrel between Henry II and Becket caused English students to leave the University of Paris and form a *studium generale* at Oxford around 1167. In the next century a fight between townsfolk and students at Oxford contributed to a segment of the academic community migrating to Cambridge. The first Oxford college, Merton, was formally established in 1264, and the first Cambridge college, Peterhouse, twenty years later. By the end of the thirteenth century Oxford had a body of students and masters numbering around 1500.

Writers and Scholars

Western civilization is indebted to the monastic scribes who preserved and copied classical manuscripts and who recorded almost all the chronicles. The abbey of St. Albans was particularly important; here, Roger Wendover and Matthew Paris wrote a detailed account of the period of Henry III in the *Flowers of History*. Other noteworthy chroniclers who described their times were William of Malmesbury (b. 1125), William of Newbury (b. 1160), and Roger of Havedon (b. 1200). Geoffrey of Monmouth (1150) was a Welsh bishop who sketched the chivalry of the era in his collection of Celtic legends which idealized King Arthur. Archbishops Lanfranc and Anselm were important scholastics in the twelfth century. John of Salisbury, the foremost platonist (a follower of the Greek philosopher Plato, who taught that true knowledge comes from transcendent ideas) of the age, wrote a defense of logic and in *Policraticus* described the government, culture, and ethics of the times.

Two Oxford scholars, Robert Grosseteste and Roger Bacon, gained fame in the thirteenth century. Grosseteste, first chancellor of Oxford University, was a mathematician, physicist, and theologian who often directed his charges against the pope and King Henry III. His writings include the *Compendium Scientiarum*. Grosseteste's pupil at Oxford, Roger Bacon, was a brilliant and independent thinker who promoted the inductive and experimental method in the study of science and mathematics. This approach ran counter to the methods of the scholastics, who were attempting to reconcile reason and religious doctrine through deductive logic. Bacon's *Opus Majus* was a veritable encyclopedia of knowledge, with treatises on philosophy, physics, mathematics, logic, and grammar. Henry de Bracton (d. 1268) was England's outstanding medieval jurist. His *Laws and Customs of England* is still considered the finest exposition of the laws of England in the Middle Ages.

Architecture

The artistic dimension in medieval England was most beautifully expressed in church architecture. Sixteen of England's present cathedrals (including Canterbury, Lincoln, Durham, Chester, and Gloucester) were originally monastic churches built by men serving both as artists and craftsmen. The architects of Durham Cathedral solved a major problem of medieval architecture—the construction and support of a ribbed vault, oblong in plan over a central aisle. The Norman Conquest introduced Norman architecture, an adaptation of *Romanesque*, with sturdy, massive design, semicircular arches, and flat buttresses. *Gothic* architecture reached England in the reign of Henry II and soon developed distinctive variations: *Early English* (ca. 1180–1280) with a steeply-pitched roof, lancet windows and pointed arches; *Decorated Gothic* (ca. 1280–1380) with broader windows and embellished spires; and the *Perpendicular* (ca. 1380–1530) with square towers and flat-pointed arches. New architectural styles were also reflected in castles that incorporated stronger fortifications with round towers and curved walls—an idea brought back by the Crusaders. The manor houses of the country gentry changed little in this period; their central feature remained the great hall.

THE RISE OF TOWNS

Feudal law protected the baron and his farm laborers, but the town dwellers also began to insist on their rights. Those who did not fit into the feudal framework formed separate communities and set up their own laws and regulations. These corporations of burgesses, craftsmen, or students played an increasingly important role in the changing economy and society of England, a society that became more wealthy and doubled its population to about 3 million persons between 1100 and 1300.

The Boroughs

During the early Middle Ages town life was replaced by the manor and its closed domestic economy. Then in the eleventh and twelfth centuries town life began to revive as a result of better security, the rise of a money economy, and the expansion of commerce and trade both within the country and with foreign countries. The contacts with the Angevin empire, the immigration of Jews, and the Crusades spurred commercial activities. By 1300 towns and boroughs had doubled to more than one hundred, but London with its 40,000 inhabitants remained the only city of any size.

Political Status

Since the time of William the Conqueror every town was subservient to a local lord and the townspeople were under the jurisdictions of the manor court and the sheriff. Gradually the burgesses bargained for special privileges and bought charters from the king or their landlords. Like the monasteries and colleges, these free towns became independent corporations with the rights to own property, to raise taxes, to hold court, and to elect a mayor and councilors in place of a royal official. They could also deal directly with the king like any important vassal. Since the rising middle class in the boroughs had wealth, one of the quickest ways for a monarch to raise money was to sell borough charters that granted one or more of these rights. The citizens of the borough determined voting and legal rights and participated in government; whereas in the county only the nobility had influence.

MERCHANT GUILDS

The first important guild was composed of the leading merchants of the town, who regulated trade and protected the vendor and the buyer against excessive competition. This meant selling at a just price to the consumer and protecting the local merchant from outside competition. Guild economic policy opposed an open market and free competition. The policy, in turn, kept the economy from fluctuating by avoiding any sharp rise or fall in prices since both the middlemen and speculators were restricted by guild laws.

CRAFT GUILDS

Townsmen practicing the same craft, such as carpentry or tanning, developed craft guilds which regulated admission to the trade and also the quality of workmanship. The guild included the master of the trade and his apprentices, who could anticipate becoming master craftsmen by serving the required seven-year apprenticeship. By the fifteenth century the fees for the mastership became so excessive and the masters so exclusive that many expert craftsmen could not set up their own shop. They continued as hired workmen or journeymen for a master and formed a separate guild or "trade union" to protect their interests.

CONSEQUENCES OF THE RISE OF TOWNS

The revival of town life brought about several significant developments. (1) Wealth was no longer only in land; liquid capital was becoming important. (2) Rural peasants found an escape valve in the towns as individual serfs won emancipation. (3) The cities took an active role in government, and the burgesses represented the urban community in the emerging House of Commons. (4) The townsfolk increasingly sided with the king against their mutual rival—the landed nobles. (5) The urban dwellers were usually the first to encounter foreign influences: the commercial revolution, the Renaissance, and the Reformation first won support in the towns; change came much more slowly in the rural north.

The Medieval Community

Since the medieval world thought in terms of communities rather than of individuals, whatever rights existed were as part of the community. The greatest unifying force was the Church. The concept of *Corpus Christianum* made possible the Church's dominant role in the shaping of society, and for education, literature, and government to be so intimately identified with churchmen. Within this ecclesiastical framework more specific communities developed. The feudal arrangement provided laws and privileges for the warrior, landlord, and, indirectly, the serf. When all segments of society could no longer fit into this military and agricultural structure, clergy, universities and townsfolk found security in their own associations and insisted on their own rights. Thus when the House of Commons emerged, it did so as a house of communities representing counties, towns, and universities.

Medieval culture reached its finest expression in the High Middle Ages. The renewed interest in learning after the eleventh century contributed directly to the rise of universities. Scholars such as Robert Grosseteste and Roger Bacon expanded the known boundaries of knowledge in mathematics and science and, along with others, sought to reconcile the new learning with their Christian faith.

Perhaps the age's most enduring creation was the Gothic cathedral. It embodied in its stained glass windows, soaring spires, and majestic forms the medieval vision of the universe as an ordered and intelligible whole. The compassionate side of this age of faith was found in the mendicant orders of monks that sought to practice their faith by good works and serving others.

Town life was reborn and burgesses grew wealthy and self-confident in these centuries. They acquired, often by purchase from the king, their own town charters and separate political rights. This had a direct bearing on the evolving government of the realm. No longer would these towns and universities be content to be represented by a political arrangement that was based only on land and feudal allegiance.

Selected Readings

Barraclough, Geoffrey. *Social Life in Early England* (1960)

Brooke, Christopher. *The Twelfth Century Renaissance* (1969)

Curtis, Edmund. *A History of Medieval Ireland, 1086–1052* (1942)

Brown, R. Allen. *English Medieval Castles* (1976)

Knowles, Dom David. *The Monastic Orders in England 940–1216* (1963)

Lyon, Bryce. *A Constitutional and Legal History of Medieval England* (1980)

Postan, M. M. *The Medieval Economy and Society: An Economic History of Britain 1100–1500* (1972)

Power, Eileen. *Medieval Women* (1975)

Southern, R. W. *Robert Grosseteste: The Growth of an English Mind in Medieval Europe* (1986)

Stenton, Doris M. *English Society in the Early Middle Ages* (1962)

Webb, Geoffrey. *Architecture in Britain in the Middle Ages* (1956)

Williams, Gwyn A. *Medieval London: From Commune to Capital* (1963)

5

Monarchy and the Rise of Parliament: 1272–1399

The fourteenth century was a period of transition for England. It saw the erosion of confidence and the splintering of the Corpus Christianum *of the High Middle Ages. A debilitating papal schism and a growing anticlericalism weakened the Church, and the political and military bonds of feudalism were challenged. The century was profoundly affected by the bubonic plague which reduced England's population by a third between 1348 and 1350.*

Fourteenth-century England struggled, in particular, with the problem of finding a satisfactory substitute for political feudalism. Gradually Parliament slipped into the stream of English life as the institution that could best accomplish this change in governance. Not until the seventeenth century would the powers of Parliament again make such gains.

In the long run the growing sense of nationality and central government—of the king in Parliament—had more lasting effects than the more immediate concerns of the Hundred Years' War in France or civil war at home.

THE THREE EDWARDS

In the century following the death of Henry III the judicial system of England became more centralized in organization and more specialized in function. Statute law was significantly increased and defined by the king in Parliament; and through conflict and conquest the boundaries of the nation were expanded. Amidst these new developments and crises—nationalism, anticlericalism, the Black Death—the monarchy remained strong and Parliament increasingly became an important ally in governance.

Edward I, 1272–1307

Edward was the first King since the Anglo-Saxon era to be considered primarily English. His personal qualities, coupled with his reputation as a statesman and military leader, made his reign outstanding. His two great contributions to the modern British state were the development of statute law and the conquest of Wales. Tall (nicknamed "Longshanks") and attractive, King Edward was energetic and resourceful; he had learned from his father's turbulent reign that the king must reign through the law. Because of his respect for law and his legal reforms Edward I has been called the English Justinian.

Legal Reforms

Edward I confirmed and codified by legislative enactment much of the legal machinery that Henry II had set up. He did this by statute law—legislation passed by the king in Parliament—and thereby introduced into the English legal system a new type of law which took precedence over all other laws. This flurry of legislative activity would not again be matched by Parliament until the era of the Great Reform Bill (1830s). Edward and his justices were influenced by the great medieval jurist Henry de Bracton, who argued that the king must govern by the rules of the law since it was the law that made him king. The King was the fountainhead of all justice. Edward translated this theory into practice by insisting that private warrants or franchises could be valid only if they could show that they had been granted by royal charter. Among the new laws were the Statute of Gloucester (1278), which required that all holders of private jurisdiction must prove their warrant was of royal origin, and the Statute of Mortmain (1279), which prohibited a vassal from giving land to the Church without his lord's consent. *De Donis Conditionalibus* (from the Statute of Westminster, 1285) and the Statute of *Quia Emptores* (1290) made significant contributions to property law and reflected further the decline of the feudal arrangement and of the private courts.

THE MACHINERY OF JUSTICE

As baronial jurisdiction declined, royal courts increased and became more specialized in function. Three separate divisions, each stemming from the *curia regis* (the King's Council), were now in operation: the court of the exchequer for tax cases, the court of common pleas for civil cases, and the court of the king's bench for crown pleas or criminal cases. In 1275 for the first time customs duties became part of the regular revenue of the king, and an import duty, called "tunnage and poundage," soon brought in more revenue than all the king's hereditary income. However, Edward lost an old source of revenue, but won popular backing, when he expelled all Jews from England in 1290. The new statute law of Edward's was more rigid and timeless than the previous judge-made law and fostered the expansion of the legal profession as judges and lawyers increasingly became specialists.

Edward and the Church

Edward I was a devout king who remained on friendly terms with the popes without copying his father's subservience to Rome. Since the Church was the greatest landholder in the realm and as a perpetual organization never relinquished any of its property to the Crown through escheat (the reversion of lands to the original grantor because no heirs were capable of inheriting it according to the terms of the original grant), forfeitures, or wardships, Edward attempted to limit further extension of Church property without royal consent by the Statute of Mortmain. Edward also demanded a heavy income tax from the clergy to pay for some of the costs of the Crusades. In 1296 Pope Boniface VIII in the papal bull *clericis laicos* claimed such taxation could only take place with papal consent. After both King and Pope raised the stakes in the test of authority and allegiance of English churchmen, a compromise was arranged whereby "voluntary" gifts were secured from the Church.

Edward and Celtic Britain

As the first English monarch to envision a union of British peoples, Edward temporarily succeeded in subduing Wales and Scotland, but recurring revolts in these areas so harassed the King that his plans for conquest in France were frequently curtailed. Edward increased royal power in Ireland, successfully fought the Welsh and absorbed Wales into his kingdom, but he failed to conquer Scotland and, instead, aroused in the Scots a hatred of England that lasted for centuries.

WALES

In the thirteenth century the Welsh were still a pastoral people ruled by chieftains who thrived on constant war among the tribes. Following the Conquest Norman barons had carved out baronies in the border area or marches. Prince Llewelyn led the Welsh in a bid for complete independence from this Norman overlordship but the two Welsh revolts (1277, 1282) ended in their defeat by Edward I. His infant son, Edward, was designated Prince of Wales at Caernarvon Castle, and this title is still conferred upon the eldest son of Great Britain's reigning monarch. Further uprisings only extended a more direct English rule with the imposition of English laws and the shire system. The border or marcher lords remained semi-independent and would not become fully incorporated into the English government until 1536. Under Edward I the Welsh were conquered, but their assimilation took centuries.

SCOTLAND

The kingdom of Scotland had resulted from the gradual union of the Picts (the original Celtic inhabitants), the Scots (immigrants from Ireland in the fifth century), the Angles (from the Anglo-Saxon kingdom of Northumbria), and the Britons (the Celts pushed into the western highlands by the Angles). Unification began in the year 843 when Pict-land and Scot-land were merged by Kenneth Mac Alpin, King of Scots. In the centuries between the Norman Conquest and the reign of Edward I, both Anglo-Saxon and Norman influences dominated the Lowlands of Scotland while Celtic and tribal life retreated to the Highlands. Both King Malcolm III (1058–1093) and King David I (1124–1153) identified increasingly with the Norman and feudal institutions to the south.

Such amity disappeared when Edward I sought to take advantage of a disputed succession to press his claim of feudal overlord and to select John Baliol from thirteen rival candidates for the throne. When the Scots rejected his demands and made an alliance with France, Edward invaded Scotland and deposed King John. The Scots responded by rallying around two soon-to-be national heroes. The first was William Wallace, who defeated the English at Stirling Bridge (1297) and invaded northern England. When Edward returned from France he crushed the Scots at Falkirk (1298) and subdued the country a second time. The second hero, Robert Bruce, had himself crowned king at Scone, and again Edward, now over seventy, started north but died on the way to the border. His son, Edward II, a far inferior military leader, met Bruce of Bannockburn in 1314 and suffered the worst defeat of any English army in all the Middle Ages. The outcome was independence for Scotland. Edward III supported Edward Baliol over David Bruce and at the battle of Halidon Hill (1333) the English revenged their defeat at Bannockburn, but their rule over Scotland remained temporary. By 1341 David Bruce duplicated his father's feat and drove out the English. Scotland remained independent, but the country remained poverty-stricken, its nobles quarrelsome, and its economy primitive.

IRELAND

At the beginning of Edward I's reign Ireland was much like Wales, a half-conquered country. English control, going back to the twelfth century, was limited to the English Pale, a coastal strip behind Dublin. Here English law and language were found. The western and northern half of the island was almost entirely Celtic. In between was a middle zone where Norman barons from Wales, under the Earl of Pembroke ("Strongbow"), had erected baronies and built castles. Edward tried to extend the Pale and he introduced a Parliament at Dublin on the English model, but he never visited the country and accomplished little. The English extension of their authority in Ireland would wait until the era of the Tudors and Stuarts.

War with France

From the Norman Conquest to the middle of the fifteenth century the kings of England held large possessions in France. As the French kings extended their power and cultivated a sense of nationality, they constantly sought to drive out the English. No English king could allow that without incurring disgrace and humiliation at home. King Philip IV hoped to win back the province of Aquitaine from England and summoned his feudal vassal, Edward, to answer for depredations by his Gascon subjects. Edward defied the order. Consequently Philip declared his vassal, Edward, had forfeited the territory. Edward answered by declaring war in 1294. He collected a large army and made alliances with Philip's enemies, but then revolts in Wales and Scotland delayed him. The expedition ended in a truce and peace was made in 1303 on the basis of the status quo before the war.

Edward II, 1307–1327

Once again a strong king was followed by a feeble son as Edward II was to prove himself weak-willed and frivolous. His inability to govern was demonstrated by increasing dependence on favorites, beginning with the Gascon knight Piers Gaveston. In the Parliaments of 1309–1310 the barons, led by Thomas, earl of Lancaster, attempted to reassert their influence. Gaveston was banished, and a council of twenty-one Lord Ordainers was set up to control the appointments of household offices. In 1312 Edward defied this arrangement and restored Gaveston to royal favor; the barons retaliated by having Gaveston executed. The King's humiliating defeat to

Robert Bruce at Bannockburn forced him to capitulate again to the control of the Earl of Lancaster.

Baronial disunity, heavy taxes, and successful raids by the Scots in the north led to civil war in 1322. The rebellion was defeated, providing a temporary reprieve for Edward and his new favorite, Hugh Despenser. While Edward's wife, Isabella, was negotiating peace with her brother, the King of France, she became enamored with Roger Mortimer of Wales, and the two began to plot against her husband. In 1326 the Queen and Mortimer landed in England and won an easy triumph over Edward. A controlled Parliament in 1327 deposed Edward II in favor of his son, Edward, duke of Aquitaine. Shortly thereafter the deposed King was brutally murdered.

**Edward III,
1327–1377**

In contrast to Edward II's years, Edward III's reign was marked by peace at home and war abroad. At the beginning of his reign actual power rested with his mother and her lover, Mortimer. Three years later Edward, now eighteen, halted the greedy guardianship by having Parliament condemn Mortimer to death as a traitor and his mother stripped of power. Like Richard I, Edward III was a warrior-king. Chivalrous and charming, he was immensely popular. Learning from the tragedy of his father, he determined to maintain the loyalty of his barons and held their loyalty throughout his reign, as well as that of his six sons, unlike Henry II. Since Edward never threatened the barons' privileges as his grandfather, Edward I, had done, the magnates followed him in his favorite pastime, fighting. His life work was the war in France and he is charged, at times, by contemporaries and historians, with squandering the resources of the Crown and making too many concessions in Parliament to carry out this obsessive goal of victory in France.

THE HUNDRED YEARS' WAR

For over a century (1337–1453) England fought intermittently on French soil as old rivalries were renewed and new claims asserted. The fighting moved from a feudal and dynastic dispute to a national war. Although the English kings failed to conquer France, their preoccupation with the war had important side effects in England, such as the rapid increase in the use of the English language, the growth of Parliament, and rising antipapal feeling.

**Causes of
the War**

Actually a series of wars were fought, not just one war, but the term "Hundred Years' War" continues in use. The underlying cause of the war was the heritage of hostility resulting from English possessions in France.

These were a constant obstacle to the efforts of more powerful French monarchs in the fourteenth century to centralize and consolidate their holdings. Philip IV had attempted to seize Gascony in 1294, and French interference with the English rule of Gascony continued with his successors.

By 1337 Edward III was convinced that only a major war with France could prevent the annexation of Gascony by the French King. The French alliance with Scotland, which increased Edward's difficulties in his war with the Scots, added to the grievances. England's economic interdependence with Flanders was also involved. English wool supplied Flemish looms, and this trade was in jeopardy because of the increasing subserviency of the Count of Flanders to the King of France. The clash of economic interests resulted in an alliance between Edward III and the Flemish burghers against Philip and the pro-French count. When Edward decided upon war he also resurrected his claim to the French Crown. The powerful Capetian dynasty had died out after Philip the Fair's three sons had died without heirs, leaving the line of succession through Philip's daughter, Isabella, mother of Edward III. The French courts, however, disposed of Edward's claim by invoking an old Salic law forbidding inheritance through the female line and declared instead in favor of the nephew of Philip the Fair, Philip VI of Valois.

WAR: ROUND ONE, 1337–1360

The conflict between England and France is divided into two phases in each of which the English invaded France and won impressive victories after which the French rallied each time to push back the invaders. (The second phase occurs under Henry V and Henry VI in Chapter 6). In 1340 Edward assumed the title of King of France after winning the naval battle of Sluys. In 1346 Edward's major invasion began.

Battle of Crécy, 1346. At Crecy Edward III and his eldest son, Edward the Black Prince, met a much larger French army under Philip VI who was confident of victory, but the English annihilated the French cavalry by superior tactics and the innovation of the longbow. The English army then seized the port of Calais after which an eight-year truce halted the war.

Battle of Poitiers. In the summer of 1356 the English army penetrated in the heart of France under the leadership of the Black Prince, crushed the French army near Poitiers, and captured King John II and over a thousand knights.

Treaty of Brétigny, 1360. When further expeditions failed, Edward III agreed to the terms of the Treaty of Brétigny and renounced his claim to the French throne. He received Gascony, Ponthieu, and Calais and promised the release of King John in return for a ransom of £500,000. The French honored the treaty and English influence expanded in France.

English Decline. The ravages of the Black Death, the Black Prince's misrule in Aquitaine, Edward III's senility in his later years, and a new and able French king, Charles V, restored French fortunes in the years following the peace treaty. Before his death Charles won back all but a string of seaports. In 1396 King Richard II married the child-daughter of Charles VI of France and concluded an uneasy peace that lasted for twenty years. With Henry V the second phase of the war would resume.

THE RISE OF PARLIAMENT

In the thirteenth and fourteenth centuries a national Parliament evolved out of the king's court and gradually divided into two houses, a House of Lords and a House of Commons. With the collapse of feudalism as an effective basis of political life, the monarchs, as well as the barons and commoners, found in the institution of Parliament the instrument to achieve a more mature political community. Parliamentary functions and powers expanded gradually, usually as a response to an immediate need. The reigns of Henry III and the three Edwards are particularly significant in the development of Parliament. The perennial need of the monarchy for money during the Hundred Years' War became the most effective lever by which Parliament wrung concessions from the king.

Origin

The word "parliament" was a loose term referring to a meeting of the king and certain invited royal officials or influential subjects who gave advice and consent on matters of policy and taxation. Its origin goes back to the Saxon witan and the Norman Great Council, but these appointive councils were limited to the great barons and important churchmen. Under Henry I and Henry II the principle of representation and election was taking shape in the counties through the jury system; whereas King John began the custom of ordering the representative knights to London to meet with him. The kings continued the practice of having knights and burgesses (the commoners) meet with his Parliaments of officials and nobles after the Provisions of Oxford (1258), and Simon de Montfort's Parliament (1265) showed the value of such a representation. Edward I summoned knights and burgesses to thirteen of his thirty-four Parliaments; Edward II, to seventeen of his nineteen Parliaments; and Edward III, to all forty-eight of his Parliaments. Thus an experiment became a regular constitutional custom.

Composition of Parliament

The most influential members remained the great lords of the realm, who, in deference to their rank, received individual summonses to Parliament from the king. The Model Parliament of 1295 helped establish the representative principle for the Commons as all forty counties and 114 chartered boroughs were instructed to send two representatives. Eventually the lesser nobility or knights preferred to join with the town burgesses in Parliament instead of with the lords. By the middle of the fourteenth century these two groups met together as the House of Commons. The clergy and the knights met as separate estates in 1295, but thereafter the lower clergy withdrew from Parliament and voted their own taxes in convocation. The higher clergy united with the lords to form the House of Lords. By contrast, in France the first and second estates of clergy and nobles kept their ranks separate and intact and thereby had twice the influence of the third estate of town representatives.

PARLIAMENTARY FUNCTIONS

Parliament continued to be called into session because it met the needs of the various communities within the realm. It became the institution through which the king could inform his subjects of royal policies and financial needs and ascertain national sentiment through the representatives. Loyal subjects could use Parliament to petition the king or to seek the removal of unpopular royal officials by impeachment. Parliament also served as the highest court of the land. In the fourteenth and fifteenth centuries Parliament met at least annually, at which times members exchanged information, lamented their common grievances, and sought to carry out their mutual interests. Hence Parliament served to unite England into a national community, perhaps more than any other institution.

EXPANSION OF PARLIAMENTARY POWERS

By the end of the thirteenth century Parliament was an established institution, but its powers and functions were still vague until they were sharpened during the fourteenth century, at the expense of royal prerogative, largely by parliamentary exploitation of the king's need for revenue. As an example, when Edward I was fighting in France and in desperate financial straits, he was forced to agree to the Confirmation of the Charters (1297) which invoked the Magna Charta and permitted no more levying of direct nonfeudal taxes without the consent of Parliament. In 1340 Parliament took advantage of Edward III's need of money to extend its control to indirect taxation as well. The Hundred Years' War accelerated parliamentary influence since the kings were habitually in need of money to conduct their campaigns.

In 1376 Parliament first used the instrument of impeachment against the king's officials, with the House of Commons presenting the indictment and the House of Lords sitting in judgment. From the right to petition the king, Parliament slowly claimed the right to initiate legislation. The king could still veto those statutes or legislate by royal ordinance independently of

Parliament. However, Parliament's influence over finances and legislation had grown strikingly by the end of the fourteenth century.

RICHARD II AND REVOLUTION

King Richard's erratic reign (1377–1399) spanned a variety of political arrangements that included a factious regency during his youth, a baronial oligarchy, a period of royal tyranny, and a forced abdication. In this seesaw struggle between monarchy and oligarchy, the magnates supported the challenger Bolingbroke and brought the Angevin line of kings to an end.

The Regency

Richard's father, Edward the Black Prince, was Edward III's eldest son and heir to the throne, but he died in 1376, a year before his father, which raised Richard to the throne at the age of ten. The child-king had little chance to mature at court. Dominated and flattered by his ambitious guardians and his beautiful, but flighty, mother, Richard became temperamental with an overwhelming desire to be independent of the magnates who ruled in his name. At the age of fourteen he showed his courage and leadership in handling the Peasants' Revolt, but he soon gave way to the art of dissembling which became a characteristic of his adult life. The great nobles, led by the King's three uncles, took advantage of Richard's youth to conspire against each other in their scramble for powerful positions.

THE LORDS APPELLANT

Emboldened by the shifting equation between king and Parliament since Edward I, the Duke of Gloucester (an uncle of King Richard) used England's deteriorating military position in France and Scotland to oppose his nephew. Gloucester's faction became known as the Lords Appellant because they "appealed" or accused Richard's advisors of treason. Soon all power was in their hands and their "Merciless Parliament" of 1388 banished or condemned to death the King's friends. Five of the Lords Appellant tried to run the government but with no more success than earlier efforts at an oligarchy.

Richard as Ruler

In 1389 Richard II surprised the Lords Appellant by asserting his independence and running his own government. For the next eight years he ruled in a reasonably "constitutional" manner even as he sought to restore the royal prerogative. Then in 1397 Richard radically changed his manner of conduct, exhibited the characteristics of a megalomaniac and made a bid for despotic power. His revenge on the Lords Appellant resulted in the murder of Gloucester, the execution of Arundel, and the banishment of Warwick. He packed Parliament with supporters, passed retroactive anti-treason laws, and began to confiscate baronial estates. When his uncle, John of Gaunt, died in 1399, Richard forbade the rightful heir, Henry Bolingbroke, from inheriting the estate. This act frightened all propertied classes and at the same time brought forth a leader to rally the opponents of the King.

REVOLUTION AND ABDICATION

Richard II proceeded to Ireland to quell a rebellion. In July 1399 Henry Bolingbroke defied his banishment and returned to England; within weeks he had won massive support. Richard was captured upon his return, and a partisan Parliament read thirty-three charges against him and forced his abdication. Henry Bolingbroke claimed the throne by conquest and heredity (see Lancaster and York genealogical table, p. 428). Parliament tried to legalize the forced abdication by statute, but it remained a successful baronial coup and hardly a triumph for constitutionalism, except insofar as it stopped short a move toward royal absolutism. Richard's reign clearly illustrated a basic reason for Parliament's growth: that neither king nor barons were quite strong enough to rule without the other for any length of time. Therefore, each element, to protect its own interests, wanted and needed Parliament and the added strength of the House of Commons.

FOURTEENTH-CENTURY ENGLAND

The outstanding constitutional feature of the century was the manner in which the king, lords, and commons "checked and checkmated" each other and gradually compromised themselves into a state of reluctant cooperation. But these years also witnessed a period wasted in foreign wars and glory, the devastating effect of the plague, and growing social and religious upheaval. The woolen industry expanded rapidly, the English language soon outranked Latin and French, and antipapal feeling steadily increased.

Trade and Industry

Agricultural prosperity, increasing population, and the growth of woolen exports took place in the first part of the century. Then with the loss of population and the agricultural depression that followed the Black Death, England began to develop its own woolen industry, instead of letting foreigners continue to profit by importing English wool, spinning and weaving it, and selling it back as a finished product. In 1363 the King granted Calais a monopoly as the sole staple town in the export of wool. The government also encouraged the cloth industry since cloth had a much wider market than wool. To manufacture cloth the "putting out" system was developed which permitted English capitalists unlimited expansion by separating functions of production. The merchants could give as many small "contracts" to weavers, dyers, or spinners as they were able to market. The textile industry became England's first big business.

The Black Death, 1348–1349

The bubonic plague, which had swept across Europe from the East, struck England and wiped out at least one-third of the population. It halted the Hundred Years' War for two years and broke up society by the flight of the privileged from the towns. It was carried by black rats and spread by fleas that they carried, and was followed by a pneumonic plague which spread by direct human contagion. The plague returned, with lesser casualties, five times throughout the century. It reappeared intermittently for three centuries until the brown rat, which was not a carrier of the plague, drove out the black rat, which was. While the plague raged, some citizens resorted to looting and licentiousness; others attempted to do penance to placate an angry God.

The consequences of the plague were momentous: Half the clergy died of it; the great loss of population resulted in decreased servants and increased wages; prices rose and rents fell; farm rentals replaced the feudal system of labor services; and sheep farming increased because it required less manpower. The landlords tried to mitigate these changes by having Parliament pass the Statute of Laborers (1351) which froze both wages and prices; however, the act met with little success.

The Peasants' Revolt, 1381

The profound frustrations and social changes brought about by the Black Death, the changing economy, and the dissatisfaction with the Statute of Laborers culminated in a peasants' revolt which began in the two southeastern counties of Essex and Kent. The poll taxes of 1377 and 1380 had touched off a deep sense of economic injustice felt by the peasants against the privileged classes. The insurgents, led by Wat Tyler and Jack Straw, marched on London, burning manor records and houses of landlords as they went. In London the government seemed paralyzed while the rioters opened up prisons, burned homes, and murdered the most hated royal officials. At this point the fourteen-year-old Richard II bravely met the rioters and pacified them with promises of manorial reform and the abolition of serfdom. When Tyler was unexpectedly slain, Richard halted the wrath of the rebels by claiming that he would be their leader. The rioters went home and smaller revolts elsewhere were subdued. The revolt failed in its objectives for the King's promises were never kept and exploitation of peasants continued; yet attention was focused on the plight of the peasants for the first time.

Religious Discontent

Peasant discontent was also inspired, in part, by the growing criticism of the Church. The spiritual vigor of the Church had declined rapidly in the fourteenth century and the outcries against Church wealth and immorality became more strident. It is perhaps indicative of the decline that not one Englishman was canonized in the fourteenth century. Furthermore, the English Church suffered when the papal seat was moved by the French to Avignon (1305–1378). England, with rising national sentiment and at war with France, resented such papal subserviency to their enemy, and Parliament proceeded to penalize the pro-French popes by a series of statutes. The Statute of Provisors (1351) made the acceptance of Church office without royal consent a criminal offense. The Statute of Praemunire, two years later, penalized efforts to circumvent the jurisdiction of the English courts by appealing to the papal court. In 1366 Parliament repudiated the agreement to pay the annual tribute to the Pope that King John had begun.

WYCLIFFE AND THE LOLLARDS

John Wycliffe (1328–1384) provided the first frontal attack on the political power and theological underpinnings of the church. An Oxford professor of influence and a forceful writer, he translated the Latin Vulgate Bible into English, preached against ecclesiastical ownership of land, and urged the Church to find its way back to the Bible as the sole source of authority. He also questioned the central doctrine of transubstantiation (the belief that the bread and wine of the Eucharist were transformed into the true presence of Christ). Many of his views coincided with those of his patron, John of Gaunt, so he escaped punishment for his opinions. Wycliffe formed a following of "poor priests" (Lollards) who spread his doctrines after his death. Their anticlerical and evangelical preaching may have encouraged the Peasants' Revolt in 1381; no matter, it made it more easy for the Church to suppress the Lollards as heretics. This time no powerful baron protected the priests and the movement was largely stamped out, but not before Wycliffe's writings had spread to Bohemia where they influenced Jan Hus, a religious reformer whose ideas anticipated those of Martin Luther and the Reformation.

Language and Literature

The anti-French and antipapal feeling aroused by Henry III's favorites and the Hundred Years' War hastened the adoption of the English language. Three years after the battle of Crécy grammar school masters began to construe Latin into English instead of French. In 1362 cases in law courts were pleaded in English, and, in the following year, the chancellor opened Parliament with an address in English. Wycliffe wrote his popular works in English and John Gower (1330–1408) wrote his later poems in English.

The most important poets of the Middle English period were William Langland and Geoffrey Chaucer. Langland's poem *Piers Plowman* (1362) was composed as a series of allegories attacking in both satirical and didactical fashion the corrupt society of the day. Chaucer (ca. 1340–1400), often called England's first major poet, blended superb literary technique and masterful storytelling. He provided the best account of contemporary life in his *Canterbury Tales*. The conversation of his pilgrims ranged across the whole spectrum of medieval life, from otherworldliness to the bawdy capers of the knight and the miller. Throughout the tales the sense of religious dissatisfaction and unabashed earthiness foreshadowed the Renaissance and Reformation eras to come.

*A*s the fourteenth century closed, the Catholic universalism of the High Middle Ages was visibly shifting toward modern nationalism marked by the supremacy of English as the language of the realm, a rising anticlericalism, and the growth of capitalism. This transition was at the expense of such medieval customs as feudalism and scholasticism.

In other respects many medieval foundations continued to prosper, such as the rule of law by the consent of the communities of the realm (the king in Parliament), the universities, the common law, and the king's council. A century in flux gives us two contradictory images: a glittering time of Crusades and castles and chivalry, and, at the same time, a century of spiritual agony and human despair exemplified by the papal schism, the great plague of 1348–1349, and peasant revolts.

With Richard II's forced abdication in 1399 the Plantagenet line of rulers came to an end and the succession became irregular for the first time in two hundred years. For the next century the competition of rival families for the throne would afflict England with civil war and prove the truth of Henry IV's words in Shakespeare: "Uneasy lies the head that wears a Crown."

Selected Readings

Barrow, Geoffrey. *Robert Bruce* (1965)
Brewer, Derek S. *Chaucer* (1973)
Haskins, G. L. *The Growth of English Representative Government* (1948)
McFarlane, K. B. *John Wycliffe and the Beginnings of English Nonconformity* (1952)
McKisack, May. *The Fourteenth Century, 1307–1399* (1959)
Perroy, Edouard. *The Hundred Years' War* (1951)
Prestwich, Michael. *The Three Edwards: War and State in England, 1272–1377* (1980)
Salzman, L. F. *Edward I* (1968)
Sayles, G. O. *The King's Parliament of England* (1974)
Tuchman, Barbara. *A Distant Mirror: The Calamitous 14th Century* (1978)
Ziegler, Philip. *The Black Death* (1969)

6

Lancaster and York

1371 Robert II, first king of the House of Stuart, begins his reign in Scotland

1399 Henry Bolingbroke (Henry IV) claims the throne of England to become the first ruler from the House of Lancaster

1403 Henry IV defeats the Welsh and Northumberland rebellion at the Battle of Shrewsbury

1413 Accession of Henry V to the throne and the renewal of the Hundred Years' War

1415 The French army is annihilated by Henry V and the English at the Battle of Agincourt

1431 Joan of Arc is burned at the stake for heresy

1440 Eton, one of many grammar schools, is founded by Henry VI

1455–1485 The Wars of the Roses

1461 Edward IV, first of three Yorkist rulers, defeats the Lancastrians at the Battle of Towton to claim the throne

1477 First printing press set up in England by William Caxton

1485 Henry Tudor, earl of Richmond, defeats King Richard III at Battle of Bosworth Field to end the Yorkist rule

At first glance the fifteenth century appears to be little more than a time of violence, conspiracy, and demoralization of society. Decades of disputed royal succession followed the death of Richard II, the last of the legitimate Plantagenet kings of England.

But the century enveloped more than the breakdown of government. Noteworthy progress in education and literacy took place, foreign trade prospered, and Parliament expanded its functions. In a century of powerful nobles and a government in disarray, Edward IV, a consummate politician-king, reversed the trend toward factionalism and reestablished royal authority.

Through this century the military, political, and economic cornerstones of feudalism were visibly disintegrating in practice, if not always in theory. The professional knight, the fief, and the manor, as keystones of medieval life, were less important with each passing generation. In their place appeared a kingdom moving perceptibly toward a nation state, the supremacy of the English language over French and Latin, the rise of commerce, and a money economy.

THE LANCASTRIAN KINGS

Although the Lancasters claimed the throne by heredity, Henry IV did not have the best claim and was actually King by conquest. This usurpation led to a century of disputed successions during which Parliament became the tool of rival factions. The Lancasters became preoccupied with securing the throne at home and pressing their claim to the throne of France.

Henry IV, 1399–1413

Weakened by an uncertain title, Henry Bolingbroke spent most of his reign defending his throne. The difficulties that marked his reign were rarely of his own making for he was astute and experienced in political maneuvering; he realized that his sovereignty depended on the allegiance of his subjects. Henry was able and energetic, and it took all his skill to resist the growing power of the lords and the demand of the House of Commons to control taxation.

REBELLION

In 1403 a serious rebellion took shape when Owen Glendower, a Welsh landowner, aroused Welsh nationalism and allied himself with the Percys of Northumberland in an effort to replace Henry with the Earl of March. Henry intercepted the Percys near Shrewsbury, defeated them, and killed Harry Hotspur, the fiery-tempered son of the Earl of Northumberland. King Henry's eldest son, Henry (Shakespeare's "Prince Hal"), halted the Welsh rebellion. In 1408 royal forces defeated the second Percy rebellion, and Northumberland was killed. Finally Henry IV was secure in his kingdom, but exhausted and ill.

PARLIAMENTARY POWER

Parliament consistently denied Henry IV adequate revenues in order to keep him dependent on its power to raise taxes. During his reign the House of Commons reached the height of its power in medieval times. The Commons was not so much interested in controlling the government as it was in controlling taxes. To gain additional revenue Henry had to reluctantly agree to such restraints on his authority as Parliament's sole right to initiate money bills, their appointment of treasurers to administer taxes, and their authority to nominate councilors to supervise his administration. Henry resisted these encroachments as best he could. His last years were difficult, as his eldest son, Henry, was impatient to replace his father and fight France. In 1413 Henry died broken in health and spirit.

Henry V, 1413–1422

When Henry V ascended the throne, he directed his military and organizing abilities to the conquest of France in a renewal of the Hundred Years' War. Once more the nation united in a patriotic fervor against their old foe. Henry's victories marked the high tide of English success in France. At home he was not seriously threatened by rebellion as was his father, and he seemed to think the Lollards ("poor priests" who followed John Wycliffe) more dangerous than Wales or Scotland. Lollard executions increased, and their new leader, Sir John Oldcastle, was imprisoned and later burned as a heretic in the fires of Smithfield.

The Hundred Years' War: Round Two, 1414–1453

When Henry V came to the throne, conditions in France were again ripe for English intervention. The French King, Charles VI, was insane, and the country was sharply divided between rival factions of Burgundians and Orléanists. In 1415 Henry allied himself with the Burgundians and landed in France with a well-equipped army; his objective was the union of France and England under one crown.

Battle of Agincourt, 1415. On the road to Calais Henry and his troops confronted a French army five times its size at a woods near Agincourt. Before nightfall the French forces were routed and slaughtered. The victory brought Henry great prestige and large sums of money from ransoms.

Treaty of Troyes, 1420. With their allies, the Burgundians, capturing Paris, Henry was in a position to exact his terms. According to the Treaty of Troyes, Henry was to marry Charles VI's daughter, Katherine, and be recognized as heir to, and regent of, the French throne. With the death of Charles, Henry was to realize his goal and inherit the French throne. This was the high-water mark of English hopes in France. Before the terms of the treaty could take place, Henry contracted dysentery and died at thirty-five, leaving a year-old son, Henry VI, to try and make good his title to France. Charles VI of France died a few months after Henry.

Henry VI and France. At first the English under Henry V's able brother, the Duke of Bedford, made easy headway against the young dauphin who assumed the title of Charles VII. By 1429 the English were besieging the weak Charles in his last stronghold, Orléans, and all hope for an independent France appeared doomed. At this juncture a young peasant girl, Joan of Arc, saved France by her vision of divine guidance. Inspired by her leadership the French broke the siege of Orléans and advanced on Paris. Joan was captured by the Burgundians, sold to the English, tried by the French clergy, and burned as a witch. The tide now turned against the English as the Burgundians changed sides, and in quick succession Paris, Rouen and Guienne fell to the French. When this longest of wars finally ended in 1453 only Calais remained in English hands.

Results of the War. France won the war even though it lost most of the famous battles. A lasting legacy of antagonism ensued between England and France that lasted until 1914 and World War I. Nevertheless, England's loss of its French possessions was to its advantage because the nation was now freed from involvement in a hopeless Continental enterprise and could turn its attention to problems at home and commercial expansion overseas. During the war years Parliament had exploited the monarchy's constant need for money by bargaining for substantial concessions from the kings. National identities were forged by the war even though the conflict began as a dynastic rivalry. The introduction of longbows revolutionized medieval warfare and hastened the demise of feudalism by mastering the previously invincible mounted knight. Finally, the surge of nationalism resulting from the war introduced a new kind of professional or mercenary army (requiring direct taxation) and made Englishmen eager to limit the influence of a foreign papacy.

Henry VI at Home

Henry inherited very little of his father's energy or genius but copied instead the traits of madness of his grandfather, Charles VI of France. During his minority his uncles, the able Duke of Bedford and the not-so-able Duke of Gloucester, controlled the government. After Bedford's death, government authority deteriorated rapidly. In 1445 Henry married a fury, Margaret of Anjou, who ruled him and tried to rule the country. Caring only for religion and books, Henry was utterly ineffective as king even though he was also perceived by contemporaries as a pious king-saint.

The humiliation of losing territory in France increased popular dissatisfaction with the King. In 1450 Jack Cade of Kent expressed the restlessness of the gentry and yeomen by leading a three-county rebellion against the government. Cade's followers marched into London with little resistance and demanded better justice, the free election of knights to Parliament, and payment of the King's debts to his creditors. In time Cade was caught and killed, but other uprisings continued. In 1453 when the inept

Henry VI went completely mad and at the same time became a father, the stage was set for political factionalism to erupt into warfare.

THE WARS OF THE ROSES

Following the end of the Hundred Years' War in France (1453) two rival English Houses with private liveried armies fought each other for the next thirty years for the throne and for political power. Tradition has labeled this dynastic civil feud the Wars of the Roses, from the white rose emblem of the House of York and the red rose of the House of Lancaster. In fact, the red rose was not a Lancastrian emblem, but was adopted when the wars were over by the next dynasty, the Tudors. These struggles between aristocratic factions decimated the ranks of the nobility but made less impact on the country at large except to add more disruption to a time of trouble and disorder.

Origins of the Wars

The circumstances that led to war did not involve any basic differences in theories of government but centered on the breakdown of the whole structure of medieval government and the failure of Henry VI to provide any kind of strong leadership to address the problems. The economic recession and the breakdown of cooperation between the King and the ruling classes in Parliament contributed to the restlessness. The humiliating defeats in France and the unpopularity of Queen Margaret and of the King's advisors made matters worse. Finally, the inability of the government to maintain law and order tempted challengers to take matters into their own hands.

The basis for the divided allegiance of the nobility was the dynastic struggle between York and Lancaster. Until 1453 Henry VI was childless, and the best claim to succeed him was made by Richard, duke of York, who had a more direct descent from Edward III than the Lancastrian kings. In 1453 the matter of genealogy was complicated by the birth of a son to Henry and Queen Margaret and by the first of his several periods of insanity. With the king incapacitated, the House of Lords appointed York as Lord Protector. The next year the King recovered and the Queen retaliated by ousting York and his friends from office. York resorted to arms and war began.

Course of the Wars

The battles of this dynastic struggle were brutal and were mostly fought on a small scale by groups of noblemen and their bands of private mercenaries. Except for brief intervals the Yorkists controlled the government through the period with Edward IV, Richard's son, reigning as the first of three Yorkist kings.

Battle of St. Albans. The fighting began with a Yorkist victory at St. Albans in 1455. The Duke of Somerset was killed and York became Lord Protector as madness once again disabled King Henry. With his recovery Queen Margaret returned control to the Lancastrians, and in 1459 the leading Yorkists fled into exile.

Battle of Towton. In 1460 the Yorkists invaded England from France and Ireland and defeated the royalist forces, but neither the Queen nor the House of Lords would recognize the Duke of York's bid to replace Henry VI as King. Before the end of the year York was killed and Richard Neville, earl of Warwick, was defeated. The Lancastrian interlude was brief as Edward rallied the Yorkists, entered London, and proclaimed himself King. Moving north with his army, Edward IV engaged the Lancastrians at Towton on Palm Sunday, 1461, in what is termed "the bloodiest battle on English soil." Although Henry VI escaped to Scotland, Towton effectively ended sixty-two years of Lancastrian rule.

Edward IV, 1461–1483

The new Yorkist King spent the first ten years of his reign protecting his throne against the challenges of his friend, Warwick, and his foes, the Lancastrians. Warwick, the "kingmaker," and the Neville family helped put Edward on the throne, but changed sides when Warwick and the King had a fallout over foreign policy and choice of a marriage partner for the King. In 1470 Warwick signed a compact with Queen Margaret and the Lancastrians, marched on London, and released Henry VI from prison. The next year Edward IV returned from Burgundy and crushed the Lancastrian army at the Battle of Barnet, during which Warwick was killed. A month later Edward defeated Queen Margaret's army at Tewkesbury; the Queen was captured and her only son was killed. Henry VI died in the Tower, presumably murdered, and the direct Lancastrian line was wiped out.

Edward governed better than the previous Lancastrians and restored a strong monarchy and confidence in government. He managed this without paying much attention to Parliament since he was never in the financial predicament that permitted Parliament to use its most effective weapon of consent to new taxation. Edward greatly improved the finances of the Crown by abandoning the futile and expensive war in France and by confiscating his enemies' estates and receiving "gifts" from friendly magnates and the merchants of London. Edward also centralized power in the hands of trusted royal officials and councilors. The King was an astute and brilliant soldier and businessman, capable of sound decisions, who paid close attention to the management of finances. It was during his reign that the power of the monarchy began to revive.

Richard III

Edward IV died suddenly in 1483 from overindulgence in food and the feverish pursuit of pleasure. He left two young princes to be protected in their minority by either the Queen Mother, Elizabeth Woodville, or their uncle, Richard of Gloucester. Richard had served his brother well as an administrator and advisor; however his overriding ambition and suspicion of the Queen and her relatives caused him to act rapidly and without scruple to win the Crown for himself. In short order he arrested the supporters of the Queen, intimidated the Great Council into making him Lord Protector, imprisoned the two princes—the uncrowned Edward V and his brother, Richard—in the Tower, and had his enemies executed. On July 6, Richard was crowned King, claiming that Edward's sons were illegitimate. Shortly thereafter the two princes were murdered in the Tower. In the next two years Richard tried to compensate for his violent seizure of the throne by efforts at good government, but his unpopularity increased and he soon resorted to oppressive measures.

End of the Wars

As disaffection grew against King Richard, many gentry and clergy joined the Earl of Richmond (Henry Tudor) in France. In August 1485, with the backing of King Louis XI of France, Henry landed in his native Wales. The armies of Henry and Richard met at Bosworth Field where the King showed great personal courage. However, key magnates, including Lord Stanley, deserted their King in battle and Richard was killed and his army dispersed. The Crown was placed upon the head of the conqueror, the future Henry VII.

Bosworth Field was the final battle of the Wars of the Roses. The country now yearned for a strong, orderly government that could bring peace. The wars had exhausted the power of the nobility for they had suffered the greatest casualties and many of their leaders were dead. Parliament, too, went into a decline or was used only to sanction the king's actions. At the same time the wars brought the king and the townsmen closer together in common opposition to their mutual opponent, the feudal nobility.

FIFTEENTH-CENTURY ENGLAND

The dynastic and military maneuvers of the fifteenth century overshadow other areas of English life, but in so doing they create a false picture. Political demoralization and preoccupation with war and violence did not necessarily carry over into all other areas of life. Consequently the century is more correctly a transitional era as medieval times dissolved into the age of the Renaissance.

The Economy

The export of raw wool declined during the century, but the manufacture and export of woolen cloth increased dramatically and led to a search for new markets and the subsequent growth of the merchant navy. Trading organizations, such as the Merchant Adventurers, began to flourish, and during the reign of Edward IV royal support was given to commerce. There followed a notable rise in the prosperity of city merchants and country gentry which, in turn, augmented their influence. The country gentry were increasingly becoming a *rentier* class, who, instead of farming their lands, rented them out to an emerging yeoman class of small farmers—a class later known as "the backbone" of England.

In this century the merchants were also escaping from the inhibiting regulations of the medieval guilds as they looked to the king for support in their attempts at national and international trade. It was the large landowners who suffered the sharpest economic decline in this century. The civil wars and economic depression affected their standard of living sharply. The population of England dropped dramatically during the century from 5 million at the end of the thirteenth century to only 2.2 million in 1485 as a result of the Black Death and related diseases.

Education

The fifteenth century saw a significant growth in new colleges and endowments and in the expansion of old schools. About two hundred grammar schools were in existence, including Eton, founded by Henry VI in 1440. Henry also founded King's College, Cambridge, and his wife founded Queens'. Half a dozen other colleges were also established during the century. In London the famous Inns of Court, established in the thirteenth century, became prestigious centers of legal training.

Literature

There was little intellectual vitality in the century compared to earlier and later centuries. The revival of learning came later in England than on the Continent, slowed down, in part, by the confusion and anarchy of the Wars of the Roses. In 1477, under the patronage of Edward IV, William Caxton set up the first printing press in England. In contrast to the new secularism of the Italian Renaissance, Englishmen in the fifteenth century still read works dealing primarily with moral or semireligious themes.

POETRY

No author in the fifteenth century approached Chaucer, although several of his disciples tried to imitate him: John Lydgate (ca. 1420 in *The Story of Thebes* and *The Troy Book*, and Thomas Occleve (ca. 1411) in the *Dialogue* and *De Regimine Principum*.

PROSE

The Paston Letters, the correspondence of three generations of the Paston family of Norfolk, provide some of the most illuminating historical and social documents of the years 1422–1509. In 1469 Sir Thomas Malory compiled *Morte d'Arthur* in which he recaptured the legend of Arthur and the knights of the Round Table. Two important writers in law and political philosophy were Sir John Fortescue (ca. 1394–ca. 1476) and Sir Thomas Littleton (c. 1407–1481). In his *De Laudibus Legum Angliae* Fortescue showed a mastery of common law, whereas Littleton is distinguished for classic treatises on estates and real property law found in his *Tenures*.

Courts and Parliaments

The spirit of lawlessness and defiance of authority that was characteristic of the century undermined the process of justice: Royal judges lost their authority as kings lost their power; justices of the peace were bribed or intimidated by local lords and their liveried retinues; jurors were bought; and sheriffs were little more than agents of local magnates. The nobles also tried to use the Lancastrian Parliaments as their instrument, but this did not keep the functions of Parliament from becoming even more firmly established. Parliament was clearly recognized as the highest court of law in the land. The House of Commons was fully accepted as a separate entity, and in 1429 legislation made voting privileges uniform for the first time. The famous "forty-shilling freeholder" franchise was adopted. This meant that the right to elect members of Parliament in the counties was limited to freeholders whose income from property was worth a minimum of forty shillings. The Commons increased its influence over taxation. As the middle class of gentry and merchants grew in influence, so did the House of Commons.

THE KING'S COUNCIL

There were wide variations in the membership and power of the King's Council during the century. Under Henry V it was a small group of close friends; under Henry VI it came under the control of barons chosen by the House of Lords. In the reign of Edward IV the council became largely an administrative body with little influence since real authority resided with the King and certain of his key advisors, such as the Earl of Warwick. With few exceptions, what the century seemed most to lack was "strong central governance"; this was to be provided in full measure by the new Tudor dynasty.

HISTORY OF SCOTLAND, 1066–1485

Not until the eighteenth century with the Act of Union (1707) would Scotland become formally united with England. Until then the very location of Scotland made it an important factor in the reign of each English king, either in his efforts to expand his power and conquer the country or to defend England from Scottish reprisals.

Scottish Government and Society

Although the majority of Scots were Celtic in blood and background, the form of government and manner of speech in Scotland came from Saxon and Norman England more than from Ireland and Wales. In the Lowlands (southeast) Norman barons established their feudal arrangements, and Scottish kings copied English laws. In the north, the Highlanders never accepted this modified "English" society but rather maintained tribal law and customs until after their final revolt in 1745.

Summary of Scottish History, 1066–1272

Malcolm II, who succeeded in unifying Scotland as a kingdom at the beginning of the eleventh century, was followed by Duncan and Macbeth; the latter was overthrown by Malcolm III in 1057. Malcolm later fought with William the Conqueror and was forced to pay him homage. After a period of upheaval David I restored order and lived peacefully with England until 1138 when he was defeated at the Battle of the Standard. English domination peaked in the reign of Henry II when he claimed and received homage from all Scotland. Richard I assisted the return of independence to Scotland by his long absences from England and his annulment of the Treaty of Falaise for a sum of money. The reigns of Alexander II (1214–1249) and his son Alexander III (1249–1286) gave Scotland a lengthy interlude of peace and prosperity.

BALIOL, WALLACE, AND BRUCE

Following the death of Alexander III a disputed succession to the Scottish throne arose. Edward I of England asserted his claim to the overlordship of all Scotland and awarded the crown to John Baliol.

John Baliol (1292–1296). King John grew restive under English suzerainty because of Edward's constant demand for men and money for the French wars. In 1295 John made an alliance with France, which began three centuries of Franco-Scottish friendship, and renounced his homage to Edward. Edward decisively defeated the Scots at Dunbar (1296), deposed King John, and ruled Scotland through English commissioners.

William Wallace (1297–1305). After leading a guerrilla campaign, Wallace collected an army and defeated the English at Stirling Bridge in 1297. In the following year the Scots under his command surrendered to King Edward after the Battle of Falkirk. In 1305 Wallace was captured by the English and hanged as a traitor.

Robert Bruce (1306–1329). A grandson of the claimant against Baliol, Bruce in 1306 had himself crowned king at Scone, built up an army, and prepared to meet Edward I; however, the English king died en route to give battle. By 1314 Bruce had taken all English garrisons in Scotland except Stirling. Edward II finally brought his army north and met Bruce at Bannockburn in 1314. The battle became a glorious Scottish victory and made independence possible. The Treaty of Northampton (1328) confirmed both Bruce's kingship and Scotland's freedom from English overlordship.

Summary of Scottish History, 1329–1371

In the fourteenth century the contest for the throne of Scotland was between Edward Baliol, son of John Baliol, and David II, son of Robert Bruce. After an unsuccessful attempt to usurp the crown from King David, Baliol was ousted and fled to England for sanctuary. In 1333 Edward III of England defeated the Scots at Halidon Hill and placed Baliol on the throne. David escaped to France, Baliol was repudiated by the Scots for his homage to King Edward, and intermittent war between England and Scotland took place for the next two decades, with France aiding Scotland. In 1346 David invaded England but was captured at Neville's Cross and remained a captive in London. By the Treaty of Berwick (1357) David Bruce was ransomed for 100,000 marks. He reigned until 1371.

The House of Stuart

Toward the end of the fourteenth century and afterward there was a struggle between the Stuarts and their rivals for power. The intrigues and battles that took place resembled those fought south of the border in the Wars of the Roses.

Robert II (1371–1390). King Robert, the first of the Stuarts, began his reign by signing a truce with England's John of Gaunt. Then in 1385 Scotland allied itself with France and Richard II invaded Scotland. Three years later the Scots retaliated by invading England and defeating the Percys at the Battle of Otterburn.

Robert III (1390–1406). Because of his physical disability Robert III was a weak ruler; the real power was administered by the King's brother, the Duke of Albany. The King gave the guardianship of his elder son, David, duke of Rothesay, to Albany, who starved him to death at Falkland. When King Robert died, Albany became a regent of considerable ability.

James I (1406–1437). For nearly a decade King Robert's youngest son, James, was held a prisoner by Henry IV. Returning from England in 1424, James promptly introduced English statute law and reformed the judiciary. He also kept the barons in check until he was murdered by Sir Robert Graham in 1437.

James II (1437–1460). James was only seven when he inherited the throne, so that during his minority Scotland was governed until 1449 by a series of regents. A new civil war between the Stuarts and the Douglases ended in victory for James. Under his rule Scotland again saw security and prosperity, as well as some important reforms in land tenure and in the administration of justice. In 1460 James was killed by the accidental explosion of a cannon during the siege of Roxburgh Castle.

James III (1460–1488). In 1474 an Anglo-Scottish treaty was concluded that brought peace, after Edward IV had found that his support of the Douglases against the Stuarts was futile. King James patronized the arts, extended his rule over the islands surrounding Scotland, and lived in a luxurious manner. He concluded another truce with Richard III that confirmed his supremacy in Scotland; however, his own nobles rebelled against his increasing powers and murdered him in 1488. His son, James IV, would deal with the first two Tudor kings of England.

The transition from the Yorkist to Tudor age at first augured little change from the factional feudalism of the preceding decades. Indeed, the first ten years of the new Tudor rule will seem to bear out the observation that this was only another chapter in the deadly political game of claiming the throne and fending off challengers.

Significant changes were about to occur, however. The new nationalism set the stage for religious nationalism as well and a willingness to repudiate foreign religious authority (the papacy). The country yearned for peace and order after a century of wars and disorder. A powerful intellectual and literary renaissance was beginning.

Certainly the new dynasty did not seek to establish a new order. Rather, Henry Tudor would draw on the tradition of Edward IV and the earlier Edwards to reconstruct a governance model and assert the influence of a strong, secure central government, but one that still ruled most of the time with the consent of Parliament.

Selected Readings

Barber, Richard (ed.). *The Pastons: The Letters of a Family in the Wars of the Roses* (1984)

Bennett, Henry S. *Chaucer and the Fifteenth Century* (1947)

Brown, P. H. *A Short History of Scotland* (1955)

Chrimes, S. B. *Lancastrians, Yorkists and Henry VII* (1964)

Goodman, A. *The Wars of the Roses* (1981)

Griffiths, Ralph A. *The Reign of Henry VI* (1981)

Jacob, Ernest. *The Fifteenth Century, 1399–1485* (1961)

Kendall, Paul Murray. *The Yorkist Age* (1962)

Mackenzie, Agnes M. *Robert Bruce, King of Scots* (1956)

Ross, Charles. *Edward IV* (1974)

Trevelyan, George M. *England in the Age of Wycliffe* (1920)

Wilkinson, B. *Constitutional History of England in the Fifteenth Century, 1399–1485* (1964)

7

The Early Tudors and the Reformation: 1485–1558

*H*enry VII and Henry VIII, each in his own way, reconstructed and strengthened the monarchy as an institution and as the symbol of England's growing national self-consciousness. The strong royal government they provided gave England the peace, security, and self-confidence that it so obviously lacked through much of the fifteenth century.

At the same time the ferment of rising nationalism encouraged a religious and intellectual reawakening that produced a religious revolt and later a literary renaissance. The religious issue dominated the reigns of Henry VIII, Edward VI, and Mary.

This period also shows that economic, social, and intellectual forces do not alone shape history. Individual whims and actions also shape society. Henry VIII's insistence on a divorce helped make England a Protestant nation while Thomas Cromwell's calculated use of Parliament as the instrument to break away from the papacy made future royal dependence on Parliament even more certain.

HENRY VII

Henry Tudor faced the enormous problem of restoring royal authority and order in the country, a task made even more difficult by the fact that he, himself, had a very tenuous claim to the throne. In spite of these obstacles, King Henry was highly successful in both his domestic and foreign policies and left his son the richest treasury in Europe. In his quiet way Henry may well have done more to unite Great Britain than any monarch since the first Edward.

Consolidation of Power

With only a remote Lancastrian claim to the throne that he traced through his mother back to John of Gaunt (the younger son of Edward III), Henry VII seemed at first to be only one more temporarily successful dynastic ruler. He immediately moved to strengthen his position by having Parliament confirm his title on the grounds of heredity, even though he was actually king by conquest. Henry then married Edward IV's oldest surviving daughter, Elizabeth of York, thereby joining the two rival houses of York and Lancaster. His next move was to curb the power of the nobles.

LIVERY AND MAINTENANCE

Henry's first Parliament revived an earlier statute against livery and maintenance (the right of nobles to retain a private, uniformed retinue of soldiers). The legislation helped reduce the individual power base of leading magnates and possible challengers to his sovereignty.

COURT OF STAR CHAMBER

To enforce the judicial authority of the central government, Henry's Star Chamber Act (1487) revived the jurisdiction of his Council over all cases of livery and maintenance, bribery, and civil disorder. The Court of Star Chamber (so named because of the starred ceiling of the room where it met) was under Henry's direct influence. The court's officers of state and two chief justices operated without juries and developed swift and effective procedures to enforce the common law. Its vigorous prosecution of lawbreakers gradually compelled the nobles to accept royal authority since they could not intimidate or bribe this court as they could a local jury. In Tudor times the court was popular with the people for it could act impartially and bring to justice those overlords who disregarded the rights of Englishmen in their local district. The unpopularity of the Court of Star Chamber stems from the seventeenth century when its original purposes no longer applied and when the Stuarts used it to oppose Parliament.

RIVAL CLAIMANTS

Domestic and foreign enemies of the King exploited Henry's flimsy title to the Crown by supporting various pretenders to the throne. Lambert Simnel impersonated the Earl of Warwick and won the backing of Yorkist sympathizers and of Margaret, duchess of Burgundy. In 1487 he landed in England with an army of Irishmen and German mercenaries. After the invaders were defeated, Simnel was put to work as a dishwasher in the royal kitchen. Perkin Warbeck, a Flemish apprentice, claimed that he was Richard, duke of York, the younger son of Edward IV who had been slain in the Tower. By 1493 he had won the support of the Kings of Scotland, France, and Germany. His attempted invasion of England in 1495 failed. Two years later a joint invasion by King James IV of Scotland and Warbeck also failed. Warbeck was captured and executed two years later. In each rebellion King Henry remained calm, acting wisely and usually with forbearance to keep his throne by sheer ability rather than by ruthlessness or by general popularity. Although other rebellions followed, Henry had secured his dynasty and was never seriously threatened after 1497.

Character of the King

Henry VII, unlike his son, never caught the popular imagination. Perhaps his reign appeared dull because his policies were so eminently shrewd and logical that they produced respect, but hardly enthusiasm. Aloof and colorless, he engendered respect, if not love, in his subjects. By sheer skill and the wisdom to work for limited, rather than grandiose, objectives, he set the monarchy above political faction. The image of King Henry "the miser" is overdrawn; he was personally frugal and meticulous in keeping financial accounts. He was, indeed, industrious and had an infinite capacity for detail. No doubt he was the best businessman to serve as king of England. But he was frugal and fiscally prudent because he realized that money meant power and freedom from royal concessions to gain parliamentary grants.

Domestic Administration

Henry VII was a prudent, businesslike king who was convinced that external peace and internal order were dependent upon a prosperous and secure country. His financial policies reflected this conviction. His success in these policies won him the goodwill of his subjects.

TAXATION

A fundamental weakness of the feudal monarch was his reliance upon vassals for revenue. Beyond these resources the king could only appeal to Parliament. Henry did not want to antagonize his subjects by raising taxes or concede royal prerogatives to win parliamentary support for tax increases; only five times during his reign did he ask Parliament for any direct taxation. To become self-sufficient Henry pared expenditures, personally checked the account books, encouraged foreign commerce in order to increase custom duties, resumed every dormant right of the Crown he could find, levied steep fines in court, and seized the property of outlawed nobles who were convicted in court. Occasionally he resorted to benevolence or extortion from his richer subjects. In this manner he filled the royal coffers and bequeathed to his son a substantial surplus in the royal treasury.

COMMERCE

By means of treaties and monopolies Henry VII increased the volume of trade and encouraged English shipping. The Navigation Act of 1485 stimulated English shipping, while the *Intercursus Magnus* treaty (1497) with the Netherlands provided for reciprocity of trade. In 1506 a monopoly of the English cloth trade in the Low Countries was given to the Merchant Adventurers. A heavy duty was placed on exported wool to encourage the woolen industry to expand its export of manufactured woolens.

DECLINE OF THE GUILDS

The craft guilds were already in decline at the beginning of Henry VII's reign. Wealthy masters were becoming so exclusive that journeymen were leaving the towns to avoid the strict regulations of the guilds. Nor did local guilds promote the national interest; rather, they were concerned with a monopoly over local crafts, often at the expense of economic expansion. Henry accelerated the decline of the guilds by an act in 1504 which forbade any subsequent ordinances of guilds from being binding until approved by certain government officials. Already the craft guilds were being superseded by the domestic system, under which capitalistic merchants became middlemen between the producer and the consumer and supplied the worker in his home with raw materials and bought his finished product. This domestic system developed first in the woolen industry.

PARLIAMENT AND COUNCIL

Henry VII governed largely through the King's Council which included fewer of the great lords than previously and more members of lower social ranks who were selected for their abilities and loyalty. At the county level Henry upgraded the work and influence of the justices of the peace and won the allegiance of the lesser gentry who held these unpaid posts. The justices of the peace supervised the collection of taxes and were the local agents for carrying out the wishes of the central government. Since the English Crown possessed no standing army, royal decrees were effective only to the extent that local agents were able, and willing, to carry them out. During Henry's reign Parliament rarely met since Henry so seldom needed its grants as a regular source of revenue. When it did meet it was usually a willing ally of the Crown, with the Commons effectively managed by Speakers of the House who were royal officials.

Foreign Policy

King Henry's foreign policy centered around the goals of peace and security. He did not want unnecessary wars that could only drain the treasury and jeopardize his throne by possible defeat. He clearly preferred political marriages to military engagements.

MARRIAGE ALLIANCES

Henry VII arranged the marriage of his eldest son, Arthur, to Catherine, daughter of Ferdinand and Isabella of Spain. Such an alliance was a political coup, but within six months Arthur was dead and Catherine a widow. Henry arranged for his thirteen-year-old second son, Henry, to be betrothed to Catherine to save the dowry and the alliance with Spain. This marriage, in 1509, was to alter the course of English history. In 1503 he married his daughter Margaret to King James IV of Scotland, thereby preparing the way for the later union of the two kingdoms. His youngest daughter, Mary, was betrothed to Charles of Castile, the grandson of Emperor Maximilian, in return for a large loan and an alliance with Austria.

CONTINENTAL POLICY

Henry VII had little interest in asserting the old Norman-Angevin claims to French holdings or in wasting his resources in one more attempt to recover them. The English people, however, still considered France their mortal enemy, and Spain made English aid against France a term of the marriage treaty of Arthur with Catherine. Maximilian of Austria also allied with Henry VII against France only to desert him in 1491, as did Ferdinand of Spain. Henry salvaged the situation by appealing to Parliament for money and landing in Calais with a large army. Charles VIII of France was preoccupied with expansion into Italy and, therefore, quickly came to terms with Henry to avoid fighting the English as well. The Treaty of Etaples (1492) would provide large annual subsidies to Henry, who preferred tribute to territory in Brittany. Henry VII ended up with successful Spanish and Hapsburg alliances and avoided the temptation that befell the other European powers of becoming embroiled in an Italian empire.

SCOTTISH POLICY

Not until James IV invaded England in support of the pretender, Warbeck, did Henry VII worry about his northern neighbor. He then responded by threatening Scotland with invasion and giving his support to a rival claimant to the Scottish throne; but Henry, as usual, preferred diplomacy to warfare. The Anglo-Scottish treaty of 1499 promised peace between the two countries and sealed the agreement with a marriage alliance between James IV and Henry's daughter Margaret.

IRISH POLICY

Because the Yorkist Irish had actively supported both pretenders to the English throne, Henry sent Sir Edward Poynings to Ireland in 1494 to act as Lord Deputy and to reassert English authority over the island. Poynings failed to control Ulster, but in the Pale (the area around Dublin) he had laws passed which made the Irish Parliament clearly subordinate to the English Crown. Henceforth, no Irish laws could operate without the approval of the Crown, whereas all English laws automatically applied to Ireland. Poynings's Laws were later damned by the Irish, but Henry avoided immediate trouble by restoring the Earl of Kildare, who was acceptable to the Irish, as Lord Deputy.

English Society

The enclosure movement—fencing off former common lands—increased substantially under the Tudors because landlords saw how much more profitable their common lands could be for sheep-raising. The victims were the peasants who frequently became unemployed vagrants when they were excluded from their share of the meadows and woods.

These economic changes reflected the transformation of English social classes as the gentry, yeomen, and merchants grew influential at the expense of the old nobility and the peasants. The great baronial families, such as the Percys and the Nevilles, who had been decimated by the Wars of the Roses, were gradually being replaced in English political and social life by the rising country gentlemen or squires. This new landed aristocracy, based more on wealth or service to the king than on birth, built attractive country houses and became the nucleus of the leisure and governing classes in the counties. These amateur administrators took their work seriously and provided the Tudors with local influence that no central bureaucracy of royal officials could have matched.

**The Literary
Renaissance**

Not until the latter part of the fifteenth century did the Renaissance reach England and quicken the torpid intellectual atmosphere of the universities. English scholars who had studied in Italy introduced the curricula of the humanities in English schools. The first generation of these scholars, which included Thomas Linacre (ca. 1460–1524) and William Grocyn (ca. 1446–1519), made Oxford the center of this literary and educational revival.

THE OXFORD HUMANISTS

The Christian humanists restored intellectual vigor to the Roman Catholic Church by their zealous efforts at ecclesiastical reform through education and classical scholarship. At times they reflected English sentiment by being anticlerical, but they were by no means antireligious. John Colet (1467–1519) was a humanist scholar vitally interested in Church and educational reform. His discourses on St. Paul's Epistles freed his theological thinking from medieval scholasticism. He became dean of St. Paul's Cathedral and founded St. Paul's School. Thomas More (1478–1535) was a noted administrator who became chancellor under Henry VIII. His *Utopia*, which provided a humanistic parody of the times, idealized human nature in its description of a new society free from feudal conceptions and religious intolerance. Desiderius Erasmus (ca. 1466–1536), a Dutch scholar and colleague at Oxford of More and Colet, was the most celebrated Christian humanist of the early Renaissance. His devastating satire and ridicule of many Church practices opened the door for theological criticism of Church doctrines.

HENRY VIII

Henry VII bequeathed to his son a secure monarchy, a full treasury, and a nation with increased stature in the diplomacy of Europe. Upon this foundation Henry VIII's reign (1509–1547) added popular enthusiasm for the Crown and spectacular royal authority, especially observed in his break with Rome and in the confiscation of monastic properties. In this instance Henry carried the country through revolutionary change and practiced royal despotism successfully because he continued to respect traditional forms of English government and because his policies usually reflected the feelings of most of his subjects.

**Character of
the King**

King Henry came to the throne at the age of seventeen, well educated, intelligent, and with a captivating personality. He was a good athlete, knowledgeable in theology, music, and literature, and a born leader. Henry was also exceedingly vain and ambitious, and his appetites knew no moderation. Ruthless and frivolous on occasion and lacking the restraint of his father, King Henry gained the affection of his subjects in a way Henry VII never could. He won immediate goodwill by executing Richard Empson and Edmund Dudley, the two ministers who were loyal to his father but responsible for his legal extortions. The axiom that "strong people have strong weaknesses" characterized Henry. Supremely selfish and egotistical, he dismantled the English Church because it would not grant him a divorce; he married six women and beheaded two of them; he longed for a son and neglected his two daughters; he added glamour and gaiety to the court, but finally grew fat, disease-ridden, and dissolute. Few English kings were as colorful or as controversial.

Cardinal Wolsey

At first Henry VIII left most administrative details, which he did not enjoy like his father did, to the experienced ministers who had served his father, but shortly he delegated almost complete authority to Thomas Wolsey. Wolsey was a self-made man who collected a string of offices in both Church and government, including those of Archbishop of York (1514), Cardinal and Lord Chancellor (1515), and Papal Legate (1518). He became Henry's closest advisor, and for fifteen years he managed England, especially in the area of foreign diplomacy. He held his power by hard work and competency and realized that his position rested on royal favor and diplomatic success; therefore, he could afford to be greedy, ruthless, and intolerably arrogant to all but the King.

Foreign Policy

Wolsey organized and directed all but one of Henry VIII's wars. His special forte was diplomacy, in which he operated on the balance of power principle—joining with lesser powers against the most powerful. Wolsey's involvement in foreign affairs won England a conspicuous place in the councils of Europe, but only provoked reaction against him at home.

ITALIAN-SPANISH POLITICS

Italy had become the battleground of Europe ever since the French in 1494 had shown how easy it was to plunder the peninsula. The papacy organized alliances to prevent one-power domination of Italy. England joined the Pope's Holy League in 1511 to drive the French out of Italy.

THE SPANISH ALLIANCE

Henry VIII reaffirmed his father's alliance with Spain by marrying his widowed sister-in-law, Catherine, within a month of his accession to the throne. Her father, King Ferdinand, persuaded Henry to join the Pope's Holy League. In 1512 an English expedition planned by Ferdinand against the French failed miserably. Henry redeemed himself by landing in France, defeating the French at the Battle of the Spurs, and capturing Terouenne and Tournai. Ferdinand deserted Henry and made a truce with Louis XII instead.

This time the English were not left in the lurch by the Spanish monarch's actions. Wolsey arranged a peace with France that gave England a sum of money and fortified the alliance by the marriage of Henry's sister, Mary, to King Louis XII. Wolsey thereupon tried to build up a coalition against the ambitious new king, Francis I, but did not succeed. In 1518 a treaty of peace was arranged whereby England returned Tournai to France for a handsome profit.

ENGLAND AND THE FRANCO-SPANISH RIVALRY

The major dynastic struggle in Europe after 1519 was between Francis I of France and Charles V, King of Spain and Holy Roman Emperor. In this rivalry England lined up with Spain even though Henry and Francis I put on a glittering public display of friendship at the Field of the Cloth of Gold (1520). The following year an alliance with Spain committed England to another war against France, but the English campaigns in France were futile and costly. Wolsey alienated Parliament and the citizens of London by his demands for money to pay for the war and his levy of a 20 percent property tax.

PRO-FRENCH POLICY

Charles V decisively defeated the French at Pavia (1525), sacked Rome and made the Pope his prisoner. This completely upset the balance of power and forced Wolsey to change sides suddenly and seek a peace with France. In 1526 and again in 1528 England allied with France to check the Emperor; but this time Wolsey's strategy was no longer effective. The pro-French policy did not sit well with England since the old enmity toward France continued strong; furthermore, the policy was disrupting the cloth-export trade to the Netherlands. More significant was Wolsey's loss of influence with the King; he had failed in his bid to become pope, and Henry was demanding action on his divorce proceedings. In 1529 Francis I and Charles V signed the Treaty of Cambrai without even consulting Wolsey.

SCOTTISH POLICY

In 1513 the Scots, under James IV, took advantage of Henry's absence in France and invaded England. However, they were defeated at Flodden Field and King James was killed in battle. His son, James V, was strongly pro-French. Intermittent border skirmishes by both sides continued until the Scots suffered a disgraceful defeat at Solway Moss (1542). The news of the disaster killed James V, and the throne was left to his week-old daughter, Mary Stuart. Henry tried to negotiate a betrothal between Mary and his son, Edward, but the Scots turned instead to their old ally, France, and later betrothed Mary to the heir to the French throne.

WALES

In the principality of Wales Henry was quietly successful. For the first time in its history Wales was fully incorporated with England by the Act of Union (1536) which provided for twelve counties and twenty-four representatives to Parliament. A second act in 1543 meshed the legal and administrative procedures of the two regions.

IRELAND

The great Anglo-Irish lords, led by the Earls of Ormande and Kildare, were the real powers in the country. The Earl of Kildare revolted in 1533 in protest over the death of his father in the Tower of London and Henry's antipapal policy. However, this revolt was brutally suppressed, and in 1541 Henry assumed the titles of King of Ireland and Head of the Irish Church. Ireland was temporarily subdued, but the settlement was completely unacceptable to the Irish.

The Fall of Wolsey

Cardinal Wolsey had appropriated royal privileges and virtually ruled the country with an autocratic hand without paying much attention to Parliament. Only once between 1515 and 1529 was Parliament summoned. Wolsey's lavish style of living and insufferable arrogance created personal enemies envious of his position and power. Even though his preoccupation with foreign affairs damaged his reputation in England, he was not threatened as long as he retained the support of King Henry. But royal favor was lost when he was unable to win from the Pope an annulment of Henry's marriage. Wolsey was stripped of his offices and arrested in 1529 for high treason. He died en route to London, and Thomas More took his place as Chancellor.

KING AND CHURCH: THE BREACH WITH ROME

On the Continent, the Protestant revolt was primarily for religious motives; in England the revolt against the papacy was essentially dynastic and personal, with religious overtones. There was little major change of doctrine under Henry VIII, but rather an exertion of his authority over the Church in the same manner that he eventually ran the state to keep it in order and to get his way.

Background Events

(1) The influence of the German and Swiss religious reformers Martin Luther and Ulrich Zwingli had already made some impression on England, and one of their converts, William Tyndale, translated the New Testament into English. However, Henry VIII had no theological argument with the Church; he wrote a tract against Luther in 1521 and for his efforts received from Pope Leo X the title of Defender of the Faith—a title still used by the English monarch today.

(2) Religious reformers in England from the days of John Wycliffe had urged the Church to reform and to curtail its lavish wealth, but for the most part the Church had not changed since the thirteenth century.

(3) Rising nationalism in England made Englishmen increasingly hostile to any foreign allegiance. The king and Parliament both fed on these strong feelings of anticlericalism to restrict papal powers in England.

(4) Deteriorating relations with Spain increased the strain between Henry and his Spanish Queen who could not bear him a son.

(5) The Tudors were dogmatic and determined and were unwilling to be crossed in their plans. The conflict with Rome came to a head with Henry's efforts to win an annulment of his marriage.

Divorce Proceedings

By 1527 King Henry had been married to Catherine of Aragon for eighteen years and only one daughter, Mary, had survived infancy. The fear that the new Tudor dynasty would die out because of the lack of a male heir haunted the proud Henry. Since he had obtained a papal dispensation in 1509 to bypass canon law forbidding marriage to a sister-in-law, he now began to claim that his conscience was troubled by the irregularity of the marriage. His desire to divorce Catherine was heightened by his great passion for the Queen's lady-in-waiting, Anne Boleyn, who would consent to be his wife, but not his mistress.

APPEAL TO ROME

In 1527 Henry commissioned Wolsey to secure from the Pope an annulment of his marriage. However, the Pope was virtually a prisoner of Charles V; furthermore, Charles was the nephew of Catherine and certainly would not support such a slight to his aunt. Wolsey worked vigorously for Henry's cause, but the Pope used stalling tactics for two years. When no decision had been reached, Henry lost patience with both the Pope and with Wolsey; he dismissed Wolsey and took matters into his own hands.

HENRY'S MANEUVERS, 1529–1534

When Henry finally broke with Rome, he carried the nation with him. The King severed relations step by step in the hope that constant pressure, short of revolt, on the papacy would give him his own way. Relying on Thomas Cranmer and Thomas Cromwell (later to be Chancellor), he made his divorce case a subject for debate in European universities in 1529; in 1530 he pressured the English clergy into recognizing him as the supreme head of the Church of England "as far as the law of Christ allows." In 1529 Henry had called Parliament into session and for seven years it served as his instrument of antipapal defiance. By 1533 the Pope had made no concessions, and Anne Boleyn was pregnant. Cranmer, his ally, was appointed the new Archbishop of Canterbury, and the English ecclesiastical court gave Henry his long-sought annulment. Henry married Anne publicly, and in September she gave birth to a daughter, Elizabeth. The King's hope for a male heir remained unfulfilled.

Act of Supremacy. In 1534 the break with Rome was complete when Parliament by statute declared Henry the supreme head of the Church of England; no change of creed took place.

The Reformation Parliament, 1529–1536

Thomas Cromwell's most masterful work was his use of Parliament (whereas Wolsey had mistrusted it) to carry out royal policy. The Reformation Parliament, managed by the King's officials but hardly coerced, passed 137 statutes, thirty-two of them relating to the Church. These included the Act of Annates which halted the payment to Rome of the first year's income from new occupants of Church benefices, the Act of Appeals which forbade all appeals to Rome, and a Dispensations Act which cut off all payments to Rome, including Peter's Pence (a tax of one penny per household paid to the Papal See). Then in 1534 the Supremacy Act and a new Treason Act made official the independence of the English Church and prohibited any other religious allegiance among Englishmen. An Oath of Supremacy was required and executions followed for those who publicly refused, including Henry's Chancellor, Thomas More, and John Fisher, Bishop of Rochester. In the Act of Succession (1534) Parliament secured the Crown for Elizabeth and declared Mary illegitimate. This was altered in the act of 1543 to provide for the succession of Prince Edward, Princess Mary, and Princess Elizabeth, in that order.

The Dissolution of the Monasteries

Henry's Parliament gave him statutes but little money; therefore Cromwell, the Vicar-General of the Church, seeing an opportunity for his King to not only rule the Church but to own much of it, sent out commissioners in 1535 to build up a case against the monasteries. Their report emphasized the superstitious practices, excessive wealth (ownership of one-fifth of the land of England), and immoral practices within religious communities. In 1536 Parliament abolished 376 religious houses with an annual income of less than £200 each; during the next four years the larger ones were also confiscated on various pretexts, and the confiscation was ratified by statute in 1539. These acts were revolutionary in character as they were neither emergency war measures nor directed against non-English houses; rather they were large-scale encroachments on private property by the authority of the King in Parliament, and with no justification in common law.

POLITICAL CONSEQUENCES

Immediately the removal of the abbots cut in half the number of ecclesiastical lords and changed the complexion of the House of Lords from a predominantly clerical to a predominantly lay group. The combination of conservative Catholic resentment along with the spreading enclosures and increasing taxes resulted in the only serious revolt of Henry's reign, the Pilgrimage of Grace. This revolt rallied those in northern England opposed to, or frustrated by, change. The rebellion, which was firmly squelched by Henry, resulted in the establishment of the Council of the North, as a branch of the Privy Council, to administer the unruly region directly.

SOCIAL AND ECONOMIC CONSEQUENCES

King Henry became very rich temporarily with the income from confiscated monastic lands, although most of this money was squandered in a costly war with France which Henry waged at the end of his reign. More important was the sale of two-thirds of the land to his friends, laying the foundation for the rise of new, influential families and giving them an economic stake in the break from Rome. Many of today's family fortunes and estates date from this period. The poor gained nothing; they lost the social services that were offered by religious houses, whereas the new landlords, more interested in profit, accelerated the enclosure of land which, in turn, produced unsettling social consequences for displaced peasants. With the dissolution of the monasteries an important model of religious life ceased to exist. Monks and nuns became virtually unknown in England for several centuries. With the dissolution came significant destruction of Church property and the loss of books and medieval art as the monastic libraries were scattered.

Character of the Church

King Henry's quarrel was with the Pope, not with Catholic doctrine. He demanded religious conformity from his subjects in the same way that he expected political allegiance. Both Roman Catholics and Anabaptists (members of a sect that rejected such Church rituals as infant baptism) were burned at the stake for daring to dissent; but they were a small company. Most of the English clergy and laity accepted their king's version of the Church.

CHURCH PRACTICES

English replaced Latin in the church services; in 1535 Coverdale's English translation of the Bible was adopted and placed in the churches for all to read. Relics and shrines were discredited and occasionally destroyed.

CHURCH DOCTRINE

The Ten Articles of 1536 passed by Church Convocation reflected some cautious protestantization in declaring the Bible and the creeds the sole authority in matters of faith. However, the King was not in favor of changing the creed, and the Six Articles of 1539 reverted to full Catholic doctrine by upholding oral confession, transubstantiation (the doctrine that the bread and wind of the Eucharist are transformed into the true presence of Christ), clerical celibacy, and prayers for the dead.

Last Years of Henry

After Henry had Thomas Cromwell executed because of his poor choice in selecting him a new wife, he ceased to employ a chief minister. He relied instead on a Privy Council—an "inner circle" of the Great Council—which included the Duke of Norfolk; Edward Seymour; earl of Hertford; Archbishop Cranmer; and Stephen Gardiner, bishop of Winchester. Henry's last years were marked with a series of marriages, an inflationary economy, an expensive war with France, and a bloated and sickly body; the charm and glamour of the young king had given way to cynicism and bad temper in old age. Throughout these years Henry's authority over the Church and the state was supreme, as he made law by proclamation (Statute of Proclamations, 1539) and broadened the scope of treason.

HENRY'S SIX WIVES

King Henry tired of his second wife after the birth of a daughter instead of a son, and in 1536 Anne Boleyn was indicted on a charge of adultery and executed. Within a month Henry married Jane Seymour who, after giving birth to a son, Edward, died the following year. Chancellor Cromwell next persuaded Henry to contract a marriage, sight unseen, with a Lutheran princess, Anne of Cleves, in order to strengthen the Protestant alliance on the Continent. When she arrived, Henry was appalled at the sight of the "Flanders mare" and vented his wrath on the Chancellor. Cromwell, who had been the architect of Henry's policy of state supremacy in ecclesiastical matters, was executed and Anne divorced. Henry's fifth wife was nineteen-year-old Catherine Howard, who lost her head upon conviction of adultery. The king's last marriage, in 1543, was to Katherine Parr, who was to outlive Henry as she had her two previous husbands.

DEBASEMENT OF THE COINAGE

If enclosures were a major source of discontent in the realm, the debasement of the coinage between 1542 and 1547 produced even greater hardships; prices jumped sharply and rents rose to catch up with the price spiral. Only the King and the cloth-export trade prospered from the debasement. Henry VIII acquired metal extracted from the coinage valued at £227,000. The sale of cloth jumped when the pound sterling dropped in value on the foreign exchange, permitting increased purchases of English exports.

Significance of Henry's Reign

Henry's reign was remarkably stable considering the religious, political, and economic revolution that was taking place. Henry had the capacity to control events and mold them to his own and the nation's interests. Selfish, ruthless with individuals, and degenerate in his old age, King Henry was largely successful in his objectives because he understood the times and his policies reflected the feelings of a sufficient number of his subjects. Parliament would not have followed him so readily if it had been otherwise. In accomplishing his goals Parliament became an essential part of the machinery of government, even if it was used, along with the Henrician Church, as an instrument of royal strategy. The consequences of this "political reformation" were profound because the assertion of the omnicompetence of the king in Parliament—of "the unlimited sovereignty of statute"—replaced the medieval concept of Parliament as a House of Communities.

EDWARD VI AND THE PROTESTANT REACTION

Throughout Edward's brief reign (1547–1553) England was again subject to the factionalism of rule by regency. In those years the Henrician Church veered sharply to more Protestant doctrines and practices under the leadership of Edward's three most influential advisors, the Duke of Somerset, the Duke of Northumberland, and Archbishop Cranmer.

The Council of Regency

Edward VI, who was barely ten years old when he became king, was a precocious, serious, but sickly child. His government was plagued with social and economic problems, war with Scotland, and financial difficulties inherited from his father. Although King Henry had prepared for Edward's minority rule by setting up a regency council of sixteen with a carefully balanced membership of conservatives and reformers, the reformers were the more powerful and the king's uncle, Edward Seymour, assumed full authority as Lord Protector.

The Protectorship of Somerset, 1547–1549

Edward Seymour, duke of Somerset, was ambitious and well-meaning, but unschooled in political maneuvering and in administration. He was a moderate reformer in religion and encouraged religious toleration and a move toward Protestant doctrines.

RELIGIOUS CHANGE

Somerset called Parliament in to session in 1547 and had the treason and heresy acts repealed. A committee headed by Archbishop Cranmer reformed the order of public worship by issuing the first Book of Common Prayer (1549) with the approval of Parliament. The Act of Uniformity required its use in all public worship. The prayer book combined the majesty and the cadence of former ceremonies with a simplified communion service in the English language. When the religiously conservative Six Articles were repealed, the country folk of the west rose in protest, demanding the restoration of the old service and the Six Articles. At the same time, the radical Protestants demanded a repudiation of all Catholic customs, and mobs expressed their fanaticism and opposition to religious images by smashing cathedral windows and destroying religious statuary. Hugh Latimer of Oxford eloquently preached the need for further religious and social change. Somerset removed Catholic sympathizers from the Council.

SCOTLAND

Somerset invaded Scotland to hasten the negotiations that Henry VIII had arranged for the marriage of Mary Stuart to Edward VI. Although the Scots were defeated in battle at Pinkie (1547), they were not intimidated and dispatched Mary to France to marry the Dauphin (heir to the French throne) instead.

SOCIAL UNREST

Religious and economic changes created frustration and uprisings that were gently dealt with by Somerset who sympathized with the poor and attempted a few social reforms. The greed of the landlords in forcing the enclosures, the inflation from the continued debasement of the coinage, the confiscation of the endowed chapels and the plunder of the churches, and the disendowment of all town guilds except those in London increased the miseries of the poor and culminated in Kett's Rebellion near Norwich (1549) which was put down by John Dudley, earl of Warwick.

THE FALL OF SOMERSET

The inability of Somerset to ameliorate the economic distress, even after he had Parliament investigate the enclosure problems (the John Hales commission), and the diplomatic setback in France after renewal of war provided grounds for opposition. More important, Somerset antagonized the propertied classes with his ideas on social reform. As a result the Earl of Warwick (now entitled the Duke of Northumberland) ingratiated himself with King Edward, built up a party of reaction that included the Roman Catholic faction, and had Somerset ousted in 1549. A few years later Somerset was arrested on a charge of high treason and executed.

**The
Protectorship
of
Northumberland,
1549–1553**

Northumberland was an opportunist motivated by an insatiable lust for power. He favored a more radical Protestantism for political purposes and gambled on controlling the succession to the throne.

RELIGIOUS DEVELOPMENTS

Under Northumberland religious changes became more far-reaching: the vacillating and timid, yet scholarly, Cranmer repudiated the doctrine of transubstantiation in the Holy Communion; Lutheran and Calvinistic refugees and professors arrived in large numbers from the Continent; clergy were allowed to marry; and the Catholic bishops Bonner and Gardiner were replaced by aggressive reformers, such as John Hooper, bishop of Gloucester, and Nicholas Ridley, bishop of London. The Second Act of Uniformity (1552) authorized the second Book of Common Prayer which made Holy Communion essentially an act of remembrance and ended oral confession. The next year the Forty-Two Articles of Faith defined the faith of the Church of England in terms that reflected both Lutheran (justification by faith) and Calvinistic (symbolic interpretation of the sacraments) influence.

SUCCESSION SCHEMES

Realizing that King Edward was dying of consumption, Northumberland persuaded him to alter the succession in order to keep Mary Tudor off the throne and prevent her from restoring Catholicism in England. Northumberland's scheme was to marry his son to the attractive Lady Jane Grey, granddaughter of Henry VIII's sister, Mary, and have Edward name her as heir. The dying king agreed and the Privy Council felt it prudent to assent.

LADY JANE GREY

Lady Jane Grey reigned only nine days after the death of Edward. Protestants did not join Lady Jane's cause as Northumberland had anticipated; furthermore, his army deserted him because they feared his designs more than they did the religious identity of Mary. All England flocked to Mary's support when she entered London in triumph to be crowned Queen. Northumberland turned Catholic, but this did not save him from the block. Otherwise Mary was lenient to his supporters.

MARY TUDOR AND THE CATHOLIC REACTION

Mary Tudor, England's first ruling queen, had experienced an unhappy and fearful childhood in the court of Henry VIII, but through it all she had remained courageous and completely devoted to Catholicism. Her policies were dominated by two overriding convictions—the need to end England's heresy by restoring the Roman Catholic faith, and the value of a close alliance with her mother's native land, Spain.

The Return of Catholicism

Queen Mary at first was rather tolerant in her efforts to turn back the clock to pre-Reformation days, but when opposition and revolts hampered her progress, she became impatient and intolerant and won the name of "Bloody Mary." She was as obstinate as her father, but without his political awareness of national sentiment.

MARY'S PARLIAMENTS

The Queen immediately pressured the three Parliaments of 1553–1555 to rescind the religious legislation of Edward's reign, to revive the old heresy laws, and to petition the Pope through Cardinal Pole to have England received back into the Catholic Church. Parliament, however, balked at her demands to restore confiscated monastic lands. By administrative action she forced Continental preachers and exiles to leave the country, replaced Protestant bishops with Catholic prelates, and revived Catholic liturgy.

CATHOLIC MARRIAGE

The Catholic Emperor who dominated Europe was Charles V. Mary Tudor was eager to marry his son, Archduke Philip, and thereby bring England into the powerful Catholic empire. Mary proceeded with plans for her marriage to Philip II of Spain, champion of Catholic orthodoxy, in spite of Lord Chancellor Gardiner's warning and the noisy opposition of her subjects. Only reluctantly did Parliament agree after guarantees were given that Philip would not drag England into his Continental wars against France, and that he would have no rights to the throne of England if Mary died childless. Even so, the marriage announcement triggered three rebellions in 1554. The most serious of these was organized in Kent under the leadership of Sir Thomas Wyatt, the son of the poet. His followers were joined by troops who had defected from the Queen. The rebels could have captured Mary if they had not been delayed in their attack on London, but by the time they entered London, loyal troops had been assembled and the rebels were defeated. Although Lady Jane Grey was not implicated in the uprising, she and her husband were put to death along with Wyatt.

PERSECUTION OF PROTESTANTS

By 1555 Queen Mary, sickly and slighted by her husband, tried to speed up the pace of orthodoxy by burning out Protestantism. However, the three hundred burnings at Smithfield, including those of Bishops Hooper, Latimer, Ridley, and Archbishop Cranmer, backfired and evoked sympathy for the persecuted and quickly turned public opinion against Mary and her cause. Ironically her policy of persecution contributed significantly to the permanence of Protestantism in England.

Foreign Policy

Mary's foreign policy was no more successful than her domestic policy. Declining trade, a recalcitrant Parliament that was opposed to voting taxes for the Queen, and the growing influence of Calvinism in Scotland made her efforts in foreign policy appear fitful. In addition, the quarrel between Pope Paul IV and King Philip, her husband, complicated Mary's religious loyalties. Philip enlisted Mary's aid in 1557 in fighting France for purely Spanish objectives. The English were humiliated by the loss of their last French possession, Calais, in the war.

Death of Mary Tudor

The disastrous but brief career of Mary Tudor came to an end with her death in November 1558. Mary had tried to restore the past but had failed to take into account English nationalism which resented subservience to either Rome or Madrid. The result was that both her life and her reign were controversial, largely barren, and tragic.

The fear of another disrupted succession to the throne, which had plagued the fifteenth century, also preoccupied the Tudors, so much so that Henry VII, through a papal dispensation, betrothed his second son to the widow of his deceased son Arthur, and Henry VIII dared to break with the Roman Catholic Church in his desperate bid for a male heir. Unlike the Lancastrian and Yorkist years, the succession held firm for the Tudors in spite of great risks encountered by each monarch.

Central to the sixteenth century was a vibrant, self-conscious nationalism. Henry VIII understood its potential and manipulated it to accomplish his goals; his daughter Mary resisted it, seeking to turn back the clock, only to fail miserably.

Religious nationalism, as expressed in the independent Church of England, was the most powerful manifestation of the Tudor revolution in government. By midcentury England had become a self-conscious, sovereign nation, repudiating loyalty to all foreign authority. Supreme power was centered in the king in Parliament. At the same time the medieval household administration of government was transferred into a national bureaucratic administration. Thomas Cromwell was a principal architect in both transformations.

Selected Readings

Bindoff, S. T. *Tudor England* (1950)

Bolt, Robert. *A Man for All Seasons* (1962)

Chambers, Raymond W. *Thomas More* (1958)

Chrimes, Stanley B. *Henry VII* (1972)

Dickens, A. G. *The English Reformation* (1964)

Elton, Geoffrey R. *England Under the Tudors* (1977)

Fraser, Lady Antonia. *Mary Queen of Scots* (1969)

George, Margaret. *The Autobiography of Henry VIII* (1986)

Mackie, John D. *The Early Tudors, 1485–1588* (1959)

Parker, T. M. *The English Reformation to 1588* (1959)

Pollard, A. F. *Wolsey: Church and State in Sixteenth-Century England* (1966)

Powicke, Frederick M. *The Reformation in England* (1941)

Read, Conyers. *The Tudors* (1936)

Ridley, Jasper. *Thomas Cranmer* (1962)

Smith, Lacey Baldwin. *Henry VIII: The Mask of Royalty* (1971)

Zeevold, W. G. *Foundations of Tudor Policy* (1948)

8

Elizabethan England: 1558–1603

1558 Elizabeth I accedes to the throne upon the death of Mary

1560 Scottish Parliament breaks relations with Rome and adopts a Calvinistic profession of faith

1562 Thirty-Nine Articles of Faith are adopted by Church convocation as the doctrine of the Church of England

1564 Birth of William Shakespeare in Stratford-on-Avon

1572 St. Bartholomew's Day Massacre of French Huguenots and Elizabeth's ally, Admiral Coligny

1577–1580 Sir Francis Drake sails around the world in his vessel the *Golden Hind*

1587 Execution of Mary Queen of Scots

1588 Spanish Armada and its attempted invasion of England is repulsed by the English navy and fierce storms

1596 Publication of Edmund Spenser's most famous poem, *The Faerie Queen*

1598 Irish rebellion against Elizabeth led by Hugh O'Neill, earl of Tyrone

1600 East India Company is chartered

1601 Elizabethan Poor Law gives authority to the state to take over the earlier role of the Church in administering charity

1603 Tudor dynasty ends with the death of Elizabeth

After Mary's dismal reign England passed to one of its most glorious ages under Elizabeth I. During her long reign (1558–1603) Queen Elizabeth practiced moderation in an age of religious and political fanaticism and provided peace and prosperity for her nation.

Elizabeth also understood and stimulated the tide of nationalism enveloping England so that a spirit of self-confidence developed in her subjects that was perhaps unmatched in English history. Like her father, Henry VIII, and unlike her half-sister, Mary, she had superb political instincts and carried the nation with her in all her decisions.

The Queen was not an originator in government; rather she gave free reign to her subjects and allied their interests with her state policies. Parliament had little quarrel with the Queen, in part because no monarch became as popular as Elizabeth or won such loyalty from the people.

THE RELIGIOUS SETTLEMENT

Elizabeth came to the throne with the nation at war, the treasury empty, and the nation bitterly divided on religion. The failure of her sister to restore Catholicism was not lost on Elizabeth. Besides, she had not forgotten the fact that she was a child of a marriage that the Catholic Church refused to recognize. Therefore, it was only logical that Elizabeth should drop the catholicizing policy of Mary. The outcome was the establishment of a national Church of England that settled for a compromise between Roman Catholicism and Protestantism. Its doctrines were broad enough to satisfy most of her subjects and to spare England the religious wars that wracked France and Germany.

Character of the Queen

When Elizabeth came to the throne at the age of twenty-five, her subjects were very skeptical about serving another female monarch after their experience with Mary. However, the Queen soon demonstrated that she possessed the abilities to rule with wisdom and to show strength of leadership without alienating herself from her subjects. Although she was vain and iron-willed like her father, she also had remarkable political acumen and a personal magnetism that attracted devoted followers. She loved power, but her shrewd mind knew when to concede small points in order to win major ones. Unlike Mary, Elizabeth understood that the strength of the monarchy, since it lacked a royal army, must be built upon popular consent. Like her father, Elizabeth was well-educated; she loved literature and could speak and write six languages. She also loved England and identified herself successfully with the aspirations and prejudices of her people.

The Elizabethan Compromise

Elizabeth was neither bigoted nor particularly religious, but she could not avoid involvement in the intense religious climate of the times. Her religious settlement restored Protestantism, created a national church and a clergy responsible to the Crown, and produced a church service that was made binding by an act of Parliament. It was, in effect, a lay revolution carried out by the Crown and by the House of Commons over the will of the bishops.

PARLIAMENTARY RELIGIOUS ACTS

Queen Elizabeth's first Parliament in 1559 repealed the heresy acts of Mary's reign and passed the Act of Supremacy, which abolished papal allegiance and recognized Elizabeth as Supreme Governor of the Church of England. Parliament then passed the Act of Uniformity to establish the only legal form of public worship, and set up the Court of the High Commission to enforce it. In 1562 Cranmer's Forty-two Articles of Faith were modified to Thirty-Nine and adopted by convocation; in 1571 they were imposed by Parliament as the doctrine of the Anglican Church. The Articles, with certain revisions, have remained the basic doctrines of faith of the Anglican Church.

All government and church officials were required to take an oath of allegiance to the new Queen and governance of the Church. Again, as under Henry VIII and Edward VI, these religious changes were passed by Parliament rather than by Church convocation. Except for the bishops appointed by Mary, the vast majority of the clergy accepted the religious settlement. These Catholic prelates lost their positions and were replaced by Protestant clergy. Matthew Parker, a noted Protestant scholar, became Archbishop of Canterbury. If the religious settlement did not evoke much enthusiasm, neither did it provoke much protest, and it went into effect with little friction or persecution at first.

LATER RELIGIOUS DEVELOPMENTS

The Elizabethan settlement, however, did not please Roman Catholics or radical Protestants. Both made efforts to promote their religious viewpoint at the expense of the settlement and brought upon themselves increasing restrictions. The Catholics suffered most because their religious loyalties were also perceived as a threat to the Tudor state.

Roman Catholics. The government's refusal to persecute passive Catholics upset the more militant Catholics who saw their cause withering when their coreligionists found they could live quite comfortably under the Elizabethan settlement. When Pope Pius V excommunicated Elizabeth in 1570 and absolved her subjects from allegiance to her, religious peace disappeared as many English Catholics were forced to choose between their faith and their Queen. By 1580 over one hundred Catholic priests, trained on the Continent under Jesuit leadership, were back in England reawakening

Catholic opposition to Elizabeth. Mary Queen of Scots was recognized by Rome as the only lawful Catholic candidate for the English throne, and the Pope and leading Catholic monarchs on the Continent backed plots on Elizabeth's life.

The government counterattacked by increasing its powers of repression. Fines jumped from one shilling to £20 a month for nonattendance at the established Church. Saying or hearing Mass brought imprisonment. After 1581, executions of proselyting Catholics increased. Elizabeth claimed that she punished for political treason, but the cause motivating the Catholic resistance was their faith. Approximately two hundred Catholics were executed during her reign.

The Puritans. While the Catholics were challenging the Anglican settlement from without, members within the Anglican Church were also demanding changes. The Puritans wanted to purge all practices that in any way still reflected papal recognition; they favored a more Calvinistic doctrine and wanted a presbyterian, rather than an episcopal, form of Church government. The House of Commons became increasingly Puritan in its sympathies and tried to remodel the doctrine and organization of the Church with legislation introduced by ardent Puritans. Queen Elizabeth blocked all changes, arguing that religion, like foreign policy and the succession to the throne, was an exclusive preserve of the monarchy and not the business of Parliament. Thwarted in Parliament, the Puritans turned to congregational meetings and pamphlet warfare. Thomas Cartwright, dismissed from Cambridge for his Puritan beliefs, was one of the leading polemicists to argue for a Church government on the model found in Calvinistic Switzerland.

The Separatists. The radical Protestants who considered the reform of the Anglican Church hopeless formed separate organizations outside of it. They were known usually by the names of their founders—Brownists (Robert Browne), Barrowists (Norman Barrow)—and were predecessors of the Congregationalists. They stressed congregational autonomy and separation of church and state.

Government Response. The government took repressive measures against Separatist groups because they repudiated the national church, and because the government considered religious uniformity essential to political unity. The powers of the Court of High Commission were enlarged to permit it to try all cases of nonconformity. Soon Brownists and English Anabaptists were forced to flee the country. In 1583 Elizabeth appointed John Whitgift, the severest critic of the Puritans, Archbishop of Canterbury. Immediately he used his position and the power of the court to penalize opponents without and within the Church.

John Knox and the Church of Scotland

The Scottish Church on the eve of the Reformation was both corrupt and wealthy and seemingly ripe for reform. The course of religious change was largely a result of the leadership of John Knox and the political and personal issues created by Mary Stuart. In contrast to England the Reformation in Scotland was promoted by the nobility over the opposition of the Crown.

JOHN KNOX (1505–1572)

Knox was a priest actively interested in the reform of the Church and strongly opposed to the French-Catholic regency in Scotland. While in exile on the Continent because of his beliefs, he became a disciple of John Calvin in Geneva. He returned to Scotland in 1558—the same year that the Dauphin of France married Mary Stuart and publicized her right to the English throne. Since the Scots feared absorption into a French-Catholic empire, four Protestant nobles formed a group called the Lords of the Congregation and requested major Church reforms from the regent, Mary of Guise (mother of Mary Stuart). When the demands were rejected, Knox rallied the reformers with his evangelistic zeal, and civil war broke out. Only the reluctant intervention by Queen Elizabeth saved the reformers from defeat by the regent's French army.

TREATY OF EDINBURGH, 1560

The terms of the treaty required the French to withdraw from Scotland and ended three centuries of Franco-Scottish ties. The treaty also contributed to the triumph of Protestantism over Catholicism in Scotland and England. The firm alliance of these two Protestant countries permitted a longer peace between them than heretofore.

THE SCOTTISH PARLIAMENT

In 1560 the Scottish Parliament broke relations with Rome, banned the Mass, and adopted a Calvinistic profession of faith and a book of discipline prepared by the first General Assembly of the Church of Scotland. When Mary of Guise died that same year, a council of twelve was set up to govern Scotland until Mary Stuart returned from France.

ELIZABETHAN FOREIGN POLICY

For a quarter of a century Elizabeth maintained a calculated and precarious neutrality in foreign affairs. The fact that neither France nor Spain, the Continent's two Catholic "super powers," subdued the much weaker England was due to the rivalry between these two Catholic countries, and even more to the astute diplomacy of Elizabeth and her brilliant statesmen. With the breathing spell won by this period of nominal peace, England increased national finances, strengthened its commercial and naval power, and developed self-confidence.

The Queen's Advisors

Undoubtedly, the success of Elizabeth's reign was related to her ability to govern well and to her selection of wise and loyal advisors for both domestic and foreign policies. Like Henry VIII, she became an astute political manager and diplomat. Elizabeth had several shallow court favorites who pleased her vanity, but to hold major offices in the Privy Council she chose experienced and devoted laymen, largely from the gentry class. William Cecil, later Lord Burghley, was secretary and chief counselor for forty years. His brother-in-law, Sir Nicholas Bacon, was lord chancellor. Robert Dudley, earl of Leicester, was another of the Queen's closest favorites. Sir Francis Walsingham served as ambassador to France and with Cecil organized an effective intelligence service to protect the Queen from foreign attempts on her life.

The Diplomacy of Neutrality

The rivalry between France and Spain was Elizabeth's chief asset in 1558. For the next thirty years she used her shrewdness and her marriageable hand to preserve England from foreign attack and to make the nation prosperous and confident of its abilities.

FRANCE

In 1559 the Treaty of Cateau-Cambrésis, which ended the war between France and her enemies, Spain and England, gave Elizabeth the peace that she considered essential to the national welfare and her own survival. France now became England's most immediate threat when King Francis II openly supported the claim of his wife, Mary Stuart of Scotland, to the English throne. However, his sudden death in 1560 left his young widow shorn of French support. The outbreak of the religious wars between Catholics and Huguenots (French Protestants) in 1562 caused Elizabeth to intervene on the side of the Huguenots and to send troops to Le Havre. The war with France was a blunder, and the English garrison in France surrendered in 1563. Calais was not recovered, and the whole affair was an object lesson to Elizabeth and Cecil. Thereafter, they gave aid secretly to the Huguenots while holding France in line by considering marriage offers from King Charles IV and later from his brothers, the Duke of Anjou and the Duke of Alençon.

SPAIN

At first Spain supported Elizabeth and her title to the throne. Despite his hatred of heretics, Philip II was unwilling to have England brought back into the Catholic fold as a province of his enemy, France. He therefore proposed marriage to Elizabeth. The Queen was hard put to decline because she could not risk a Spanish-French coalition against her, but neither could she bear Spanish-Catholic domination if she accepted. With typical contrivance she procrastinated so long over Philip's proposal that he finally took a French wife. Gradually, English-Spanish relations worsened as France dropped its designs on England, and as Elizabeth and Philip became the recognized leaders of the Protestant and Catholic camps. By avoiding any deliberate offense against Spain, Elizabeth kept the peace. But she condoned raids on Spanish shipping and colonies by English seamen and gave secret aid to Spain's rebelling subjects in the Netherlands. In turn, Philip aided plots to place Mary Stuart on the English throne.

IRELAND

During much of her reign Elizabeth was engaged in suppressing rebellions in Ireland where Catholic loyalty continued to be intense. A serious revolt occurred in 1598 when Hugh O'Neill, earl of Tyrone, enlisted the aid of Spain and the Pope and crushed the English army at Blackwater. After Elizabeth's court favorite, the Earl of Essex, proved to be a worthless field commander in restoring English authority, Lord Mountjoy defeated both the Irish and Spaniards in Ireland and again, for a time, there was the peace of submission in Ireland.

The Threat of Mary Stuart

The young widow, Mary Stuart, returned to Scotland from France in 1561 content with neither the Protestant supremacy won in her absence, nor with her position as only Queen of Scotland. She spent her days intriguing to become Queen of England as well. Mary Stuart was a fascinating and passionate woman who found the drab and austere Scottish court contrary to her style of living. In 1565 she married her cousin, Lord Darnley, who was a descendant of Henry VII of England. This marriage further strengthened her claim to the English succession. During the next three years Mary succeeded in alienating most of her subjects, both Protestant and Catholic. She quickly lost the support of the Protestant Lords and confided constantly in her private secretary, David Rizzio, who was murdered before her eyes by her jealous husband. After giving birth to a son, Mary fell desperately in love with a Protestant border lord, the Earl of Bothwell, who superintended the murder of Darnley. Upon obtaining a divorce from his wife, Bothwell and Mary were married according to Protestant rites.

These events aroused Protestants and Catholics to rebel against the Queen. Mary was imprisoned and forced to abdicate in favor of her son, James VI. In 1568 Mary escaped from prison, tried and failed to regain her throne, and fled to England to beg sanctuary from her cousin, Elizabeth. For the next nineteen years Mary Stuart served as a magnet for plots against Elizabeth. The royal advisors urged Elizabeth to sentence Mary to death because her very presence was a threat to the Queen's security; but Elizabeth, aware of her own mother's fate, disliked the idea of beheading monarchs and refused to act.

Marriage Diplomacy

Parliament and the people were anxious for Elizabeth to marry in order to preserve the Tudor and Protestant succession. There was no doubt that if the heir presumptive, Mary Stuart, came to the throne, a religious and civil war was almost a certainty. Yet, if the Queen was to marry an English lord, this too would create jealousy among her nobles. In the first two years of her reign Elizabeth received fifteen foreign proposals of marriage, most of them from Catholic princes; however, she preferred her independence. Certainly, her father's six marriages and Mary Tudor's sorry match had not served as very inspiring examples. Besides, Elizabeth's marriageable state gave her great flexibility in foreign diplomacy and an opportunity to play her hand with almost Machiavellian detachment. She apparently had real affection for only one suitor: Robert Dudley, earl of Leicester.

Plots Against Elizabeth

As long as Mary Stuart remained alive and in England, there were repeated conspiracies against the life of Elizabeth. The plots had as their objectives the full recognition of Mary Stuart as Queen of England and the reestablishment of Catholicism. The first serious threat was the rising of the northern earls in 1569. The old nobility of the north were reluctant to submit to the authority of Cecil and other "new men" who were administering the Tudor state. Their plan called for the Duke of Norfolk to wed Mary and reign with her after Elizabeth's death, thereby restoring the power of the old nobility in London. The rebellion, led by Norfolk and the Earls of Westmorland and Northumberland, was easily crushed because English Catholics failed to support it. Northumberland and eight hundred rebel recruits were executed on orders from Elizabeth.

Other conspiracies were the Ridolfi Plot (1571), the Throckmorton Plot (1583) and the Babington Plot (1586). The last of these was planned by Anthony Babington. It was discovered by Elizabeth's councilor, Walsingham, who allowed it to develop until he had names and evidence. It was this evidence that finally persuaded Elizabeth to consent to Mary's execution. Babington and his associates were killed, and Mary was found guilty by both Parliament and the law courts. Elizabeth procrastinated until February 1587, before she finally signed Mary's death warrant.

THE WAR WITH SPAIN

The drift of events led England into a war with Spain that Elizabeth and Cecil had struggled to avert for decades. By 1588 the confrontation was watched with keen interest all over Europe for its outcome would have religious and political consequences affecting the whole Continent. The Armada, which Spain claimed was "invincible," failed, and Spain's great prestige began to wane; nevertheless, the Armada was the beginning, and not the end, of the war against Spain. In English history, the legend of the Armada, like the Magna Charta, became a heroic symbol of the defense of freedom against tyranny, whether foreign or royal.

Steps to War

By 1580 only England seemed to stand in the way of Spain's military and political hegemony over Europe. King Philip II persuaded himself that for religious, commercial, political, and personal reasons he had cause to invade England.

RELIGIOUS RIVALRY

Philip was convinced that his divinely inspired mission was to restore religious orthodoxy to Europe. Of the Protestant triumvirate (William of Orange in Holland, Admiral Coligny, leader of the French Huguenots, and Elizabeth) only Elizabeth was left in his path. Coligny was murdered by French Catholics in 1572, and William by an assassin in Spanish employment in 1584. By elimination Elizabeth was the obvious leader of Protestant Europe, and Catholic plots on her life were attempted routinely, but without success.

MARITIME FRICTION

In 1580 Spain annexed Portugal, and their combined colonial empires gave Philip fabulous overseas wealth. But for over a quarter of a century English adventurers ("sea dogs") had been sailing the Atlantic and the Spanish Main, capturing treasure ships, breaking the Spanish monopoly on the slave trade, and suffering few casualties. These adventurers, among whom the most famous were Sir John Hawkins, Sir Francis Drake, and Sir Richard Grenville, were never publicly supported by the Crown; however, Elizabeth backed them privately, knighted them, and took her share of the profits. Goaded to fury, the Spaniards saw no way of assuring control of the seas and stopping this piratering without defeating England.

THE WAR IN THE NETHERLANDS

The Protestant provinces of the Spanish Netherlands were still in open revolt against Spain because of the steady support from the English. Philip knew that Dutch resistance would be maintained so long as the rebels received aid from England and England controlled the sea route to Antwerp. Elizabeth supported the Dutch rebels because she feared that a Spanish reconquest would end a profitable trade with the Netherlands and prepare the way for an invasion of England.

EFFECTS OF MARY STUART'S EXECUTION

Mary's death forced the issue of succession since she had been the intended instrument of the Catholics for regaining the throne of England from within. While Mary Stuart lived, Philip hesitated to risk Spanish money and blood to win England for her, because she favored France over Spain. Within a week of the news of Mary's execution, Philip moved rapidly with plans for an invasion, even though there was no assurance that English Catholics would rally to the banner of a hated Spaniard when Spanish troops landed in England.

The Spanish Armada

Philip's plan was to send a great armada of ships to the Netherlands and ferry the Duke of Parma and the best army in Europe to England, where he hoped that English Catholics would rise in revolt. The whole venture from the beginning was plagued by mishaps. Spain's leading admiral, the Marquis of Santa Cruz, died and was replaced by the old Duke of Medina Sidonia. Sir Francis Drake sailed into Cadiz harbor in 1587 and sank Spanish ships at anchor, which delayed the expedition for a year. The army of the Duke of Parma was blockaded by Dutch and English forces and did not rendezvous as planned. Nevertheless, on July 29, 1588, the Armada of 131 ships was sighted by the English in the Channel.

THE CHANNEL BATTLE.

For nine days Admiral Howard's English fleet of smaller and faster ships kept up a running battle but could not break the crescent-shaped formation of the Spaniards. While the Armada anchored for provisions at Calais, the English drove the fleet into confusion with fire ships. On the next day the English cannonade inflicted heavy damage in the decisive battle fought off Gravelines. Unable to reach Parma, collect supplies, or retrace its course, the Armada sailed north around the British Isles where fierce storms did even more damage than the English navy. In September the incompetent Medina Sidonia returned to Spain with two-thirds of his fleet—the invasion had failed.

SIGNIFICANCE OF THE ARMADA

The defeat at sea did not crush Spain or immediately transfer command of the seas from Spain to England. More treasure ships reached Spain in the next fifteen years than in any other similar period. Nevertheless, the defeat of the Armada had important consequences. It saved England from Parma's powerful army and at the same time united English Catholics and Protestants against a common enemy. Equally important, the defeat of the Armada prevented the imposition of both a Catholic and a Spanish hegemony over Europe by force and gave heart to the Dutch rebels to continue their fight for independence.

There were also repercussions in the colonial world as the breaking of Spanish sea power opened up new regions in both the Far East and in America. English and Dutch squadrons challenged the fading Portuguese empire in the East, and the French and the English no longer hesitated to settle America. Finally, to Elizabeth and her people the events in the year 1588 reinforced their belief that God and good fortune were on their side, and over the years the legend of victory became an increasingly eulogized example of the heroism of the English spirit.

The War Continues

The Armada marked the beginning of a war with Spain that dragged on for the remaining fourteen years of Elizabeth's reign. The English counterattack in 1589 under Drake was a fiasco. An invasion force of 150 ships and 1,800 men attacked Spain but failed miserably, as disease decimated the land army, and Drake refused to attack Lisbon. English mariners intermittently harassed the Spanish in the Azores, and in 1595 both Drake and Hawkins died in an expedition to the West Indies. Elizabeth was drawn more deeply into the struggles on the Continent when she provided English troops to serve in the Netherlands and in northern France against Spain. Between 1589 and 1595 the Queen sent five expeditions to support the Protestant Henry of Navarre in France and to block Spain's designs on France. Although Henry became a Catholic in 1593 to win Paris, neither he nor Elizabeth abandoned their Anglo-French alliance until France concluded a peace with Spain in 1598.

King Philip supported the Irish rebellion with a second armada, but it too was dispersed by a gale. The Irish rebellion preoccupied England and cost the treasury much more than did the repulse of the Armada in 1588. To finance the war Elizabeth was forced to grant monopolies, increase customs, and sell £876,322 of Crown lands, as well as raise an additional £2 million in taxes.

ECONOMIC AND COLONIAL EXPANSION

During the Elizabethan Age prices, trade, and prosperity increased as the commercial revolution and the rise of small industry improved the lot of the merchant, the gentry, and the yeoman. In contrast, the depressed out-of-work classes often became a floating population of vagabonds and unemployed. The government recognized the need for dealing with the unemployed poor and introduced important economic and industrial legislation in Parliament.

Agriculture and Labor

Since the country gentry who administered the laws did not push any enforcement that conflicted with their own interests, the enclosure movement continued in spite of laws passed to restrict it. Wheat-raising competed with sheep-raising as the rapid growth of towns increased the demand for foodstuffs.

Elizabeth called in the debased currency early in her reign and replaced it with sound money to restore the country's credit. However, she still had the problem of unemployed poor drifting around the country and supporting any rebellion. Because of this the government passed more economic legislation—the Parliament of 1563 alone passed fourteen statutes—than in any previous reign. The Statute of Artificers (or Statute of Apprentices) of 1563 transferred the regulation of labor and industry from local to national control in an effort to halt vagrancy by promoting full employment. The act attempted to control and recruit labor by enforcing the seven-year apprenticeship in the trades, requiring unskilled labor to work in agriculture in rush seasons if needed, and providing for local justices of the peace to regulate wages and hours.

Welfare Laws

The plague and the harvest failures of the 1590s caused the government to nationalize poor relief because local, municipal relief was too limited and erratic to handle the distress. Here the state took over the earlier role of the Church in administering charity, motivated more by fear than by humanitarianism of what wandering, hungry people could do. The Poor Laws of 1597 and 1601 made the parish the local unit of welfare administration and responsible for the poor relief of its residents. Stiff penalties were levied for vagrancy. Each parish appointed four overseers who levied rates (compulsory taxes) on property owners in order to build workhouses and provide work and wages for the unemployed. Although considered harsh, the Poor Laws became the cornerstone for much later social welfare legislation.

Commerce and Industry

The cloth trade continued as the leading industry. In foreign trade the Merchant Adventurers replaced the Staplers as the most powerful export group after they received a royal charter in 1564. Shipbuilding and coal-mining grew rapidly, and new industries, such as salt and alum, became important. The Tudors tightened state controls in order to encourage home industries and to promote a favorable balance of trade. This policy, sometimes termed "mercantilism," was done on a piecemeal basis for specific objectives (as to help fishermen or export traders by legislative acts) and not as part of any doctrinaire view on economics.

Colonies and Chartered Companies

The reign of Elizabeth is also noted for the expansion of England's overseas exploration and trading activities after a late start. Portugal and Spain took the lead in overseas expansion because those countries had the fleets and power to back up their ventures, whereas England was preoccupied with establishing a new dynasty and a new church.

John Cabot in 1497, exploring for an English company, discovered Newfoundland and thus provided England with a basis for future claims to North America. John Hawkins broke into the lucrative Spanish monopoly of the slave trade between Africa and the West Indies at the same time the English naval adventurers were exploring the New World and Sir Francis Drake was making his spectacular voyage around the world (1577–1580). Three relatives, Sir Humphrey Gilbert, Sir Walter Raleigh, and Sir Richard Grenville, backed by a royal charter, tried to colonize Newfoundland (1583) and Virginia (1585, 1587), but their efforts were unsuccessful. Martin Frobisher explored northeastern Canada (1576) while searching for a Northwest Passage. With the rise of the merchant navy English foreign commerce expanded through new trading companies chartered by the Crown; these included the Muscovy Company (1553), the Levant Company (1592), and the East India Company (1600). The influence of English sea power was just beginning to make itself felt.

THE MACHINERY OF GOVERNMENT

The so-called Tudor despotism of the sixteenth century was actually an authoritarian, yet popular, government that provided peace and order without resorting to despotism. In the political transformation from a medieval to a national state two important developments took place: The central administration became national and public in scope to replace the medieval practice of the king's household administering primarily his private estate; and the House of Commons increased in size and significance and became a major instrument of government.

The Administration

Henry VIII's minister, Thomas Cromwell, was the chief architect of the administrative reform which transformed a royal household administration into centralized administrative machinery that could function effectively regardless of the leadership of the king. Royal administration, both on the local level and in Parliament, relied especially on the rising gentry class; both worked well together, particularly during the years when the Crown and the gentry had the same aims and felt threatened by either civil war or external invasion.

THE CENTRAL GOVERNMENT

The center of administrative control from the time of Henry VIII was the Privy Council; it became a formal executive body that took over the functions formerly handled by household officers. The highest policy decisions, of course, were still made by the monarch. The Council itself was responsible to the sovereign and not to Parliament (in contrast to the British Cabinet today). An enormous increase in Council business took place under Henry VIII and Elizabeth, and specialization of function occurred. The Council also claimed judicial powers as well as supervisory functions over the Councils of the North and the Marchers (Wales). Elizabeth made no attempt to demand unanimity among her councilors; in fact, rival factions reflecting different viewpoints appealed to her. In this way she was informed of possible alternatives in policy and no controlling clique could assume to control her. When Parliament was in session, her councilors drafted government bills and piloted them through the two Houses as the Cabinet ministers do today.

LOCAL GOVERNMENT

The substitution of the parish for the earlier manor or village as a local unit of administration was one of the developments of Elizabeth's reign. The church wardens and the overseers of the poor, supported by the county justices of the peace, administered the poor laws under the supervision of the Privy Council. On the county level the post of lord-lieutenant was created in the 1550s whereby a peer, and frequently a Privy councilor, served as the formal contact between the central government and the local administration; he was responsible for the local militia and all emergency measures.

However, the justices of the peace were the indispensable officers in local government. The great increase in their number and the greater diversification of their duties reflected the rising power of the gentry and the efficiency of their work. These unpaid local magistrates presided over local courts, regulated new laws on labor and apprentices, kept the peace, enforced the poor laws, and punished vagabonds. Other local officials linking the county with London were the sheriff, the coroner who investigated sudden deaths and empaneled juries, and the vice-admirals of the coastal counties.

The Courts

The legal profession and legal business expanded greatly in the Tudor period. At the same time the authority of statute law was enhanced by the prominence given to it by Henry VIII and the Reformation Parliament. The Inns of Court and the common law resumed their stature under Elizabeth after faltering in the reigns of Henry VIII and Mary. The regular courts consisted of (1) the Petty Sessions, presided over by two or more justices of the peace, which heard minor charges; (2) the Quarter Sessions, meeting four times yearly, which considered more serious county cases; (3) the Assizes where royal judges on circuit presided; and (4) the Common Law Courts at Westminster—King's Bench, Common Pleas, and Exchequer. The prerogative courts of the Crown with no jury were the Chancery, which heard cases of equity and important civil cases; Court of the High Commission, for religious offenses; Court of the North, for northern England; Council of Wales; Court of Castle Chamber, for Ireland; and Court of the Star Chamber.

Parliament

Parliament became increasingly important as an instrument of government after Henry VIII used it extensively it to complete his break with Rome. Parliamentary proceedings were effectively managed by the Tudors, but the gentry cooperated willingly. Thus the Parliaments did not have to be packed to secure a favorable vote. Under Elizabeth Parliament perfected some procedures: three readings for each bill was established; a standing committee for privileges and disputed elections existed after 1588; and the committee system for examining bills was accepted. At the beginning of each session Parliament claimed from the Queen freedom of speech and freedom from arrest.

HOUSE OF COMMONS AND HOUSE OF LORDS

The Commons gained greatly in power since it represented the growing influence of the middle class—the gentry, the lawyers, and the merchants. The membership of the Commons increased during the sixteenth century from 296 to 462. The Lords often influenced the selection of members to the House of Commons, but as a class they never exerted the power that they had before the Wars of the Roses. All baronial rebellions against the Tudors failed. The new aristocracy was frequently a creation of the Tudors and, therefore, indebted to them; besides, the removal of the abbots from the House of Lords and the royal appointment of the remaining bishops gave the monarch direct control of one-third of the Upper House.

THE TUDOR SYSTEM

The medieval concept of a king with unlimited authority only in certain recognized spheres was somewhat undermined in practice by the Tudors, such as in the dissolution of the monasteries. However, they were astute enough not to enunciate any doctrine of absolutism for, unlike the French king, they had no standing army or professional bureaucracy to back such a claim. Instead, Tudor government relied on the voluntary services of local administrators and on the cooperation of the Crown and its loyal subjects. However, by the end of Elizabeth's reign the House of Commons was becoming vigorous and vocal under such a system and was expanding its privileges.

THE LAST YEARS OF ELIZABETH

By 1590 England felt secure from religious wars and Spanish attack. Therefore, Parliament became restive and grumbled about the cost of the war against Spain and Ireland, censured the Queen for the granting of royal monopolies in 1597, and delayed the passage of bills for as long as four years. Yet direct protest was muted out of respect and affection for the aged Queen; the Commons reserved its opposition for her successor. Elizabeth had refused to name a successor until she reached her deathbed; she then nominated King James VI of Scotland. Her chief advisor, Robert Cecil, son of William Cecil, completed arrangements for a smooth transition of power. In 1603 the dynasty ended with the death of the greatest of the Tudors.

LEARNING AND LITERATURE

The spirit and vitality of the Elizabethan Age is perhaps best expressed in its literature. The Renaissance and the Reformation, in different ways, helped mold this literature which assumed a distinctly English character that reflected the new nationalism and revealed a self-questioning and a self-conscious maturity. The awakening was all the more striking because, except for Chaucer, this caliber of writing was previously lacking in English literature. However, no comparable achievement occurred in education.

Tudor Education

Renaissance scholars turned away from scholasticism and contributed new ideas on learning, especially in the study of Greek classics. The Reformation reduced Church influence on education. But the dissolution of the monasteries under Henry VIII and of the chantries under Edward VI closed many elementary schools when the endowments were lost. Not until the end of Elizabeth's reign did the patronage of clergy and nobility restore the grammar schools. In the universities the Renaissance provided some reforms, but the Reformation also brought on disputes and division, and only later a greater diversity of knowledge and a freer spirit. Oxford was more affected than Cambridge by the Reformation in its monastic and faculty losses, but it continued to be the larger university. Cambridge advanced greatly in size and influence after the Reformation. Elizabeth's inner circle of councilors were all Cambridge men, and the Church, from Cranmer to Bancroft, was led by Cambridge scholars. Since Cambridge was more Protestant than Oxford, it stimulated intellectual vigor and controversy as the Puritans grew in power; three of the seven new colleges at Cambridge were established as a direct result of the Puritan impulse. Little change in curriculum took place; theology, logic, and philosophy were still the central studies, although the tutorial system began to alter teaching methods.

Literature

The religious and political controversies prior to the middle of the sixteenth century did not encourage scholarship or literary productivity. The real flowering of Renaissance letters with its amazing range of writing occurred during Elizabeth's reign.

PROSE

The works of Elizabethan prose writers typically reflect the varied interests of the Renaissance. (1) Roger Ascham, Elizabeth's tutor and secretary, produced an admirable treatise on political education in *The Scholemaster*. It was a plea for the study of classical literature and gentle manners in the public schools. (2) Ralph Holinshed's patriotic *Chronicles* became the source materials for the historical plays of Shakespeare and Marlowe. (3) John Lyly portrayed society in two books on court etiquette and mannerisms, *Euphues* and *Euphues and His England*. His ornate, elaborately structured prose became a popular vogue. (4) Richard Hakluyt in his *Principal Navigations, Voyages and Discoveries of the English Nation*, John Leland in *The Laborious Journey*, and William Harrison with his *Description of England* stimulated popular interest in geography and history. (5) The versatile Sir Walter Raleigh, besides being a courtier, financier, explorer, and poet, composed a remarkable *History of the World*. (6) Sir Francis Bacon's *Essays* offered worldly wisdom in an epigrammatic style. His intellectual and philosophical brilliance was observed more sharply in his writings during the reign of James I. (7) Richard Hooker furnished the ablest apologia for the Elizabethan Church with his judicious and balanced *Laws of Ecclesiastical Polity*.

POETRY

Before Elizabeth's reign only three Tudor poets claim recognition: John Skelton (ca. 1460–1529) with his satirical *Speke, Parrot* on Cardinal Wolsey; and Thomas Wyatt (ca. 1503–1542) who, along with Henry Howard, the Earl of Surrey (ca. 1517–1542), introduced the sonnet form to England— Wyatt the Italian or Petrarchan form, Surrey the English or Shakespearean. During Elizabeth's reign came the three leading poets of the century: Sir Philip Sidney, Edmund Spenser, and William Shakespeare. Sidney, a gentleman, scholar, courtier, and knight, was the ideal Elizabethan man of letters. His two most admired works are *Astrophel and Stella* (sonnets) and *The Defence of Poesie*, a lofty and imaginative treatise on the art of poetry. Spenser was the poet's poet and his works provided a new stanza of nine lines, a richness of imagery, and a high seriousness that many later poets imitated. His two most noted works are *The Shepherds' Calendar* and *The*

Faerie Queene. Shakespeare's nondramatic poems were written early in his career and consisted of the *Sonnets* and the long narrative poems, *Venus and Adonis* and *Lucrece*.

DRAMA

No age approaches the Elizabethan in the excellence and variety of drama. Robert Greene, a bohemian university wit and journalist, wrote the farcical *Friar Bacon* and the historical play *James IV*. Christopher Marlowe died in a tavern brawl before he was thirty, but in his short life he wrote the first great tragedies in blank verse including *Tamburlane*, *The Jew of Malta*, and *The Tragical History of Doctor Faustus*. Shakespeare climaxed the age with his thirty-four plays which so fully captured the temper of the Elizabethans and the human spirit. His plays have continued to be classics because of the universal themes and the characterizations that underlie them. He attempted all types—comedy, tragedy, and history—and triumphed in each area. Other playwrights of the period were Thomas Sackville (*Gorboduc*), Thomas Kyd (*Spanish Tragedy*), Nicholas Udall (*Ralph Roister Doister*), and Ben Jonson (*Every Man in his Humor*).

At first plays were given in courtyards of inns; then beginning in 1576, theaters were built in London which soon became the focus of popular entertainment. The court was the acknowledged center of art and culture, and here the sophisticated, the social climbers, the professional politicians, and the new rich all vied for the honor of Elizabeth's favor.

The last half of the sixteenth century is rightly called "the Elizabethan Age" for the Queen embodied the confidence and character of the emerging nation state and made England a major participant in European and overseas affairs.

Elizabeth left as her legacy a firmly established Church of England, domestic peace, a victorious navy, a sound coinage, and a flourishing environment for poets and playwrights. At the end of her reign she also left an increasingly assertive House of Commons that would test its prerogatives with her successor.

Elizabeth was a symbol of unity for England and she wooed her subjects so that the affection they expressed for their sovereign would not be matched again until late in the reign of Queen Victoria. Although religious and political restlessness was evident in Elizabeth's last years, deference for a beloved Queen meant that overt opposition would wait until after her death to assert itself.

Selected Readings

Black, J. B. *The Reign of Elizabeth, 1558–1603* (1959)
Dickens, A. G. *The English Reformation* (1964)
Elton, Geoffrey R. *The Tudor Revolution in Government* (1959)
Fraser, Lady Antonia. *Mary Queen of Scots* (1969)

Jenkins, Elizabeth. *Elizabeth the Great* (1959)

Mattingly, Garrett. *The Armada* (1959)

Neale, John E. *Queen Elizabeth* (1957)

Palliser, D. M. *The Age of Elizabeth: England Under the Later Tudors, 1547–1603* (1983)

Read, Conyers. *Mr. Secretary Cecil and Queen Elizabeth* (1955)

Rowse, Alfred L. *The Elizabethan Renaissance* (1974)

Hakluyt, Richard. *Voyages and Discoveries* (1982)

Stone, Lawrence. *The Crisis of the Aristocracy, 1558–1641* (1965)

Tillyard, E. M. W. *The Elizabethan World Picture* (1959)

9

King vs. Parliament: 1603–1642

1603 James VI of Scotland becomes James I of England, uniting the English and Scottish thrones

1605 Guy Fawkes' Gunpowder Plot to blow up James I and Parliament fails

1607 England's first permanent colony established in Jamestown, Virginia

1609 The six northern counties of Ireland (Ulster) are confiscated by the English government and settled with Scottish and English immigrants

1611 Publication of the King James or Authorized Version of the Bible

1620 English Puritans sail on the *Mayflower* to Plymouth, New England

1625 Charles I succeeds his father as King of England and Scotland

1628 Petition of Right signed by Charles I

1640 Long Parliament convenes

*T*he first two Stuarts attempted to exert Tudor-like authority in England without the tact of the Tudors and came into conflict with the latent, but growing, power of the rising gentry class. "Parliamentary privilege" versus "royal prerogative" became the focal point of the conflict and resulted in the alienation of the House of Commons.

At the same time the clash between two unfortunate and often inept Stuart kings and their religiously and politically restless subjects was intensified by problems not resolved by the Tudor monarchs. Inflation, the *rising influence of the gentry, lawyers jealously guarding the common law against royal encroachments, and Puritan dissatisfaction with the Church of England sapped the foundations of the early Stuart monarchy.*

THE RELIGIOUS QUESTION

The growing Puritan influence among the gentry and the freedom from foreign invasion meant that the Elizabethan settlement could no longer remain safe from attack. James I, however, had no intention of sacrificing the episcopal structure and his headship of the Church of England. Since the ecclesiastical government was linked so closely to royal authority, King James argued that a retreat in religion was a retreat for royalty. Since neither compromise nor toleration in religion were considered virtues in this age, both the king and the Puritans took unyielding positions.

James's Scottish Background

When Mary Stuart abdicated the throne and fled for safety to England, her only child became King of Scotland before he was a year old. For the next thirty-nine years James survived the plots of kidnappers, a grasping nobility, militant and strident Presbyterian churchmen, and "a thousand intrigues" to prove himself the adept master of an unruly kingdom. He had received a superior education under the tutorship of George Buchanan and was scholarly and intelligent in a pedantic way. The King was a theorist, understanding books far better than he did his subjects—a French contemporary called him the "wisest fool in Christendom." In the Stuart tradition he believed that he was born to rule. To combat the Scottish Presbyterian Church and his lawless nobility, James argued for the theory of government known as the divine right of kings and wrote a treatise on it to support royal absolutism. James enjoyed hunting, riding, and court favorites, and was inclined to be lazy. He conducted government affairs in an erratic, although successful, manner in Scotland. By the time of Elizabeth's death in England, James was in full control of Scotland and in despotic fashion had effectively practiced his theory of divine right.

ACCESSION OF JAMES

James was overjoyed to become ruler of England and to leave poverty-stricken Scotland and its Presbyterian Church for a richer and more secure kingdom where he could govern the church as well as the state. To that end he had handled his relations with Elizabeth most properly, even to the point of only mildly protesting to her the execution of his mother. Thus in 1603 when the two kingdoms were joined under one crown, it was the easiest accession of any new English dynasty. Elizabeth's acknowledgment, the support of Robert Cecil and the Privy Council, and the enthusiastic greeting of the people attested to the logic in their choice of James. But the Scottish King never fully grasped the differences between the two kingdoms, and his initial popularity soon faded.

RELIGIOUS HOPES

Puritans and Catholics were optimistic that King James would be more sympathetic to their cause than was Elizabeth. The Puritans hoped that his years as King of Presbyterian Scotland would permit them to bring about reforms in England; the Catholics noted that his mother was Catholic and that James had been tolerant of the Catholic faith in Scotland and seemed friendly toward Spain. James could not please both parties and was rather content with the Elizabethan Church.

Hampton Court Conference, 1604. Some eight hundred Puritan preachers presented the Millenary Petition to James in which they requested a simpler ritual than that decreed by Elizabeth, a greater emphasis on preaching, and the abolition of certain ceremonies, such as the cross in baptism. They also requested a new translation of the Bible. James granted the petitioners an audience at Hampton but became enraged by their suggestion to abolish the office of bishop. The conference ended with the Puritans dissatisfied and the King critical of their demands. The King's agreement to authorize a new version of the Bible (the King James Version, 1611) was the only constructive result.

Catholic Plots. When the early friendliness of King James to the Catholics changed to official disfavor, certain Catholics resorted to plots which threatened his life. The "By-Plot" of 1603 hoped to capture James, whereas the Gunpowder Plot of 1605 aimed at blowing up both the King and Parliament. Guy Fawkes was caught with kegs of gunpowder in the cellar of Parliament just before the session opened. This spectacular plot shocked the country and aroused Parliament to enact additional penalties against the Catholics. The Anglican settlement was not to be altered in the reign of James.

JAMES AND HIS PARLIAMENTS

Religion and finances became the leading issues generating friction between James and his Parliament. The King never appreciated two important differences between his kingdoms: The power of the nobility and the weakness of Parliament in Scotland were not duplicated in seventeenth-century England. In that sense his rule in Scotland was not a helpful preparation for his rule in England. In medieval England powerful barons had led the opposition when Parliament challenged the Crown; after 1604 the opposition in Parliament came primarily from the Commons.

Parliamentary Privileges

In 1604 few established rules existed that clearly indicated the rights and privileges of Parliament. The Commons, however, soon asserted its undefined privileges as inalienable rights and developed a political doctrine to back its position.

THE FIRST PARLIAMENT, 1604–1611

The Goodwin Case which arose out of a disputed election created the first clash between the Crown and Parliament. The Commons argued that it, and not the court of chancery, was the judge of its own membership. Finally the King yielded, but with little grace. In 1606 the exchequer court found in favor of the King in the Bates Case. The decision recognized the right of the King to levy impositions of duties because there were no limitations on the King's power except his own forbearance. Both merchants and Parliament protested the additional customs. In the session of 1611 James offered to surrender some of his rights, such as wardship, in return for a guaranteed annual income of £2,000,000. However, the negotiations over this "Great Contract" broke down, whereupon James lectured the members on their failure to respect the prerogatives of the Crown and dismissed them. Parliament then sent an "Apology" to James that was actually a defense of their privileges. Such privileges, said the Apology, were derived from law and tradition, and not from the King.

THE SECOND (OR ADDLED) PARLIAMENT, 1614

After three years of trying to govern without parliamentary grants, King James was forced to call Parliament into session. The Commons demanded the redress of grievances before voting any money bills. After a stormy two-month session James dissolved Parliament because it had not passed any acts or granted him any money. For the next seven years James governed without Parliament, and to obtain revenue he exploited every possible resource at his disposal from forced loans to the selling of titles.

THE THIRD PARLIAMENT, 1621

The Thirty Years' War (1618–1648) on the Continent between Catholic and Protestant states caused James to summon this Parliament which promptly retaliated for the dismissal of Chief Justice Coke, the leading opponent of the royal prerogative, in 1616. Resurrecting its old weapon of impeachment, Parliament indicted two courtiers for abusing monopolies and the brilliant Sir Francis Bacon, the King's Chancellor, for receiving bribes. Parliament then examined foreign policy which James, like Elizabeth, considered none of its business. In the second session the King lost his temper over Parliament's insistence on debating foreign policy and dissolved Parliament.

THE FOURTH PARLIAMENT, 1624

The King's last Parliament was the most friendly to him because it was anxious to fight Spain and the Catholic League and to assist the German Protestants. In this session James permitted the members to debate foreign affairs, to impeach his financial genius and Treasurer, the Earl of Middlesex, and to invade the royal prerogative by limiting royal control over monopolies. Parliament subsidized an elaborate expedition against Spain. However, James died in 1625 before the fleet set sail.

Parliamentary Theory

The attack of the Commons on royal prerogatives was supported by the common law courts which had formerly been allies of the Crown. Led by the tough, irascible Sir Edward Coke, Chief Justice of the Court of the King's Bench, the courts supported the assumption that Parliamentary privileges had an ancient, and not necessarily royal origin, that the king was under law (*rex sub lege*), and that the courts were independent of the Crown. They were not, however, as James proved by removing Chief Justice Coke. Nevertheless, the claims of the judges emboldened Parliament to continue its piecemeal encroachments on royal prerogatives. James was never browbeaten by his Parliaments and only gave in on the matter of royal monopolies because he knew when to compromise. He was wise enough to sense the danger signals and to warn his son, Charles.

Royal Favorites

At first James relied on Elizabeth's chief councilor, Robert Cecil, but gradually new royal favorites replaced Cecil (who died in 1612 as Earl of Salisbury) and the Privy Council in influence. The two leading courtiers were Robert Carr, whom James made Earl of Somerset, and George Villiers, who eventually became Duke of Buckingham. The King's dependence on these incompetents aroused the resentment of the Court. With the rise of favorites the King's councilors lost their influence on parliamentary legislation since they no longer introduced legislation, as they had previously in the days of Elizabeth. "By the third decade of the seventeenth century, the commons were in charge of the initiation, formulations, and passage of laws. They were the tail that wagged the dog."[*]

---

[*] George L. Haskins, *The Growth of English Representative Government* (London, 1948), pp. 126–27.

FOREIGN AFFAIRS

James, ever the pacifist, vigorously pursued a policy of peace even under the most trying conditions and succeeded, except during the first and last years of his reign. The Thirty Years' War in Germany caught him in a dilemma: He curried favor with Catholic Spain and hoped to marry his son to the Spanish Infanta (princess); at the same time his daughter Elizabeth and her Protestant husband, the Elector of the Palatinate in south Germany, were being besieged by a Catholic coalition determined to oust all Protestant rulers. England's old enmity toward Spain finally brought war in 1624 and reconciled Parliament to the King.

Scotland and Ireland

King James hoped for the union of England and Scotland, but Parliament was opposed to the idea and even refused free trade and English citizenship to the Scots. Except for removing the danger of border warfare and French influence in Scotland, the two countries remained separate nations with a common king for another century. James tried to pacify the Irish by having his deputy terminate martial law, dismiss old charges against Irish rebels, and restore certain tribal lands to Irish tenants. However, the attempt to enforce the Anglican supremacy led to new uprisings in northern Ireland. The English government responded by seizing land in six northern counties and settling Scotch Presbyterians, Welsh, and English in the area known as Ulster. Queen Elizabeth had introduced this Anglo-Protestant colonization, and the Stuarts and Cromwell continued the settlement.

Spain

In 1604 James and Robert Cecil ended the war with Spain that had dragged on since the year of the Armada. The peace halted an expensive and fruitless war, but was unpopular in Parliament, particularly among the Puritans and the commercial class. When James pursued a pro-Spanish policy, he was greatly influenced by Buckingham and the Spanish ambassador, Count Gondomar. James had Sir Walter Raleigh executed to placate Spanish demands and attempted to negotiate a marriage between his heir, Charles, and the Spanish Infanta. Buckingham and Charles went to Spain to complete the negotiations but returned in 1623 humiliated and empty-handed—a slight which turned them into angry foes of Spain. Charles and Buckingham and Parliament eventually prevailed on the King to declare war on Spain in 1624. The twenty-year peace was over, and Buckingham dispatched a series of expeditions to the Continent, all of which were frightful failures. The first expedition to free the Palatinate ruled by James's son-in-law, Frederick, failed because of mismanagement, sickness, and starvation.

The Thirty Years' War, 1618–1648

In 1618 bitter religious warfare broke out in Germany between the Protestant Union of principalities and the Catholic League. In Bohemia the Protestants deposed their fanatical Catholic King and invited Frederick, the Elector of the Palatinate and James's son-in-law, to take the throne. The vengeance of the Catholics and the Hapsburg rulers was swift and cruel. After one winter of rule Frederick and Elizabeth (daughter of James) were ousted, and the Palatinate was annexed by Maximilian of the Catholic League. The flight of his daughter from Catholic forces and the failure of his son's marriage negotiations in Spain reversed James's policy of support for Catholic Spain and won him popularity with his subjects. But England had suffered military stagnation for twenty years and was in no position to take effective action.

CHARLES I

Parliamentary and Puritan opposition coalesced in King Charles's reign (1625–1649) to challenge his high-handed and small-minded manner of ruling. The King's expensive and futile foreign policy only added to his predicament. By ending the wars and governing without Parliament Charles put off some of his problems, but neither he nor his advisers really understood or cared to grapple with the basic problem that plagued his reign: how to negotiate with a Parliament that refused to accept the traditional royal prerogatives.

Character of Charles

The twenty-five-year-old King was more dignified and attractive than his father, but, like his father, he held exalted notions of kingship and relied on royal favorites. Charles was a patron of the arts, a nervous, shy person, highly religious and an affectionate family man. Unfortunately Charles was a disaster as king; he was petty and indecisive and conspicuously lacked the art of political management.

Foreign Affairs

After the pacifist policy of his father, Charles and his advisor, the Duke of Buckingham, promoted within four years six reckless military adventures against the German Catholics, Spain, and France, none of which succeeded. Thereafter, Charles, lacking financial subsidies from Parliament, became essentially a spectator in the political-religious maneuvers of the Thirty Years' War.

SPAIN

Charles asked his first Parliament (1625) for funds to sustain the war against Spain but refused to discuss his campaign plans with Parliament. When the Commons refused to grant funds, Charles went ahead with his plans. The result was a badly organized and ill-equipped expedition that landed near Cadiz. The demoralized and drunken soldiers failed to take the city, and on the way back to England the fleet was mauled by a storm.

FRANCE

Meanwhile England was also drifting into conflict with France. Charles's marriage in the first week of his reign to Henrietta Maria, sister of Louis XIII, purchased a fleeting friendship with France but raised suspicions that the King was susceptible to Catholic influence. When English ships loaned to France were ordered by Cardinal Richelieu to attack the French Huguenots at La Rochelle, the crews mutinied. Months later war broke out between England and France (1627), and three expeditions were sent to relieve the beleaguered French Protestants at La Rochelle. Buckingham led the second expedition to the Isle of Rhé, where he was repulsed by the French after losing half of his men. In 1630 England made peace with France and Spain, and the nation now became preoccupied with internal controversies.

Charles and Parliament

Since Charles considered such matters as war and peace outside the authority of parliamentary jurisdiction, he did not justify his requests for money. In turn Parliament, led by such squires as John Eliot, Thomas Wentworth, John Pym, and John Hampden, raised a whole list of grievances and claimed additional powers.

THE FIRST PARLIAMENT, 1625

Parliamentary opposition to Buckingham and the King's Catholic marriage prevented Charles from receiving more than one-seventh of his financial request, while royal tax revenue on tonnage and poundage were voted for only a year instead of for life as was customary.

THE SECOND PARLIAMENT, 1626

The members of Parliament refused to vote war supplies for the King, and John Eliot's oratory led to impeachment proceedings against the Duke of Buckingham. To save his favorite minister, Charles dissolved Parliament and demanded forced loans from taxpayers. This aroused opposition, and arrests were made for refusal to pay. Soldiers were quartered in private homes to save expenses; but the King still required additional revenue.

THE THIRD PARLIAMENT AND THE PETITION OF RIGHT, 1628

Charles was forced to summon a third Parliament to raise more money. However, the leaders of Parliament—Eliot, Coke, Pym, and Wentworth—were determined that no subsidy would be granted until the King redressed their grievances. A Petition of Right was drafted which limited royal prerogative and requested the King to protect ancient liberties. It forbade imprisonment without showing cause, martial law in time of peace, forced loans or taxes without parliamentary consent, and the billeting of soldiers in private homes without consent of the occupants. Charles reluctantly signed the petition in order to have his subsidies approved. The petition, like the Magna Charta of 1215, became, in time, a constitutional landmark in limiting the power of the monarchy, although its immediate effects were slight.

Second Session, 1629. Charles dismissed the first session of Parliament to stave off an attempt to remove Buckingham from office. But during the adjournment Buckingham was assassinated by John Felton, a naval officer, and the nation rejoiced as the King grieved. When Parliament reconvened religious grievances took priority over fiscal matters, and the Commons launched an attack on the High Church policies of the Bishops. When the Speaker attempted to adjourn the fruitless session, members held him in his chair while the Commons hastily passed three resolutions condemning anyone who introduced innovations in religion, or who advised levying taxes on tonnage and poundage without parliamentary consent, or who would pay such taxes. When Parliament was finally dissolved, Eliot and eight other members were arrested; three of them were sent to the Tower, and Eliot died there three years later.

Personal Rule, 1629–1640

For the next eleven years King Charles ruled without summoning Parliament. To save money he made peace with France and Spain; to raise sufficient money to govern, royal officials invoked every possible source of revenue short of parliamentary grants. Customs revenues were not sufficient to pay expenses; therefore the King levied fines on individuals who had violated long dormant forest laws, invented new monopolies, and invoked an old statute that required all landholders with an annual income of £40 to be knighted. A large fee was charged if they became knights; a steep fine if they refused.

The levy arousing the greatest opposition was the ship money tax which seacoast towns had paid in earlier centuries to provide ships for defense against a threatened invasion. But England was at peace and Charles demanded the tax of inland as well as coastal counties. John Hampden, a wealthy Puritan, refused to pay his tax, arguing that it usurped Parliament's power to levy taxes. In court the King won the legal verdict, but not the popular one.

Royal Advisors

After the assassination of Buckingham (1628) Charles relied largely on two advisors, Thomas Wentworth (later the Earl of Strafford) and Archbishop Laud. Wentworth was previously a parliamentary leader; he changed sides after the passage of the Petition of Right for personal advantage and because he feared that parliamentary extremism would result in a breakdown of government. As President of the Council of the North Wentworth imposed law and order on the region so effectively that Charles made him Lord Deputy of Ireland in 1633. His Irish policies were thorough even though his methods for reorganizing finance and stimulating trade were high-handed. Such methods kept Ireland temporarily docile, but he alienated both the "old English" Catholic gentry and the "new English" Puritan immigrants to Ireland during his administration.

In 1633 William Laud became Archbishop of Canterbury and won royal support for religious uniformity in public worship according to High Church (Anglo-Catholic) tradition. Puritans accused him of reverting to Catholicism but Laud, through the Courts of Star Chamber and High Commission, took stern measures against his critics. His measures prompted a Puritan migration to New England and provoked the chain of events that led to civil war in England.

Charles and the Scots

In 1637, when Charles and Laud attempted to force a new prayer book and an Anglican system of church government on Presbyterian Scotland, the Scots rioted and resisted the innovations. A National Covenant was signed which pledged allegiance to Charles but swore to resist to the death all religious changes contrary to their Kirk (Church). Charles determined to invade Scotland but could find neither men nor money to meet the Scottish army that was commanded by Alexander Leslie, and was forced to abandon his campaign. The First Bishops' War (1639) ended in a truce without a battle. Wentworth (now the Earl of Strafford) advised the King to call a Parliament and appeal to English patriotism in order to raise money for fighting the Scots.

The Short Parliament of 1640 assembled in an angry mood and refused to vote funds until it had discussed grievances. Within three weeks Charles dissolved Parliament (therefore the name "short") and made desperate appeals for funds and men to fight a Second Bishops' War; however, he again met with little success. The Scots invaded England with ease and forced Charles to terms which stipulated that they would stay in English territory and receive £850 daily from the King until a settlement was signed. To pay the bill Charles was forced to summon another Parliament in 1640 which turned out to be a Long Parliament.

The Expansion of England

The unsuccessful efforts of the Elizabethans to colonize Virginia did not deter Englishmen from trying again a generation later. The London Company succeeded in establishing Jamestown in 1607 as England's first permanent colony in America. The export of tobacco propped up the colony's meager economy, and in 1619 Virginia set up the first colonial legislature fashioned on the parliamentary model of the mother country. In 1620 a second settlement colony was established in Plymouth, Massachusetts by

Puritan separatists who left the Old World on the *Mayflower* in order to follow freely their religious beliefs in America. Nine years later, under a charter granted by King Charles, the Massachusetts Bay Colony provided a haven for English Puritans to set up their version of a Christian community. This colony prospered and a steady stream of immigrants gave it a population of 14,000 by 1640.

At the same time Ulster (northern Ireland) was colonized by Scottish and English settlers. By 1609 the English Crown had seized all six counties of modern Ulster from Irish lords and chieftains. The land was divided into parcels and leased to English and Scottish immigrants. By 1629 there were 13,000 English and Scottish families in Ulster, cultivating the best of the land and sowing the seeds of the religious and political tension that has found no solution to this day.

Charles's call to arms in an effort to prove he was King would be fatal to his system of personal government. His makeshift absolutism had alienated the House of Commons, the Puritans, and his native Scotland.

Unlike his European counterparts, he lacked both a trained and paid bureaucracy and a standing army. English monarchs depended upon the loyalty of unpaid local officials. By the time the Long Parliament was summoned in 1640 there was already a willingness on the part of these gentry to disobey the King and his law, as witnessed in John Hampden's ship money case. Archbishop Laud's heavy-handed High Church policies spurred English Puritans and Scottish Presbyterians to follow their religious conscience rather than obey their King. War and political revolution was the outcome.

Selected Readings

Ashley, Maurice. *England in the Seventeenth Century, 1603–1714* (1961)

Bowen, Catherine Drinker. *The Lion and the Throne: The Life and Times of Sir Edward Coke* (1957)

Coward, Brian. *The Stuart Age* (1981)

Davies, Godfrey. *The Early Stuarts, 1603–1660* (1961)

Gregg, Pauline. *Charles I* (1981)

Haller, William. *The Rise of Puritanism, 1570–1643* (1957)

Notestein, Wallace. *English People on the Eve of Colonization, 1603–1630* (1954)

Stone, Lawrence. *The Crisis of the Aristocracy, 1558–1641* (1954)

Trevelyan, G. M. *England Under the Stuarts* (1963)

Trevor-Roper, Hugh R. *Archbishop Laud* (1965)

Wedgewood, Cicely V. *Thomas Wentworth, First Earl of Strafford, 1593–1641: A Reevaluation* (1961)

Willson, David H. *King James VI and I* (1956)

10

Civil War and Interregnum: 1642–1660

1640	Long Parliament holds its first session
1641	King Charles's councilors, Thomas Wentworth and Archbishop Laud, are sentenced to death by Parliament
1642	Charles raises his royal standard at Nottingham: the Civil War begins
1645	Parliament's New Model Army decisively defeats the Royalists at the Battle of Naseby
1648	Charles and a Scottish army invade England to precipitate the Second Civil War
1649	Execution of Charles I by order of a rump House of Commons
1649–1660	Interregnum: the Commonwealth and Protectorate
1651	*Leviathan*, a defense of absolute monarchy, written by Sir Thomas Hobbes
1653	The Instrument of Government drawn up by the army ends the Commonwealth and establishes Cromwell as Lord Protector
1658	Death of Cromwell; his son, Richard, becomes Lord Protector
1660	Convention Parliament restores monarchy by recalling Charles II from exile

The Long Parliament provided the stage for a renewed confrontation between the King and Parliament, as the House of Commons claimed for itself additional royal prerogatives and sought a transferral of political power from the King to Parliament. The ensuing two Civil Wars began largely as a struggle for supremacy between the King and the parliamentary gentry, but ended with the army as victor and Oliver Cromwell as the commanding figure.

Cromwell's republican experiments were serious attempts to find a satisfactory, constitutional substitute for the monarchy; however, each alternative failed. Since military rule was not an acceptable long-term substitute for the monarchy, the Stuart dynasty returned upon Cromwell's death.

From this English revolution in government sprang two political ideals that profoundly affected English society in the following centuries: the importance of individual liberty and the merits of representative government.

STEPS TO CIVIL WAR

The Long Parliament was in general agreement in its efforts to curb the King's royal prerogatives and abuse of power by parliamentary legislation. There was little thought of revolution or deposing the King. However, John Pym and his radical colleagues sought more: the transfer of sovereignty to Parliament. Pym steered the radical wing of the House of Commons toward divisive religious issues and an attempt to control the army. Instead of capitalizing on this danger to gain supporters, Charles I, with his genius for miscalculation, forced the issue by sending armed men into the House of Commons to arrest his opponents, thereby coalescing the opposition against him.

Parliamentary Triumphs

Under Pym's leadership the Long Parliament accomplished a mild constitutional revolution in its first two years. But when revolutionary changes were also demanded in the Church and in the control of the militia, the positions of the royalists and of the radicals became irreconcilable. Most of the constructive work of this Parliament was accomplished in its early months and included: (1) the abolition of such prerogative courts as the Star Chamber and the High Commission; (2) no dissolution of Parliament without its consent; (3) the Triennial Act demanding that Parliament meet at least every three years; and (4) no type of taxation without parliamentary consent.

Parliament attempted to punish the Earl of Strafford (Thomas Wentworth) for his administration of royal policies of the previous decade. When the impeachment proceedings failed to convict, the Commons resorted to a bill of attainder which needed neither legal proof nor a trial, but still required the King's consent. Charles had promised to protect his chief advisor, but mob and parliamentary pressures intimidated him into signing the death warrant, and in May 1641, Strafford was executed. Archbishop Laud was also imprisoned and later (1645) executed.

Parliamentary Division

The proposal of the Puritans to abolish bishops (the "Root and Branch" bill) and radically reform the Church alienated a considerable number of Parliamentarians who had previously backed political bills. In the summer of 1641 the division was widened by the news of a far-reaching rebellion in Ireland and the massacre of English and Scottish settlers in Ulster. Parliament wished to crush the rebellion by sending over an army, but did not want to place a large force under the control of the King for fear that he might use it to enforce his authority in England. Therefore, the radical members drew up a resolution, the Grand Remonstrance, in which they stated their grievances and demanded parliamentary approval of both the King's advisors and the army officers. After a stormy debate the bill passed the Commons by only eleven votes, which was evidence that the conservative members were opposed to any sweeping changes in the traditional political arrangement.

ATTACK ON THE COMMONS

Instead of waiting and winning over a few more members, Charles committed a political error by marching into the House of Commons with an armed guard to arrest five of its leading members; however, the members had been forewarned and had fled. Soon after this abortive coup, Charles rode north to raise an army and to show by force that he was King. His subjects gradually took sides and prepared for war. In June 1642, Parliament sent the King an ultimatum (the Nineteen Propositions) requiring that he surrender virtually all his remaining prerogative powers. Such preposterous demands indicated that any hope of compromise was past, and in August civil war began.

COURSE OF THE WAR

At first the Royalists were victorious because of the quality of their cavalry and leadership. But time favored Parliament because of its control of the richer and more populous areas of the country, superior number of troops, and the backing of the navy. By 1646 Parliament was victorious, even though Charles was not willing to recognize the fact. The King's dealings with the Scots brought on a short second Civil War that Cromwell's forces won easily, and that left the army in control of the country. The army promptly purged Parliament of some 140 members it disliked. The resulting Rump Parliament that remained constituted a court to try the King for treason. This illegal court convicted Charles and had him executed. The King was dead; Cromwell and the army were the new rulers.

Choosing Sides

Geographically, the King's supporters (Royalists or Cavaliers) centered in the less populous north and west. His party included most of the nobility, many of the gentry, Roman Catholics, and the Church of England. Lacking sources of revenue, Charles called upon the loyalty of his peers and gentry to provide him with money and services. And in his two nephews, Prince Rupert and Prince Maurice, Charles found competent military leaders.

Although the lines of demarcation were never sharp between the two sides, Parliament's supporters (named Roundheads) drew their major strength from the south and east of the country. Support also came from the navy, merchants, yeoman farmers, the City of London, and opponents of High Anglicanism. Parliament had greater financial resources at its disposal for fighting a war, but its commander-in-chief, the Earl of Essex, lacked generalship and a plan of attack. Not until Thomas Fairfax and Oliver Cromwell took over command could parliamentary leadership rival that of its opponents.

Civil War, 1642–1646

The Royalist superiority in cavalry gave Charles the edge in the campaigns of the first two years. Parliament then negotiated with Scotland and signed the Solemn League and Covenant (1643) in which Parliament agreed to establish the Reformed (Presbyterian) Church in England in return for the assistance of the Scottish army. At Marston Moor (near York) in 1644 the combined Parliamentary and Scottish armies won their first important battle, but were unable to follow up their victory. In the next year, with the help of the Self-Denying Ordinance which forced the resignation of members of Parliament holding military commands (including their inept generals), Parliament reorganized the army and made Sir Thomas Fairfax the new commander. Drawing heavily on Oliver Cromwell's disciplined and dedicated troops, a New Model Army was created which decisively defeated the Royalists at the Battle of Naseby (1645). Thereafter, the King's position was hopeless and the following year he surrendered to the Scots. By the end of 1646 the first Civil War ended when the Scots agreed to surrender Charles to Parliament and go home.

The Disputed Peace

Parliament had triumphed over the King; however, Parliament did not represent the views of Cromwell's army and the army was now the real power in the land. Defeating the King was easier than creating a government acceptable to all parties. Factions appeared in Parliament and in the army, as the victors quarreled among themselves and attempted to negotiate separately with the King. Charles responded by trying to play off Parliament, the army, and the Scots against one another. He made conflicting promises

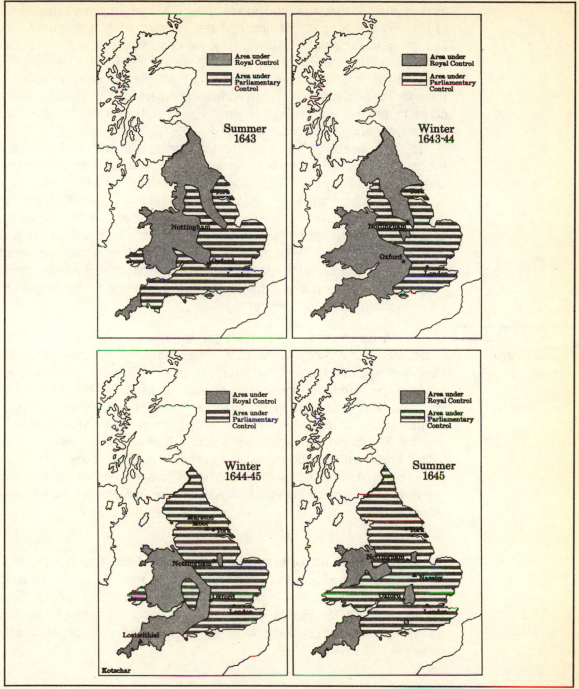

Fig. 10.1 The Civil War

to each group so that in the end his scheming made all the parties suspicious of his integrity. No party, at first, had any intention of deposing the King, and the argument revolved around religious controversy. The Presbyterian members of Parliament wanted to impose the National Covenant on England, but the sectarians in Parliament and in the army opposed a Presbyterian establishment. When Parliament ordered the New Model Army either to disband without back pay or to go to Ireland under Presbyterian officers, the army threatened mutiny.

In the summer of 1647, Oliver Cromwell, who had served as the mediator for the various parties, threw in his lot with the army. Cromwell and his followers proceeded to draft the Heads of the Proposals as a compromise measure to save the nation from both royal absolutism and the democratic republican proposals advocated by the Levelers (the followers of John Lilburne) and other radicals in the army. Cromwell's moderate proposal was ignored by both Parliament and the King. Charles escaped from his army captors to the Isle of Wight where he negotiated with the Scots to invade England and restore him to the throne in return for his support of a Presbyterian Church settlement.

The Second Civil War, 1648

The Scottish invasion of 1648 precipitated the second Civil War. General Fairfax crushed Royalist uprisings in the south of England while Cromwell's veterans moved north to rout a superior Scottish-Royalist army near Preston. After Preston the army dominated the situation and vented its wrath on both Parliament and Charles. The soldiers were convinced that Charles was a "man of blood" for breaking his word and reviving the war, and that Parliament was little better because of its efforts to negotiate with such a king even after the second war broke out. In December of 1648 the army council directed Colonel Pride to purge Parliament of its Presbyterian supporters. The remaining members—the Rump Parliament—took orders from the army.

REGICIDE

The purged House of Commons, consisting of less than one hundred members, appointed a court of commissioners to try the King for treason. Charles never accepted the legality of this tribunal and refused to speak in his own defense. The verdict was never in doubt, for the army had decided upon the execution of the King. In January 1649, Charles met his death with calmness and dignity.

THE COMMONWEALTH
AND THE PROTECTORATE, 1649–1660

The execution of the King transformed England into a republic which few in England had foreseen or actually desired. The government now rested on the power of the army and its rather reluctant hero, Oliver Cromwell. In the ensuing interregnum Cromwell experimented with various alternatives to monarchy, but each attempt foundered over the incompatibility of a constitutional government and the "rule of the saints" who considered themselves God's elect, but were not politically elected by the nation. Cromwell's leadership saved England from the grim prospects of either anarchy or tyranny. He achieved prosperity and order in the country and won respect abroad by a vigorous and successful foreign policy but failed to find a satisfactory alternative to monarchy. Cromwell's death brought increasing civilian discontent and the restoration of the Stuarts.

Cromwell and the New Government

The Rump Parliament passed an act which abolished the monarchy and the House of Lords and set up a Council of State of forty-one members to administer the realm. For the next four years this Council served as the nominal executive, but real, if somewhat disguised, power was in the hands of Cromwell. Only Cromwell's statesmanship and self-restraint kept him from abusing his almost unlimited authority, because the constitutional checks demanded by earlier Parliaments of the Stuarts were never applied to him. He was devoutly religious and confident that God was on his side; yet, he was neither intolerant of other faiths nor a "puritan in the narrow sense." Unlike many Puritans, he enjoyed the pleasures of life, including music and dancing. Led on by the force of circumstances more than by personal ambition, Cromwell successfully met internal and external challenges to the government.

THE RADICAL OPPOSITION

Cromwell's government was opposed not only by royalists but also by radicals within the army. The war had undermined the previous religious and social order, and zealous pamphleteers played upon the feelings of the disenchanted. Some of the independents in the army were seeking to legalize religious pluralism; others went further in their demands. John Lilburne and his Levelers advocated a democratic republic, whereas Gerrard Winstanley and his fellow Diggers aimed at an agrarian communism that would abolish all manors and landlords. But in political and social viewpoints Cromwell and his middle-of-the-road party were not innovators. Thus, when choosing members of the Council of State, they excluded radicals. Both Fairfax and Cromwell acted decisively to smother further revolutionary threats and minor mutinies in the army. Lilburne was imprisoned, and a few executions took place. Cromwell turned next to foreign threats.

Foreign Affairs

Cromwell's active foreign policy brought together Ireland, Scotland, and England under a single government and made England respected in Europe as a powerful naval and commercial power. "Cromwell and Blake, rather than Queen Elizabeth and Drake, really made England mistress of the seas.[*]

IRELAND

Royalists and Catholics had joined forces under the Marquis of Ormonde in support of Charles II, son of the executed King, and were attempting to gain control of all of Ireland. In August 1649, Cromwell and his troops landed in Ireland, relieved Dublin, and within ten months had crushed the rebellion. Cromwell's massacre of the defenders in Drogheda for refusing to surrender was an object lesson to other cities, but was also a blight on his reputation. The land settlement that followed produced additional Irish resentment against Cromwell. About two-thirds of the land south of Ulster was confiscated and given to English Protestants who soon built up extensive estates. For the next two and a half centuries the hostility between the English-Protestant (and often absentee) landlords and the Irish tenants remained unresolved.

SCOTLAND

From Ireland Cromwell returned to England to lead another army (1650) against the Scotch Covenanters who were supporting Charles Stuart's second attempt to gain the throne. Cromwell's efforts for a peaceful negotiation failed, and the superior forces of the Scots hemmed in his army at Dunbar. But his troops won a decisive victory, taking ten thousand prisoners. During the winter Charles was crowned King at Scone and in the spring a new Scottish army moved into England—and into the trap Cromwell had planned. The royal army was surrounded and decimated at Worcester. Charles escaped and fled to the Continent. The Battle of Worcester ended the Civil War and united Ireland, Scotland, and England under one Commonwealth government.

---

[*] Robert Eckles and Richard Hale, *Britain, Her Peoples and the Commonwealth* (New York: McGraw-Hill, 1954), p. 152.

THE WAR WITH THE DUTCH, 1652–1654

Triumphant over British opposition, Cromwell next faced Holland which was England's chief commercial and naval rival. The Republican navy under Robert Blake had won respect by forcing the rebellious Virginian and West Indian colonies to acknowledge the Commonwealth, and by routing Prince Rupert's fleet. In 1651 Parliament passed the Navigation Act which favored England's commercial class by restricting the maritime trade of the Dutch. The act, which reflected the economic rivalry of the period, decreed that trade with England and her colonies could be carried only in English ships or in ships of the producing country, and that all goods from the colonies must be in English ships. Other causes that contributed to the outbreak of hostilities with Holland included: (1) disputes over fishing rights off the coast of England; (2) the harboring of royalist supporters of the son of Charles I by the Dutch; and (3) the refusal of Dutch ships to dip their flags in respect to English warships in the Channel. Although indecisive sea battles followed, Dutch shipping interests were so badly hurt that peace was made in 1654 on terms favorable to the English. Treaties were also concluded with Sweden, Denmark, and Portugal that benefited English commerce.

SPANISH POLICY

Cromwell also shared the Elizabethan and Puritan sentiment that Spain was more dangerous to England than France. Admiral Robert Blake's expedition to the Mediterranean (1654–1657) was so impressive that England became the dominant naval power in the Mediterranean for the first time. The attack on Spain in the West Indies was only partially successful. Jamaica was taken, but the attempt to seize Santo Domingo failed. The harassment of Spanish possessions led to all-out war with Spain and an alliance between England and France. In the Anglo-French land campaign against Spain in the Spanish Netherlands, the English troops won the Battle of the Dunes and received Dunkirk from Louis XIV for their aid.

Constitutional Experiments

Although successful abroad, Cromwell failed to find a satisfactory constitutional basis for his government. All efforts foundered over the issue of sovereignty between the rule of the elect—the army leadership—and the elected—the various Parliaments. The execution of the King and the dissolution of Parliament by force left no shred of legality for the government during the interregnum. Yet Cromwell had no wish to become either a king or for the army to have governmental power.

The Commonwealth

For four years (1649–1653) Cromwell attempted to negotiate the differences between the Rump Parliament and the army since he was the pivotal figure in each. Dissatisfaction with the Parliament grew in the army and in the nation. The Rump Parliament was charged with corruption and appeared to be interested primarily in its own tenure in office when it refused to hold a general election.

In April 1653, Cromwell forcibly dissolved the Rump Parliament and replaced it with a nominated "Parliament of Saints." This body was hand-picked by Cromwell's Council from candidates supplied by the independent churches. This assembly was nicknamed the Barebones Parliament after the name of one of its members, an Anabaptist preacher named Praise-God Barebones. Its members were zealous but amateurish. When its views on religion became too radical for moderates among the army officers, the Assembly was dissolved, and the Commonwealth came to an end in December, 1653.

The Instrument of Government, 1653

The outcome was a new constitution drawn up by army officers to replace the Commonwealth. The Instrument provided for an executive (Cromwell) who was to be the Lord Protector. A Council of State would advise the Protector and share control of the army with him. A one-house Parliament would be elected every three years by an enlarged franchise representing England, Scotland, and Ireland. Toleration was granted to Christians who were not Anglicans or Roman Catholics. Checks and balances were included to prevent the tyranny of either Protector or Parliament. The first Protectorate Parliament met in 1654 and immediately attempted to amend the Instrument to its advantage. One hundred members were dismissed for refusing to accept Cromwell's four constitutional "fundamentals," but when the remainder continued to wrangle, Cromwell dissolved Parliament in January 1655.

MILITARY RULE

As a temporary expedient England and Wales were divided into eleven military districts with a major general placed over each. The people disliked the military arrangement, and war with Spain created the need for increased subsidies. Therefore, in 1656 a second Parliament convened which was carefully chosen by the army officers and screened by the Council of State. Even this select group asserted its independence from the army and could not be effectively controlled. One of its first acts was to discontinue the rule of the major generals and to propose a new constitution.

HUMBLE PETITION AND ADVICE

Leaders in Parliament, wishing to return to a more traditional system of government, next proposed that Cromwell should become king, that a second chamber, called the "other house," should be filled with the king's appointees, and that the powers of Parliament should be increased. Cromwell declined the crown because acceptance would have violated the whole republican argument. But he accepted the other features of the constitution and the new Parliament met in January 1658. Almost immediately the House of Commons demanded control over both Cromwell and the Upper House, instead of paying attention to the war with Spain. Once again, Cromwell dissolved Parliament, but before he could assemble another one, he died in 1658.

Fall of the Protectorate

Cromwell's death also doomed the protectorate, because only the force of Cromwell's personality and the loyalty of the army to its commander-in-chief had held the government together. Oliver's son and successor, Richard, lacked prestige and ability to keep the support of the sectarians, the army, and the Puritans. Besides, the nation was weary of Puritan and army control and was ready for the return of traditional government—a king and Parliament.

Army commanders, led by Charles Fleetwood and John Lambert, defied Richard and grasped for power, while royalist and republican uprisings also took place. Richard surrendered to the army which promptly replaced the protectorate government with the earlier (Rump) Parliament. However, this Parliament got along with the army no better than in earlier years and was dismissed in October. Finally General George Monck, commander of the army in Scotland, marched south to support civilian rule and oppose General Lambert. In London he recalled the Long Parliament of 1640 and had it dissolve itself in favor of a freely elected Convention Parliament. In 1660 this Convention Parliament invited Charles II, son of Charles I, to return to England from exile. The experiment of an English government without a king had lasted eleven years.

Achievements of the Interregnum

The accomplishments of the interregnum were largely the triumphs of Cromwell since he was the leader responsible for preserving order and individual liberty. His foreign policy brought security through strength. Religious pluralism and free thought were saved from the extremism of sectarians and the uniformity demanded by Anglicans and Presbyterians. The Jews were allowed to return to England after an exile of 350 years; civil marriages were legalized; public schools and universities were reformed. The two decades between 1640 and 1660 also produced economic change. The capitalist classes, in agriculture, commerce and industry, freed themselves from the control over economic life that the Crown had formerly exercised. Landed classes were freed from feudal tenure, agricultural productivity jumped as landowners were free to drain marshes and enclose land, while in industry monopolies came to an end and the government no longer attempted to regulate prices or wages.

THE PURITAN DILEMMA

Although Cromwell represented the loftiest ideals of Puritanism and frowned upon the "blue laws" that his compatriots favored, he had no doubts about the rightness or moral superiority of the Puritan position. He was convinced that he and his supporters were God's agents to save England from the forces of tyranny, whether foreign, royalist, or religious. This conviction made it impossible to resolve the constitutional conflict in the rivalry between the politically elected and the religiously elect. Thus the Puritan position created its own dialectic or contradictions, for although it stressed individualism, it also claimed the guardianship of the saints over the sinners. By 1660 England was weary of this guardianship and ready to return to the old ways, perhaps because "the sinners were more numerous than the saints."[*]

*E*arlier views of these two decades often made "the early Stuarts too evil and the parliamentary leaders too virtuous." Perhaps closer to the truth is to see James and Charles as conservative monarchs with few political skills defending the status quo economically, politically, and religiously against the aggressive challenge of the House of Commons and the Puritans who wished to extend their influence and authority.

Puritanism and the mythology of the common law—protecting the liberty of individuals and the inviolability of property—were two ideologies that motivated revolt. However, it turned out to be easier for Parliament to revolt successfully than to rule a kingdom without a king.

By 1660 nostalgia for the old order brought back the Stuarts, but neither the monarchy nor Parliament would be the same as before the Civil Wars. And certainly the ferment of ideas, from the Levelers' demand for democracy, to John Milton's plea for freedom of the press, to the merchants' push for freedom of enterprise, to the religious ferment of the Puritans and Independents, meant that England could never fully turn back the clock in the Restoration of 1660.

Selected Readings

Ashton, Robert. *The English Civil War: Conservatism and Revolution 1603–1649* (1978)

Aylmer, G. E. *The Interregnum: The Quest for Settlement, 1646– 1660* (1972)

Bagwell, R. *Ireland Under the Stuarts* (1936)

Brailsford, H. N. *The Levellers and the English Revolution* (1955)

---

[*] E. l. Woodward, *History of England* (New York: Harper & Row, 1962), p. 106.

Clarendon, Edward Hyde. *Selections from the History of the Great Rebellion.* (1955)

Fraser, Lady Antonia. *Cromwell the Lord Protector* (1974)

Hill, Christopher. *God's Englishman: Oliver Cromwell and the English Revolution* (1970)

Howat, G. M. D. *Stuart and Cromwellian Foreign Policy* (1974)

Solt, Leo F. *Saints in Arms* (1959)

Stone, Lawrence. *The Cause of the English Revolution 1529–1642* (1972)

Wedgewood, Cicely V. *The King's Peace, 1637–1641* (1955)

_____*The King's War, 1641–1647* (1959)

11

Restoration and Revolution: 1660–1702

1660 Restoration of the monarchy and the Church of England

1661–1665 Parliamentary acts, known as the Clarendon Code, effectively enforce Anglican supremacy

1665 New Amsterdam (New York) seized from Holland in Second Dutch War

Great Fire of London

1667 John Milton writes epic poem *Paradise Lost*

1673 Passage of anti-Catholic Test Act requiring all officeholders to take the Anglican sacraments and deny transubstantiation

1685 James II, the last Catholic King, succeeds his brother on the throne

1687 Publication of Sir Isaac Newton's *Principia*

1688 Successful, bloodless Protestant overthrow of James II, known as the Glorious Revolution

1689 Bill of Rights sets forth parliamentary conditions for recognizing William and Mary as rulers

1690 King William and Protestants rout James II and Catholics at the Battle of the Boyne in Ireland

John Locke publishes *Two Treatises on Government* proposing a social contract between the governor and the governed

1701 Act of Settlement assures a Protestant succession after the death of King William

The Restoration of 1660 was a rejection of the Puritans' constitutional experiments. The monarchy, Parliament, and the Anglican supremacy were restored, but not simply as a replica of the days of Charles I. The King had lost power; Parliament had increased its influence. Charles II accommodated himself to the changes, but his brother, James II, could not. As a result James lost the throne in the revolution of 1688.

The revolutionary settlement transferred ultimate sovereignty from the King to Parliament and replaced a Catholic monarch with the Protestants, William and Mary. The new co-monarchs were rulers, not by divine right or by strict heredity, but by an act of Parliament.

Both Charles and James had gained financial advantage by aligning England's foreign policy with the interest of Louis XIV and France. In contrast, King William marshaled English resources and led a European coalition against France to halt Louis XIV at the zenith of his power.

CHARLES AND THE RESTORATION

Charles II learned from the execution of his father some of the risks involved when Parliament and king became hostile rivals and distrusted each other. Therefore, the Restoration brought unusual harmony between monarchy and Parliament until Charles's religious and foreign policies produced such opposition that he reigned his last years without Parliament in order to control the succession to the throne.

The Return of Charles

To allay the reservations of English subjects who had reasons to fear the restoration of the monarchy, Charles issued the Declaration of Breda from Holland in which he promised to grant a general pardon to all political opponents except to those designated by Parliament; to permit as much religious toleration as Parliament would allow; and to let Parliament determine the legitimacy of property titles acquired during the interregnum.

The Convention Parliament was satisfied with the Declaration, and in May 1660, Charles returned to London from exile. But the Restoration did not restore all the powers of earlier kings, for the acts of 1640–1641 to which Charles I had given assent (e.g. prerogative courts, unparliamentary taxation, and the arbitrary arrest of members of Parliament without cause) remained illegal. Before its dissolution in 1661 the Convention Parliament, sympathetic to Charles's proclamation of clemency, carried out a relatively moderate policy toward former supporters of the Commonwealth. Troops were paid and dismissed, except for a standing army of five thousand soldiers, and only thirteen leading officials of the Cromwellian period were put to death.

The New King

Charles II held few principles of any kind. He cared little about national policies and seemed to live only for pleasure and the pursuit of his many mistresses. Yet he was witty and possessed keen intelligence. When circumstances demanded a display of power, Charles could exert his latent ability and carry on important negotiations successfully. Clever, charming, selfish, and completely cynical, Charles mocked the morals and fears (Catholicism and Louis XIV) of England and held on to his throne and the powers of the monarchy, even though he wasted his authority in the pursuit of pro-French and pro-Catholic policies. When threatened by political opposition, or when the succession to the throne was challenged, the King would display his masterly abilities. Ordinary duties bored him, however, and he preferred to devote himself to more pleasant courtly pastimes; but he remembered well his father's fate and was never lazy to the point of letting affairs of state get out of hand.

The Religious Settlement

The parliamentary election of 1661 brought hundreds of enthusiastic royalists and Anglicans into the House of Commons. The resultant "Cavalier Parliament" proceeded to penalize Puritans and Dissenters, as well as Roman Catholics, by a series of four acts known as the Clarendon Code (after Charles's chief minister, Edward Hyde, earl of Clarendon): (1) The Municipal Corporations Act excluded from municipal office all who refused to renounce the 1643 Solemn League and Covenant establishing the Presbyterian Church in England, or who refused to swear allegiance to the King. (2) The Act of Uniformity required all clergy to use the revised Book of Common Prayer in their services. One-fifth of all clergy refused and a significant Dissenting religious community was born. These faced further restrictions. (3) The Conventicle Act imposed harsh penalties for attending a religious service (conventicle) which did not conform to the Anglican liturgy. (4) The Five Mile Act forbade these nonconforming ministers to visit or live within five miles of any town where they had previously preached or taught school.

These acts clearly restored Anglican supremacy. More than ever, Anglicanism, as the established church of the country, became the religion of the landed classes. At the same time this pressure to conform, after the religious pluralism of the interregnum, created modern nonconformity in England because many clergy and laymen no longer found in the Anglican Church the religious latitude which had existed in the Elizabethan Church. Thousands of Nonconformists in England and Scotland went into hiding or were imprisoned. One Nonconformist, John Bunyan, wrote part of *The Pilgrim's Progress* while imprisoned in Bedford jail for his dissenting views.

Foreign Affairs

The foreign policy of Charles II was motivated by personal rather than national interests. The independent strength and stature of England in European affairs under Cromwell soon shifted under Charles to one of subserviency to French interests in return for the secret payment of money to Charles by Louis XIV. European politics in the last half of the seventeenth century centered upon the decay of Spain and its empire and the expansionism and influence of Louis XIV of France.

THE MARRIAGE OF CHARLES

In 1662 Charles made an unpopular but profitable marriage alliance with Catherine of Braganza, daughter of the King of Portugal. The marriage brought him a rich dowry which included the ports of Tangier in North Africa and Bombay in India; the treaty also aligned England with France against Spain. In the same year Charles sold Dunkirk to France in spite of the opposition of his subjects.

IRELAND

Irish Catholics and royalists had supported Charles during the interregnum and welcomed the Restoration. In return for their loyalty Charles restored to the Irish some of the land that had been confiscated by Cromwell's government, but this action antagonized his relations with English landlords in Ireland. Moreover, the English Parliament continued its traditional anti-Irish policies by excluding Irish ships from colonial trade and by making illegal the shipment of cattle from Ireland to England.

THE DUTCH WARS

The continuing commercial rivalry between Holland and England led to the Second Dutch War (1665–1667) and the seizure of New Amsterdam in America, which was renamed New York. After the peace treaty Charles asserted a temporary independence from Louis XIV by signing the Triple Alliance (1668) which united England, Holland, and Sweden against the expansionist designs of France. But Louis used bribery to persuade Charles to break this alliance and to attack Holland again. Charles dragged England into the Third Dutch War (1672–1674) which Parliament finally halted by refusing to grant additional funds. The strain of naval warfare against England, combined with the land war against France, weakened the resources of the Dutch and contributed to their decline as a major colonial and naval power.

CHARLES AND LOUIS XIV

Charles admired the glittering court, the Roman Catholicism, and the unlimited royal power of Louis XIV and instead of opposing France—in line with the balance of power principle—he became an agent of Louis's scheme of expansion. In 1670 Charles secretly signed the Treaty of Dover, whereby he promised to break away from the Triple Alliance, to attack Holland, and to convert to Catholicism as soon as expedient. For this alliance Louis provided Charles with substantial sums of money. Charles kept his promise of declaring war on Holland, but his efforts to relieve the restrictions on English Catholics provoked instead a strong parliamentary protest.

Political Developments

The King and Parliament cooperated on most matters until growing suspicions of Charles's French and Catholic sympathies resulted in legislative efforts to increase restrictions on English Catholics. In particular, Parliament wished to keep James, the Catholic brother of Charles, from succeeding to the throne since Charles had no legitimate children. To save the Stuart succession, Charles acted forcefully to destroy the political opposition and ended up ruling without Parliament. Louis XIV helped make this possible by granting additional money to Charles.

FALL OF CLARENDON

Lord Clarendon made many enemies during his years as chief minister (1661–1667). He distrusted the House of Commons, censored the immoral activities of the royal court, and was identified (unfairly) in the minds of Puritans with the harsh Clarendon Code. The unpopular foreign policy, including the King's marriage, the sale of Dunkirk, and the war with Holland, increased his unpopularity. Finally, when the Dutch fleet humiliated the English by sailing up the Thames in 1667 and burning English war ships anchored at Chatham, the King abandoned Clarendon to his enemies. He was dismissed and impeached, then fled to the Continent where he wrote his *History of the Rebellion*.

THE CABAL, 1667–1673

Instead of replacing Clarendon with another chief minister, Charles chose to direct affairs himself, relying on five unofficial advisors who, for various reasons, favored the efforts of the King to relax the Anglican supremacy. Two were Catholics, Clifford and Arlington; another, Buckingham, was a skeptic and Charles's favorite. Ashley Cooper, later Earl of Shaftesbury, was a latitudinarian (broad and liberal) in religion and an able essayist; and the Earl of Lauderdale was formerly Presbyterian. The cabal of advisors (so-called because their initials spelled "cabal") broke up in 1673 when opposition to Charles's Declaration of Indulgence for non-Anglicans triggered the passage of anti-Catholic legislation and bitterness between King and Parliament. Three members left the cabal, and Shaftesbury, convinced he was deceived by the King, became the leading critic of the King's policies.

The Rise of Political Parties

The reaction of the fiercely anti-Catholic Parliament to Charles's Declaration of Indulgence was the passage of the Test Act (1673) which required all officeholders, civil and military, to take the Anglican sacrament and to deny transubstantiation (the change during the eucharist or communion from the bread and wine to the substance of the body and blood of Christ). By 1674 the friendly Cavalier Parliament had been transformed into a hostile critic of Charles's pro-French, propapal policy. The King dropped his scheme for Catholicizing England and tried to court Parliament by making the Earl of Danby his chief minister and the platform of royalty and Anglicanism the rallying point for his supporters.

Tory and Whig Party Origins. The "court party" which emerged under Danby won the epithet Tory (a term for Irish cattle thieves) from opposing groups. Rival factions who gravitated toward Shaftesbury and his anti-Tory "country party" were later to be called Whigs (as political heirs of the Puritan opposition to Charles I, although the term refers to Scottish robbers who murdered their victims). Their supporters came largely from the city merchants and several powerful aristocratic families who favored limitations on royal power, toleration of Protestant dissenters, and who were militantly anti-Catholic.

THE POPISH PLOT, 1678

The factions opposed to Charles were aided by the false tales of an unprincipled informer, Titus Oates, who inflamed the populace to hysteria by describing a Jesuit plot to murder Charles, massacre Protestants, and set up, with the help of the French, a Catholic government under James, duke of York. A shocked and angry Parliament, led by Shaftesbury, impeached and executed several Catholics and began to impeach Danby when the secret dealings of Charles and Danby with Louis XIV were revealed. To save Danby and his own family from attack, Charles dissolved the Cavalier Parliament.

THE PARLIAMENTS OF 1679–1681

Charles's second Parliament convened in 1679 with an anti-Catholic Whig majority dedicated to excluding James from succession to the throne. Charles blocked the exclusion bill by dissolving Parliament, but not before it had passed the Habeas Corpus Amendment Act which prevented arbitrary imprisonment and insured a speedy trial. A third Parliament met in 1680 and the House of Commons immediately passed an Exclusion Bill that made Charles's illegitimate son, James Scott, the duke of Monmouth, heir to the throne instead of James; but the House of Lords rejected it. A fourth Parliament which was summoned to Oxford in 1681 to avoid the influence of the London mob was dissolved within a week. Charles ruled his remaining years without Parliament.

PERSONAL RULE OF CHARLES II, 1681–1685

Once again Charles was receiving subsidies from Louis XIV and no longer needed Parliamentary grants. His last four years were a time of personal and autocratic rule during which he struck hard at the Whig opposition. Shaftesbury fled to the Continent and died in Holland. Other Whig leaders were fraudulently charged with plotting the King's death, and Lords Russell and Sydney were executed. Whig boroughs lost their charters and Tory town governments and sheriffs replaced the influence of such Whig organizations as the Green Ribbon clubs. When Charles died in 1685, the Whig opposition was scattered, the English monarch was a willing pensionary of France, and the succession had been preserved for the legitimate heir, James.

Restoration Society

Reaction to Puritan morality was observed most noticeably in Charles's court where a studied effort was made to imitate the lively and lavish court of Louis XIV. Wit, worldly charm, and love affairs were the stepping-stones of success in many a political career. But society at Whitehall never represented England. The nation which was still largely agricultural in its economy and provincial in its outlook, was often suspicious of commercial and social life in London. Furthermore, the capital suffered two disasters: the plague of 1665 which took 70,000 lives in London alone; and the Great Fire in 1666 which destroyed over 13,000 buildings and gave the architect Sir Christopher Wren a magnificent opportunity to rebuild the city.

THE LAST CATHOLIC KING

James II succeeded to the throne with a minimum of dissension, because the nation expected only a mild Catholic interim until his Protestant daughters, Mary and Anne, came to the throne. James pushed to the extreme his royal prerogative of suspending laws. When his son and heir to the throne was born, who would most assuredly be reared Catholic, leading Englishmen invited William of Orange, husband of James's daughter Mary, to lead a revolt against the King. The coup, which turned out to be bloodless and successful, settled the constitutional issue of the century: the sovereignty of Parliament triumphed over the divine and hereditary right of kings.

Accession to the Throne

With the Anglican Church preaching the Biblical doctrine of nonresistance, the Whig opposition dead or scattered, and the recent civil war still a vivid memory, there was little serious opposition to James's accession as long as the King promised to uphold the established church and to keep his religion private. James was serious-minded, honest, and devoutly Catholic, but he was also arrogant and obstinate and, unlike his brother, insensitive to the political and religious facts of English life. His one overriding goal, like that of Mary Tudor, was the restore Catholicism to England.

PROTESTANT REBELLIONS

The Duke of Monmouth, an illegitimate son of Charles II, landed in southern England in a reckless effort to win the throne, but only a few thousand peasants and tradesmen joined his ill-starred venture. Royal troops under John Churchill, crushed the rebels at Sedgemoor. Monmouth was executed, and the "Bloody Assizes" under Lord Chief Justice Jeffreys inflicted brutal vengeance on hundreds of Monmouth's followers. In Scotland a Protestant rebellion was led by the Earl of Argyll; however, his little army of Covenanters was dispersed and Argyll was executed.

JAMES AND CATHOLICISM

With the Whigs in disarray, a cooperative Tory Parliament was elected in 1685 that was willing to grant money to James provided there were no religious changes. However, when James asked for a standing army commanded by Roman Catholic officers, Parliament became suspicious and reduced the King's subsidies. Angered by their criticisms, James adjourned Parliament and never called another.

Undeterred by the warnings of his political advisors or the religious sensibilities of his subjects, King James proceeded to restore privileges to Roman Catholics. He encamped an army near London commanded by Catholic officers; appointed an ecclesiastical commission, headed by the notorious Justice Jeffreys, to silence or dismiss his Anglican critics; appointed Catholics to official positions in universities and in the royal administration; and issued two Declarations of Indulgences (1687, 1688) which would permit free public worship for Roman Catholics and Protestant Nonconformists. When seven bishops, including the Archbishop of Canterbury, petitioned that the Declaration be withdrawn, James had them arrested on a charge of seditious libel. Their trial became a popular cause, and crowds cheered the bishops when the jury acquitted them.

Foreign Policy   King James, like Charles II, aligned his foreign policy with the interest of France which, at this time, was encroaching on neighboring countries. This threat produced a defensive coalition (the League of Augsburg) of Protestant and Catholic states which included Holland, Brandenberg, several south German states, and the Hapsburg Emperor. Even Pope Innocent XI did not endorse the Catholicizing efforts of Louis XIV on the rest of the Continent. When James persisted in his support of these efforts, William of Orange intervened in English affairs on the grounds that his wife was rightful heir to the throne of England, that he needed English backing to fight King Louis XIV, and that influential Englishmen would back him if he invaded England.

The Glorious Revolution, 1688

With the birth of King James's son in the summer of 1688, the expectation of an interim Catholic monarchy was shattered, since the Crown Prince became heir presumptive in place of his Protestant half-sister, Mary. The prospects of a Catholic dynasty and the exclusion of Mary from the throne dismayed many Englishmen, and in July seven influential Whig and Tory leaders invited William of Orange to lead an English uprising to prevent King James from consolidating his movement toward absolutism and Catholicism. Although the English were slow in rallying around William's forces, they did not oppose his advance. Since the revolution was successful, bloodless, and supported by the respectable members of society, the label "Glorious" was soon attached to it.

THE DUTCH INVASION

William and Mary accepted the invitation and made preparations for the invasion. James became alarmed over the turn of events and began making concessions and promises to the Church of England and to political opponents, but his efforts were too late. On November 5, 1688, William and his army landed at Torbay in southwest England. The involvement of Louis XIV in a war on the Rhine frontier relieved the Dutch from the fear of a French invasion. James's position deteriorated rapidly as soldiers, his commander-in-chief, John Churchill, and his daughter, Anne, defected and turned against him; even Whig and Tory peers began raising forces to support William and Mary in their local communities. James began negotiations with William but became frightened when he remembered his father's execution. In December he fled to France, conceding a bloodless victory to William.

Change of Monarchs

A convention Parliament met in January 1689, to arrange a constitutional settlement (following the precedent of 1660). After searching for a legal loophole that would not force abandonment of the principle of hereditary succession to the throne, the House of Commons finally declared that James had violated the fundamental laws of the land, had fled the country, and had left the throne vacant by his abdication. The Tories claimed that the throne was not vacant but belonged to Mary, because in their eyes James's son was unacceptable. However, William refused to be only a "gentleman-usher" to his wife, so the Crown was offered jointly to William and Mary. Most Tories joined with the Whigs to forfeit the principle of strict succession (and with it the divine right of kings) in favor of a practical and Protestant settlement. Those who refused the settlement and believed that James was still the legal monarch became known as Jacobites.

The Bill of Rights, 1689

Parliament granted the throne to William and Mary on the conditions set forth in the Declaration (later Bill) of Rights. This document cited the failings of James II and, like the Magna Charta and the Petition of Right, was not concerned with political theories so much as with specific restrictions on royal authority: (1) the use of their suspending power or dispensing power without parliamentary consent was declared illegal; (2) Roman Catholics were prohibited from succeeding to the throne; (3) provisions would be made for frequent sessions of Parliament and freedom of debate; (4) standing armies were prohibited (a notable distinction from the Continent); and (5) the levying of taxes or forced loans without the consent of Parliament was repudiated.

There was no attempt in the bill to revolutionize the political or social structure, because the leaders of the revolution wished to conserve the established order in church and state which they claimed James II had jeopardized. But a fundamental change actually occurred, inasmuch as sovereignty was now transferred from King to Parliament by the Bill of Rights. If Parliament could enthrone monarchs by legislative act, it could also dethrone them. John Locke became the patron saint of this respectable revolution when his argument for the contract theory of government (written earlier) in *Two Treatises of Government* was published in 1690 and appeared to justify the legitimacy of the actions taken.

THE DILEMMA OF THE CLERGY

Under Charles I the clergy and Anglican royalists had few divided loyalties because the Church and King were on the same side. In 1688 the situation was different. The clergy had a legitimate monarch in James and preached nonresistance to royal authority (the divine right of kings). Were the clerics to continue to support the King if he failed to support the established church? When the Convention Parliament of 1689 forced a decision between elected kings and hereditary kings, many clergy had difficulty switching their allegiance. Over four hundred clerics refused to take the oath of allegiance to William; they became known as Non-jurors. The majority, however, accepted the King designated by Parliament as their legal monarch.

WILLIAM AND MARY

William's first task was to make good his disputed title of King in the British Isles. Thereafter, he was preoccupied by his lifelong goal of halting the expansionist designs of Louis XIV. William was not a popular ruler and made clear his preference for his beloved Holland. His greatest achievements were as a diplomat and statesman. He held together the warring factions in England and was the architect of the coalitions that kept in check Louis XIV. Under William and Mary a diplomatic revolution occurred as England reversed its foreign policy from being a satellite of Louis XIV to becoming the leader of the European coalition against France.

Constitutional Settlement

The acceptance of William and Mary as joint monarchs took different patterns in England, Scotland, and Ireland. The Glorious Revolution brought a series of constitutional reforms in England and a transfer of ultimate power to Parliament, prosperity to Scotland, but only repression and bitterness in Ireland. In England the Bill of Rights which set up the parliamentary conditions by which the monarch must govern was strengthened by several subsequent acts. The Toleration Act (1689), which was supported by William and the Whigs, gave freedom of worship to most Protestant dissenters; Catholics, Unitarians, and Jews were still restricted, and all the civil disabilities of the Clarendon Code and Test Act remained in force. A mutiny among the soldiers led to the Mutiny Act (1689) which allowed the king to raise an army and rule by martial law for a period of six months. To be renewed the Act demanded the annual assent of Parliament. To prevent a repetition of the seventeen-year Cavalier Parliament, the Triennial Act (1694) stipulated a maximum three-year life for any Parliament. The Treasons Act (1696) provided safeguards for accused Englishmen: the accused may see the indictment, be permitted to have counsel, and cannot be convicted without two witnesses to an overt act of treason. The Act of Settlement (1701) concluded the constitutional changes (see Domestic Politics.)

SCOTTISH SETTLEMENT

The Church of Scotland and the Lowlanders preferred the Dutch Calvinist William to the Pro-Catholic James. Consequently, the Scottish Parliament met in convention, declared that James II had forfeited his crown, and offered it to William and Mary. But the Highlanders, with typical affection for the Stuarts and contempt for the Lowlanders, gathered around Viscount Dundee and defeated William's troops at Killiecrankie (1689). When Dundee was killed in battle, resistance fell apart, and most of the Highland clans took the oath of allegiance to William. By 1692 only the MacDonalds of Glencoe had delayed their submission. William's advisors urged him to extract obedience, and soldiers of the Campbell clan were sent to discipline the clansmen of Glencoe. After being entertained by their unsuspecting hosts for twelve days, the soldiers treacherously slaughtered a large number of MacDonalds in the night. William and Mary made Presbyterianism the established church in Scotland and offered numerous concessions to the

Scottish Parliament. But friction with England mounted when the English Parliament excluded Scottish trade from England.

THE WAR WITH IRELAND

With good reason the Irish preferred James II, who favored their religion, to the discrimination that they usually suffered at the hands of their Protestant overlords. Thus the Irish Parliament espoused the cause of James and took advantage of the English revolution to confiscate Protestant lands. In 1689 James arrived to lead the Irish, bringing French troops and money with him. All of Ireland except beleaguered Londonderry and Enniskillen recognized James as king. William and his troops arrived in Ireland in 1690 and on July 12 routed the army of James at the Battle of the Boyne River (the "Glorious Twelfth" for Orangemen—members of the Orange Lodge). James fled to the Continent, leaving the Irish Catholics to fight on until their last stronghold, Limerick, capitulated in 1691.

The Irish Settlement. The Treaty of Limerick (1692) offered the Irish relatively generous terms, including retention of the religious privileges given them under Charles II, permission for Irish soldiers to join the French army, and the restoration of estates confiscated since the reign of Charles II. But the Irish Protestants and the English Parliament had no intention of honoring the treaty. Instead, even more oppressive legislation was passed against Ireland. These laws barred Catholics from the Irish Parliament, from teaching in schools, from serving in the army or navy, or from holding any civil office. Protestant heirs received priority of inheritance over Catholic heirs, and interfaith marriages were penalized. At the insistence of English traders Parliament also passed restrictive acts which effectively destroyed the trade and industry of every Irish staple. Thus the Irish espousal of James resulted in political and religious tyranny for them, followed by poverty.

The War with France

King William added the resources of England and Scotland to his continental coalition against France and halted Louis XIV at the zenith of his power. The ensuing war was the beginning of a series of encounters between England and France which lasted for over a century. This second "Hundred Years' War," unlike the first, was not an effort to seize Continental France or the French crown, but was a duel for leadership in commerce, colonies, and sea power.

CAUSES OF THE WAR OF THE LEAGUE OF AUGSBURG, 1689–1697

The League of Augsburg was formed in 1686 to prevent French conquest of the Spanish Netherlands (modern Belgium). In 1689 William III eagerly attached England to the League to protect the national interests which the Stuart kings had neglected. France was the most powerful nation on the Continent, and if Louis triumphed in his expansionist schemes, political absolutism and an intolerant Catholicism (as reflected by Louis's revocation of the Edict of Nantes in 1685) would threaten England as well as the Continent. Moreover, France had become England's major opponent in commerce and a colonial rival in India and in North America. Finally, Louis defied and insulted England by refusing to recognize William as King; instead he had kept James at the French court and had provided him with men and money for the invasion of Ireland. In May 1689, Parliament declared war, and England returned to the leadership of forces opposed to Catholic absolutism.

COURSE OF THE WAR

The land war was dominated by a series of siege operations in Belgium in which the French won the major battles until William inflicted the first serious check on Louis's army by recapturing Namur. In 1690 the French fleet defeated the combined English-Dutch fleets at Beachy Head, and James and Louis made preparations for an invasion of England. However, the invasion army was kept in port when England and Holland regained control of the Channel in 1692 by routing the French fleet at La Hogue. On the southern front the French army invaded Savoy and made good progress until the English fleet blockaded the French navy and cut off their supplies. Meanwhile, in North America King William's War was being waged between English and French colonies. The French under Count Frontenac and with the help of Indian allies made a series of attacks on the New England colonies. Fighting on a small scale also took place in India and Africa.

THE PEACE OF RYSWICK, 1697

France was financially exhausted from the heavy expenses of Louis's half-century of intermittent wars, and the coalition had temporarily halted his schemes for expansion. By the treaty of Ryswick France restored all territory conquered since 1678 except Strasbourg; William was recognized as King of England; and the Dutch were allowed stronger fortifications along the French frontier. Although the peace was indecisive, the spread of French power was checked. An important by-product of the war was the establishment of the Bank of England in 1694 which stabilized England's financial system. To meet the heavy expenses of a world war a permanent national debt was legalized. This meant that the credit of the nation could be used in borrowing, and a portion of the debt payments would be charged to future generations, a practice eagerly copied by other nations.

Domestic Politics

After the death of Queen Mary in 1694, the aloof and alien King William had little popular appeal to British subjects or political appeal to the Whig and Tory factions, except as the symbol of Protestantism and national independence. For his part William was annoyed by the constant party bickering which prevented unified support of the war effort against France.

The Whigs hoped that the King would become a party leader and keep the Tories out of office as Charles II had kept the Whigs out; but William sought to avoid political intrigues. By 1694 Tory opposition to the war was so strong, however, that the Whig faction won the cooperation of the King and gained a majority in the Commons. During the interval of peace with France the Tories (the peace party) returned to power and flouted William by reducing the size of the army and navy. William hoped for a Whig victory in the election of 1701 in order to win support of his plans for a new coalition against Louis XIV; however, the Tories retained control and opposed William's renewed military effort against France.

THE ACT OF SETTLEMENT, 1701

This legislation insured a Protestant succession and reflected the anti-William sentiment of Parliament by placing further restrictions on the monarchy. The act provided that the crown should next descend to Anne (sister of Mary and daughter of James II) and then, if she had no living children, to Princess Sophia, granddaughter of the first Stuart King who ruled the small state of Hanover in northwest Germany; future English monarchs must join the Church of England and must not leave the country or involve England in war without consent of Parliament; royal officials were excluded from the House of Commons, and, after the Hanoverian succession, no foreigner could hold office or title to land; finally, judges could not be removed from office by the Crown (establishing a judiciary independent of the executive); they could only be removed by an act of Parliament.

Renewal of the War with France

The War of the Spanish Succession (1701–1713) broke out when King Charles II of Spain died childless and willed his kingdom to a grandson of Louis XIV, despite the Partition Treaties laboriously arranged by William to prevent this threat to the balance of power. King Louis, of course, supported the will and antagonized England further by recognizing the son of James II (known as the Old Pretender) as king of England—a violation of the terms of the Peace of Ryswick. Once again William fashioned a Grand Alliance of England, Holland, Austria, and several German states against the Bourbon kingdoms of France and Spain and appointed John Churchill, earl of Marlborough, as commander-in-chief. By December of 1701 the House of Commons was sympathetic to the war, but William died three months later, leaving the administration of the war to Queen Anne and Marlborough.

*T*he restored monarchy of 1660 never again had the degree of autonomy of action found before the Civil War. The Crown retained control of the executive branch of government, but the king was left utterly dependent upon Parliament for money, if he was not to use illegal or secret means to meet royal expenditures.

A second or "glorious" revolution in 1688 unseated yet another Stuart. It was supported by many in the political establishment as a necessary step to "conserve" traditional and religious arrangements, not as an effort to change the status quo.

The heritage of the Puritan Revolution and the Glorious Revolution affected the constitutiuonal settlements of 1688–1701. Parliament became the dominant partner and source of sovereignty in government thereafter. After the death of Queen Mary, King William succeeded in holding together an alliance against France and planning a world war that would span the reign of his successor, Queen Anne.

Selected Readings

Ashley, Maurice. *The Glorious Revolution of 1688* (1968)
Bryant, Arthur. *Restoration in England* (1960)
Burnet, Gilbert. *History of My Own Time* (1900)
Clark, George N. *The Later Stuarts* (1961)
Jones, J. R., ed. *The Restored Monarchy, 1660–1688* (1979)
Locke, John. *Two Treatises on Government* (1960)
Miller, J. *James II: A Study in Kingship* (1978)
Ogg, David. *England in the Reign of Charles II* (1955)
_____*England in the Reigns of James II and William III* (1955)
Pepys, Samuel. *The Diary* (1970–1972)
Pinkham, Lucille. *William III and the Respectable Revolution* (1954)

12

The Last of the Stuarts: 1702–1714

Queen Anne was the last of the Stuarts, in spite of bearing sixteen children; all died before her. She was more successful in uniting the two kingdoms of England and Scotland which her great-grandfather, James I, had attempted earlier without success.

For all but the final year of Anne's reign, England was at war with France and emerged with impressive victories on the Continent and colonial and commercial rewards in the peace treaty. John Churchill, duke of Marlborough, led the successful coalition against France.

The Queen presided over a kaleidoscopic political alignment that began and ended with a Tory administration. Although her reign was dominated by the great war with France, it was also a time of internal achievement: Newton in science, Wren in architecture, Godolphin, Harley, Churchill, and Bolingbroke in politics.

THE WAR AGAINST FRANCE

The War of the Spanish Succession (1702–1713) involved England in a world war. In addition to leading the coalition against Louis XIV, England had two armies on the Continent, fleets in the Mediterranean, Atlantic, and North Sea, and also confronted the French in North America and in the West Indies. For the first time in two generations a large French army was decisively defeated. England's victories brought about a substantial enlargement of her colonial empire as set forth in the Treaty of Utrecht ending the war.

Course of the War

The prevalent fear in Europe that Bourbon monarchs on both the thrones of France and Spain would permit Louis XIV to dominate the Continent prompted the formation of the Grand Alliance. John Churchill, serving as commander-in-chief and coordinator, succeeded by military genius and diplomatic skill in keeping this Grand Alliance together and achieved its first spectacular victory in 1704. At Blenheim, Churchill, who had joined forces with the equally brilliant commander of the Hapsburg army, Prince Eugene of Savoy, defeated the French and the Bavarians and saved Vienna from a French advance. In the same year an Anglo-Dutch fleet captured Gibraltar, and with it the control of the Mediterranean. In 1706, while Prince Eugene was routing the French from Italy, Churchill (now the Duke of Marlborough) won a second decisive battle at Ramillies. By 1708 a third victory at Oudenarde forced the French out of the Spanish Netherlands.

The coalition had achieved its essential goal: the ouster of the French from Italy and the Netherlands. France was exhausted and eager for peace, but several of the allies on the Continent and the Whigs in England insisted on the expulsion of Philip V from Spain. So the war dragged on, becoming more costly in manpower and more controversial in English politics. In Spain the allies took Madrid but could not hold the capital or the country. A treaty with Portugal, however, provided for an Anglo-Portuguese alliance and the exchange of English woolens for Portuguese wines. In 1710 English troops captured Acadia (Nova Scotia) from the French in North America. A year later Marlborough was dismissed by Tory political manipulation and negotiations for peace began between England and France.

THE POLITICS OF THE WAR

At the beginning of the war Marlborough and Sidney Godolphin, the chief ministers to the Queen, had only lukewarm support from their Tory party. The Whigs who favored a vigorous war policy gained the majority in the election of 1705. Marlborough and Godolphin continued as chief ministers, working successfully with the Whig faction in control of the Commons. When the Whig party refused to negotiate for peace after English security was achieved in battle, the war-weary electorate voted in a Tory majority in 1710. Tory ministers (Robert Harley and Henry St. John) now replaced the Whig advisors and pushed for a peace without ousting Philip V from the Spanish throne. Marlborough, the exalted war hero, was discredited by charges of misuse of public funds and went into exile to escape prosecution. St. John began peace negotiations with France in the Dutch city of Utrecht without the consent of all the allies.

THE PEACE OF UTRECHT, 1713

The provisions of Utrecht permitted Philip V to keep the Spanish throne, but excluded him from accession to the French throne. Austria acquired Milan, Naples, and the Spanish Netherlands, and England retained Gibraltar, Minorca, Acadia (Nova Scotia), Newfoundland, and title to all the Hudson Bay territory in Canada. The English also broke the Spanish monopoly on trade with her colonies by securing the right to supply slaves to South America (the Asiento Treaty with Philip).

The Peace, which recognized England as a major military power and the leading naval power, greatly expanded the colonial and commercial empire of Britain at the expense of France and Spain. England's commercial rival, Belgium (and particularly the city of Antwerp), was transferred to Austria, a country without a navy. Thus the fear of the Low Countries being ruled by a powerful, unfriendly country was removed. The war left France exhausted and nearly bankrupt, while the Dutch, after their century of glory, sank to an unimportant second-rate power in the eighteenth century.

QUEEN ANNE AND THE POLITICIANS

Anne's advisors supplied the leadership during her reign; the Queen took her royal responsibilities seriously, but she did not rule. Considered slow-witted and obstinate, she was devoted to the Anglican Church and favored the principles and prejudices of the Tory party. Although the Queen tried to remain aloof to the political factions in Parliament, she was forced to include Whigs among her ministers whenever the Whigs controlled Parliament. The Queen's original advisors had great influence over her, but were all dismissed from office before her death.

The Political Triumvirate

In the first half of Anne's reign three persons dominated the government: Sarah Churchill, duchess of Marlborough, was the Queen's closest confidante; her husband, the Duke, was the Queen's military and political advisor; and Sidney Godolphin, who provided the parliamentary leadership for Marlborough's campaigns, served as Lord Treasurer. Both men were moderate Tories; however, when the High Church Tories attacked Marlborough's conduct of the war and the Nonconformists, Godolphin stayed in power only through the backing of Anne at court and the Whigs in Parliament. After the Whigs increased their numbers in the election of 1705, several ultra-Tory ministers were dismissed by the Queen; nevertheless, the moderate ministers Godolphin, Marlborough, and Robert Harley were acceptable to the Whigs and remained in office.

In 1707 the Duchess of Marlborough lost her influence when Robert Harley's relative, Abigail Masham, replaced her as the Queen's closest court confidante. The following year the Whigs increased their majority in the Commons and demanded more ministerial (cabinet) offices; Anne consented under pressure but never forgave the Whigs. Godolphin and Marlborough made a political alliance with the Whig leadership, and the war was now conducted with vigor. But by this time the nation was becoming weary of the war.

Act of Union, 1707

The Godolphin-Marlborough-Harley ministry achieved a major feat with the Act of Union which joined the kingdoms of England and Scotland. The temporary union imposed on both nations by Cromwell had been dissolved with the Restoration in 1660. The Scots were lured into the union for economic reasons. The English feared their security would again be menaced if the Scots chose a separate monarch after the death of Anne, the last of the Stuarts, which the Scottish Parliament indicated it would do.

Commissioners from each kingdom met and negotiated the terms of union: (1) the Scottish Kirk would continue independent of England, as would the court system; (2) Scotland would give up its Parliament and, in its place, send forty-five members to the House of Commons and select sixteen peers to represent the Scottish nobility in the House of Lords; (3) Scotland would agree to the Hanoverian succession; (4) Scotland would receive a large financial grant for assuming its share of the English national debt; and (5) Scotland would receive the same trading rights as England. Although many Scots were unhappy with the prospects of being governed from London, the act brought trade and relative prosperity to Scotland and expanded their potential for political and business leadership in Great Britain.

THE NEW POLITICIANS

The Whigs, already disliked by the Queen, began to lose popular support as the war dragged on. In 1709 the government impeached Dr. Henry Sacheverell for preaching two sermons in which he criticized Godolphin, the Whig ministry, and the revolution of 1688. The London mobs made Sacheverell a popular hero and attacked Whig homes and Dissenter chapels. The Queen took advantage of this political climate to dismiss Godolphin and other Whig ministers. In the election of 1710 the Tory faction won a majority, and Robert Harley became Lord Treasurer and Henry St. John, his chief colleague. The Tories punished leading Whigs—Robert Walpole was sentenced to the Tower—and negotiated a peace with France. To pursue peace overtures it was necessary to oust Marlborough, the last important leader of the war ministry. In 1711 he was replaced as commander by the Tory Duke of Ormonde. The House of Commons backed Harley in his negotiations with France; however, to win a majority in the House of Lords, Queen Anne was forced to create twelve new peers.

The Tory cabinet took advantage of Jonathan Swift's and Daniel Defoe's literary talents to subsidize essays supporting the government. It was this cabinet that began the practice of coming to a consensus on policy in order to strengthen its case before seeking the Queen's approval. Although Queen Anne favored the Tories and carefully chose her ministers, she realized that a ministry was useless if it could not win votes in Parliament and that changing political alignments in Parliament could not be ignored.

TORY STATUTES

With the support of Queen Anne, the Harley-St. John ministry (1710–1714) passed a series of acts aimed at punishing the Whigs and the Dissenters. The Occasional Conformity Act put an end to the practice of Dissenter officeholders (mostly Whigs) who complied with the Test Act by taking the Anglican sacrament only once a year. The Property Qualification Act required members of the House of Commons to hold landed property with an annual value of £300 or £600 (depending on the constituency). This act handicapped the Whigs, whose wealth was more likely to be in business than in land. The Schism Act was aimed at Dissenter academies; it required all teachers to be licensed by a bishop and to attend the Anglican Church.

THE SUCCESSION QUESTION

As the time approached to put into effect the clauses of the Act of Settlement (1701) which would transfer the dynasty to the Hanoverians as the closest Protestant succession to the throne if none of Queen Anne's children survived childhood, there was little enthusiasm for the Hanoverian cause. The Whigs favored the Hanoverian dynasty for political and religious reasons; however, they were not in control of Parliament. The Tories were divided between allegiance to the Stuarts, known as the Jacobite faction, and to the Anglican Church. With his party divided, Henry St. John (now Viscount Bolingbroke) schemed to become indispensable in determining the succession, but his plans went awry and he was unable to control the situation.

Divided Loyalties

When Anne became ill in 1713, the issue of the succession loomed large. The Tories had tried and failed to get James, the Old Pretender (son of James II), to change his religion. When that hope was rebuffed, they became divided on the succession. Lord Treasurer Harley (now Earl of Oxford) led the moderate Tories, who favored the Hanoverian succession. Meanwhile Bolingbroke intrigued with the opportunist Abigail Masham, the Queen's chief lady-in-waiting, to persuade Anne to dismiss Oxford. Finally, on July 27, 1714, Oxford was dismissed as the Queen's chief minister.

Viscount Bolingbroke, with a mind uncluttered by loyalties to anyone but himself, was one of the most witty, brilliant, and cultured political leaders of Queen Anne's reign. During the few days after he had accomplished the fall of Oxford, Bolingbroke was the most powerful person in the realm but he hesitated to act. His schemes for controlling the succession, whatever they were, collapsed. The Duke of Shrewsbury, a moderate Tory and one of the seven signatories to the petition to invite William to England in 1688, took the lead in forestalling Bolingbroke's plans. Supported by the Duke of Somerset and the Duke of Argyll, the Privy Council met on July 30 and rushed through a motion urging the Queen to make Shrewsbury Lord Treasurer, in which capacity he would be responsible for matters relating to the succession. Bolingbroke was not prepared to challenge the Privy Council, and Shrewsbury received the Treasurer's staff from the dying Queen.

THE CHANGE OF DYNASTIES

The Tories lost an opportunity to consolidate their position by failing to agree to the succession of the Hanoverians. Instead, they hedged their loyalties so that the early Hanoverian monarchs considered the Whigs their friends and the Tories tainted with Jacobitism. Two months before Anne's final illness, Sophia, electress of Hanover and granddaughter of James I, had died and left the succession to her son, George. Upon the death of Anne, Shrewsbury arranged the transition, and in September 1714, George, the elector of Hanover, along with his German advisors, mistresses, and hounds, arrived in England. With the Hanoverian succession Protestantism and a limited monarchy were maintained.

STUART ENGLAND

The seventeenth-century population of England increased to over five million by 1701. Commerce and colonies became increasingly important and brought prosperity, but their future growth would be contingent on the control of the seas that was won under Queen Anne. Political participation and social mobility certainly existed to a greater degree in England than on the Continent, but those who overcame political and class barriers were the exception, not the rule. The century still belonged to the favored few, not to the common people, because the great majority of citizens did not participate in the political events or share in the increasing wealth. London was the one metropolitan center. Most people (74 percent) lived in villages and continued to do so until the Industrial Revolution.

Religious controversy spanned the century, but passions over religious differences were moderated by 1700. The security of the country and of the established church, along with the rationalism of the dawning Enlightenment, muted religious intolerance. The changing standards and thinking of the century are mirrored in the arts, architecture, and literature.

Stuart Literature

The scientific revolution and the "age of Newton" mark the dawn of modern cosmology and modern thought. Seventeenth-century writing was characterized by a variety of forms and themes, ranging from the majestic sweep of John Milton's blank verse to the shallow, affected drama of the Restoration and the pamphlet literature of Queen Anne's reign.

POETRY

The Anglican clerics Robert Herrick (1591–1674) and John Donne (1573–1631) are probably the most representative and respected poets of the early seventeenth century. Herrick's lyrical poems, dealing with classical myths of love or pastoral beauty, with occasional touches of fresh irreverence, are unsurpassed in craftsmanship. Donne's earlier works included satires and elegies but his metaphysical poems, such as *Songs and Sonnets*, are imbued with moods of introspection and distinguished by remarkable innovations in stanzaic patterns. His poetry influenced Dryden and a host of later poets.

John Milton (1608–1674) was the official apologist for the Cromwellian period. Following the Restoration he created three great poems in blank verse, *Paradise Lost*, *Paradise Regained*, and *Samson Agonistes*, in which his genius blended classical and Biblical themes into epics magnificent in scope and imagery; these heroic, profound, and tragic themes far transcended traditional Puritan theology.

Satire and the heroic couplets were the most marked characteristics of poetic efforts in the Restoration period. Samuel Butler (1612–1680) ridiculed the Puritans in his *Hudibras*; whereas Andrew Marvell (1621–1678) displayed imaginative wit in *To His Coy Mistress* and justly praised the Lord Protector in the *Horatian Ode upon Cromwell's Return from Ireland*. The poet laureate of the Restoration was John Dryden (1631–1700), whose versatile endeavors—criticism, poetry, drama, and satire—moved English literature to the threshold of the Augustan Age, identified with the reign of Queen Anne. His poems include *Absalom and Achitophel*, *The Hind and the Panther*, and *Alexander's Feast*. More than anyone else he dominated the last half of the century and dictated its literary taste.

PROSE

Essentially, the prose of the seventeenth century is formal, utilitarian, and precise. The *Essays* of Sir Francis Bacon (1561–1626) are polished treatises on civil and ethical matters written in terse, epigrammatic style. John Bunyan's (1628–1688) *The Pilgrim's Progress* combines moral instruction with Biblical allegory in a storytelling framework of remarkable invention and technique. The midcentury was dominated by a variety of writers on theology such as William Chillingworth, Jeremy Taylor, George Herbert, and Richard Baxter, and such political writers as John Lilburne, William Walwyn, and William Prynee. Isaac Walton (1593–1683) wrote brief biographies of contemporary poets and *The Compleat Angler*, a pleasant, witty treatise on fishing. Samuel Pepys's *Diary* and John Aubrey's *Brief Lives* are invaluable sketches of social history spanning the last half of the seventeenth century. The King James Version of the Bible (1611) became the most influential book in the English language. It taught the richness of that language to three centuries of readers.

DRAMA

The theater had its greatest vogue under James I and Charles II. Shakespeare, who lived until 1616, had many of his plays performed before King James. Ben Jonson (1572–1637) became the most influential and admired playwright of the early seventeenth century. His vivid characterizations and satirical humor are found in *Volpone*, *The Alchemist*, and *Bar-*

tholomew Fair. Perfection in dramatic structure and a keen interest in the politics of the day were distinguishing features of the plays of Philip Massinger (1583–1640).

Puritan disapproval restricted the theater during the interregnum, but with the Restoration theaters were reopened and became popular with Charles II and his court. In reaction to the Puritan spirit, the Comedy of Manners accented lasciviousness and cynical worldliness. Among the playwrights who wrote these mock-heroic and romantic comedies were Dryden, William Wycherley, William Congreve, and John Vanbrugh. By the turn of the century, sentimental, domestic comedy, full of moral instructions and middle-class respectability, as in Richard Steele's *The Tender Husband* (1705), became the vogue of the "reformed" theater.

History and Philosophy

History was generally written for public readership, not for an academic audience. Frequently historians incorporated memoirs or political philosophy in their writings. Pre–civil war historians included Sir Walter Raleigh and his influential *The History of the World*, Sir Francis Bacon, and Lord Herbert of Cherbury. Popular postwar works were Lord Clarendon's *History of the Rebellion* and Bishop Burnet's *History of His Own Time*. Political theorists dealt with the issues of ultimate sovereignty, royal prerogative versus common law, and the rights of the state and of the citizenry. King James I justified the prerogative rights of kingship in *The True Law of Free Monarchy*.

The philosopher Francis Bacon replaced Aristotelian concepts with an inductive approach to knowledge in *The Advancement of Learning* and *The New Atlantis*. Sir Edward Coke argued for a "fundamental law" that preceded and was superior to royal law. Sir Thomas Hobbes (1588–1679) was a cynical secularist who argued powerfully for absolute monarchy on the grounds of materialistic self-interest in *Leviathan*. James Harrington's (1611–1677) answer to Hobbes was his *Commonwealth of Oceana* (1656) which influenced political thought in the interregnum by an economic interpretation of political power and an argument for a mixed constitution and a "balance of property."

In the reign of Charles II, George Savile (1633–1695), marquis of Halifax, published anonymously *The Character of a Trimmer*; he was an apologist for the golden mean in politics, which, in his terms, meant a limited monarchy. John Locke (1632–1704) in his epoch-making *Essay Concerning Human Understanding* argued for empiricism—all knowledge comes through experience—and rejected the theory of innate knowledge. In political theory Locke was a utilitarian like Hobbes, but opposed Hobbes's all-powerful state. In the second of his *Two Treatises on Government* (1690) Locke supported a government limited to certain areas of jurisdiction by a social contract between the governor and the governed. If government abused the liberty or the property rights of the subjects, the right to cancel the contract and to revolt was permissible. Locke's ideas of individual liberty and freedom from tyranny, religious or political, spread to France and America, and would be heard again in the American Declaration of Independence.

Scientific Interests

In the seventeenth century a scientific revolution shattered traditional ways of thinking and the medieval world view on cosmology and physiology. The plea for scientific inquiry, introduced by Roger Bacon in the *New Atlantis* and the *Novum Organum*, and coupled with the observations of Copernicus, Kepler, and Galileo in astronomy, stimulated a fundamental reordering of the old Ptolemaic universe. William Gilbert (1540–1603) offered new ideas in magnetism, and William Harvey (1578–1657) explained the circulation of the blood.

With the establishment of the Royal Society of London for Improving Natural Knowledge, scientists gained additional freedom and respectability. Robert Boyle's law in chemistry and his critique of classical views replaced outmoded Aristotelian theories. But the major scientific breakthrough was made by Sir Isaac Newton, professor of mathematics at Cambridge, with the publication of his *Principia Mathematica* (1687), a monumental treatise dealing with the motion of celestial bodies according to the law of universal gravitation. The spirit of inquiry and the inductive method of thinking flourished in Restoration England uninhibited by the Counter Reformation that crushed science after 1660 in Catholic Europe.

Religious Developments

In no other century were religious and literary issues so interwoven. The controversies and convictions which spanned the civil war and interregnum inspired a variety of religious expressions and freedoms: the Fifth Monarchy men, George Fox and the Quakers, the Brownists and Congregational church government, and Cromwell's sponsorship of religious toleration. The efforts of Archbishop Laud to enforce religious uniformity increased Puritan opposition and writings. The Clarendon Code deliberately made the Anglican Church more exclusive and forced Nonconformists from its membership. These Dissenters influenced English politics in the following century and joined with the rationalists and the utilitarians to make freedom from unfair restrictions, religious or political, a common goal. By the end of the Stuart period the Anglican Church was beginning to feel the effects of increasing rationalism and a decline of religious fervor. This development in the church was foreshadowed by the Oxford rationalists William Chilingworth (1602–1644) and John Hales (1584–1656) and the Cambridge Platonists John Worthington (1618–1671) and Ralph Cudworth (1617–1688).

Social Developments

Since England's population was still four-fifths rural in the seventeenth century, the relationship of individuals to the land largely determined their social and economic class. The gentry or country squires, who owned large estates, were the most influential class, living in ease in their country manors most of the year but increasingly moving to London for the winter season. Politically, this class supplied the justices of the peace. Under the Stuarts the gentry won control of the House of Commons and forced political concessions from the king, such as the Petition of Right, the Triennial Act, and the Bill of Rights. Below the gentry were a diminishing class of yeomen, perhaps numbering 160,000, who were owners of smaller landholdings, but enfranchised and proud of their independence. Tenant farmers were increasing in number, although outnumbered greatly by the rural wage owner who knew the full meaning of poverty and had little opportunity to participate in national affairs except in such episodes as the Leveler movements of the civil war.

The moral tone of Puritanism dominated social customs until the Restoration. The court and the upper classes then repudiated Puritan tradition and took advantage of their new social liberties until a more sober court, prompted by the moralizing essayists of the Augustan writers in Queen Anne's reign, muted these excesses and encouraged a refinement of social conduct.

AGRICULTURAL IMPROVEMENTS

Agriculture continued as the occupation of the great majority of the population, with minor production improvements resulting from the use of fertilizers and the rotation of crops. The enclosure movement continued with less opposition as the need for converting the open-field system into hedged fields became generally recognized; and yet by the end of the century less than half the land was enclosed. Peasants who lost employment because of enclosures sought work in the industries of Bristol, York, Newcastle, and London.

TRADE AND COMMERCE

A significant growth in commerce, particularly in foreign trade, characterized the second half of the seventeenth century. Except for the East India and the Hudson Bay companies, monopolistic companies were broken by laws favoring competitive enterprise. Foreign commerce was promoted by legislation designed to further imperial trade and guarantee a favorable balance of trade. Commercial legislation, such as the Act of Navigation (1660), was an application of the mercantile theory which assumed that national prosperity was based on a favorable balance of trade and that any English expansion of commerce could only be at the expense of commercial rivals (Holland and Spain). Laws promoting exports and restricting imports, the expansion of the merchant navy to move exports, and a stronger navy to protect shipping became accepted features of the mercantile theory.

In terms of imperial policy the acts of trade were devised to make the colonies serve as suppliers of raw materials and as markets for manufactured goods; also, the acts attempted to exclude all but English or colonial ships from the carrying trade. The preference given to colonial over foreign goods, along with the protection of the royal navy, were advantageous to English colonies at first. However, since colonial manufacturing was restricted, the acts would hinder the expansion of the American economy as the colonies developed. In practice, the mercantile acts were not a serious deterrent to colonial industry because they were only occasionally enforced; nevertheless, the mercantile policy became a growing source of grievance in the thirteen colonies.

The Growth of Empire

The English colonies exercised far greater independence of action than the colonies of any other European nation in the seventeenth century. In their charters and in their customs the colonies were to be "little Englands"; in the eyes of English lawmakers they were conceived of as settlements to promote English commerce. Economic and religious motives were paramount in the establishment of the North American colonies.

To most of the Scots and English, however, their settlement in Ireland and the colonies in Bermuda and in the West Indies were at least as important as the American colonies. Bermuda received its royal charter in 1615. During the remainder of the century Barbados, Jamaica, and the Bahamas were settled and became prosperous through a lively trade in sugar, molasses, tobacco, and cotton. These colonies, like the American colonies, were administered by an English governor and local assemblies. The East India Company received a new charter as a joint-stock company and, from its centers at Bombay and Madras, competed with the princes of Maratha in southwest India and with the Dutch for trade and spheres of influence.

The years 1713–1714 ended a quarter-century of wars, from which Britain emerged as the major sea power in the world and a major power in European affairs. The peaceful transfer of dynasties from the Stuarts to the Hanovers made secure the provisions of the Act of Settlement (1701) and the Church of England.

During Anne's reign political factions—the Whigs and the Tories—became more clearly identified. Increasingly rulers needed, for practical, political reasons, to choose their ministers from the dominant party or cliques in the House of Commons. Since she depended to a large degree on her ministers for making policy, the practice of limited monarchy advanced during the rule of Anne.

The Age of Queen Anne was also known as the Augustan Age since the greatness of its literary achievement was said to resemble that of Rome under Augustus. Jonathan Swift, Daniel Defoe, Richard Steele, Christopher Wren's "new London," and Isaac Newton's "new science" gave evidence of this age of transition toward the eighteenth-century Enlightenment.

Selected Readings

Butterfield, Herbert. *Origins of Modern Science* (1949)

Churchill, Winston. *Marlborough: His Life and Times* (1958)

Holmes, Geoffrey. *British Politics in the Age of Anne* (1967)

Kronenberger, Louis. *Marlborough's Duchess* (1958)

Lever, Tresham. *Godolphin, His Life and Times* (1952)

Trevelyan, George M. *England Under the Stuarts* (1960)

Wedgewood, Cicely V. *Poetry and Politics Under the Stuarts* (1950)

Westfall, Richard. *Never at Rest: A Biography of Isaac Newton* (1980)

Willey, Basil. *The Seventeenth-Century Background* (1953)

13

Georgian Politics: 1714–1763

The Glorious Revolution of 1688 had conserved and sanctified, rather than radically altered, the English political structure and religious settlement. The landed aristocracy dominated politics; the king remained the constitutional center of government and chose his ministers, subject to the increasing need to find a ministry (cabinet) that could work effectively with Parliament.

Because the Whig politicians believed that the settlement of 1688 could best be protected by supporting the Hanoverian succession, the first two Georges repaid this consideration by choosing parliamentary ministers from among the Whigs. During this period the power of the House of Commons grew as ministries became increasingly dependent upon it for support and influence. Such a development disturbed neither the aristocracy nor the monarchy, because the Commons was not yet a popular body. It could be managed by the titled oligarchy or the royal Court, either through nomination of their candidates in the constituencies or by royal patronage and influence.

No politician understood the power of the Crown's extensive patronage better or managed the system more deftly than Robert Walpole. For that reason he was "Prime Minister" for two decades. The period witnessed the expansion of English influence abroad through colonies, commerce, and sea power.

ENGLAND AT THE ACCESSION OF GEORGE I

In 1714 the majority of the country preferred a Hanoverian succession that would ensure a parliamentary and Protestant supremacy to any of the more controversial alternatives of the day promoted by the Jacobites (supporters of a Stuart heir). In contrast to the Stuart period during which political and religious controversies divided the nation, the political leaders of the early eighteenth century were largely satisfied with the settlement of 1688 which had limited the monarchy even though it had failed to reform Parliament.

Abuses in corporate institutions (Parliament, church, municipal government, and universities) continued unchecked as English stability became identified with the status quo and was not to be tampered with. As a result, Britain's expansion and strength in the eighteenth century came largely through the abilities and energies of individuals who were given free rein by the country's uninhibiting laws more than through the reforms or vigor of its institutions. Such reforms would come a century later.

The New Dynasty

On the death of Queen Anne in August 1714 George, elector of Brunswick-Luneburg (commonly called Hanover after its principal city), succeeded to the throne in accordance with the terms of the Act of Settlement. Four months earlier, his mother, Sophia, a granddaughter of James I, had died; hence the throne went to her son who was not so eager about his inheritance as his mother had been. The Hanoverian succession was not the most direct line but was the most Protestant, and English acceptance of the new dynasty meant that there would be little likelihood of a Catholic monarch, French troops, or another civil war. On September 18, George I landed in his adopted realm. Dull, stodgy, and already fifty-four years of age, the new King never learned English and his subjects never learned to love or admire him. If they were attached to him, it was largely because he interfered so little with national institutions and because the return of the Stuarts might jeopardize the Anglican and parliamentary arrangement.

THE STRUCTURE OF SOCIETY

In the early eighteenth century, England had a population of about five and one-half million, the vast majority of which was in the rural areas of the south. London grew rapidly, passing the half-million mark, and new towns and industrial villages in the Midlands began to drain off the rural poor of the south and east. Parliament reflected these changes in its increasing preoccupation with trade, because trade meant wealth and wealth meant power; however, liquid capital had not yet replaced ownership of land as the hallmark of social and political power. Because property was sacrosanct, the laws dealing with crimes against property were numerous and extreme: a child stealing a handkerchief worth a shilling or more was liable for the death penalty.

The Country. At the apex of the social scale were the landed aristocracy, rich in estates and political influence, who lived in magnificence and provided a thin veneer of elegance to society. Their interest in, and profit from, agriculture made them supporters of improved farming methods. Next in rank were the country gentry who exercised local authority, often as justices of the peace. However, because of their most modest means and back-country residences, they seldom influenced national politics and, as a class, were identified with the Tories who resented the Whig oligarchy. As enclosures of common land became widespread, country laborers drifted into towns and became unskilled laborers. Many yeoman farmers who could not compete with the large estateholders sold their holdings and became tenant farmers.

The Towns. The great merchants had close financial ties with the government and often bought or married their way into the aristocracy. The smaller merchants and shop owners continued a seventeenth-century tradition of thrift and industry as well as a Puritan attitude toward corruption in high places; many were Dissenters who favored religious toleration at home and an isolationist policy abroad. Craftsmen and artisans worked long hours and made a modest wage so long as trade was good. But the deteriorating economy and spread of a free labor market threatened their position, and two parliamentary acts (1720, 1744) prohibited combination (uniting in protest), after unrest in the textile industry had caused workmen to act together to secure their rights. In the coffee houses of London the disaffected expressed their grievances in attacks on Walpole's government.

The Ruling Class

Dominating the political scene were the great families of England whose ideas of a balanced constitution explained their allegiance to the Hanoverian rather than the Stuart dynasty. From 1707 to 1801—when one hundred Irish seats were added—the membership of the House of Commons remained frozen at 558. Nevertheless, the power of the Lower House grew steadily during the century without any serious efforts by the Lords to halt the trend, because the political and family interests of the two houses were similar— they represented the same class. By means of political and monetary manipulation the peers could control the selection of candidates in their areas, and in only a minority of constituencies was the outcome of an election ever in doubt.

With no uniform franchise (except for the county seats) and no redistribution of seats, the overrepresented south produced numerous "rotten boroughs" in which a handful of voters could easily be managed with bribes or patronage. "Pocket boroughs" were completely under the control of one individual or family. Thus "the number of votes a peer or squire could secure either by threats, promises, or bribes was the measure of his influence; and a man in eighteenth-century politics was assessed by his influence."[*] With such influence a person could barter for pensions, sinecures, or government appointments. It was not by accident that the position of Prime Minister evolved from the post of First Lord of the Treasury, for patronage secretaries played an essential part in the intimate, yet complex, system of political bargaining that characterized the institutions of the century. With no appointments by examination, political connections and influence were the avenues to success. In this context the borough managers and influential families who controlled anywhere from eight to forty-five seats in the Commons could translate their local power to national parliamentary influence.

---

[*] J. H. Plumb, *England in the Eighteenth Century* (Baltimore, 1950), p. 38.

The Cabinet

It was perhaps characteristic of the English that their cabinet system had no definition in law but was essentially the growth of political conventions. These parties slipped casually into British institutional history under the first two Georges as the most effective arrangement for governing the country. The cabinet served as the link through which the legislature could communicate with, and eventually control, the executive. The problem of limiting the king's power and exerting parliamentary sovereignty was solved, not by excluding the king's ministers from the House of Commons (as the Act of Settlement, 1701, specified and as currently practiced in the United States), but by insisting that the king's advisors sit in Parliament and command parliamentary support.

The term "Prime Minister" came into use initially as a criticism of Robert Walpole for being more prominent in the cabinet than his colleagues. By the time of Pitt the Younger, the term "Prime Minister" had become generally accepted, and the executive functions of the post increased at the expense of the reigning sovereign. Although full responsible government, whereby the cabinet owed collective responsibility to an elected legislature, did not become a necessity until the nineteenth century when party identity was more clearly defined, Walpole and his successors developed an arrangement whereby the prime minister and his cabinet colleagues could control sufficient support in the Commons (assisted by government patronage) to make sure of a majority. In practice the cabinet consisted of a group of politicians, led by one of their number, who could win the support of a majority of those who counted at court and in Parliament. Such a cabinet would stay in power until one of three things happened: the king tired of its members, the members fell out among themselves, or they failed to keep the support of Parliament.

THE WHIG SUPREMACY

The Hanoverian monarchs favored the Whigs because the Whigs in turn favored them and were not tainted with Jacobitism (those supporting the claims to the throne of James II and his son, James III, whose name in Latin translated as Jacobus) as were some of the Tories. Therefore the king chose his ministers from the Whig factions, which were controlled by the great landed families and supported by the Nonconformists and the majority of city merchants. The Whigs halted the increasing religious intolerance of the Harley-Bolingbroke years (1710–1714) by repealing the Schism and Occasional Conformity Acts, partly because the Whigs were a minority and needed the support of Dissenters penalized by these acts, partly because the Whig leadership was more latitudinarian in their view of the established Church. Although the Whigs dominated at court and at Westminster, they seldom tampered with the local power of the landed gentry. Like Squire

Western in *Tom Jones*, the landed gentry were usually Tory and exercised influence in the countryside as justices of the peace and as landholders.

POLITICAL DEVELOPMENTS, 1714–1754

After the tempestuous political and religious developments of the Stuart period, the early years of the Hanoverians provided Britain with domestic peace and governmental stability. During these years the Whigs, although split into competing factions in Parliament, nevertheless enjoyed the favor of the first two Georges and composed the various ministries. Chief among Whig ministers was Robert Walpole whose long tenure (1721–1742) as Prime Minister has never been duplicated. The major threat to the Hanoverian supremacy came from the Jacobites. The two Jacobite uprisings of 1715 and 1745 failed to attract English support for the Stuarts and were easily crushed; each defeat discredited the Tories politically and made them appear synonymous with Jacobitism.

THE HANOVERIAN-WHIG SUPREMACY

The new dynasty was not popular in Britain. The King's coarse taste, coldness, and German court were not warmly received. George's inability to speak English and his awareness that he could not rule England in the absolute fashion in which he had ruled Hanover made him rely on English ministers and particularly on Whig leaders, because their loyalty to him, unlike that of the Tories, was not in question. In 1714 George appointed a new ministry led by Lord Townshend, and an election early the next year gave the Whigs a majority in the Commons. The Whigs now reciprocated the vindictive partisanship of the Tory years by passing acts of attainder that outlawed Bolingbroke and Ormonde, depriving them of all civil rights, and beginning impeachment proceedings against Oxford. When riots and demonstrations flared up in favor of James Edward Stuart, the Old Pretender, the Whigs passed the Riot Act (1715). This act empowered a magistrate to order the dispersal within the hour of any assemblage of twelve or more persons who were disturbing the peace. Felony charges could be proferred against those failing to comply.

The Jacobite Rebellion. Stuart supporters who placed their hopes on an uprising joined a band of Highland clansmen under the leadership of the Earl of Mar. A landing was also planned on the south coast of England, but even before the Pretender landed in Scotland, the Jacobites had been twice defeated. The rebellion fizzled because Englishmen were not inclined to risk a civil war to restore a Catholic dynasty that they still mistrusted; also James proved to be an incompetent and dispiriting leader. Furthermore, King Louis

XIV died on the eve of the rebellion; his promise of help was not honored by the Duke of Orleans who was regent during the minority of Louis XV.

The Septennial Act. The rebellion further discredited the Tories for their Jacobite leanings and permitted the Whigs to gain a decisive political ascendancy which lasted until 1760. The last Tory was dismissed from the cabinet, and the Whigs passed the Septennial Act which extended the life of Parliament from three to seven years. The act gave the Whigs four additional years to entrench their political power. The excuse of unsettled conditions permitted the postponement of an election.

The Stanhope Ministry

King George's interest in foreign (Hanoverian) affairs helped make James Stanhope, supported by the Earl of Sunderland, the dominant figure in the remodeled all-Whig ministry. This ministry would later divide over Stanhope's adventurous foreign policy. In 1716 George I had completed two alliances of mutual aid with Austria and with France. Stanhope continued this involvement in Continental affairs by completing the Quadruple Alliance (1718) which joined Britain, France, Holland, and Austria against Philip V of Spain, who had designs on Austrian territory and ambitions for the French throne. In 1719 French troops and a British fleet inflicted a double defeat on Spain. Philip abandoned his expansionist plans, dismissed his brilliant minister, Cardinal Alberoni, and negotiated the Treaty of Madrid (1721) which established a defensive alliance with England and France and confirmed earlier political and commercial agreements.

Stanhope was just as successful in the Baltic where Charles XII, the powerful King of Sweden, was challenging Hanoverian interests and encouraging opposition to the new dynasty in England. Stanhope sent the British navy to the Baltic, risking war to protect British interests in northern Europe. The sudden death of Charles made Russia the chief threat in the Baltic. To contain Peter the Great, Stanhope succeeded in allying with Sweden and settling their differences over recognition of Hanover by the treaties of Stockholm and Frederiksburg in 1720. Stanhope's foreign policy helped secure the peace of Europe and recognition of the Hanoverian succession.

Stanhope was less successful in domestic policies. The Schism Act and the Occasional Conformity Act were repealed, but his efforts to abolish the Corporation and Test Acts were defeated. In 1719 Stanhope introduced his peerage bill which would ensure Whig domination of the Lords by virtually freezing its membership. The political purpose was to keep the Prince of Wales, who bitterly opposed his father, from creating sufficient Tory peers as Queen Anne had done to swamp the Whig majority. Walpole denounced the bill as one making the Lords a private corporation and closing the one avenue to rank and honor open to the country gentry. The opposition and independent members coalesced to defeat the bill which, if nothing else, convinced Stanhope of the wisdom of restoring Walpole and Townshend to the cabinet they had left over his foreign policy.

The South Sea Bubble

In 1711 the South Sea Company was chartered as a joint-stock organization to take advantage of South American trade which opened up through the Asiento clauses of the Treaty of Utrecht. At the time, the government was trying to liquidate the national debt more quickly by having portions of it absorbed by several great companies, such as the Bank of England and the East India Company. The South Sea Company devised a sinking fund scheme to pay off the entire debt and permitted the court and members of Parliament to buy a large number of shares. A mania of speculation broke loose as the government appeared to be backing the company. Stocks soared 1,000 percent, and other promoters took advantage of this bull market to advertise the flimsiest of schemes. The bubble burst in August 1720, ruining thousands of investors and precipitating a financial and political crisis.

The dispossessed clamored for scapegoats, and a parliamentary inquiry revealed gross corruption in high places. Members of the cabinet were involved and publicly disgraced, and although Stanhope was not implicated, he suffered a stroke defending his innocence in the House of Lords. The King desperately needed a new political manager, one who was not incriminated in the sorry scandal, and one who could restore public confidence and national credit by his financial abilities. Walpole met these requirements and became chancellor of the exchequer. He performed a remarkable job of extricating the government and the court from the scandal and in restoring the finances and confidence of the nation. The South Sea scandal was the turning point of Walpole's career.

"Prime Minister" Walpole, 1721–1742

Walpole became head of the Whig faction with the death of Sunderland and held on to his newly won position for twenty-one years. During this time Walpole exerted a primacy among his cabinet colleagues previously unmatched. Through his loyalty to the Crown, bribery ("every man has his price" is attributed to him), patronage, enormous energy for work and mastery of detail, he effectively controlled the machinery of government. As Prime Minister he used his uncanny knack for probing the weaknesses of human nature and sensing public opinion to steer England on a course that was wise and profitable, if not always heroic. He was neither an idealist nor a reformer, but his contribution was substantial. Through his policy of peace and prosperity, he left England powerful and its new dynasty secure. A master manager of people, Walpole reflected and played upon the political morality and shifting political alignments of his day.

RISE TO PROMINENCE

The son of a Norfolk squire, Sir Robert Walpole became a successful businessman and a typical country squire of his day—coarse in morals and uncouth in manners, a heavy drinker, generous to his friends and indifferent to his opponents. In 1700 he began his political career as a member for a pocket borough belonging to his family. Under Queen Anne he built up a reputation in the area of finance. He was a member of Stanhope's cabinet, but survived its disintegration because of his timely severance from the South Sea Company and his reputation in finance.

Minister and King. Under the first two Georges the cabinet became increasingly independent of the king's domination. Because George I was unable to speak English and was more absorbed in Hanoverian affairs, he rarely attended cabinet sessions. Under George II this custom hardened into precedent, which meant that as the king's influence in the cabinet and in parliamentary affairs declined, it became increasingly important to have a cabinet which could command the support of Parliament. Thus under both kings Walpole came close to being an indispensable political manager. Throughout his long career, he sat in the Commons and made it the center of government. Similarly, he made himself the center of the cabinet either by demanding his colleagues' support of his policies or, on occasion, their resignation.

In 1727 George I died and his son came to the throne. George II (1727–1760) was dull, pompous, and hostile to the advisors of his father, and, as was expected, the ministers were dismissed, but not for long. Walpole was too valuable a political manager to lose. He returned to office by outbidding his competitors' promise of an increased royal income and through the support of Queen Caroline, the intelligent and politically astute consort, who commanded King George's confidence, if not his fidelity. Thereafter, George II interested himself chiefly in foreign and court affairs, and Walpole consolidated his position through patronage and pensions. Borough patrons and independent members were rewarded with spoils as Walpole and his political colleague, the Duke of Newcastle, manipulated pensions and Church and state appointments to sustain parliamentary support.

Economic Policies. Not until Gladstone would another Prime Minister master financial details as completely as Walpole. Convinced that a prosperous country required peace, Walpole shunned foreign entanglements and gave his attention to a more efficient development of the nation's commerce and industry. He reduced interest on government borrowing to 4 percent, relaxed colonial restrictions, simplified the confusing tariff rates, and removed export duties from manufactured articles. His economies kept taxes low, especially the tax on land, which won him the support of landowners at court and in Parliament. In 1733 Walpole attempted a major reform with an excise bill which would extend the excise system of taxation already highly successful on tea, coffee, and chocolate imports. The bill would apply to tobacco and wine. Immediately public and political opposition loudly denounced the proposed bill as an increase in bureaucratic power. Finally Walpole yielded to popular and court pressure and withdrew the bill, and then proceeded to punish his supporters who had deserted him on the measure.

POLITICAL WARFARE

Walpole's notion of good government emphasized peace abroad, prosperity at home, sound finances, and freedom from controversial issues; he did nothing to upset either the Anglican churchman or the local Tory squire. Such policies were difficult to fight at first, especially when prosperity ensued. But gradually the opposition gained in strength over the years as each colleague Walpole alienated joined their ranks. Bolingbroke, whom Walpole had permitted to return from exile, stood at the center of opposition in the discredited Tory party. Joining the Jacobite opposition were two able, but lazy, Whig leaders, John Carteret and William Pulteney, who were bitter over their exclusion from Walpole's cabinet.

Reaction to the excise bill had increased the ranks of the opposition; those who changed sides protested Walpole's use of pensions and place to keep supporters or were jealous because they were not recipients of patronage. Before 1733 there was not a sufficient number of anti-Walpole Whigs to form a government; after 1733 Chesterfield, Bolton, Cobden and many other Whig peers were eager to provide an alternative ministry. They were joined by a group of young, aspiring Whigs, including William Pitt and George Grenville, who opposed the aging Walpole and his manipulative style of administration. Dubbed the "boy patriots" by the Prime Minister, they claimed to be champions of the people. This heterogeneous "out" group gravitated to the court of Frederick, prince of Wales, who quarreled publicly with his father and was anxious to assume the throne. The opposition finally found Walpole vulnerable on foreign policy.

WALPOLE AND FOREIGN AFFAIRS

The object of Walpole's foreign policy was simple: to keep England out of a Continental war because wars were expensive and their outcome uncertain. Through a network of alliances Walpole and Townshend strove to keep the Continent from breaking into two armed camps. By the first Treaty of Vienna, Spain and Austria resolved their differences which, in turn, brought on a bellicose attitude in England against Spain. Walpole believed that with the help of France (Treaty of Hanover, 1725) Spain and Austria could be separated; so with indifference to the anti-Spanish sentiment he concluded the Treaty of Seville with Spain in 1729. Two years later, the second Treaty of Vienna settled the major differences between Hanover and Austria. War was arrested but the alliances depended for their success on a friendly France.

In 1733 the French partnership was jeopardized by a Bourbon family compact made between the rulers of France and Spain even though France's involvement in the war over the Polish Succession (1733–1735) kept the covenant temporarily dormant. England remained neutral in spite of King George's interest in participating in the war; however, Walpole's peace policy was becoming his one vulnerable point, and his opponents quickly capitalized on the anti-Spanish sentiment of the country to condemn his pacifist policy as unpatriotic: declaring war was patriotic, peace was not. Hatred of Spain had increased in the thirties as grievances grew out of England's efforts to break the monopoly of Spanish trade in the Americas. British traders evaded the restrictions of the Asiento clause, and smuggling was heavy. In retaliation, Spanish patrols searched ships in Spanish waters and, on occasion, maltreated British seamen. Walpole attempted negotiations once more and secured a treaty even though the opposition and the nation wanted war. When the cabinet agreed, Walpole yielded to popular pressure and in 1739 England became involved in the War of Jenkins' Ear (named after an English mariner, Robert Jenkins, who claimed that his ship had been boarded and his ear torn off by the Spaniards. He told his tale and showed the withered ear to the House of Commons as evidence of Spanish atrocities. The tale captured the popular imagination). This Anglo-Spanish conflict became the prelude to the War of the Austrian Succession (1740).

Fall of Walpole. For three years Walpole conducted a war of which he strongly disapproved. During these years he missed the assistance at court of his ally, Queen Caroline, who had died in 1737, while in Parliament his supporters gradually deserted him so that the election of 1741 left him with only a slim majority. His closest colleagues, including Newcastle, announced their willingness to work in another ministry. Under these circumstances Walpole resigned in February 1742, and accepted a peerage; three years later he was dead.

WAR OF THE AUSTRIAN SUCCESSION

In 1740 Emperor Charles VI died, leaving his vast Hapsburg dominions to his only daughter, Maria Theresa. Her accession was confirmed by the Pragmatic Sanction signed by the other leading European states. It was repudiated immediately, however, by Frederick the Great, who came to the Prussian throne in 1740 and who wanted to annex the Austrian province of Silesia. The war, in part, was a struggle between the Hohenzollern and Hapsburg dynasties for domination of the smaller German states. It was also a resumption of the struggle between England and France in which national, commercial, and imperial considerations were interwoven, because neither nation had yet achieved a decisive colonial or commercial supremacy over the other.

The War in Europe. On the Continent, Great Britain, Hanover, Austria, and Holland opposed Prussia, Bavaria, France, and Spain. Britain aided the Austrians with money and dispatched an army to Holland. Frederick invaded and held Silesia. A British victory at Dettingen (1743)—where George II was the last English king to lead an army into battle—was offset by a French triumph at Fontenoy (1745).

The War Elsewhere. From 1744 to the conclusion of hostilities Great Britain and France were the chief combatants without either one winning a decisive engagement. The British were successful in several naval encounters; the French captured Madras from the British, and the English took Louisburg (Acadia) from the French. With commerce suffering and the war drifting on aimlessly, both sides agreed to peace.

Treaty of Aix-la-Chapelle. In 1748, the Peace of Aachen ended the War of the Austrian Succession. The treaty signed at Aix-la-Chapelle resulted in (1) a restoration of the *status quo ante bellum* except for Silesia, which Frederick kept; (2) confirmation of the Pragmatic Sanction and the election of Emperor Francis (Maria Theresa's husband); and (3) Spain's agreement to the continuation of British trade with the Americas according to the Treaty of Utrecht. In effect, the treaty became an armed truce, because it left Austria angry over the loss of Silesia, said nothing about the right of search which had led to English-Spanish hostilities, and only offered a breathing spell in the colonial rivalry between England and France until the struggle could be resumed in the Seven Years' War.

REBELLION OF 1745

Charles Edward Stuart, the son of the Old Pretender, landed in Scotland to press his father's claim. The Young Pretender commanded an army of loyal Highlanders who seized Edinburgh and defeated the British army at Prestonpans. The energetic and charming Bonnie Prince Charlie moved his Jacobite army as far south as Derby hoping for English support which never materialized. With the help of regiments from the Continental wars, the Duke of Cumberland pursued the Scots and finally destroyed their army at Culloden Moor in April 1746. Charles Edward escaped to the Continent, many of his supporters were executed, and the hereditary jurisdiction of the Highland chiefs was taken away. The "Forty-five" was the last serious effort to overthrow the Hanoverian dynasty and restore the Stuarts.

THE UNEASY PEACE, 1748–1754

The War of the Austrian Succession taught the British, and particularly William Pitt, that a commercial and colonial empire could only be won and held by naval supremacy. Although there was peace in Europe in 1748, the threatening aspects of Anglo-French rivalry in the colonies overshadowed this calm interlude.

Rivalry in India. The truce of 1748 did not extend to India where the rivalry between France and England was shifting from purely commercial competition to a political and military contest. By the eighteenth century the Portuguese and the Dutch were no longer serious competitors. The last of the great Mogul emperors had died in 1707, and, in the scramble for power that ensued among the Indian rulers, conditions were ripe for intrigue. By supporting rival Indian princes, the French and English expanded their influence beyond their respective "factory" posts. Joseph Dupleix, the energetic French governor of Pondicherry, supported the pro-French candidate to the throne of the Carnatic. The British backed Mohammed Ali and his claim to the throne. When war broke out between the French and the British, only the magnificent daring of Robert Clive, a clerk of the East India Company turned military captain, saved the Carnatic and Madras from yielding to the French siege. In 1754 Dupleix was recalled to France, and Clive and the English engaged French interests in the northeast, around Calcutta.

Rivalry in North America. English colonies were strung along the Atlantic seaboard but were not yet interested in a federation (Albany Conference, 1754), which would have utilized their superior manpower to halt French efforts to link the Mississippi and St. Lawrence territories by controlling the Ohio Valley. The French, who had erected forts in this area, defeated George Washington at Fort Necessity (1754). The English attempted to punish the French by sending General Braddock and English regiments against Fort Duquesne; however, the French and Indians ambushed the army and killed Braddock. In 1755 the British retaliated by deporting some ten thousand French Acadians (lamented in Henry Wadsworth Longfellow's 1847 poem *Evangeline: A Tale of Acadie*) from Nova Scotia and scattering them from Maine to Louisiana. Thus war had actually begun in India and America before it was formally declared in Europe.

Diplomatic Revolution. By 1754 the alliances of the War of the Austrian Succession had disintegrated. National self-interest and new jealousies, such as the dislike of the "Three Furies"—Czarina Elizabeth, Empress Maria Theresa, and Madame de Pompadour—for Frederick the Great brought about a new diplomatic alignment. When Britain and France declared war in May 1756, Britain and Prussia were allied against France, Austria, and Russia.

Domestic Politics

After Walpole's resignation, a "Broad-bottom Administration" led by Lord Wilmington, though dominated by Carteret, brought in some opposition Whigs and a few Tories. Carteret's venturesome conduct of the war and his inability to control the Commons united the opposition and forced his resignation in 1744. For the next ten years (1744–1754), Henry Pelham headed the cabinet ably assisted in the Lords by his brother, the Duke of Newcastle. The Duke in his painstaking, nervous manner skillfully held together a parliamentary majority for his brother as he had done for Walpole. When George II tried to get rid of Pelham in 1746, the cabinet resigned in a body, and since no alternative cabinet could manage Parliament, George was forced to take back the Pelhams on their terms, which included the admission of William Pitt to the ministry. In 1754 Henry Pelham died, and Newcastle took over the leadership of the cabinet just as Britain was entering the Seven Years' War.

WILLIAM PITT AND THE SEVEN YEARS' WAR

Although the Seven Years' War broke out over a European dispute, colonial and commercial rivalry dominated the worldwide areas of conflict. At first the French were successful everywhere, until the tide turned in favor of the British under the leadership of William Pitt. Convinced of his own and England's destiny, Pitt's genius steered the nation from peril and his war leadership masterminded a string of impressive victories. Pitt led England from defeat and despair to colonial and naval supremacy but he could not rescue his own political career, because he lacked the political base to hold on to power when the King and Parliament no longer needed him.

English Defeats   At the outset, the war was an unrelieved disaster for Great Britain. In India the British garrison at Calcutta fell to the Indian ruler of Bengal, and all but 23 of 146 prisoners suffocated or were trampled to death in a small cell, infamously termed the "Black Hole." In North America the brilliant French general Montcalm captured Fort Oswego in New York and tightened the encirclement of the English colonies. In the Mediterranean the British lost Minorca when Admiral Byng failed in his mission. The likelihood of a French invasion of England added to the despair when, on the Continent, Hanover fell to French troops. Although Britain's ally, Prussia, won some notable victories in 1756, in the next few years Frederick II could only keep at bay the huge armies of his enemies.

MINISTERIAL CRISIS

These misfortunes forced the resignation of the Newcastle ministry in 1756. King George reluctantly accepted a Devonshire-Pitt ministry, even though his old prejudices against Pitt—for his attacks on the King's partiality to Hanover—were as strong as ever. The new ministry labored under a political disadvantage because it could not win a parliamentary majority. When King George dismissed Pitt in 1757, he was immediately faced with a hostile nation demanding the return of the "Great Commoner." A political coalition between Newcastle and Pitt was arranged, and, for the next four years, Pitt led the Commons and directed the war, while Newcastle provided the parliamentary majority and raised money to fight a world war.

The Leadership of William Pitt

William Pitt, unlike most of his cabinet colleagues, was not born into a politically and socially established family. The Pitt fortune had been made by William's grandfather, "Diamond Pitt," the governor of Madras in India. Pitt entered Parliament through his grandfather's purchase of the rotten borough of Old Sarum. The young Pitt soon made himself known by his impassioned oratory and attacks on Walpole's government and the King's Hanoverian interests. In 1746 the Pelhams brought Pitt into the cabinet where he won a popular following and a reputation of incorruptibility by refusing to use his position as Paymaster of the Forces to indulge in the usual plundering of public funds. When Newcastle did not give him a major post, Pitt resigned in 1755 and assailed the government's failed war policies with telling effect. A year later Pitt was finally in the position he wanted—minister in charge of the war.

As war leader, Pitt increased the subsidies to Frederick II and strengthened the Hanoverian army in order to keep France occupied on the Continent. Meanwhile he pursued his primary aim—the crushing of France's navy and trade by the use of superior sea power. The British navy and army were reorganized, and young, able commanders, like James Wolfe and William Howe, were placed in charge of expeditions. A new enthusiasm and energy infected the whole nation.

Pitt was not a political operator, like Walpole, adroit in the handling of people. Pitt worked alone. He was proud, imperious, egotistical, with marvelous oratorical powers. His greatness was in his rare ability to translate his own patriotism and vision for Britain into the nation's belief in its destiny. Such a wide-ranging yet erratic genius, who disregarded normal political conventions, did not win lasting political support; nevertheless, he was the right leader to mobilize Britain in a time of crisis. Two hundred years later, in World War II, Winston Churchill would be called on by the nation in somewhat similar circumstances.

THE TIDE OF VICTORY

Almost immediately major English victories occurred on land and sea so that by 1759 Horace Walpole could write, "One is forced to ask every morning what victory there is, for fear of missing one."[*] In North America Louisburg, Frontenac, and Duquesne fell to the British. General James Wolfe commanded the British expedition in 1759 against Quebec and defeated the French under Montcalm on the Plains of Abraham, the decisive battle to determine the destiny of Canada. A year later Montreal and all Canada became British.

In India Clive won a major victory at Plassey. By 1761 the French fleet was driven away and Pondicherry surrendered, virtually ending the French empire in India. On the seas, the navy captured Guadeloupe in the West Indies and Dakar on the west coast of Africa. In 1759 Admiral Boscawen demolished one French fleet off Lagos, and a second fleet was decisively beaten at Quiberon Bay by Admiral Hawke. As a result the French troops at Le Havre preparing for an invasion of England were left stranded. Not since Marlborough's campaigns had the British been so overwhelmingly victorious over the French.

PITT'S DECLINE

Pitt and his supporters in London believed that trade was wealth (and power) and, therefore, that the war should continue until France was stripped of her commercial empire. However, opposition arguments grew louder after 1760. Some opponents lamented the increasing cost of the war, others were jealous of the prestige and power Pitt had acquired as war minister. Foremost among his critics was the newlycrowned King George III who disliked his grandfather's ministers, especially one who overshadowed the King in power. Consequently, King George supported the opponents of Pitt. When Pitt's cabinet colleagues refused to support him in a declaration of war against Spain in 1761, Pitt resigned; Newcastle followed. The cabinet, headed by Lord Bute, ended up declaring war against Spain anyhow after it became evident that Spain was about to declare war against Great Britain. In 1762 Havana and Manila were taken from Spain. In the same year Russia withdrew from the war, and King Frederick regained the Prussian territory which Russia and Austria had occupied. Lord Bute quickly began negotiations for peace with France.

---

[*] *Letters* (16 volumes; Oxford, 1903–1905), IV, p. 330.

PEACE OF PARIS, 1763

The peace settlement left Prussia one of the major powers in Europe. Pitt and London merchants condemned the peace because it failed to follow his grand design of utterly destroying the French trading empire. Even so, Great Britain retained most of its conquests including: (1) Canada, Cape Breton, and undisputed possession of the territory east of the Mississippi; (2) Florida, in exchange for the return of Havana to Spain; (3) all but four of the islands captured from France in the West Indies; (4) the slave port of Senegal in Africa; (5) the recovery of Minorca; and (6) several French trading factories in India.

The seven decades after the Glorious Revolution were largely dominated by four major wars in the extended duel for influence between Britain and France and in Britain's successful efforts to checkmate the domination of Europe by France.

The Seven Years' War and the Peace of Paris settled the century-old English and French rivalry for control of North America, paved the way for British rule in India, bankrupted France, and destroyed her navy. In 1763 Britain was the foremost naval and colonial power in the world.

Within Britain, in contrast to the previous century, the political and religious settlements were never seriously challenged. The practice of limited monarchy and the influence of the House of Commons and of the cabinet both advanced during the reigns of the first two Georges.

Selected Readings

Black, Jeremy. *British Foreign Policy in the Age of Walpole* (1985)
Colley, Linda. *The Defiance of Oligarchy: The Tory Party, 1714–1740* (1982)
Derry, John W. *William Pitt* (1963)
Lecky, W. E. H. *A History of Ireland in the Eighteenth Century* (1972)
Marshall, Dorothy. *Eighteenth Century England* (1974)
Namier, Lewis B. *The Structure of Politics at the Accession of George III* (1957)
Plumb, John. *Sir Robert Walpole: The Making of a Statesman* (1956)
_____*The First Four Georges* (1956)
Rogers, Pat. *The Augustan Vision* (1974)
Speck, W. A. *Stability and Strife, England 1714–1760* (1978)
Williams, Basil. *The Whig Supremacy: 1714–1760* (1962)

14

Colonial Policies and the American Revolution

W*ithin twenty years of the Peace of Paris which marked the apex of the First British Empire, Britain was once again in Paris relinquishing the crown jewels of its empire, the thirteen colonies. Britain blundered into war* *through failure to remodel her imperial policies to satisfy the growing independence of the American colonies.*

Colonial problems were further complicated by the political sparring which was occurring in Britain. The outcome was a constant turnover in cabinet membership and leadership and a lack of continuity or coherence in handling the colonies at a critical time.

At first, the declining influence of the Whigs was encouraged by George III since it permitted him more personal power. However, the loss of the colonies and the government's failed imperial policy ended the Lord North ministry and the King's attempt at personal government.

GEORGE III AND THE POLITICIANS

George III had a loftier and more active concept of kingship than his grandfather, George II, although he never aimed at more than constitutional conventions allowed him. Given the chronic bickering of the Whig factions, there seemed some justification for making cabinet ministers the "king's servants" in fact and for seeking to rule above political factions. During the 1760s the young King endured and contributed to cabinets in a state of flux, but his own vision of government was too narrow to offer a more effective system of administration. Certainly the Whig legend of George III as a domineering tyrant seeking to thwart Parliament by unconstitutional conduct is patently overdrawn. His system of personal government was unsatisfactory largely because it was unsuccessful and failed to deter political factions.

The New King

George III was the first of the Hanoverians to be English born. His youth, piety, and seriousness made him popular at first, until other traits of character became evident, such as his obstinateness and narrowmindedness. The King held exalted ideas of the royal prerogative and he was determined to exercise dormant royal powers, such as the right to dispense patronage. His stubborn sense of duty and recurring attacks of mental illness made cooperation between himself and his cabinets exceedingly difficult, and eventually his popularity faded. The loss of the American colonies was hardly his fault alone, but he received more blame on both sides of the Atlantic than he actually deserved.

GEORGE III AND THE WHIGS

By 1760, when George came to the throne, Whig rule was disintegrating. This was a development that George III encouraged since he disliked his grandfather's ministers and especially "indispensable" figures such as Pitt.

From 1760 to 1770 there were seven prime ministers and, as a result, an obvious lack of continuity and coherence of policy in handling the colonies at a most critical time.

Lord Bute, 1762–1763. After the resignation of Pitt in 1761, Lord Bute, the King's mentor, arranged the ouster of Newcastle and became Prime Minister. Bute led the cabinet until he had pushed the peace treaty through Parliament by exercising the patronage of the Crown to replace Newcastle's appointments. However, Parliament disliked Bute because he was a royal favorite and an outsider, a Scotsman. King George reluctantly accepted his resignation.

George Grenville, 1763–1765. George Grenville, Pitt's brother-in-law, obtained a parliamentary majority by allying himself with the Duke of Bedford and the Duke's unprincipled parliamentary clique, the Bloomsbury gang. Grenville was an efficient administrator though he was never liked by the King. In 1765 George III dismissed the cabinet to show his displeasure over the passage of a regency bill that would make his eldest son regent if the King became incapacitated.

Rockingham, 1765–1766. To rid himself of Grenville, the King turned to the "Old Whig" faction and the Marquess of Rockingham. The new cabinet repealed Grenville's Stamp Act, but Rockingham could not maintain Whig unity in Parliament, especially after Pitt refused to support the cabinet. Within a year Rockingham was forced to resign.

Pitt's Coalition Cabinet, 1766–1768. Pitt, who had accepted a peerage, was now known as the Earl of Chatham. His return to the cabinet was a miserable failure. Suffering with gout and from mental disorders, he was unable to coordinate policies or control his colleagues, each of whom went his own way. Pitt, who had been habitually snappish and arrogant, became increasingly uncooperative. yet nothing except a strong leadership could have held the diverse elements of the nonparty cabinet together. When Pitt failed to recover from a mental breakdown, the Duke of Grafton replaced him as Prime Minister.

The Grafton Government, 1768–1770. The cabinet remained divided under the Duke of Grafton's ineffectual leadership. Colonial policies continued to drift although a new cabinet post, Secretary of State for the Colonies, was created. By this time, not only the King but also many members of Parliament were restive with the revolving Whig ministries.

Lord North, 1770–1782. George III finally found a suitable manager of the House of Commons in Lord North. As Prime Minister, North used tact and royal patronage to hold a majority for twelve years, with the support of the Tories and the King's Friends not affiliated with Whig cliques. George found North and his cabinet acquiescent. Through patronage George won personal supporters in the Commons (the King's Friends) who looked to the King for pensions and jobs. Where possible North avoided controversial policies and gave stability to the administration. However, he was more successful as a peace minister than in waging war.

John Wilkes and Radicalism

King George resented the literary critics of his peace negotiations (1762–1763) with France and singled out John Wilkes, a member of Parliament, to serve as an object lesson. Prime Minister Grenville issued a general warrant for the arrest of everyone connected with the publication of the *North Briton*, issue No. 45, in which Wilkes had sharply assailed the ministerial policy reflected in the King's speech to Parliament. In the ensuing court squabble over the legality of general warrants, Wilkes claimed the privilege of immunity as a member of Parliament and fled to France after his release from prison. However, the House of Commons formally expelled Wilkes for his seditious libel and the cabinet outlawed him for refusing to stand trial.

Such highhanded action united the London mob and parliamentary opposition to make a constitutional test case out of the Wilkes affair and to defy the King. The "Wilkes and Liberty" agitation harassed the government until 1769, when Wilkes was ejected from the House for the fourth time after his fourth reelection by the independent-minded electorate of Middlesex County. Not until 1774 was he allowed to take his seat. Thus Wilkes, a disreputable drunkard, rather ironically became the hero of the mob and the rallying point for radicalism which would lead ultimately to parliamentary reform. English radicalism which stemmed from this episode learned well the techniques of mob psychology and pamphlet warfare. These methods were quickly copied by the American colonists when they, in turn, were coerced by the British government.

COLONIAL POLICIES, 1763–1775

With a brooding France and a restless Ireland as neighbors, along with radical agitation and cabinet instability at home, Britain was much too occupied to give serious attention to any new policy for the old and trusted thirteen colonies in America. The British government was unaware that the colonies were outgrowing their dependency on Britain for survival or success. During these years the British cabinet lacked any imaginative, or even coherent, policy; cabinet policy seemed to be largely one of doing too little too late. As a result Britain blundered into a deteriorating relationship with the American colonies during these years which was neither anticipated nor planned.

**Imperial
Problems in
1763**

The acquisition of huge new territories in the Seven Years' War demanded immediate attention with regard to boundaries and to relations with the French and Indian inhabitants. The recent war had also revealed the casual and inefficient administration of the empire and the need to coordinate imperial policy. Yet such coordination was impossible without a central authority with power to establish and administer colonial policy. With at least six separate central agencies, ranging from the Board of Trade to the Admiralty Courts, responsible for colonial administration, it was easy to avoid the burden of responsibility or to handle only one facet of a larger problem in the colonies.

ACTS OF TRADE

The mercantilist laws prohibiting trade between a colony and a foreign territory were never severely enforced by the British or their customs officials, until the Seven Years' War revealed how heavy traffic was between the colonies and the French West Indies. In 1760 when Pitt tried to enforce previous acts of trade, such as the Molasses Act (1733), colonial merchants in New York and Massachusetts stoutly resisted this invasion of their lucrative, though illicit, trade.

IMPERIAL DEFENSE

The separate colonies were usually unreliable in supplying either troops or supplies when the empire was at war or even when a neighboring colony was attacked by Indians. And yet some type of imperial defense was necessary to control the interior and to keep peace between the colonists and the Indians, especially after Chief Pontiac's uprising in 1763. The British determined that a standing army of ten thousand was necessary for colonial security, when the end of French encirclement made the colonists claim they no longer needed Redcoats for protection.

COLONIAL TAXATION

The expenses of the French and Indian War and the continued maintenance of troops in America drained the British Treasury. Because the colonists derived major benefit from British protection, they were asked to contribute one-third of the cost of the standing army; the British taxpayer would pay two-thirds and the entire cost of naval defense. The type of taxation attempted by English ministries to raise these revenues and the larger issue of their right to tax the colonists united the colonists for the first time in a common protest against the mother country's parliamentary practices.

Colonial Acts, 1763–1774

The thirteen taxation acts passed by Parliament in eleven years were protested by the Continental Congress in 1774. Apart from trade regulations, colonial laws had previously originated in the local assemblies. Now Parliament legislated directly for the colonists in an effort to raise revenue, a legal right which the British Parliament undoubtedly possessed, but which appeared arbitrary to the colonists who had enjoyed practical independence for so long. There was no tyrannical intent in the British policy. Most British statesmen, including such friends of the American colonies as Pitt and Burke, believed that Britain had the right to tax the colonies. The slogan of "no taxation without representation" made little constitutional sense to the English when only one out of ten adult males in England had the vote, but all were taxed. Furthermore, the British system of representation was based on interests, such as land, commerce, or the church, not on population; therefore, all subjects, wherever they resided, were considered represented in Parliament. The British Parliament and taxpayers disregarded the intensity of the colonial feeling; the American colonists refused to accept the supremacy of the British Parliament.

STAMP ACT, 1765

Grenville renewed the Sugar Act in 1764 while cutting the duty by one-half to reduce smuggling and raise revenue. The next year Parliament passed his Stamp Act which would raise £100,000 a year for imperial defense. The tax was already in operation in Britain, and although colonial opinion had been consulted before its passage, the act nevertheless provoked stormy protest in the colonies. A boycott of British goods ensued, and a Stamp Act Congress condemned the levying of an internal tax. The Rockingham government repealed the act in 1766 because it was unenforceable in the colonies and because British merchants protested the loss of trade. The cabinet accompanied the repeal with a declaratory act, however, asserting the right of Parliament to tax the colonies.

THE TOWNSHEND DUTIES

In 1767 Charles Townshend, chancellor of the exchequer, skirted the colonists' opposition to an internal tax and imposed instead duties on lead, glass, paint, paper, and tea imported into the colonies. Again the colonists resisted a revenue tax. In 1770 Lord North's cabinet repealed all duties except that on tea which was retained as an assertion of parliamentary authority. The Americans refrained from purchasing imported tea, and in 1773 a group in Boston dramatized their feeling against the tax by dumping cargoes of tea into the harbor. This act shifted England's vacillating policy of resoluteness and conciliation to one of coercion.

COERCIVE ACTS

Parliamentary legislation in 1774 closed the port of Boston, arranged for the quartering of British troops in America, strengthened royal authority in the administration of Massachusetts, and stipulated that persons accused of capital offenses could be removed from Massachusetts for trial.

The Quebec Act, which was included in the colonists' list of intolerable acts, gave Quebec control over the region of the Great Lakes and offered recognition to the Roman Catholic Church in Quebec. In reality, it was a pragmatic and liberal decree which Canadians hailed as the "Magna Charta" of their civil liberties. It not only allowed the French to keep their civil law and their religion, but it also recognized the futility of efforts to Anglicize and assimilate French Canada as a "fourteenth colony."

AMERICAN UNITY

A unique result of the friction between the colonies and Britain was the degree of cooperation achieved among the formerly disunited colonies. Committees of correspondence were set up in each colony which permitted an isolated grievance to become a common grievance, and well-organized protest societies, such as the Sons of Liberty, fanned the increasing discontent. The events of 1774 strengthened the influence of a vociferous radical element in the colonies and resulted in a Continental Congress in Philadelphia, which challenged the authority of Parliament and demanded the withdrawal of British troops. In 1775, when the British countered with a search of the Boston countryside, military conflict began at Lexington. In the following year, the Continental Congress declared the colonies independent and functioned as the *de facto* government for most of the war.

BRITISH DISUNITY

If friction with England unified the colonies, it had the opposite effect on English cabinets. All through this period cabinet opinion on colonial policy was confused and divided. Token gestures at colonial planning were made in 1768 with the creation of the post of Secretary of State for Colonial Affairs; however, the ministers appointed to the post were utterly incompetent. On numerous occasions the cabinet split on policy according to the parochial outlook of their personal feelings. Chatham and Burke suggested the possibility of self-governing dominion roles for the colonies, but not enough Englishmen had such sufficiently broad vision, and their ideas received no encouragement from the King. Lord North's and Edmund Burke's efforts at conciliation in 1775 were too late. By that time the majority of leaders on both sides of the Atlantic were ready to decide the issue by force of arms.

THE AMERICAN WAR OF INDEPENDENCE, 1775–1781

In November 1774, King George declared that England must either master the colonies or leave them totally to themselves. The English attempted the first alternative, but the outcome of the war forced them to accept the second. The conflict, which began as a civil war within the empire, with divided opinion on both sides of the Atlantic, changed its complexion after 1778 and became a world war with Britain fighting alone against an increasing number of European powers. In 1781 the British army surrendered to the French and American forces at Yorktown, and American independence was established.

The Military Ledger

The American colonists declared war on the most formidable naval and industrial power in the world: a nation with a professional army which controlled both flanks of the colonies (Canada and Florida), and which had the support of Indian allies. Furthermore, the Americans had no adequate central government to coordinate activities; they lacked money and supplies to sustain a long war, and had only an untrained and unreliable local militia. However, the British were fighting a war three thousand miles away from home under the incompetent leadership of the King's Friends. Often British military orders were obsolete by the time they reached America.

Neither side had brilliant military leaders, but George Washington, commander of the colonial army, grasped a critical factor: that if his army could only endure in the field, time was on their side, and the British would grow weary of trying to subdue such a vast country. Simply defeating the Americans in battle, as they often did, would not enable the British to occupy the interior without vastly larger forces.

Unlike previous wars, England had no ally on the Continent, and such isolation encouraged a European coalition against her. Certainly the value of the French alliance to the American cause can hardly be overestimated. Throughout the war, the Whigs, under the leadership of Pitt, Burke, Charles James Fox, Rockingham, and Shelbourne, denounced the war as the King's fault. In the colonies only a minority were active "patriots," and perhaps a quarter of the colonists—known as "Loyalists" or "Tories"—supported the British in the war. Thus the initial conflict was essentially a civil war within the empire rather than a clear clash between Britain and the thirteen colonies.

Conduct of the War

In the beginning of hostilities, English opinion was favorable toward the policy of coercion against the troublesome colonies. King George determined war policy but lacked the ability to plan effective strategy; nor was he aided by his administrators. Lord North was a reluctant and fretful Prime

Minister. Similarly, Lord Sandwich, in charge of the navy, and Lord George Germaine, Secretary of State for the Colonies, sadly lacked talent and the respect of the armed services. A naval blockade would have been the wisest policy to pursue because it would not have embittered the colonists as did the army of occupation; nor would it have required such a large number of troops. But blockades were slow in their effects, whereas a territorial war might produce a decisive battle. Besides, the seemingly insurmountable difficulties of the colonists made it unlikely that they could maintain any concerted opposition: colonial paper money was worthless; their army was weak; and colonists loyal to the King would probably aid the British in halting the rebellion. A land war was ordered regardless of the logistics of supplying armies in occupied territory.

Course of the War

The British pursued a half-hearted naval war which was inadequate in conception, while they attempted a territorial war in which they overextended themselves. After 1778 the Colonial war became a minor theater when France threatened to invade England.

CAMPAIGNS, 1775–1778

The colonists forced General Gage and the British army to evacuate Boston in the spring of 1776, though the American effort to conquer Canada that winter was repulsed. The following summer General Howe defeated Washington on Long Island and made New York the principal British base thereafter. Howe failed to pursue the retreating colonials, and Washington's dwindling army rallied during the winter with two victories, Trenton and Princeton. In 1777 British strategy planned to split the colonies by winning control of the Hudson River–Lake Champlain route. General Burgoyne and his army moved down from Canada to join Howe's forces moving up the Hudson. Instead, Howe captured Philadelphia and dallied in the city, leaving Burgoyne at the mercy of growing numbers of colonial forces who forced him to surrender at Saratoga in October. Saratoga became the turning point in the war because it demonstrated to France the prospect of the colonists defeating the British, and because it resulted in foreign alliances which were crucial to American success. The battle also revived American patriotism and turned English opinion against the war effort in the colonies.

WORLD WAR, 1778–1781

The French alliance in February 1778 furnished the colonists with the essential elements they lacked—sea power, money, munitions, and a professional army. The war took on a different character when the British Isles became vulnerable to attack as well as the widely scattered British empire. Spain joined France in 1779, and Holland entered the war against England the following year. In 1780 the League of Armed Neutrality (led by Russia and including Sweden, Denmark, and later Holland and Prussia) was organized to resist the British claim of the right of search of neutral vessels on the high seas.

For once England failed to enjoy naval superiority. The French had built up a new navy which, when allied with the Spanish, outnumbered the British fleet. The British lost Minorca, most of Florida, two islands in the West Indies, posts on the African coast, and barely withstood a massive siege of Gibraltar. In 1779 the two Bourbon fleets entered the Channel and were prevented only by technical errors from landing forty thousand Frenchmen on England's shores. The threat of invasion kept seventy thousand troops guarding England, leaving few reinforcements for the British army in the colonies.

In America Henry Clinton replaced Howe as commander, and after Saratoga the land war moved to the southern colonies. Clinton and Cornwallis won most of the battles but could not control the interior. In the summer of 1781, Lord Cornwallis moved from the Carolinas to Yorktown, Virginia, where supplies could reach him by sea. This avenue of relief was cut off in September when the French navy under Admiral de Grasse won the crucial Battle of Chesapeake Bay. This forced Cornwallis to surrender six weeks later to a combined French and American army more than twice the size of the British forces. The surrender virtually assured the independence of the United States.

POLITICS AND THE PEACE SETTLEMENT

Defeat abroad forced the downfall of the personal rule of George III. When the Whigs returned to office, they quarreled with the King and among themselves, thereby blunting the prospects of parliamentary reform which growing discontent within and without Parliament was now demanding. In Paris, Whig negotiators offered generous terms to the Americans in order to restore friendly trade relations between the two countries and to reduce the influence of France on the new nation.

Fall of the King's Friends

The British defeat at Yorktown brought about the disintegration of Lord North's administration. Early in 1782 the opposition carried a motion to halt the war in America. Lord North recognized that the King's imperial policy had failed and that royal manipulation of Parliament had been repudiated. King George reluctantly accepted North's resignation when he, too, realized that the whole system of government by which North maintained influence in Parliament was in disrepute. For the next two years political instability plagued the country and the King. The King had to find a new Prime Minister not too closely associated with the failed war effort. The coalitions that resulted had little in common, either in philosophy or in policy.

Agitation for Reform

The American war accelerated the demand for reform of the corrupt parliamentary system. In 1776 John Wilkes had introduced into the Commons a comprehensive measure for parliamentary reform. In the same year Adam Smith and Jeremy Bentham published arguments indicting the economic and institutional premises of English life. The Whigs, in political opposition during the war, seized on reform to blame the failed war on the Tories and the King; they introduced bills to reduce the influence and patronage of the King. In 1780 the Commons adopted John Dunning's motion that "the influence of the Crown has increased, is increasing, and ought to be diminished." The Gordon riots that terrorized London for five days in 1780 were, on the surface, a manifestation of Protestant animosity to the proposed reduction of penal laws against Catholics. However, the savage rioting mirrored a deep discontent in the working classes and indicated to many members the need for constitutional reform rather than harsh repression.

In public meetings in towns across England petitions for reform were sent to Parliament. The Rockingham Whigs translated this reform agitation into parliamentary legislation in a cautious effort to reduce royal patronage and to make Parliament more representative of the nation. Edmund Burke and Charles James Fox were two of the more eloquent orators for reform. When the Rockingham Whigs came to power in 1782, they passed two Economical Reform Bills which reorganized the royal household, limited royal influence by barring government contractors from sitting in Parliament, and disenfranchised a large number of government officials. The bill for parliamentary reapportionment failed to win a favorable vote; nevertheless, the influence of the King had been checked, and a movement for reform was under way.

WHIG FACTIONALISM

Complying with George III's request, Rockingham formed a Whig cabinet after Lord North resigned. Two powerful colleagues in his cabinet, the Earl of Shelbourne and Charles James Fox, disliked each other and soon quarreled openly, splitting the Whigs into two jealous factions. Lord Shelbourne was a friend of Adam Smith, Jeremy Bentham, and Benjamin Franklin, and a brilliant, shrewd critic of Britain's economic and political institutions; he was the heir to Chatham (Pitt the Elder) and won the support of Pitt's son (the Younger).

His rival, Charles James Fox, was the most influential and eloquent supporter of political liberty in the House of Commons. Fox's great-hearted and engaging disposition won him a loyal following in spite of his gambling habits and notorious private life. The dispute between these two Whig leaders came to a head over their respective authority in controlling peace negotiations in Paris with France and the colonies. Fox refused to serve in Shelbourne's ministry upon the death of Rockingham in 1782. Instead he joined with his old enemy North in an effort to defeat the peace negotiations which Shelbourne had completed.

Peace Negotiations

A British naval victory in the West Indies (Battle of the Saints) under Admiral Rodney and the successful defense of Gibraltar against the French-Spanish siege somewhat salvaged Britain's position in the peace negotiations with its European enemies. American independence was ceded at the outset. The British representatives encouraged the American peace commissioners, Benjamin Franklin, John Jay, and John Adams, to disregard the instructions of Congress and negotiate a separate peace with Britain rather than take the advice of France as they had been ordered. The French were furious at the generous British terms offered to the Americans; the British were delighted with the discord developing among their opponents.

TREATIES OF VERSAILLES AND PARIS, SEPTEMBER 1783

In the Treaty of Versailles signed with France and Spain, France recovered the islands of St. Pierre and Miquelon off the coast of Newfoundland, won several trading posts in Africa, and regained its trading posts in India. Spain secured Florida and Minorca, in return for the surrender of the British Bahamas. By the Treaty of Paris, the United States acquired all territory east of the Mississippi and south of the Great Lakes, fishing rights off Newfoundland, and free navigation on the Mississippi. In return, the American Congress recommended that the states restore confiscated Loyalist property; however, the states failed to do this, and the mistreatment of Loyalists continued. Over fifty thousand fled, the majority migrating to Canada.

END OF THE FIRST BRITISH EMPIRE

The loss of the American colonies marked the end of the First British Empire. The loss of most of the English settlements left an empire which with the exception of Canada was largely tropical. One direct result of the American revolution was the settlement of Australia to replace Georgia as a penal colony. Another result was Lord North's Renunciation Act of 1778 which set up a policy, learned too late for the thirteen colonies, of never again taxing a colony for imperial revenue. The American revolt also reshaped Britain's attitude toward its colonies of settlement; if colonies were like children, then the mission of the parent was to lead them toward political maturity, not to expect an indefinite period of dependency.

IRISH CONDITIONS

The American Revolution had immediate repercussions in Ireland. The Irish were struggling for their rights against the restrictions of Poynings's Law which since the reign of Henry VII had prevented a free and equal Irish Parliament. When British troops were withdrawn from Ireland in 1778 to fight in America, regiments of largely Irish Protestant volunteers were raised and encamped outside Dublin, while a convention under the Earl of Charlemont encouraged the Irish Parliament to pass measures granting themselves legislative independence. Under the Rockingham ministry in 1782 Henry Grattan succeeded in procuring the repeal of Poynings's Law. The following year Fox and North passed the Renunciation Act which made the Irish legislature and judiciary independent of the British Parliament; only the Executive was to remain tied to it. A separate and elected Irish government seemed possible in Ireland had not the French Revolution intervened to frustrate such prospects.

After reaching the apex of power in its colonial and commercial empire in 1763 and becoming the world's number-one sea power, Great Britain saw the loss of its "old and trustworthy" thirteen colonies within the next two decades. The First British Empire ended with the Peace of Paris in 1783.

The transplanted overseas settlements were growing up and in need of more autonomy than British colonial policy and practices permitted. Britain learned a lesson from the loss of the thirteen colonies that would be wisely applied to the rest of its settlement empire. As a result these colonies will evolve peacefully to self-government and continue by choice in the British Commonwealth.

George III failed to find strong or successful leadership for his cabinet until after the Peace of Paris was signed in 1783 and William Pitt the Younger became Prime Minister. The two decades of 1763–1783 saw growing pressure for parliamentary reform and the promise of it until the French Revolution intervened.

Selected Readings

Alden, John Richard. *American Revolution* (1954)
Brooke, John. *King George III* (1972)
Derry, John. *English Politics and the American Revolution* (1976)
Harlow, Vincent T. *The Founding of the Second British Empire, 1763–1793* (1952)
Hill, B.W. *British Parliamentary Parties, 1742–1832* (1985)
Mackesy, Piers. *The War for America, 1775–1783* (1964)
Namier, Lewis. *England in the Age of the American Revolution* (1961)
Pares, Richard. *King George III and the Politicians* (1953)
Parkman, Francis. *Montcalm and Wolfe* (1895)
Rudé, George. *Wilkes and Liberty* (1962)
Thomas, P. D. G. *Lord North* (1976)

15

Britain vs. France: The Era of the French Revolution and the Napoleonic Wars

1783 William Pitt the Younger becomes Prime Minister

1784 India Act establishes political and commercial arrangement in British India until 1858

1788 First settlement of Australia by British

1789 Declaration of the Rights of Man by the French National Assembly

1793 Start of the wars with revolutionary and Napoleonic France

1800 Act of Union abolishes Irish Parliament; representation of Ireland begins in the British Parliament

1805 Admiral Nelson defeats the combined French and Spanish fleets at Trafalgar

1807 Slave trade abolished by Parliament

1812 Napoleon invades Russia

United States declares war on Britain, seeking to annex Canada

1815 Peace Settlement in Europe worked out by the members of the Coalition and France at the Congress of Vienna

The telescoping of three revolutions—the American, the French, and Industrial—into a few decades of time demanded adjustments in the structure of English society and government. The landed aristocracy and unrepresentative Parliament could no longer absorb these massive changes, but the movement for reform was diverted by a more immediate crisis, the menace of revolutionary France.

When France threatened Britain in its most sensitive area—control of the Low Countries and the Channel by an unfriendly power—Britain went to war and remained at war for over twenty years. The war with France dominated all domestic issues.

In Britain the fear of French radicalism turned reform into reaction. It also turned Pitt from a peace-loving Prime Minister bent on progressive reform into a war leader, who used sea power to limit Napoleon's grandiose designs and who, with Castlereagh, designed a strategy for a successful peace settlement.

WILLIAM PITT THE YOUNGER

William Pitt, who knew the art of political management far better than his father, dominated the political scene from 1783 until his death in 1806. Unlike his great political opponent, Charles James Fox, Pitt was a pragmatist who moved with the times and became the honored symbol of Britain's traditions and virtues during the war with France. Ambitious, astute, often aloof, he understood and used political channels to win and keep a parliamentary majority, having first assured himself of King George's support. He also understood the changes occurring in commerce and supported Adam Smith's ideas on free trade. Pitt at the age of twenty-five received the prime ministership, because he was acceptable to George III, and because he had the skill of holding the support of the King and winning parliamentary support.

The Problems of Britain in 1783

Britain had been humiliated by defeat in the American War of Independence and in 1783 found itself without European allies. Under the stresses of defeat and incompetence, George III's political system and support had collapsed and no stable ministry was likely as rival political factions wrangled for office.

ECONOMIC DISLOCATION

In 1775 Britain was already in the midst of fundamental industrial changes which had begun two centuries earlier with the enclosure (fencing in) of land. Between 1700 and 1760 over three million more acres were enclosed. In manufactures, the substitution of horsepower for manpower and a series of mechanical inventions (see chapter 16) moved industry from the home to the factory. These developments introduced a new influential class of industrial capitalists who resented being excluded from political power. Adam Smith's doctrine of unrestricted production, free trade, and freedom from governmental regulations (*Wealth of Nations*, 1776) coincided with the expanding capitalistic economy, but was contrary to the mercantilist theory and the legislation in operation.

THE EAST INDIA COMPANY

The conquests of Robert Clive in the Seven Years' War had altered the East India Company from a trading post to a private imperial empire. The transformation brought on strong criticism from Edmund Burke and the Whigs, because the company governed Bengal without any legal responsibility for its actions. Impressive fortunes were made by company officials who levied local taxes through Indian puppets. As corruption and lawlessness increased, the House of Commons investigated the company. Lord North modified the exercise of power with the Regulating Act of 1773, which, nevertheless, left the company with its monopoly. Warren Hastings, the first governor under the Regulating Act, saved, and then extended, the company's position in a prolonged war with native potentates who were backed by the French. Hastings won over his enemies in the field, on his council, and in England, but his methods were often arbitrary and his empire building was expensive and involved major administrative expansion. When Hastings was called home to face impeachment proceedings, the testimony against him forced Parliament to recognize that a drastic alteration in the government of India was essential if Britain was intent on remaining there.

THE IRISH PROBLEM

The Renunciation Act of 1783 had provided the Irish Parliament with legislative independence, but no further attempts were made to eliminate the centuries of discrimination and plunder which the conquering English had inflicted upon the Irish. Henry Grattan in Ireland and Pitt in England realized that basic problems, such as absentee landlordship, religious restrictions, and economic discrimination, needed to be solved or the Irish Parliament would be little more than an agency of the English administration which could be bribed.

Prime Minister Pitt

The defeat of Shelbourne in the Commons in 1783 following the passage of the peace treaties with France and the United States brought a short-lived Portland-Fox-North ministry that the King did his best to oust. He considered North a traitor after he resigned in 1782 and Fox, whose debauchery was a bad influence on the Prince of Wales, the most dangerous of the Whig leaders. The King successfully exerted personal influence in the House of Lords to block Fox's East India bill. He used the bill's defeat as the excuse to dismiss the ministry and to invite young William Pitt to become Prime Minister.

Pitt was masterful in the art of administration and parliamentary maneuvering. Accepting office in 1783 without a majority in the Commons, he showed the invulnerability of the King's favor by surviving weekly defeats in the Commons at the hands of Fox while whittling away at the Fox-North majority. When the opposition was reduced to a majority of only one, Parliament was dissolved and an election called. Pitt had won the respect of politicians as well as popular sympathy by this remarkable performance in weakening Fox's position in the Commons. In the election of 1784 he was helped by his alliance with William Wilberforce and the financial resources of the Treasury to ensure an electoral victory.

The election gave Pitt a large majority at the expense of his opponents. He carefully cultivated the support of the City of London with honors and titles and favorable commercial policies. In the House of Lords he swamped the Whig majority by having the King create scores of new peers. This marked the end of Whig supremacy and the beginning of a new political alignment which would become increasingly Tory in principle and in personnel. Although the King preferred Pitt to anybody else, he never controlled him as he had North. Under Pitt the powers of the prime ministership were to be expanded.

OPPOSITION OF FOX

The decimated Whig opposition under Fox's inspired but erratic leadership had difficulty opposing Pitt's successful reform of the national economy and use of patronage. The French Revolution frightened many Whigs, including Edmund Burke, into leaving Fox's liberal camp and joining Pitt. Only in the years 1787–1788 was Pitt's supremacy threatened when the temporary insanity of George III made a regency appear necessary. Pitt stalled as long as possible in transferring power to the Prince of Wales, because he knew that the Prince, as Regent, would immediately call upon Fox to form a ministry. When the King suddenly regained his sanity, the threat was removed.

PITT'S INDIA ACT

After the Lords defeated Fox's East India bill, Pitt offered an acceptable substitute. In 1784 his India Act established a dual control whereby the government accepted responsibility for political and civil affairs, while the company retained control of commerce and patronage. A Board of Control, headed by a secretary of state, assumed responsibility for Indian administration and had the power to remove officials appointed by the company. This system operated until 1858 and, with the governorships of Charles Cornwallis and Richard Wellesley, efficient government came to India, but at the expense of a moral arrogance which increasingly isolated the ruling British from the Indians and their culture.

FINANCIAL REFORMS

Pitt was compelled to reorganize Britain's public finances in his budgets of 1784–1787 since the American war had almost doubled the national debt and jeopardized the credit of the government. The complicated system of collecting taxes was simplified, and taxes were lowered to provide new revenue and eventually a budgetary surplus. Smuggling decreased because lower tariffs no longer made it highly profitable. Pitt also created a Sinking Fund (1786), the interest on which was to be used to pay off the national debt. In three years Pitt had stabilized the country for George III, as Walpole had done for George I. He encouraged as much free trade as the mercantilist interests in England would permit and in 1786 negotiated a reciprocity treaty with France which permitted the mutual reduction of duties on specified imports.

FURTHER REFORM ATTEMPTS

Throughout the 1780s Pitt worked for reform in several areas, pressing his proposals where politically prudent and accepting defeat of other measures with equanimity. Only the fear of France made him quietly drop reform and become a protector of the status quo. In 1785 Pitt acknowledged his debt to the reformers by introducing a bill for parliamentary redistribution which would have abolished thirty-five rotten boroughs. The bill was defeated, and Pitt did not risk his political majority in pursuing it further. His efforts to repeal the religious disabilities against Catholics and Dissenters were no more successful than his proposals for parliamentary reform.

Pitt next worked on bills for the abolition of the slave trade. The decision handed down in the Somerset case of 1772 freed slaves in Britain and encouraged reformers in their efforts to ameliorate the horrors of slave trading in the empire. (The question of the legality of slavery in Great Britain and Ireland was decided in the Somerset case by Lord Mansfield's judgment that "as soon as a slave set his foot on the soil of the British islands, he became free.") In 1787 Sierra Leone, West Africa, was established as a haven for emancipated slaves. Pitt's close friend William Wilberforce led the agitation in the House of Commons against the slave trade. At first they met with little success, but did not give up their efforts. In 1807, the year after Pitt's death, the slave trade was abolished by Parliament—the only reform to occur in the war years.

Pitt sought to relieve the worst of the commercial disabilities in Ireland by permitting free trade between Ireland and the colonies in return for Irish revenue to support the navy. The Irish Parliament approved, but commercial interests in England spurned Pitt's efforts and defeated the measure. The Irish realized that they could only win concessions when Britain was threatened by foreign invasion.

COLONIAL POLICIES

Over forty thousand Loyalists fled the United States to British North America to escape harassment and to continue their loyalty to the Crown. Some ten thousand arrived in Upper Canada (present-day Ontario), and quickly became restive over the political and religious arrangements of the Quebec Act. In 1791 Quebec was divided into Upper and Lower Canada with each province having religious freedom, its own lieutenant governor, a nominated upper house, and a representative assembly. Thus the Loyalists introduced the English system of government to Canada and to the French Canadians.

While Canada was being reorganized, Australia was being settled. Captain Cook had charted the land in 1769, and in 1788 the first settlement, largely convicts, founded Sydney. Transportation to Australia was preferable to an English prison, and until the year of the Great Reform Bill (1832), the practice was accepted with little question; afterward it was condemned on both humanitarian and utilitarian grounds. All told 166,000 penal offenders were transported to Australia.

Foreign Affairs

Pitt had hoped for a period of peace to carry on his administrative reforms, because domestic affairs in the eighties interested him more than foreign affairs. Nevertheless, he proceeded to end England's diplomatic isolation by a Triple Alliance (1788) with Holland and Prussia which sought to halt the extension of French influence in the Netherlands. Pitt then reversed England's traditional policy of friendship to Russia by using the Triple Alliance to protest Russia's designs in the Near East. He urged Parliament to use force to keep Russia from devouring more Turkish territory, but Parliament refused to back him.

The French Revolution and its implications for Britain now loomed large. At first Pitt failed to recognize the strength of the revolutionary movement or to believe it could last long. As late as 1792, Pitt was predicting fifteen years of peace. Then France advanced into the Low Countries and threatened the English Channel; the next year (1793) Britain was at war.

WAR WITH FRANCE

Pitt and most Europeans underestimated the strength and appeal of the French revolutionary movement. After the force of revolutionary nationalism and the appeal of democratic slogans were graphically observed, Britain and Europe were intent not only on defeating France but the revolution as well. Warfare radically changed as the national spirit of France made the whole nation part of the war effort, with citizen armies routing the professional armies of the old regimes. Britain relied on its navy and subsidies to Continental allies to stave off defeat. Its colonial and industrial resources, sea power, and five coalitions created by Britain served in the end to checkmate Napoleon. If the Battle of Waterloo left Britain as the foremost power in the world, it also left the nation with a host of internal problems which the war had not solved but only set aside.

Revolutionary France

From 1789 to 1791 the National Assembly in France successfully abolished ancient abuses and privileges and expressed its aspirations in the eloquent Declaration of the Rights of Man. The radical changes that were decreed, particularly in the monarchy and in the church, split France into two groups—one accepting, the other rejecting, the revolution. The active revolutionists gained the ascendancy, and the ensuing war against Austria and Prussia consolidated their position. Louis XVI tried to flee the country while the demoralized French army, shorn of most of its officers who were loyal to the old regime, retreated before the Austrian-Prussian armies. The invading forces were halted at Valmy by the French revolutionary army on September 20, 1792. By that time the Jacobin clubs—radical pressure groups led by George Jacques Danton and Maximilian Robespierre, who rejected the monarchy in favor of a republic—controlled Paris.

The "September Massacres" of people suspected of hostility to the revolution mirrored the breakdown of central authority. The National Convention (1792) which replaced the Assembly abolished the monarchy and declared France a republic. The next year Louis XVI was executed, and a Reign of Terror, introduced by the Committee for Public Safety, purged the nation of political opponents. The revolutionary government also put the national economy on a war footing and began a mass conscription. As the French Republican army began a crusade to liberate the Continent, it spread fear and hatred throughout Europe. Republican France was more expansionistic and successful than the monarchy it had overthrown. It defied treaties and annexed Savoy and Belgium.

Reception of the Revolution in England

English public opinion was sympathetic to the French Revolution, likening it to the Glorious Revolution of 1688. Charles James Fox, Charles Grey, and especially William Wordsworth, the Romantic poet, were enthusiastic about the upheaval in France. Stimulated by the revolution, various societies for the reform of Parliament were revived and new ones established, such as the Society of the Friends of the People and the London Corresponding Society. The latter was founded in 1792 by Thomas Hardy to promote universal suffrage (voting rights) among working-class people.

As the excesses of the revolution dampened this early enthusiasm and as France attempted to stir up revolution beyond its borders, the reformers in Britain became suspect as being only one step away from becoming revolutionaries. This changing mood was witnessed in Burke's pamphlet, *Reflections on the Revolution in France*. His lucid warning that the ideas of the French Revolution, if not checked, would destroy overnight the values and order of Western society won an immediate response. Burke's viewpoint appealed to conservatives who were frightened by Thomas Paine's *The Rights of Man*, which advocated the overthrow of monarchical government. Burke and a majority of conservative Whigs joined Pitt, leaving Fox with a small and ineffectual opposition. Pitt, hitherto a reformer, now turned reactionary and repressed all reforms, fearful they would open the door to revolution.

The First Coalition, 1792–1797

The first years of the war were full of mistakes and failures because Pitt, and most of the leaders in Europe, underestimated the strength of revolutionary France mobilized for total war. When war was declared on February 1, 1793, Pitt at once lined up the First Coalition, which eventually consisted of Austria, Prussia, Great Britain, Sardinia, Spain, Portugal, Naples, and the Papal States. Pitt hoped to imitate his father's policy of subsidizing Continental powers and using sea power to combat France's commercial empire. However, the members of the Coalition were jealous of each other and did little but preserve their respective interests.

The allied powers were at first successful when the French suffered defeat in the Netherlands and desertion by its generals. Pitt agreed to using British troops because victory seemed imminent. Henry Dundas, the incompetent secretary of war, sent British troops to various theaters in an attempt to sever French colonies. In one theater alone, the British lost 40,000 troops in their efforts to subdue the French sugar islands in the West Indies.

Under the generalship of Carnot a new French conscript army was organized into a superior fighting force. The allies were severely defeated and British troops were routed from Holland. By 1795 Holland was overrun, and after Prussia and Spain withdrew, only Austria, Russia, and Sardinia remained in the Coalition. Napoleon Bonaparte, the commander of the French armies on the Italian front, demonstrated his military genius with superb tactics against the Austrians and Sardinians. By 1797 Britain stood alone, its allies beaten by France.

Britain in 1797

Britain's fortunes reached their lowest ebb in 1797. Only a violent storm prevented the French army from landing in Ireland. At Spithead and the Nore two naval mutinies over living conditions, food, and the brutal treatment of sailors lowered British morale, but forced redress of grievances. Within the country, the Bank of England suspended cash payments to stop a run on the bank, food became scarce, and Pitt's peace overtures to France were rebuffed. Before the year was out, however, Britain restored its naval supremacy by two major victories: at Cape St. Vincent the English Mediterranean fleet under the command of Jervis and Nelson routed a Franco-Spanish fleet; at Camperdown the North Sea fleet under Admiral Duncan defeated the Dutch navy.

British Victory and the Second Coalition

Because the two naval disasters had prevented France from invading England, Napoleon led a French army against England's commercial empire in the Mediterranean by invading Egypt in 1798 and marching eastward. Admiral Nelson sighted the French supply ships at anchor in Abukir Bay and in a brilliant maneuver (Battle of the Nile) sank the fleet. At Acre (in modern-day Israel), British sailors checked the French army and forced Napoleon to give up his eastern plan. Abandoning his army, Napoleon slipped back to France. There, after being feted as a national hero, he easily unseated the corrupt and incompetent Directory and installed himself as First Consul and virtual dictator. Napoleon's consulate marked the end of the revolutionary decade in France. His immediate plans were to consolidate France's reforms, use the nation as the instrument of his ambition to rule Europe, and eventually become emperor.

To accomplish his aims, Napoleon would have to defeat the Second Coalition (Great Britain, Russia, Austria, Turkey, Naples, and Portugal), which Pitt had arranged after Britain's naval successes in the Mediterranean. While Napoleon was carrying out his campaign in Egypt, the allied forces, rearmed through subsidies obtained by Pitt's new income tax, had recaptured northern Italy. In 1800 Napoleon invaded Italy and quickly crushed the Austrians at Marengo. Another French army defeated a second Austrian army at Hohenlinden. The double disaster forced Austria out of the war. Russia had already dropped out and turned against England by heading the League of Armed Neutrality of Northern Powers (Russia, Prussia, Sweden, and Denmark) to halt England's search of neutral ships for contraband. Lord Nelson, in a finely calculated risk, destroyed the powerful Danish fleet at Copenhagen (1801) and sailed into the Baltic to meet the Russians. Meanwhile Czar Paul had been murdered and the new Czar, Alexander I, wanted peace. The League disintegrated, and the Baltic and the Mediterranean remained open to British ships.

TREATY OF AMIENS, 1802

The war ended in a stalemate with France supreme on land and England supreme on the seas, and both countries agreeing to peace. The Treaty of Amiens: (1) formally recognized the new French government; (2) required Britain to withdraw from Malta and restore all conquests except Ceylon and Trinidad; and (3) demanded that France recognize Turkish claims to Egypt and withdraw from Rome and Naples. The treaty was unduly favorable to France since England gave up far more territory, whereas large areas of Europe remained closed to British commerce. Napoleon regarded the peace as only a breather because his ambitions were not yet satisfied. He acquired Louisiana from Spain, reconquered San Domingo, accelerated his program of naval construction, and by act and utterance seemed to have designs on British possessions. The peace was of short duration.

DOMESTIC REPRESSION

Even before war was declared with France in 1793, the British government had turned against all political reformers, lumping them in the same bracket as revolutionaries. The repression grew heavier as the war dragged on, and for over a quarter of a century all effective oppositon to the government was considered seditious. In 1792 a proclamation was issued against all seditious writings; the authors of such works would be subject to prosecution. This was followed by an Aliens Act, a Seditious Meetings Act, a Treasonable Practices Act, and the Combination Acts. Their cumulative effect prevented public meetings without the approval of a magistrate, broadened treason to include writing and speaking as well as acting against the government, and made trade unions illegal. The Habeas Corpus Act was suspended in 1794 and, except for Fox and a dwindling handful of faithful supporters, all opposition to the government was muzzled.

The French Revolution and Ireland

The French Revolution gave the Irish the opportunity to take advantage of England's extremity, just as the American Revolution had helped their cause a generation earlier. The successful American Revolution, reinforced by the infiltration of radical ideas from France, had encouraged Irish rebellion. Some reforms had recently been granted: Irish Protestants no longer had to submit to the Test Act, and Irish Catholics could lease land for ninety-nine years. However, acts of the Irish Parliament were still subject to veto by the cabinet of Westminster, and the religious and economic grievances remained.

Wolfe Tone, a Belfast lawyer, led the independence movement with his Society of United Irishmen (1791). Other groups followed and several reforms were secured, one of which was an extension of the franchise to Irish Catholics. When Tone asked the French for aid, they responded by attempting to send several expeditions. In 1798 a rebellion broke out in Ireland which the British quickly and cruelly suppressed. These developments convinced Pitt that a new political arrangement for Ireland was imperative.

ACT OF UNION, 1800

Only by a legislative union, like the agreement between the Scotch and English Parliaments of 1707, could the British cabinet end the independence of the Irish Parliament. However, the Irish legislature refused to dissolve itself until British gold and peerages were distributed freely and the implicit promise of Catholic emancipation was given. Both Parliaments passed the Act of Union in 1800. Ireland was henceforth represented by thirty-two peers in the House of Lords and one hundred members in the House of Commons. The act also allowed free trade between the two countries, provided for the continuance of the Church of Ireland (Anglican), and abolished the Irish Parliament. To make the union effective and to pacify Ireland, Pitt proceeded with a bill for Catholic emancipation which George III adamantly refused to consider. Because Pitt could not continue without the King's approval, he resigned in 1801, and Viscount Addington became Prime Minister. Thus Britain was deprived of its leading statesman, and Ireland of its promised relief.

Renewal of the War

The interval of peace appeared to the British government only to be helping Napoleon prepare for further expansion; therefore Britain declared war in 1803 after just one year of peace. Napoleon made the invasion of England his primary objective, and barges were built to ferry the French army encamped at Boulogne. In the fervor and anxiety of defending the island Addington proved ineffectual, and the nation demanded the return of Pitt. In 1804 Pitt came back to office. Immediately he strengthened British sea power and resurrected another coalition on the Continent.

To safely transport his troops to England, Napoleon had to break British control of the Channel. In October 1805 the combined French and Spanish fleets under Admiral Villeneuve were engaged by Nelson at Cape Trafalgar. Although the British fleet was outnumbered, Nelson's strategy—using a double row of ships to penetrate the enemy line at two places—annihilated the enemy fleets in the last major battle fought under sail. Nelson was killed in the engagement, but his victory kept control of the seas for Britain.

The Third Coalition

Using subsidies and diplomacy, Pitt raised a Third Coalition (Great Britain, Russia, Austria, Sweden, and later Prussia) in 1805 to fight Napoleon on land; however, it was no more a match for Napoleon than the previous coalitions. Even before the naval defeat at Trafalgar, Napoleon had turned eastward and defeated the Austrians at Ulm, and in December 1805, Austria was forced out of the war after a crushing defeat at Austerlitz. Prussia entered the war but quickly accepted a humiliating peace after being defeated at Jena in October 1806. After Russia suffered two defeats, Czar Alexander came to terms with Napoleon at Tilsit (1807).

The Russian Emperor allied himself with Napoleon, who was now Emperor of France, and both agreed that Russian influence would be allowed to expand eastward provided that the Czar recognized Napoleon's control of central Europe and supported a boycott on British commerce. After Tilsit Napoleon reached the apex of his power and for the next five years dominated Continental Europe. Only Britain's island location and naval supremacy saved it from the invincible French army.

DEATH OF PITT, 1806

On January 2, 1806, only weeks after the Austrian disaster at Austerlitz, Pitt died of overwork at the age of forty-six. His rational approach to problems, his powerful though narrow mind, and his pleasing personal character and administrative abilities did much to enhance the post of prime minister. Such a statesman could not easily be replaced in the war against Napoleon.

The Continental System

Napoleon devised a method whereby he hoped to crush Britain without invasion: all Europe was to be closed to British trade. Without sea power Napoleon could not attack Britain or her colonies, but he hoped to ruin its commerce and break the "nation of shopkeepers" with an embargo. To that end he issued the Berlin Decree in December 1806, to blockade the British Isles. The decree forbade neutrals under French influence from trading with Britain, and declared merchandise exported from British ports lawful prizes for any nation. The British government countered with its own order in council forbidding neutrals, under penalty of forfeiting ships and cargoes, to trade with France or her allies or to observe the Berlin Decree. Additional decrees and orders in council followed in 1807.

If either side had fully enforced the decrees the resulting economic warfare may well have destroyed European commerce. However, each side protected its own trade, and Napoleon made no effort to police exports from the Continent, only imports. Even this was difficult because it demanded a detection system which Napoleon lacked, and a self-sacrifice which satellite nations were not inclined to make. Smuggling developed to unheard-of proportions as resentment arose against the tyranny of the system. Finally, the nationalism which Napoleon had exploited in his own conquests back-fired and became a weapon the conquered countries used in opposing French imperialism. The Continental System became essentially a paper blockade.

PENINSULAR CAMPAIGNS

To enforce his Continental System, Napoleon attempted to bring Portugal and Spain more completely under his control. After occupying Portugal and deposing the Bourbon King of Spain, Napoleon placed his brother, Joseph, on the throne. This provoked the Spanish popular uprising of 1808 and an invitation to Britain to intervene. Under Sir John Moore (who was killed in 1809) and Sir Arthur Wellesley (later the Duke of Wellington), the British forces gradually liberated Portugal; they then coordinated their strategy with the guerrilla warfare of the Spanish peasants to restrain the operations of 300,000 French troops by hit-and-run tactics. Under Wellesley's superb generalship the British made an orderly retreat when faced with overwhelming odds, attacked the overextended supply lines of the French, and in 1812 took the offensive to drive the Bonaparte government out of Spain.

Downfall of Napoleon

The uneasy alliance between Napoleon and Alexander I collapsed as each became suspicious of the other's motives. When the Czar violated the Continental System and accepted British goods, Napoleon invaded Russia with over half a million troops. His army captured Moscow in September 1812, but the Russians refused to surrender. Since winter was fast approaching and the French army was without provisions, Napoleon ordered a retreat that became a nightmarish disaster. The freezing weather, starvation, and the Cossack attacks permitted only a remnant to reach France safely.

Meanwhile Britain's foreign secretary, Castlereagh, was forging a Fourth Coalition (1812–1814). Russia, Prussia, Austria, Great Britain, and many lesser powers combined to take advantage of Napoleon's misfortunes in Spain and Russia. At Leipzig in 1813 the allied armies inflicted the first crushing defeat on the army of Napoleon. In the following year they entered Paris, exiled Napoleon (Treaty of Fontainebleau) to the island of Elba in the Mediterranean, and placed Louis XVIII, brother of Louis XVI, on the French throne. The allied powers then gathered at Vienna to negotiate the remaining problems.

BATTLE OF WATERLOO

While the victorious delegates were still quarreling over terms, Napoleon escaped from Elba, made a triumphant entry into Paris, and reoccupied the throne. Wellington and Castlereagh organized yet a Fifth Coalition to confront once again their common enemy in the field. Napoleon's Hundred Days ended with the climactic Battle of Waterloo fought near Brussels on June 11, 1815. Wellington and Napoleon dueled for supremacy, but successive charges of French cavalry failed to break the British squares. Before nightful, General Blucher and the Prussian army arrived to reinforce the British and rout the French. Napoleon surrendered to the British and was banished to St. Helena, where he lived out the remaining six years of his life. The diplomats returned to Vienna to complete the peace settlement.

Causes of the War of 1812

While the British army was fighting Napoleon, the United States declared war on Britain for the purpose of annexing Canada and protesting Britain's violation of the maritime rights of neutrals at sea. The United States gained none of the objects for which the war was fought. To Britain the war was only a sideshow, completely overshadowed by the peninsular war in Spain and Napoleon's invasion of Russia.

When the Anglo-French war broke out in 1793, American sentiment favored an alliance with the French, but President Washington immediately declared the neutrality of the United States. American neutral ships did a lively business with both France and England during the war, and American commerce prospered until the Napoleonic decrees and Britain's orders in council caught the ships in a crossfire of the belligerents' regulations. Because British sea power enabled it to exercise the right of search more effectively than France, American resentment was directed largely against Britain. Although Congress declared war on the ostensible grounds of the violation of maritime rights, there were other reasons as well: (1) The sectional ambitions of the south and the west urged expansion into Florida and Canada. These rich lands could easily be annexed, because Spain and England were concentrating all their available forces in the European war; by 1812 only four thousand British troops remained in Canada. (2) The Indian problem was aggravated when Chief Tecumseh, aided by Canadian supplies, established an Indian Confederacy to prevent the encroachment of white settlers. (3) American nationalism was intensified by the War Hawks in Congress who believed that the United States should control the continent. (4) Anti-English sentiment developed from the aftermath of the American Revolution, Jay's unsatisfactory Treaty of 1794, and the exclusion of American commerce from the West Indies trade.

COURSE OF THE WAR AND THE TREATY OF GHENT

On land the poorly prepared efforts to conquer Canada failed as the invaders were repulsed in a series of small, but bitter, attacks in which both the British commander, Sir Isaac Brock, and the Indian chief, Tecumseh, were killed. When the war in Spain progressed favorably, Britain sent seasoned troops from the Peninsula to America. In 1814 one army captured Washington and burned it in retaliation for the American burning of York (present-day Toronto). A second army was defeated by Andrew Jackson at New Orleans two weeks after the peace had been made. Admiral Perry's naval victory gained control of Lake Erie for the Americans. On the Atlantic, American privateers and lone raiders damaged British shipping and pride before the British blockade effectively restrained American commerce.

The Treaty of Ghent (December 1814) provided for a restoration of territories as they were before the war. Nothing was mentioned about the original causes of the war, except that disputes over boundaries and fisheries were to be turned over to the arbitral adjudication of joint commissions. This procedure brought lasting peace between Canada and the United States. Fishing and boundary disputes were peacefully resolved by 1818, and the Rush-Bagot Agreement (1817) brought complete naval disarmament to the Great Lakes. The war put an end to Tecumseh's Indian Confederacy and to all efforts of the United States to annex Canada by force. For Canadians, the anti-American sentiment engendered by the war became the precursor of future Canadian nationalism.

British Politics after 1806

When Pitt died in 1806, George II reluctantly accepted a coalition cabinet led by Lord Grenville with Fox as foreign secretary. Fox put through the bill for the abolition of the slave trade before he died the same year (1807). His Whig colleagues were forced to resign that year because of parliamentary and royal displeasure over their attempt to remove restrictions preventing Catholics from holding military commissions. For a short span a Tory cabinet was assembled under the Duke of Portland, and in 1809 Spencer Perceval became Prime Minister. He prosecuted the war vigorously until his assassination in 1812. His successor was Lord Liverpool, who was astute, but indolent by nature, thereby letting his cabinet colleagues lead in their areas of responsibility. The most able and influential of Liverpool's cabinet was Lord Castlereagh who did little to oppose the reactionary views of his colleagues, but whose sound judgment and successful performance in conducting the peace negotiations won him the respect of Parliament and of Europe.

The long tenure of Liverpool's government (1812–1827) was aided by a rivalry among Whig leaders and a liberal-conservative split in their ranks, with the conservative faction supporting the government in its suppression of reform. Prosecution of critics of the government continued in the closing years of the war. Sir Francis Burdett, leader of a small group in Parliament who were called "Radicals," and William Cobbett, publisher of *Cobbett's Weekly Register*, were imprisoned for their opinions on reform.

ECONOMIC CONDITIONS

Britain's industrial revolution gave it an edge over France in the economic competition of the war years. British commerce expanded significantly, but wealth was not evenly distributed. The poor suffered greatly because prices rose faster than wages, food was scarce, and because the government legislated against labor agitation yet refused to remedy the causes of distress. The wildly fluctuating law of supply and demand caused periodic booms and busts. Thus when manufacturers found a sudden change in demand for products, they were forced to lay off workers. During the depression of 1811–1813 the misery of the poor produced the Luddite riots, during which unemployed workers went through three counties smashing the new machines of the textile industry that had put them out of work. The government had no answer for the grievances of the poor other than repression.

THE PEACE SETTLEMENT

Five coalitions had been forged to contain France and finally, after a generation of warfare, Napoleon was defeated and the allied powers gathered to arrange the peace. Coalitions are usually formed in a time of danger against *someone*, not for *something*; but often when the threat is removed, solidarity collapses and old rivalries return. The Congress of Vienna was no exception. The final settlement, which came about after months of maneuvering and compromises, did not completely satisfy any of the powers; yet it met the minimum requirements of each for security and preserved the balance of power until 1871.

Pitt's Proposals

As early as 1804 Pitt was looking beyond the war to plans for peace which could protect British interests, attract other members of the coalition, and ensure the peace of Europe. He corresponded with Czar Alexander I, who was contradictory in his goals for Russia. The young Czar could never bring into accord his dreams of being both the liberator and the autocrat of Russia. Alexander recommended a policy providing for an international organization to maintain the peace of Europe and proposals for expanding Russia's influence. Pitt tactfully reformulated these propositions to make them still acceptable to Alexander yet palatable to neighboring Austria and Prussia.

The First Peace of Paris

After Paris capitulated in March 1814, the victors met to conclude peace with Bourbon France. Since the allies could not agree, they shelved the most controversial matters, such as the future of Poland, and concluded a treaty with France which was signed on May 30, 1814. Under the treaty France renounced all claims to Holland, Belgium, Germany and Malta; French frontiers were set, with a few exceptions, at those which it had held in 1792; and France ceded three colonies to Britain. The treaty was lenient; there were no indemnities or reparations to embitter defeated France or to jeopardize the position of the restored Louis XVIII.

PRINCIPLES AND PERSONNEL

Certain professed principles guided the diplomats in their deliberations at Vienna, although national self-interest prevailed during the negotiations in the actual decision-making. The principles were: (1) "legitimacy"—the restoration of disrupted dynasties; (2) encirclement of France with stronger powers for security; (3) compensation for countries that lost territory in the shuffle; and (4) a balance of power. The Big Four (Great Britain, Russia, Austria, and Prussia), which quickly became the Big Five with the inclusion of France, decided all important matters and left the small powers to participate on committees and to complain about their inferior status. The major delegates were Emperor Alexander I (Russia), Viscount Castlereagh (Great Britain), Prince Metternich (Austria), Prince Hardenberg, chancellor for King Frederick William III of Prussia, and Talleyrand, the opportunist and irrepressible foreign minister of four French regimes.

The Vienna Settlement

Dissension at Vienna centered on the question of Poland, a country which in 1750 possessed a vast area and a population of over ten million, but which since then had been completely absorbed by Russia, Prussia, and Austria. The Czar proposed a plan that would restore an enlarged kingdom of Poland with a liberal constitution, but one totally subservient to Russia. The other powers did not want to see Poland become a satellite of Russia. Prussia was willing to give up its Polish provinces in return for the annexation of Saxony. But this would violate the principle of legitimacy by dethroning the King of Saxony and would place Prussia on the doorstep of Austria and France.

The final agreement on Poland and Saxony allowed Russia to retain the Polish province of Posen, and Austria to keep the province of Galicia. The remainder of Napoleon's duchy of Warsaw was set up as the kingdom of Poland with a model constitution, but with an illusory independence since it was placed directly under the suzerainty of the Russian throne. Prussia, in compensation for relinquishing its Polish provinces, received two-fifths of Saxony, Swedish Pomerania, and several Rhenish areas, thus replacing Austria in northern Germany as the dominant power. The other provisions included: (1) the return of British colonial conquests to their previous rulers except for Ceylon, the Cape of Good Hope, Heligoland, Trinidad, Malta, and four of the French colonies—Mauritius, Tobago, St. Lucia, and the Seychelles—which Britain added to its empire; (2) the union of Belgium with Holland to deter French expansion in an area vital to British interests; (3) the ceding of Venetia to Austria to compensate for the loss of the Austrian

Netherlands; (4) a loose German confederacy of thirty-eight states with a Diet at Frankfurt; and (5) the transfer of Norway from Denmark to Sweden.

THE SECOND PEACE OF PARIS

Peace negotiations were interrupted by Napoleon's Hundred Days following his escape from Elba. When the conference was resumed, Russia's previous preeminence was reduced, and Britain's stature was enhanced by Wellington's triumph at Waterloo. Castlereagh and Wellington directed British policy, and a second peace with France was negotiated. Prussia wanted revenge and reparations. Castlereagh stood for "security but not revenge," and his moderation and consistency in placing the interests and peace of Europe above the acquisition of more spoils won the support of the other members. In November 1815, the Second Peace obliged France to pay an indemnity of 700 million francs, to support an allied army of occupation for five years, and to abandon Savoy and a few strips of territory on the Swiss and Belgian frontier. In all essentials, France retained her integrity and her honor.

CONGRESS SYSTEM

At Castlereagh's and Metternich's prompting, Britain, Russia, Prussia and Austria formed a Quadruple Alliance in 1815 to maintain the peace settlement and quarantine the revolutionary ideas of France. In 1818 France joined, making it a Quintuple Alliance. However, the Alliance's effectiveness was diminished by the Czar's insistence on a Holy Alliance which Castlereagh saw as little more than a piece of peculiar mysticism and nonsense. The Holy Alliance sought to join the kings of Europe in a Christian union of peace and charity. In practice this alliance supported the old regimes and resisted change. The kings of Russia, Prussia and Austria were members.

Failure of the Congress System. Castlereagh planned to use the system to protect the small nations and to keep France from rearming. Metternich, and later Czar Alexander, viewed the two alliances differently. They were to be used as approved organs of reaction with the right to intervene in any country to crush national or democratic uprisings. Other rulers of Europe looked upon the Holy Alliance as a pact of three emperors to dominate the Continent. Liberal opinion everywhere condemned the Quadruple Alliance as an effort to protect the status quo in a world demanding change. Britain's old policy of isolation from the Continent soon grew popular again, particularly when the System was used as police action to defeat internal revolts in Spain and Italy. In 1823 George Canning, Castlereagh's successor as Foreign Minister, publicly disassociated Britain from the Congress System.

*T*he success of the American Revolution was not lost on European thought and actions. Within six years of the Peace of Paris the old regime in France was challenged in theory—by the Declaration of the Rights of Man—and in political structure with the revolutionary changes of Republican France. For twenty-two years Britain would be the architect of five coalitions that sought to contain French revolutionary ideas and French imperialism.

Within Britain the movement toward political and economic reform was under way, led by Prime Minister Pitt, Fox, and Wilburforce. The French Revolution halted this progress; reform efforts turned to reaction and repression by the government, as fears of the revolution spreading across the Channel made former reformers turn to the safety of the status quo and the use of repressive measures to maintain it.

Britain emerged from the Congress of Vienna as the premier power in the world and unchallenged in naval supremacy. British policy did not exploit this advantage in the peace negotiations. As a result the balance-of-power principle held in Europe until 1871, and following a century of war, Europe entered a century of relative peace.

Selected Readings

Barnes, Donald G. *George III and William Pitt, 1783–1806* (1965)

Creevey, Thomas. *The Creevey Papers* (1913)

Derry, John W. *Charles James Fox* (1972)

Feiling, Keith G. *The Second Tory Party, 1714–1832* (1951)

Longford, Elizabeth. *Wellington: The Years of the Sword* (1969)

Nicolson, Harold. *The Congress of Vienna: A Study in Allied Unity, 1812–1822* (1961)

O'Gorman, Frank. *The Emergence of the British Two-Party System, 1760–1832* (1982)

Palmer, R. R. *The Age of the Democratic Revolution* (1964)

Thompson, J. M. *Napoleon Bonaparte: His Rise and Fall* (1952)

Watson, John S. *The Reign of George III, 1760–1815* (1960)

16

Eighteenth-Century Britain: The Age of Reason and Revolution

1711 *Essay on Criticism* written by Alexander Pope

1714 George I accedes to the throne: beginning of the Hanoverian dynasty

1742 George Frederick Handel conducts the first performance of his oratorio the *Messiah* in Dublin

1755 Founding of the British Museum

1767 James Hargreaves invents the spinning jenny as part of the textile revolution

1769 Significant improvement in the steam engine patented by James Watt

1776 Death of David Hume, political philosopher

Publication of *Enquiry into the Wealth of Nations* by Adam Smith

1790 Edmund Burke's *Reflections on the Revolution in France*

1791 Death of John Wesley, founder of the Methodist movement

1798 Wordsworth and Coleridge publish their *Lyrical Ballads*, reflecting the new Romantic movement in literature

*T*he eighteenth century is commonly characterized as a period of intellectual brilliance, an Age of Reason, a time during which there was a belief
that common sense could discover the natural laws which govern society

and the arts. The accent on reason permeated the literature of the Augustan Age, the Church of England, the economics of Adam Smith, and Locke's idea of a "balanced constitution." The religious fervor and political violence of the previous century were regarded with considerable abhorrence by a century given to art, elegance, balance, and stability.

Such calmness and correctness were jolted in the second half of the century by a religious revival, by two revolutions, one in industry and one in France, by the clamor for parliamentary reform, and by the Romanticists who rebelled against the coldness of the Augustan literature; they believed that human emotions were more important than human reason. All through the century class distinctions separated the comfortable rich from the miserable poor.

Economic changes at home and worldwide wars abroad for commercial and colonial supremacy transformed the island kingdom into the world's leading industrial power. From 1689 through World War II Britain moved to center stage in world history as one of the major powers in the modern world.

SOCIETY AND RELIGION

The gulf between the rich and the poor in Britain created essentially a country of two nations with political power and the comforts of society belonging only to the upper class. Good taste and elegance were commonly found among this class, if not always at the court of the first two Georges. The search for excellence or quality was observed in the chinaware of Wedgwood and Spode, the furniture of Chippendale and Sheraton, and the crafted verse of Alexander Pope. In contrast to the lavish life of the upper classes, the lower classes lived in squalor, ignorance, and were exceedingly coarse in manners. The Industrial Revolution increased the shameless display of materialism within the country while wars of commercial aggression were fought against the country's rivals. The established Church, as the handmaiden of the state, did little to raise doubts about the rightness of the social order or to question the morality of the age.

The Condition of England

In eighteenth-century England a person's position was fairly well defined by birth, and the distinction of class was the accepted order of things. Death everywhere was also the accepted order of things. In 1750 one in three English children died before the age of twenty-one, and the average life span was only twenty-nine years. After 1750 the population grew rapidly, freed from the many epidemics that previously halted its growth. Sanitation and medical care began to improve and the national diet was profoundly altered by the introduction of tropical fruits and by expanding domestic cultivation of the potato, spinach, and the strawberry. The consumption of chocolate, sugar, and tea became a national habit, and coffee houses became lively centers of news, fashion, and politics.

Heavy drinking was common, and the consumption of gin and rum among the lower classes was widespread. Gambling became a national pastime, so much so that society in the 1760s was called "one vast casino." Government lotteries financed the building of Westminster Bridge (1736) and the British Museum (1755). The immorality, gambling, and brutality of the period resulted in a ready lawlessness. Mobs gathered at the slightest pretext as a chance for looting and an escape from urban squalor. Public executions were common, serving often as spectacles, but not as deterrents to crime. Prison conditions were wretched, and philanthropists worked to moderate the politicians' obsession with the sanctity of property to save children from the harsh penal laws and conditions. There were more stable patterns of life in the countryside where tradition and customs changed slowly.

POLITICAL SOCIETY

The smallness of the voting population meant that the politically powerful families could control their electorate with considerable ease. It also meant that politics was personal and clannish, because the members within an oligarchy which dominated the town or county knew one another and had common backgrounds and interests. (In 1721 there were only 179 English peers.) The basic unit of government continued to be the parish in which elected officials, such as the church wardens or the overseers of the poor, were under the supervision of the justice of the peace. The justices and the landed gentry relished the intrigue and electioneering which went on to ensure the control of seats in each constituency. Yet, paradoxically, a growing problem of the unreformed House of Commons was the huge expenditure that was becoming necessary to hold a seat; for a large county election expenses could easily cost a candidate or his patron £100,000.

THE PROFESSIONS

Bishops, university chancellors, admirals, and captains, as well as politicians, were usually indebted to Westminster for their appointments. Army commissions were bought and could be canceled for opposition to the ministry. In the church the bishoprics were political plums which went to assured supporters of the ministry. Independence of political thought could blight a promising career in the church or the army. Beneath the bishoprics was a pyramid of patronage that went to the discreet politician-preacher or to a relative of an influential member of Parliament. Such a system neither won respect for the clergy nor had any particular connection with theological conviction or competence. Other professions also had much patronage; the legal profession, except for its highest offices, had perhaps the least of all.

EDUCATION

The poor could not afford an education, and the state provided none for them. Primary education for the sons of shopkeepers and artisans expanded in the eighteenth century through the efforts of the charity school movement which provided moral instruction for youth. One result of the increased literacy was the demand for more books and periodicals. However, the English universities were dormant in the earlier part of the century. Young gentlemen attending there were frivolous and did little but socialize. Scholarship waned and Oxford and Cambridge virtually ceased to burden their students with any examinations. In contrast, the Scottish universities were much more involved in the European Enlightenment, especially Glasgow and Edinburgh. Glasgow (Adam Smith, Joseph Black, David Hume) became distinguished in mathematics and philosophy; Edinburgh was recognized as the best medical school in the nation.

CONDITIONS OF THE POOR

The misery of the poor was taken for granted as part of the divinely ordained nature of things. The urban laborer was dependent for survival on the whims of the employer or the handouts of his betters or his parish. There was much sentiment for the virtuous poor and their weary lives as compassionately portrayed in Goldsmith's *The Deserted Village*. Individual philanthropists, such as John Howard who helped improve the conditions of prisons, and Thomas Coram who established foundling hospitals, did much to relieve distress. It was the poetry of William Blake at the end of the century that aroused the public conscience to a sense of responsibility for social evils. The government corrected by statute some of the worst social scandals (e.g., the debilitating effects of cheap gin), but there was no significant remedial legislation until the nineteenth century. Gin drinking became a mania since it provided the poor with a temporary escape from their desperate conditions; but it also compounded their problems by ruining their health and increasing crime. Not until the Wesleyan movement was there any real interest shown in the neglected working class.

Condition of the Church

In 1717 George I discontinued the sessions of Church convocation on the advice of the Whigs who wished to reduce the influence of their political opponents, the High Church Tories. This act left the Church without a legislative body and made it more than ever an appendage of the state, led by clergy who often won high office by their political connections and who ministered primarily to the governing class. For the vast majority of Englishmen, the Church neither ministered to their needs nor won their respect. To the upper class the cold rationalism of the Church made little impact on their skepticism or immorality; to the lower class the very fact that the church catered to the well-to-do and copied their way of life served to remove the poor from its ministry.

The Age of Reason reached into religion in the form of deism. This interpretation of theology minimized the supernatural, basing its natural religion on human reason rather than revelation; reason was enthroned, enthusiasm and fervor were suspect. This intellectual religion resulted in sermons which featured serene discourses on metaphysics and ethics, but all too often spiritual or human needs were frequently unmet, especially for the masses.

Wesleyan Movement

When the Anglican Church appeared to be too closely identified with the establishment to reform itself, the spiritual wasteland of the eighteenth century was restored to life by Methodism. This revival reached people neglected by the established Church, transformed thousands of lives, and released an emotional flood which was regarded as unseemly in an Age of Reason. The Methodist movement began in Oxford where John Wesley (1703–1791) was preparing for the Anglican ministry and meeting regularly with some friends for Bible study and devotions. The religious devotion of this group was ridiculed by scoffers who labeled the devout members "Methodists." In the organization were the three future leaders of religious revival: John Wesley, a versatile genius and organizer with a sincere and intense religious nature; his brother Charles, a prolific hymn writer; and George Whitefield, an orator who could move the masses with his preaching.

John Wesley's life was suddenly transformed by an assurance of "salvation through faith in Christ alone." When Anglican fellow clergy refused to let him preach the doctrine of salvation by faith in their pulpits, Wesley and Whitefield preached in the open air to thousands who would never have entered a church. The moral fervor and enthusiasm of these evangelists swept over the land, and hostile mobs turned into responsive crowds. John Wesley never left the Church of England, but when his converts had no place in which to receive further instruction, he built Methodist chapels. Societies were established under Wesley's organizing skill and vision of Christian discipleship into effective and dynamic groups. After Wesley's death the Methodist movement became completely separated from the Anglican Church.

RESULTS OF THE RELIGIOUS REVIVAL

Because of his political conservatism John Wesley opposed John Wilkes, the American Revolution, and Catholic emancipation. Nevertheless, his contribution was immense. His preaching awakened the Anglican Church and revitalized its spiritual life. His stress on human brotherhood and his indictment of social evils produced movements for the abolition of slavery, better working conditions, and prison reform. Some historians argue that the revival saved England from the wave of social and political revolutions that swept Europe. Certainly, Methodism gave meaning and a new self-respect to thousands of the working class who otherwise would have been most ripe for revolution. Methodist influence, by merging with the Puritan tradition, sharpened the Nonconformist conscience in British society. Within the Church of England a revival also occurred; its members became known as Evangelicals or "Low Church" Anglicans. By the end of the century a renewal of religion had helped change the moral fiber of the nation.

THE ARTS AND SCIENCES

The thought and letters of eighteenth-century England not only mirrored the values of society but also frequently caricatured its standards. The century was rich in intellectual and literary fare and was enhanced by a rational and tolerant spirit which placed increased reliance on observation and on a growing skepticism of traditional attitudes. The Age of Enlightenment was curious about nature and intensely interested in scientific discoveries.

The Augustan Age

During the first four decades of the century writers turned to the Augustan Age of Rome for their model. The classics continued to serve as the basis of upper-class education, and the eighteenth-century reader responded to the aristocratic tone, the diction, and the reasoning of Latin authors. The neoclassical writers, therefore, imitated the ancients by writing correct and polished essays on mankind and by replacing passion and spontaneity with style and dignity. A new and larger reading public was created by the introduction of periodicals.

JOSEPH ADDISON (1672–1719)

Collaborating with Richard Steele on *The Tatler* and *The Spectator*, Addison became a popular and successful essayist who exposed and commented upon all matters of social life in a style that was witty, urbane, and practical. His most famous literary character was the squire Sir Roger de Coverley.

DANIEL DEFOE (ca. 1659–1731)

Coming from the home of a tradesman, Defoe probably cared little for the classics. He was primarily interested in earning a living and became a political hack until late in life. His novels, written in precise, descriptive prose, tell the story of lower-class existence. *Robinson Crusoe, Moll Flanders*, and *Roxanna* were three of his popular works.

ALEXANDER POPE (1688–1744)

Pope's wide-ranging mind and flawless style echoed perfectly the sentiment "Whatever is, is right" of the Augustan Age. His output covered the fields of literary criticism, social satire, and scholarly editing, but his genius was best displayed in his didactic, subtle poetry. Working within the confining limits of rhymed couplets, his poetry portrayed the aesthetic (*Essay on Criticism*) and intellectual (*Essay on Man*) interests of his age, and included perhaps the finest mock-heroic attempt (*Rape of the Lock*) in the English language.

JONATHAN SWIFT (1667–1745)

Swift's unhappy personal life, in which he hid his virtues and paraded his faults, along with his savage contempt for society, gave him a reputation of being a misanthrope. His original and bold prose scored the follies of people in sinning against the clear light of nature. Swift's devastating satire and irony fill the pages of *Gulliver's Travels* and *A Modest Proposal*.

THE AGE OF SAMUEL JOHNSON

In midcentury Samuel Johnson (1709–1784) dominated the world of letters, not so much for what he wrote—a *Dictionary* and *Lives of the English Poets*—but for his qualities of character and conversation. These were incomparably described by his constant companion, James Boswell, in his *Life of Samuel Johnson*. Johnson defended the established traditions of church, state, and classical learning, and yet all his contemporaries, from Goldsmith to Hume, held him in highest esteem for his independent mind and freedom from cant.

THE ENGLISH NOVEL

The English novel reached perfection in the work of Henry Fielding (1707–1754) with the characterization and well-balanced plot of *Tom Jones*. Samuel Richardson (1689–1761) in his novels on middle-class manners, *Pamela* and *Clarissa*, contributed to the development of the genre by adding psychological or sentimental detail. Challenging the heavy Augustan standards of Queen Anne's era were the tender, sentimental novels of Laurence Sterne (1713–1768), *Tristram Shandy* and *Sentimental Journey*; and Oliver Goldsmith (1728–1774), *The Vicar of Wakefield* and *The Deserted Village*. Tears and laughter became respectable, and in Goldsmith's satire there was no sting. Poetry again became passionate and personal in William Cowper's (1731–1800) sensitive, religious verses.

POETRY

The century closed with the forerunners of the Romantic movement: Thomas Gray, Robert Burns, and William Blake. Gray (1716–1771) was a transitional poet, essentially classic in form but novel in his treatment of beauty and sorrow. Burns (1759–1796) was an unschooled poet whose songs dealt with such homely and human topics as love, drinking, and married life. His admiration for medieval and rustic society was a departure from Augustan scholarship. The mystical movement of Blake's (1757–1827) thoughts and the elusive symbolism of his painting and poetry seemed, to his contemporaries, little more than the gropings of an undisciplined imagination. Not until the late nineteenth century was his work understood and appreciated. The literary revolt against the classical traditions and aristocratic way of life had begun.

THE THEATER

In 1698 Jeremy Collier, the essayist and critic, lashed out at the coarseness and frivolity of the Restoration theater with its Comedy of Manners. Second-rate sentimental comedies, sincere but insipid, played to capacity audiences of the Augustan Age; however, there was relief with the revival of Shakespeare by the actor David Garrick; John Gay's delightful musical comedy, *Beggar's Opera* (1728); and Henry Fielding's burlesque of dramatic conventions in *Tom Thumb* (1730). Oliver Goldsmith with *She Stoops to Conquer* (1773) and Richard Sheridan in such plays as *The Rivals* (1775) and *The School for Scandal* (1777) revived the theater by using comic wit free from the heavy sentimentality of earlier decades.

ART AND ARCHITECTURE

Eighteenth-century artists painted the fashionable world because society served both as the subjects and the patrons of their work. Sir Joshua Reynolds (1723–1792) was the dean of portrait painters and first president of the Royal Academy; his influence was significant on Thomas Gainsborough (1727–1788) and George Romney (1734–1802). In contrast to conventional subject matter and style, William Hogarth (1697–1764) was a pictorial satirist who painted and engraved the vices of London society. The social caricatures of *Gin Lane* or *Marriage à la Mode* enabled the city to recognize the folly of dissolute living and raised the consciousness of the governing class.

Classical architecture with its refined sense of proportion exemplified in the work of Sir Christopher Wren remained popular in England. Country and town house architecture revealed several attractive variations of Palladian and Neoclassic design in columns, brickwork, and arches. The leading architects of the century were Sir John Vanbrugh, James Gibbs, William Kent, the Adam brothers, and Sir William Chambers. "Capability"

Brown set the style for hedges and gardens and became England's most famous landscape designer. Thomas Chippendale and, later, Thomas Sheraton created delicate, attractive styles in furniture and Josiah Wedgwood captured the world's trade in exquisite china.

HISTORICAL WRITING

History was popular because it was conceived of as literature and written for a wide audience. The three most influential historians of the century were Hume, Robertson, and Gibbon. David Hume (1711–1776), a philosopher-historian, wrote a six-volume *History of England*. William Robertson (1721–1793), like Hume, was also a Scotsman, whose writing included histories of Scotland and America and a biography of King Charles V. Edward Gibbon (1737–1794), with his monumental *Decline and Fall of the Roman Empire*, offered a comprehensive and controversial interpretation of the fall of a great classical civilization.

PHILOSOPHY: IDEAS CONCERNING A FREE SOCIETY

In the eighteenth century English philosophers were asking the question: "What are the crucial characteristics of a free society?" Several answers were forthcoming, and these served as the rationale that stimulated political, social, and economic change as well as the justification for perpetuating certain practices. Eighteenth-century thought was greatly influenced by the work of Newton and Locke. John Locke had relied on his contract–natural rights theory to lay the basis for certain fundamental rights (life, liberty, property) of the individual that, in the final analysis, had priority over the claims of the king. If the sovereign overstepped the bounds of his power and became tyrannical, the oath of allegiance should become null and void. Given certain conditions Locke's argument was a justification for rebellion. Thomas Jefferson largely rephrased Locke's *Second Treatise of Government* to argue the colonial case against George III.

David Hume (1711–1776): The Dissolving Question. A skeptical Scotsman, Hume reduced Locke's political problem to a single question: Why is a "contract" which formed a government centuries ago still binding on the present generation? For two reasons only, answered Hume. Because of habitual allegiance (common habit), or because it is to the self-interest of the present generation to have such a government (common good). These two answers became the points of departure for Edmund Burke, and the case for conservatism, and Jeremy Bentham and his theory of utilitarianism a generation later (see chapter 17).

Edmund Burke (1729–1797): The Case for Conservatism. In his two best-known works, *On Conciliation with America* and *Reflections on the Revolution in France*, Burke eloquently established a conservative tradition that cautioned against radical change. He approved of the Glorious and the

American Revolutions because he claimed they were essentially protecting fundamental rights against abuse or change; furthermore they were led by the right people—responsible citizens who held on to the basic values of the past. In contrast the French revolutionaries repudiated their past and pressed for radical change in the structure of society. Burke expressed no more confidence in the will of the majority than in the absolute will of a king.

Instead, he urged slow change—reform through renovation rather than through innovation—and defended the tradition and balance of the British constitution. To some extent Burke's views ran counter to the ideas of the Enlightenment, because he considered "natural man" evil rather than good and defended strong checks and balances as necessary to save human beings from themselves. The greatest liability of Burke's viewpoint was its orientation toward a slow-changing agricultural, handicraft society instead of toward the new machine age with its rapid changes.

Adam Smith (1723–1790): Free Trade. In his *Enquiry into the Wealth of Nations* (1776) Smith discussed the nation's affluence in terms of individual prosperity. He argued that in a free society individuals, inspired by self-interest, would produce a prosperous economy in accord with reason and nature, if not restricted by government regulations. Influenced by the discoveries of the Age of Newton, Smith urged England to apply natural laws to economics: produce what you can most cheaply at home and trade these items freely for other goods, and all will prosper. He was supported by two other classical economists, Thomas Malthus and David Ricardo.

In time the link was drawn between free trade and a free society by Adam Smith's followers. His doctrine proved attractive to the classical liberals who believed that government governed best when it governed least, and to the new industrial capitalists who found that the prevailing laws, such as the Apprentice Act and the Navigation Acts, which favored the agricultural and handicraft society, were cramping both their expansion and their profits. These manufacturers, therefore, picked up the cry of "free trade" since they had nothing to fear from international competition.

SCIENTIFIC DISCOVERIES

Edward Jenner (1749–1823), physician and naturalist, found an immunity to smallpox with his preparation of a serum from cowpox. The two leading English scientists of the century were Henry Cavendish (1731–1810) and Joseph Priestley (1733–1804). Cavendish discovered that water was composed of oxygen and hydrogen. Priestley was a Nonconformist clergyman and experimentalist in many areas—philosophy, history, religion (Unitarian), and science. He built on the work of Stephen Hales and Joseph Black in isolating gases. In 1774 he isolated oxygen and made possible Lavoisier's work in quantitative chemistry. In physics Priestley discovered the Law of Inverse Squares (1766) which formed the basis of the work of the French scientist Coulomb. Fascination with electricity led to numerous experiments with lightning conductors by experimenters such as Benjamin Franklin.

The hunger for more information and the spread of knowledge was accelerated by the establishment of circulating libraries and philosophic societies; soon every city had both a library and a literary and philosophic society. By 1815 the *Encyclopaedia Britannica* had gone through four editions and new professional journals were appearing. In 1800 the Royal Institution was founded which paralleled the work and interests of the older Royal Society. This scientific interest, however, did not carry over to the application of science to industry. Tradition and superstition retarded the application of practical measures, such as vaccinations or the study in schools of science based upon current investigation. Even the invention of machines was regarded by employer and employee alike as labor- and money-saving devices rather than as instruments of industrial growth.

THE ECONOMIC REVOLUTION

Three interlocking revolutions occurred in the eighteenth century: in agriculture, in industry, and in transportation. These revolutions did not occur suddenly, rather they accelerated and expanded the countless changes which had been going on since the commercial revolution. But the consequences of industrialization for English society, and later for the world, were profound and revolutionary.

Prerequisites for Change

The industrial and agricultural revolutions began first in England because conditions were ripe for change. A half-century of internal peace had encouraged the growth of internal and external trade and this, in turn, promoted increased production. Britain had sufficient capital to pay for expansion and a banking and checking system to facilitate it. More important was the significant growth of population in England after 1740 through improved midwifery, medicine, and foundling hospitals. The expanding population reduced the labor shortage, expanded the home markets, and from 1720 to 1760 helped British exports to double in value. The world wanted these exports, particularly textiles; therefore, inventions to save labor and increase production were urgently needed.

Agricultural Revolution

To secure better farming and increased efficiency, the agrarian changes which had begun slowly in the sixteenth century accelerated rapidly in the eighteenth century. The new methods of farming brought prosperity and a readiness by landlords to experiment in agricultural production.

ENCLOSURES

The open-field system was destroyed by the wholesale agricultural enclosures of the Georgian period. Between 1761 and 1801 two thousand private acts enclosing three million acres were passed by Parliament. Local landowners petitioned Parliament for such legislation and usually the bill passed, because the wealthy landholding class dominated Parliament and the protests of the poorer villagers went unheeded. Commissioners then carried out the law; land was valued, surveyed, and redistributed among those entitled to receive portions. The enclosures brought many more acres under cultivation, and the new, compact farms permitted individual farmers to improve their crops and breed cattle without wasting their efforts as they would have done under the open-field system. Enclosures brought efficiency and wealth to landlords and independent farms at the expense of the traditional communal life of the village.

ACHIEVEMENTS

Wealthy landowners experimented in farming and several had significant success. Jethro Tull (1674–1741) improved seed planting and yield with his inventions of the horse drill which dropped the seeds in rows, instead of the former method of broadcast. After his retirement from politics Charles Townshend (1674–1738) popularized the turnip as winter fodder for livestock. He also experimented with a four-course rotation of crops to eliminate the waste of fallow land. Robert Bakewell (1725–1795) turned the attention of farmers to better breeding for an increased supply of meat. The records of London's Smithfield Market show that the average weight of sheep and cattle more than doubled between 1710 and 1795. These farming methods were popularized by Arthur Young in his writings on agricultural economy. In 1793 Young became head of the first semi-public, semiprivate Board of Agriculture.

EFFECTS

The diet of Englishmen changed as roast beef and white bread became staples; also the combination of new methods and enclosures helped feed a larger population. However, enclosures had an adverse effect on the lesser tenants who, losing their free fuel and pasturage, could no longer compete and paid the penalty for the changes. The result was the disappearance of the peasant proprietor who sank into proletarian status and became either a rural or urban wage earner.

Industrial Revolution

The changes in industry were even more fundamental. The Industrial Revolution transformed the very nature of society by substituting horsepower for manpower, the factory for the home workshop, and the city for the village. With these changes came greater productivity and wealth for the factory owner and misery for the worker in the factory town, a shift in population to the industrial Midlands, and a challenge by the new industrialists to the political domination of the landed aristocracy.

INVENTIONS

The most remarkable developments of the economic revolution were in technology and in methods of industrial organization. The application of mechanical inventions began in the first half of the century but became extensive only in the latter half as recognizable needs were met by new mechanical improvements. In each case an invention brought about new needs, new problems, and an expansion of the market. A marked advance in one area of manufacturing, such as weaving, produced pressure on the complementary area of spinning to catch up, thereby producing a chain reaction and accelerating the whole pace of technological improvement. Once started, these technological advances never ceased. The Industrial Revolution became a continuing and self-generating phenomenon.

TEXTILES

Inventions made their first major impact upon the textile industry. The infant cotton industry was aided by the fashion changes in favor of cotton goods and the restrictions on the importation of Indian calico. The increased demand for domestic cottons could not be met by the old domestic system of "putting out" orders to homes on a piecework basis. The outcome was a series of inventions and the transfer of work from the home to the factory, which quickly made England the world leader in the production of cotton goods.

John Kay hastened the weaving process with his flying shuttle (1733) and James Hargreaves's spinning jenny (1767) kept the weavers supplied with more spun yard. Richard Arkwright's water frame took the weaving industry into factories because the new looms were too large for homes and required water power. These inventions were followed by Samuel Compton's spinning mule (1779) and Edmund Cartwright's power loom (1785) for weaving. By this time the supply of raw cotton could no longer keep up with the demand. This problem was remedied when Eli Whitney, an American, invented the cotton gin (1793) to extract seeds from cotton. The machine made the southern United States a land of cotton which soon supplied three-fourths of the total British demand.

IRON, STEEL, AND POWER

Although England had ample iron deposits, the charcoal used in southern England for smelting was becoming scarce, because the groves of oaks providing the charcoal were depleted. After successfully experimenting in smelting with coke made from coal, the Darbys of Coalbrookdale encouraged the iron industry to move north to the coal regions. In 1784 a new type of blast furnace, the "puddling" process, perfected by Henry Cort, made iron tough, malleable, and cheap. New iron machinery, such as rolling mills, made iron available for a wide variety of uses, with the result that between the years 1740 and 1840 iron production jumped from 17,350 tons to 1,348,000 tons. Small steel factories were opened at Sheffield and Birmingham, but mass production awaited the inventions of Bessemer in the next century.

The problem of removing water from the coal mines led to use of Newcomen's inefficient steam engine in 1705. James Watt improved the steam engine in 1769 and twelve years later he and Matthew Boulton perfected it for use in the iron and coal industries. Because steam replaced water as the principal source of power for industry and transportation, factories could now operate in large cities away from rivers; furthermore, the development of the locomotive and steamboat was made possible.

THE REVOLUTION IN TRANSPORTATION

The industrial revolution called for improved methods for shipping iron and coal. In 1760 travel conditions in England were so wretched that travelers and goods moved more slowly than they did in Roman times. The pack horse, slow and expensive, was often the only way goods could be moved, until canals and turnpikes eventually revitalized inland transport. The Duke of Bridgewater had the first canal completed in 1761; immediately the cost of coal was halved in Manchester and new markets were opened.

The lesson was quickly learned and by 1815, 2,600 miles of canals crisscrossed England. Ironmasters such as John Wilkinson pressed for major road improvements, and Parliament responded by authorizing turnpike trusts to build, maintain, and charge tolls for new roads. Civil engineers Thomas Telford and John McAdam provided all-weather roads of crushed rock. Stagecoach travel, mail service, a decline in provincialism, and the expansion of industry were some of the advantages to come from rapid and easy transportation.

RESULTS OF THE ECONOMIC REVOLUTION

The enormous increase in industrial output and the cheapness of manufactured goods increased national wealth and gave England a commanding lead in competition for world markets. This wealth was not widely diffused, however, and the factory employee reaped few benefits from these economic changes. Although the picture of the village farmer has too often been romanticized (as in Gray's *Elegy Written in a Country Churchyard*), the social dislocation, slum housing, and exhausting working conditions of the wage earner were neither acknowledged nor ameliorated until the nineteenth century. These hardships were aggravated by twenty years of war with France and muted only by the Methodist religious revival and the development of local authorities to administer basic utilities and social services. The city commissioners believed in efficiency and cleanliness and opened the door for the utilitarian reforms of the nineteenth century.

The early stages of industrial capitalism did not distribute its burdens and benefits any more evenly than in pre-industrial Britain. It provided great vitality as an economic force, but much injustice as a social system. The lack of intervention by the ruling classes to ameliorate problems was reinforced by Adam Smith's views on the political economy: the government should not interfere with the natural laws of supply and demand, but should hold to a policy of laissez faire ("hands off").

The eighteenth century experienced more changes and a faster rate of change than any preceding century. The revolutions in industry, in political ideology (in America and in France), in migration from village to city, fundamentally altered the material conditions of the nation and the way people lived and worked. Once the wars with France were finally over, pent-up pressures for parliamentary, social, and economic reforms would dominate the national agenda.

The century is regarded as the classical age of the British constitution, a balance between the king, the Lords, and the Commons, even though the future was clearly with the power of the Commons. In a narrow sense the century was the last "age of aristocracy," an age of refinement; the era survives today in the superb country houses and estates, from Blenheim to Woburn, that capture the classical architecture and balance of the period. The achievements of the age, however, were increasingly accomplished by the inventions of individual members of the middle class, from Kay to the Darbys.

Selected Readings

Armstrong, Anthony. *The Church of England, the Methodists and Society, 1700–1850* (1973)

Ayling, Stanley. *John Wesley* (1979)

Boswell, James. *Life of Johnson* (1953)

Briggs, Asa. *The Power of Steam* (1982)

Brown, Ford K. *Father of the Victorians: The Age of Wilburforce* (1961)

Gascoigne, John. *Cambridge in the Age of the Enlightenment: Science, Religion and Politics from the Restoration to the French Revolution* (1989)

Gilbert, Alan. *Religion and Society in Industrial England: Church, Chapel, and Social Change, 1740–1914* (1976)

Hartwell, R. M. *The Industrial Revolution and Economic Growth* (1971)

Marshall, Dorothy. *Industrial England, 1776–1851* (1978)

Stephen, Leslie. *History of English Thought in the Eighteenth Century* (1902)

Stone, Lawrence. *The Family, Sex, and Marriage in England, 1500-1800* (1977)

Thompson, E. P. *The Making of the English Working Class* (1966)

Turberville, A. A. *English Men and Manners in the Eighteenth Century* (1957)

17

Repression and Reform: 1815–1841

1815 Vienna peace settlement after Napoleonic Wars

Passage of the Corn Law which raises the cost of bread

1820 Death of George III; accession of George IV

1823 Robert Peel begins reform of the Penal Code

1829 Catholic Emancipation Act passed under Prime Minister Wellington

1830 Death of George IV; accession of William IV

1832 Passage of the First (Great) Reform Bill, changing the representation in the House of Commons

1833 Abolition of slavery throughout the British Empire

Passage of first major Factory Act

1837 Death of William IV; accession of Queen Victoria

1839 Lord Durham's Report recommends responsible government for Canada

1841 Election of 1841 ends Melbourne ministry; Robert Peel becomes Prime Minister for the second time

Britain hailed the peace in 1815 with pride and with relief: pride in defeating Napoleon and in ruling the seas; relief that twenty-three years of war were over and now the nation could address its own internal need for change and reform. This transition from war to peace, however, was ex-

tremely difficult. The war years had left Britain with a residue of restrictions and an exaggerated fear of revolution that made the Tory government hostile to all demands for reform.

Gradually, the aristocracy saw the necessity for change if they were to maintain their influence and not suffer the fate of the nobility in France. The outcome was a respectable "revolution from above." Unlike the aristocracy on the Continent, English aristocrats helped introduce parliamentary measures for reform, since a continuing effect of the Industrial Revolution was the need to broaden the base of political power by enfranchising more social classes.

These changes toward political and social democracy took place gradually without violence because in most cases they were made piecemeal and made common sense. The most obvious abuse in postwar Britain was the unreformed Parliament which had failed to keep up with the social and political changes of the eighteenth century. In the wake of the Great Reform Bill (1832) that addressed this need, other reforms followed as the public conscience forced changes in the institutional life of the country.

POSTWAR PROBLEMS AND POLICIES

After the war with Napoleon, the people expected some rewards and several specific reforms for the sacrifices they had made in that struggle. Instead, the adjustments to a peacetime economy brought depression and unemployment. The outcome was disenchantment and rioting until Prime Minister Liverpool salvaged his unpopular cabinet by bringing in some younger ministers who quietly began to change the actions of the Government from repression to reform. Many of England's institutions, from the Poor Law to the Church, were still basically Elizabethan in practice. Devised for a simpler age, they were inadequate for the changed society of the nineteenth century.

Grievances of the Populace

Fundamental in the discontent of the workers was the complaint that the government persisted in a wartime mentality of repression, fearing any demonstration of discontent by the poor as a prelude to insurrection in the streets. As a result no postwar effort was made by the government to alleviate serious economic and social problems spawned by the war.

Specific problems or grievances included: (1) a postwar depression which lasted five years; Britain was overstocked with goods and no longer provided war shipments to Continental allies. (2) Unemployment; the glutted market caused bankruptcy and sharply reduced employment; the situation was aggravated by the return of 400,000 veterans to the labor force. (3) The Corn Law; following a series of crop failures Parliament revised the

Corn Law in 1815 to raise the tariff on imported grain. This act was attractive to the Tory landlord class, but increased the already high cost of bread for the rest of the nation. (4) Taxation; financing the war had raised the national debt to £850,000,000, and although Parliament repealed the income tax in 1816, taxation remained heavy.

The Agitators

The reform movement was reintroduced after the war in typically eighteenth-century style with correspondence societies, working-class clubs, and middle and upper-class supporters raising the issue. However, when the reformers received little understanding from Parliament, more radical leaders came forward. These radicals agreed that parliamentary reform was the first step in alleviating economic distress. Mass meetings were held by William Cobbett (publisher of *Cobbett's Weekly Register*), Henry Hunt, and John Cartwright. Soon these moderate protests became blurred in the public mind with the economic unrest of the unemployed and the rioting and physical violence that erupted.

Between 1812 and 1820 increasingly violent protests occurred as demonstrators became impatient with the lack of response by the Government. These included the Luddite riots, which erupted when unemployed workmen systematically wrecked factory machinery in the industrial towns of northern England; the rioting of a huge crowd assembled in Spa Fields in 1816 near London that required police intervention; the March of the Blanketeers (unemployed workers in Manchester) on London which was halted under orders from the Home Secretary; the St. Peter's Fields, Manchester, demonstration in 1819, in which a large crowd gathered to hear Henry Hunt's speech on parliamentary reform. Local magistrates ordered the cavalry to arrest Hunt. The cavalry charged the crowd, leaving eleven dead and many more wounded. When the government publicly commended the magistrates' action, the brutal incident was popularly labeled "the Peterloo Massacre" in memory of the battle of Waterloo. Finally, the Cato Street Conspiracy occurred in London where a group of radicals met in 1820 to plot the assassination of the cabinet; they were caught red-handed while dining and were eventually tried and executed.

The cabinet looked upon every demonstration as evidence of a budding insurrection and passed legislation even more restrictive than in wartime. As a consequence of the Spa Fields riot the habeas corpus act was suspended in 1817 and the law restricting public meetings was tightened. The repressive measures reached a climax after Peterloo with the passage of the Six Acts (1819) which further limited the freedom of the press and the right of assembly and strengthened the powers of the magistrates in dealing with disorders.

ACCESSION OF GEORGE IV, 1820

In 1820 George III died, after a sixty-year reign, and was succeeded by his disreputable son, George IV, who had treated his wife, Caroline of Brunswick, with brutality. Although Queen Caroline had exceedingly few virtues, the populace supported her as a woman abused by a man who had even fewer. George pressed his cabinet to obtain a divorce from her on the grounds of her alleged adultery. The unpopular Six Acts and the royal scandal turned the balance of public opinion against the government. The suicide of the brilliant Foreign Secretary, Castlereagh, in 1822 added to the pressure to bring younger, more moderate Tories into the ultraconservative cabinet.

NEW TORY LEADERSHIP

Liverpool remained as Prime Minister, but three able, younger Tories entered the cabinet: George Canning, Robert Peel, and William Huskisson. They moderated the cabinet's position. The Tories who held office in these postwar years included Castlereagh, Liverpool, Wellington, and Eldon. They were men of intelligence and a high sense of duty. However, they feared change and their policy was largely one of reaction rather than one of adaptation to a changing political and economic order.

George Canning and Foreign Policy. Canning succeeded Castlereagh as Foreign Secretary and leader of the House of Commons. Continuing his predecessor's policy of nonintervention on the Continent, Canning acquired a liberal reputation (a term brought into currency by the Spanish revolution of 1823), because of his sympathy with reformist groups in other countries and his methods of open diplomacy, whereby he took the nation into his confidence—in a reversal of Castlereagh's practice of secret negotiations. By warning the European powers not to interfere with the new South American republics in 1823, he won popular support as well as commercial backing from British merchants eager to break Spain's monopoly on South American trade.

In 1826 Canning repudiated the powers of the Quadruple Alliance by ordering British troops to Portugal to prevent an invasion by Spain. In the following year his diplomatic maneuvers helped the Greek insurgents win independence from Turkish despotism. This action gave British foreign policy a reputation in favor of nationalism and liberalism which lasted for decades. Although he won more support from the Whigs than from the conservative wing of his own party, Canning became Prime Minister after Liverpool's resignation in 1827; but within five months he was dead.

Sir Robert Peel, Home Secretary. In domestic affairs Peel supported the "common sense" reforms of the moderate Tories and yet retained the respect of the entire party. His reforms reflected the new humanitarianism that was taking hold of the public conscience and the new industrial leadership of the nation. As home secretary Peel brought about the long needed overhaul of an antiquated and harsh criminal code. He abolished the death penalty for over one hundred offenses, established other punishments on a more rational and humane basis, and organized the nation's first professional police force in London.

William Huskisson and Freer Trade. As president of the Board of Trade, Huskisson worked closely with the Chancellor of the Exchequer, Frederick Robinson (later Viscount Goderich) in moving away from the traditional policy of agricultural protectionism toward a liberal policy of freer trade. In 1825 the entire tariff was revised and lowered in the manner that Pitt had pioneered in the 1780s. Cognizant of Britain's industrial and commercial supremacy, Huskisson modified the outmoded Navigation Acts, repealed in 1824 the harsh Combination Acts of wartime vintage (aided by the able trade union organizer and political manipulator, Francis Place), and persuaded Canning to introduce a sliding scale of duties on imported grain in place of the old fixed price. (Wellington secured defeat of the bill in the House of Lords, but reintroduced it later, when he became Prime Minister.) Huskisson worked with Canning to exercise diplomatic pressure in bringing about reciprocity treaties with cooperative nations and reprisals for the uncooperative.

CABINET CHANGES

All of the administrative reforms mentioned above had occurred under the prime ministership of the benign and adroit Lord Liverpool. When Liverpool resigned in 1827 because of ill health and Canning died suddenly, Lord Goderich was unable to hold together the coalition with the Whigs that Canning had arranged. Disliked by the King, Goderich was replaced by the Duke of Wellington, the fourth prime minister within the year. Wellington was a national military hero who at first united both wings of the Tories but soon alienated the Canningites by his opposition to the reform current. Peel was the only reformer to stay in the cabinet as the ultra-Tories rallied around the Prime Minister's "stand pat" views on the constitution and the church. Nevertheless, Wellington could not stop the current of change and his political leadership, in contrast to his military, consisted largely of a series of retreats. When threatened by riots at home and civil war in Ireland, the Duke gave way and pushed through Parliament the necessary changes.

Catholic Emancipation

The Protestant dissenters won their victory against religious discrimination in 1828 when a young Whig, Lord John Russell, introduced a bill in the House of Commons to remove the political disabilities imposed on them by the Test and Corporation Acts (see chapter 11). Wellington and Peel had agreed to this bill, yet they feared that its passage would only encourage the Catholics to demand similar emancipation, and their fears proved correct.

William Pitt the Younger had promised Irish Catholics the vote and the right to sit in Parliament at the time of the Act of Union in 1800; but George III reneged on his promise to Pitt, and the restrictions against Catholics continued. Led by Daniel O'Connell and his powerful Catholic Association, Irish Catholics were forcing the emancipation issue. Despite the law against Catholics, O'Connell was elected to Parliament over a member of Wellington's cabinet. Fearing civil strife, the Duke beat a strategic retreat and commanded sufficient respect from the King and Peel to win their support on the issue, even though the passage of the bill was against the convictions of all three. The Catholic Emancipation Act was rammed through Parliament in 1829, thereby permitting O'Connell to take his seat in the House of Commons and allowing Catholic peers to resume their vacant seats in the House of Lords.

It was perhaps ironical that the bill passed under the sponsorship of the leading ultra-Tory, rather than under earlier reformers. However, this was the last Tory reform because the High Tories in Wellington's party never forgave him for deserting them, and in 1830 they combined to bring down his ministry. For that matter, Tory administrative reform had run its course, and, when the even more controversial issue of parliamentary reform came up again, most of the party lined up in opposition to change.

THE GREAT REFORM BILL

Once again the radicals and reformers focused their attention on the one area of unanimity among them, the need for parliamentary reform. And again public opinion was ably manipulated by popular leaders, but this time it was strengthened by the demands of the rising industrial class for representation. Sufficient members of the aristocracy sensed the wisdom of aligning the new, wealthy class with them, rather than against them, and took action in time to avoid violence. The bill was a first step and gave encouragement to the nation that more changes would follow.

The Case for Reform

By 1830 the reform climate was such that change would come either with or without parliamentary support. The Whig leadership, therefore, introduced the reform bill as a rational measure, rather than a democratic one, to meet the minimum needs of this agitation without destroying the basis of their control in the process.

The case for reform of the parliamentary system drew heavily on abuses in the current parliamentary representation. These included the following: (1) The notoriety of rotten boroughs that were available through bribery or influence so that elections, in many cases, became largely a matter of selection. (2) The major shift in population to the north and west of England with no corresponding change in parliamentary representation. Such large centers as Birmingham, Leeds, and Manchester had no representation. (3) A parliamentary system that reflected the traditional influence of the country gentry but not of the burgeoning commercial interests. (4) A House of Commons which no longer enjoyed the confidence of the nation nor reflected changes in popular opinion to any great extent. In 1830 revolutions racked the Continent, and the "Last Laborers' Revolt" broke out in southern England. Fears grew that if reform did not come, revolution would.

ACCESSION OF WILLIAM IV

George IV was admired as a patron of the arts, but for little else. His brutal treatment of his wife and the scandal brought about by his efforts to divorce her had brought the popularity of the Crown to its lowest level since James II. By the time of his death he had become an adamant foe of constitutional reform. His younger brother, William, succeeded him as King. He often lacked resoluteness, but was genial and conscientious, and sympathetic to parliamentary reform, unlike his brother.

The New Whig Cabinet

The death of George IV in 1830 required (by law) a general election. It was held in July 1830 and the Wellington government was returned to power. But the voting loyalty of the various Whig and Tory factions was most uncertain, and the Whig opposition joined with the new industrial class to reopen the issue of parliamentary reform. Prime Minister Wellington was forced to state his position on current events—the revolution that year in France, the newly created Belgium, Greek independence from Turkey, and the riots in England. His speech at the opening of the new Parliament on the perfection of the British government—in effect, a defense of the status quo—caused such violent reaction that he was forced to resign after enough Tories deserted him on a minor bill in order to show their disapproval of his leadership.

The new Whig cabinet of Prime Minister Grey was not a middle-class alternative government. It had a decidedly aristocratic identity, with all but two members either peers or sons of peers. It included followers of Canning (Melbourne, Palmerston, and Graham) who combined with such Whig ministers as Henry Brougham and Lords Russell, Durham, and Althorp to make electoral reform a top priority. Led by the elderly, respected Lord Grey, who had advocated parliamentary reform since 1797 with Charles Fox, the cabinet aimed at retaining the old basis of political power, but remodeling Parliament to eliminate its worst abuses and give the new industrial centers a political voice.

Passage of the First Reform Bill, 1830–1832

The new Whig government drew up reform proposals that were hardly democratic, but were far-reaching enough to bring about the strong opposition of the Lords and the members of boroughs about to be disenfranchised. This opposition caused the resignation and reelection of Grey's government before the final passage of the bill.

The Reform Bill was introduced by Lord John Russell in March 1831, and passed the second reading by only one vote. Grey, therefore, asked for a dissolution of Parliament in order to take his cause to the country. In the election campaign the combination of government patronage along with Whig, Radical, and working-class political meetings won the reformers some ninety new seats. The bill now passed the House of Commons but was thrown out by the House of Lords. When the King refused to create sufficient peers to pass the bill, Grey resigned. By this time the popular mood of the country showed itself so angrily that revolution seemed quite possible. Newspapers were trimmed in black, riots broke out, and bishops were booed for voting with the lay lords.

When Wellington was asked by the King to form a government, the Duke found he was without support in either the House of Commons or in the country. Unable to form a ministry under Wellington, William IV recalled Grey and promised to create the necessary number of peers to pass the bill. The threat was as good as the act, and the King's surrender became the Lords' surrender. In July 1832, the Reform Bill became law.

MAJOR CLAUSES OF THE BILL

(1) All boroughs containing less than two thousand inhabitants were disenfranchised; this eliminated fifty-six. (2) One member was dropped from each borough containing less than four thousand inhabitants; this eliminated thirty-two. (3) Sixty-five seats were given to new boroughs previously underrepresented. (4) Sixty-five additional seats were given to English counties; eight to Scotland and five to Ireland. (5) Borough voting lists were eliminated, and all £10 freeholders were enfranchised. The county franchise was also enlarged. (6) A system of voting registration demanding the compilation of electoral lists was introduced.

SIGNIFICANCE OF THE REFORM BILL

The bill met the immediate needs which old abuses and changing times had demanded, and representatives of the new industrial wealth now became associated with the landed aristocracy; but there was no basic shift in power. In the debates neither Whig nor Tory argued for democracy because both parties agreed that any government of the people should still be by the best of the people. Thus the right to vote was still limited to the owners or lessees of land; the working class still had no part in political affairs.

As a result, the radicals were not satisfied since the enfranchisement in England was raised by only some 200,000 voters, to include one out of every seven adult males. Nor was the composition of Parliament altered radically, for the newly reformed House of Commons of 1833 contained 217 sons of peers. In some ways the most significant consequence of the bill was one wholly unanticipated by the reformers or their opponents. The clause requiring registration of voters caused the creation of local political groups to get the voters registered and get out the vote. From this grew the well-organized and countrywide party organizations.

The First Reform Bill was, therefore, essentially a compromise. Several of the old institutions, such as the monarchy, the House of Lords, and the cabinet, remained unscathed, but the power of popular opinion and political organization made itself felt as never before. The agricultural interests remained, but were now rivaled by the growing industrial interests. However, in some sense it was a revolution, because popular pressure had forced changes in the age-honored principle of parliamentary representation. This was the specter that caused Robert Peel to oppose the bill, saying, "I was unwilling to open the door which I saw no prospect of being able to close." The rest of the century was to prove Peel correct as the parliamentary system was no longer treated as something forever fixed and impervious to change.

THE REFORM MOMENTUM CONTINUES

The combination of popular agitation, the expanded readership made possible by the sale of newspapers for a penny, reform-minded members of Parliament, and the taste of success which the passage of the Reform Bill had encouraged increased demands for parliamentary intervention in other areas of British economic and social life. Wretched working conditions in the new factory towns and squalid housing threatened not only the poor but eventually endangered the industrial system that spawned them. Parliamentary legislation was the state's belated response to these social and industrial ills.

Abolition of Slavery, 1833

The issue of slavery dominated all other colonial questions in the first part of the nineteenth century. The act abolishing the slave trade (1807) was found impossible to enforce in international waters, and efforts to reform the institution of slavery were blocked by the West Indian planters. Therefore evangelicals and humanitarians, led by William Wilberforce and Sir Thomas Buxton, campaigned for the abolition of slavery itself and were strongly supported by the Anti-Slavery Society (1823) and the Colonial Office. Gradually, the opposition of the powerful West Indian lobby withered as trade with the West Indies became less important to Britain and as mass petitions put pressure on Parliament. Lord Stanley, the colonial secretary, introduced a bill abolishing slavery throughout the empire; the bill became operative in 1834 and a vested interest was beaten, largely on humanitarian groups. The slave owners were compensated by a government grant of £20,000,000, and the emancipation was to take place gradually through a system of apprenticeship covering four to six years. The act won great acclaim in Britain but led to planter hostility and economic decline in the West Indies and to bitter protests from the Boers in South Africa, culminating in their great trek across the mountains to form two new Boer republics.

The Factory Act, 1833

Because the previous factory acts of 1802 and 1819 lacked provisions for effective enforcement, few factory owners heeded the clauses which attempted to ameliorate the harsh working conditions and long hours of child labor. Three men, in particular, resumed the earlier efforts of Dr. Percival and Robert Owen and pushed through Parliament the first effective factory reform. Michael Sadler, a Tory MP, brought about a royal commission in 1831 to investigate working conditions and the treatment of child employees. His graphic and grim report aroused public sympathy for working children. At the same time Richard Oastler, a practical philanthropist, promoted popular support for factory legislation by describing working conditions at mass meetings. Lord Ashley (later the Earl of Shaftesbury), a Tory nobleman and Evangelical religious leader, became known as "the children's friend" for his labors in behalf of factory children. He introduced a bill to correct the abuses in the textile industry and Lord Althorp sponsored its final passage. The act decreed: (1) No employment of children under nine years of age. (2) No child under thirteen was to work more than nine hours per day and each child was to receive two hours of schooling per day. (3) No child under eighteen was to work more than twelve hours a day (excluding meal breaks). (4) Inspectors were to be appointed by Parliament to enforce these provisions.

The Poor Law Amendment, 1834

The Elizabethan Poor Law and its accompanying system of parish doles had changed little in two hundred years. But the number of paupers in England had increased to the point that one out of every six inhabitants was on relief. Farmers and manufacturers, knowing that laborers could survive by living off the poor rates, kept wages low. A royal commission, headed by Nassau Senior, investigated and recommended procedures to encourage frugality and discourage laziness by providing relief in such a manner that individuals would lose their self-respect by asking for it.

The ensuing amendment to the Poor Law contained the following provisions: (1) All relief was centralized by combining parishes into larger units, with three commissioners in London controlling the welfare program. (2) Outdoor relief (assistance to the poor in their own homes) was restricted to the sick, the aged, and children. (3) Able-bodied men who demanded relief were required to live in workhouses (denounced as "Poor Law Bastilles" by Thomas Carlyle), where they were separated from their wives, and where food and heat were kept at a minimum. This amendment was not passed to assist the poor, but to reduce the tax rates for the middle classes. It was supported by followers of Jeremy Bentham, but was harsh in its application.

The Municipal Corporation Act, 1835

This act (along with similar acts for Scotland and Ireland in 1833 and 1840) radically reorganized urban government according to a uniform plan. Municipal councilors were elected for three years by resident taxpayers. These councilors then elected one-third of their number to serve as aldermen for a six-year term. The council elected the mayor annually, regulated all public utilities, and appointed the salaried officials. The act ended the corrupt and unrepresentative character of municipal government in which a self-perpetuating oligarchy usually chose members of the governing council to serve for life and felt no responsibility to provide such needed services as waterworks, sewers, or police protection for the citizens. The Municipal Corporation Act increased both efficiency and democracy in local government and paved the way for future public health reforms by abolishing the abuses of private monopolies in utilities. Although additional legislation increased the functions and powers of councilors, the act still serves as the basis of English municipal government.

Colonial Policies

Conflicting views on the merit and function of colonies prevented any consistent policy from being applied to all parts of the empire in the first half of the nineteenth century. Pitt's India Act provided for dual control of British India; Britain continued to annex territory (Natal) in South Africa; Canada moved toward responsible government; and Australia had a unique situation with its penal settlements. The supporters of free trade and the Manchester School of Political Economy (James Mill, David Ricardo, and Thomas Malthus) argued that free trade had no colonial boundaries, and that the law of supply and demand should work free of government regulations. Therefore, colonies were of little value. In contrast, the radical imperialists (Gibbon Wakefield, Lord Durham, Charles Buller, and William Molesworth) had an active interest in reviving the empire by selective emigration from Britain and by the promotion of local self-government in the colonies of white settlement.

Colonial administration was strengthened by the quality and vigor of leadership found in the Colonial Office. In 1812 the Earl of Bathurst became Secretary for War and the Colonies and picked Henry Goulburn as under-secretary. These two officials practically created the colonial office. They organized departments, hired specialists, and for decades their active humanitarianism was reflected in colonial policies. Their work was effectively continued in the Colonial Office by Lord Glenelg and James Stephen. Under Bathurst and Stephen the influence of the humanitarian and Evangelical movement produced a colonial policy favoring missionary expansion and racial equality.

Colonial Policy in Canada

Pitt's Canada Act of 1791 had eased the tension between French and English by dividing Canada (present-day Quebec and Ontario) into two colonies. Yet, friction continued between French and English, and Catholic and Protestant. In Upper Canada (Ontario) the early settlers resented the influx of newcomers and tried to keep control of the Assembly in their own hands; in Lower Canada (Quebec) the friction was between the elected Assembly and the upper house, nominated by the governor. The grievances flared into open rebellion in 1837, led by Louis Papineau in Lower Canada and William Lyon Mackenzie in Upper Canada. The rebellion awakened the British government to the seriousness of the situation and the need to prevent another colonial revolution from developing. Lord Durham, a liberal Whig cabinet minister, was sent to investigate and make recommendations.

Durham's Report sensed two basic problems in Canada: "two races warring in the bosom of a single nation," and representative government without political responsibility for its actions. His report to Parliament in 1839 recommended: (1) the union of Upper and Lower Canada so that racial differences would not become permanent in the two provinces, and immigration would eventually bring an English majority; (2) responsible government. The governors should choose their ministers from members commanding a majority in the Assembly, making the executive responsible to the legislature.

The British government bungled the application of Durham's Report by giving an equal vote to Upper and Lower Canada in the Act of Union of 1840. More important, though, the principle of responsible government was accepted and became a constitutional landmark in the evolution of the British empire. The principle implied that the bond of empire would be by voluntary association and not by coercion. The lesson of the American Revolution had been well learned. In Canada responsible government came in 1848 and, in the next decade, was extended to Newfoundland and the five Australian colonies. Cape Colony in South Africa followed in 1872.

CHURCH REFORM

The agitation for reform had a religious as well as a political and social dimension. At the beginning of the nineteenth century religious torpor within the Church of England and mounting protests against religious restrictions on non-Anglicans brought about numerous changes which indicated a significant revival of interest in religion, both without and within the established Church.

Religious Emancipation Outside the Church of England

The rationalism and latitudinarianism of the eighteenth century combined with the growing political power of the Nonconformists to bring substantial relief from sixteenth- and seventeenth-century religious restrictions. The freedom from disabilities applied to Roman Catholics and to Protestants outside the Church of England.

Catholic emancipation in 1829 and the conversion to Catholicism of two Anglican leaders of the Oxford Movement (John Henry Newman and Henry Manning) helped restore respectability to the Catholic Church. The improved relations with Rome had been aided by the end of Jacobite plots to restore a Catholic monarchy and by the new attitude of the papacy toward the Church of England. The papacy now publicly accepted the existence of the Anglican Church and made Catholicism less alien in England by giving English titles to English bishoprics. By mid-century Catholicism was a religious choice and not a political error.

Protestant Dissenters (Nonconformists) followed up their religious emancipation by parliamentary statute in 1827 with renewed efforts to abolish the remaining restrictions. The Registration Act of 1837 freed Dissenters from the obligation of being baptized, married, and buried by the Anglican Church. In 1829 Dissenters were first admitted to the University of London, although Oxford and Cambridge excluded them until 1861–1862. Several tithe acts simplified the collection of the tithe for the support of the established Church. These gains came gradually as a result of a new climate of tolerance and the use of political pressure. Nonconformist members of Parliament demanded support of their objectives as conditions for winning their votes. The influence of Nonconformists went beyond the political realm. Their evangelical and humanitarian concerns expressed themselves in support for the abolition of slavery and in lending moral and vocal support to rid their communities of corruption and vice. They actively supported industrial reform and social legislation.

The Free Kirk Movement seceded from the Church of Scotland in 1843 when the courts ruled that one person (the patron rather than the congregation) could select the parson. The five hundred secessionist ministers, led by the Reverend Thomas Chalmers, claimed that the state was interfering with the policies of the church.

From 1801 to 1869 the Church of Ireland (Anglican) was supported by the tithes of the Catholic South and the largely Presbyterian North—an impossible situation. Both groups opposed the compulsory support of an alien church. The issue was not resolved until 1869 when Prime Minister Gladstone pushed through a bill which disestablished the Church of Ireland and made it a self-governing member of the Canterbury communion.

Reform within the Church of England

The year that the Great Reform Bill was passed Thomas Arnold wrote, "The Church as it now stands no human power can save." Critics attacked the established Church for its political subservience, inertia, and sinecures (salaried appointments that required few duties), while reformers talked in favor of disestablishment. Defenders argued that the church was an institution beyond the pale of parliamentary action; their position was strengthened when the Anglican Church was aroused by a religious revival of its own.

THE OXFORD MOVEMENT, 1833

No longer could Anglican clergy take the Church for granted in England simply as the authorized version of Protestantism established by law. It needed a higher loyalty than statute law. John Keble in his Assize Sermon at Oxford in 1833 called for a spiritual regeneration by reasserting the authority and historical traditions of the Church, particularly the authority of Apostolic Succession. Other leading Oxford clergymen—John Henry Newman, Hurrell Froude, and Edward Pusey—joined Keble in a liturgical and theological revival that stressed the writings of medieval churchmen and the early Fathers of the Church. This movement inevitably led to a greater admiration for the Roman Catholic Church, with the result that two leading figures of the movement, John Henry Newman and Henry Manning, joined the Roman Catholic Church and eventually became cardinals.

The results of the Oxford Movement were significant and widespread. Orders of nuns and monks were founded, and the self-government of the Church of England was restored with the revival of the convocations of the provinces of York and Canterbury in 1852. Anglicanism still had its internal divisions commonly known as "High," "Low," and "Broad" Church, but most significantly its members cared about the Church as they had not cared in the eighteenth century. By midcentury the real threat to Anglicanism was not in schism, vestment controversy, or disestablishment, but in the onslaught of Biblical criticism and skepticism.

EDUCATION: A NEGLECTED AREA

Not until 1870 was Parliament able to agree on a national education act. Britain paid for this failure by having to contend in world competition with the least trained artisans and the most poorly educated middle class in Europe. The basic causes for the delay were sectarian rivalries and opposition to state subsidies for church schools.

The Voluntary Tradition in Education

The English system of education had a long tradition of private schools. Some such as Winchester, Eton, Harrow, and Rugby had developed excellent reputations and were heavily endowed; paradoxically, they became known as the public schools. These public schools, grammar schools, and Dissenter academies prepared a select number of students for admission to the universities; there was no public system of secondary education. Elementary education was, if anything, even more irregular, with the children of the working class completely neglected except for the scattered efforts of philanthropic or religious groups. The latter had most success through the Sunday schools, begun by Robert Raikes in 1780, in which children were taught reading, writing, and religion on the one day they were not working. In 1797 the Bell and Lancaster system provided the first phase of mass education with the help of monitors. Under this system teachers taught the most able students, who, in turn, repeated the lessons to the rest. The program was amazingly successful, but it put a heavy premium on memorization.

By 1830 the educational scene resembled a patchwork quilt, completely without design or administrative pattern. No industrial society could long rest on such a substratum of ignorance as dense as the statistics of 1830 indicated was the level of education in Britain. The average term in school was less than two years. In city after city barely half the inhabitants could sign their own name and even less could add sums. It became obvious that public education and some scheme of teacher training were imperative, but no agreement could be found for any plan.

STATE SUBSIDIES AND SECTARIAN SUSPICIONS

In 1833 the first state grant for education was a modest appropriation of £20,000 to the two largest voluntary associations: the National Society for Promoting the Education of the Poor in the Principles of the Established Church, and the British and Foreign School Society (Dissenters). Six years later the distribution of the parliamentary grants was entrusted to a Committee of Council, but no agreement on curriculum or administration could be found. Most plans foundered over the issue of religious instruction in state schools. The Dissenters objected to the Anglican cleric in the public (state) school while the Anglicans did not want public education shorn of religious instruction.

In 1846 a new system of grants—£1 from the Treasury for every £2 of local school funds—again raised the whole issue of state subsidies. This time Thomas Babington Macaulay's eloquent speech in defense of the state grants for religious schools and in defense of the role of the Church of England in education carried the day; thereafter education was also acknowledged to be a duty of the state. It would take another twenty-five years before a national education bill was finally enacted.

POLITICAL LEADERSHIP AND THE MONARCHY

The Whigs, with a loose and changing coalition of votes, remained in office for most of the decade following the Great Reform Bill, with Melbourne serving as Prime Minister for six of these years. He gave a great deal of time and attention to the tutoring and advising of Queen Victoria, but finally resigned in 1841 when it became apparent that Peel's argument was becoming constitutionally correct. Peel had pointed out that it was "at variance with the principles and the spirit of the constitution for a Ministry to continue in office without the confidence of the House."

The Melbourne Ministry

Earl Grey, as Prime Minister, and Althorp, as leader of the House of Commons, had won the respect of most of their Whig colleagues. But following the reform measures of 1832 and 1833 neither one was interested in pursuing the political maneuvering that additional reforms demanded. The radicals and the Irish, however, were not content to stop. Led by Daniel O'Connell and backed by an aroused peasantry and priesthood who opposed payment of the tithe to the Anglican Church, Irish agitation for reduction of the tithe grew stronger. Their efforts were opposed by conservative Whigs who would countenance no change in the Irish Church. A bill to reduce the tithe split the cabinet. Lord Stanley (later the Earl of Derby) and James Graham left the cabinet and joined the Tories. In the ensuing name-calling the elderly Grey resigned in July 1834, pleased to have fulfilled his youthful pledge of reform and anxious now to be relieved of office.

The new Prime Minister was Lord Melbourne, an affable and sophisticated former Canningite, whose weak and divided cabinet held a fragile majority in the House of Commons. William IV dismissed the cabinet and asked Peel to form a Tory government. In the election campaign Peel issued the Tory party's first platform, the Tamworth Manifesto, supporting a program of cautious reform. The large Whig-Liberal majority was cut in the election, but not enough to give a Tory victory. Nevertheless, Peel refused to resign and tried to govern for six weeks with minority support before surrendering office to Melbourne.

For the next six years (1835–1841) Melbourne in the House of Lords and the quietly persuasive Lord John Russell, leader of the House of Commons, survived threats from both wings (Whig and radical Irish) of their supporters. With the help of O'Connell they pushed through a few reforms (Municipal Reform Act, Irish Poor Relief Act) and accepted the Durham Report proposing responsible government in the colonies. Melbourne was adept in the art of political maneuvering and shifted his political positions with the times. He was equally proficient at managing Queen Victoria, who relied heavily on him as she learned the duties of the monarchy.

VICTORIA, MELBOURNE, AND PEEL

When William IV died in 1837 with no legitimate heirs, his niece, Victoria, became Queen at the age of eighteen. Since Hanover had a law forbidding a female from ruling, the royal connection with that German state was finally broken. Lord Melbourne, as Prime Minister, tutored the young monarch in correct constitutional and court conduct. He was an able teacher, and Victoria accepted the idea of offering only constitutional advice rather than instructions with considerable grace. In 1840 Melbourne helped arrange the marriage of Victoria to Prince Albert of Saxe-Coburg-Gotha. Albert became a knowledgeable and hard-working consort to whom Victoria was deeply devoted, but whom the nation never understood or appreciated during his lifetime.

In the election of 1837, required by the death of William IV, the Tories almost equaled the Whig vote. Two years later Melbourne was defeated over the Jamaica Prisons Bill, and his cabinet resigned. Peel now sought to put together a Tory ministry and ordered Queen Victoria to dismiss her Whig Ladies of the Bedchamber because he feared they might have undue influence on her—as Abigail Masham clearly had in Queen Anne's court. This tactless request disturbed the Queen, who was upset over the prospect of losing both Melbourne and her court companions. Instead of complying, Victoria asked Melbourne to remain in office. He accepted and was able to maintain a tenuous majority until 1841. The election of 1841 gave the Tories a clear majority, and by this time both the Queen and Parliament recognized that the monarch must choose a Prime Minister who could command a majority in the House of Commons. Peel took office and immediately faced the agitation of the Chartists and the Anti–Corn Law League.

Political Ideas

Motivating the British reformers of the eighteenth and nineteenth centuries were new ideas on society and its improvements. In time, many of their proposals slipped into the institutional life of the nation. Often the actual form of the final achievement was quite different from the original plan, or—to put it another way—reformers planned, and their plans often made a difference in society, but not always the difference planned. In the early nineteenth century Jeremy Bentham added his views on society to those already spelled out by Locke, Hume, Smith, and Burke.

JEREMY BENTHAM AND UTILITARIANISM (1748–1832)

Bentham seemed to appeal to the pragmatic mind of the British more than the doctrinaire schemes of utopian socialists such as Robert Owen (1771–1858). Bentham argued with Burke's position by declaring that respect for tradition dare not excuse the perpetuation of abuses in society; a free society must continuously reappraise its institutions in the light of *utility*. Two questions should be leveled at each institution. *Utility for what?* Promoting happiness. *Utility for whom?* The greatest number of individuals. Thus each law should be tested to see if it provided happiness (according to an arbitrary listing of pleasures and pains) for the many or for the few.

Bentham's followers—Edwin Chadwick, Southward Smith, William Cobbett, and Henry Hunt—employed this utilitarian doctrine to prove that the Game Law, parliamentary representation, and factory regulations favored the few and were in need of revision. Perhaps no other single theory was so influential as utilitarianism in bringing about item-by-item reform in the nineteenth century. Benthamites, serving on royal commissions, focused the nation's attention on public abuses, and the result was increasing government intervention and corrective legislation.

The immediate postwar reaction of the government to any type of change was strictly negative. Fear of revolution was still strong. In the 1820s Liverpool accommodated himself to the changing times and advent of more liberal ideas by bringing in young moderate Tories to his cabinet.

The 1830s was the decade that unleashed the pent-up pressures for reform, beginning with the unreformed House of Commons. The aristocratic Whig ministries led these reform efforts, not because they were advocates of democracy, but because they sensed the pragmatic need to expand the basis of political power and align the new industrial interests with them. In addressing the worst of the abuses, they showed reformers and radicals that it was possible to change society within the system.

By 1841 responsible government—the executive being directly responsible to the will of the majority in the Commons—became an established precedent. Sovereignty had moved in 1689 from the king to Parliament; by 1841 it had moved to the elected House of Commons.

Selected Readings

Aspinall, A. *Letters of George IV, 1812–1830* (1938)

Briggs, Asa. *The Age of Improvement, 1783–1867* (1959)

Brinton, Crane. *English Political Thought in the Nineteenth Century* (1962)

Cecil, David. *Melbourne* (1955)

Halévy, Elie. *A History of the English People in the Nineteenth Century.* vol. II (*The Liberal Awakening, 1815–1830*) and vol. III (*The Triumph of Reform, 1830–1841*) (1961)

Harrison, J. F. C. *The Early Victorians, 1832–1851* (1971)

Laski, Harold. *English Political Thought from Locke to Bentham* (1920)

Longford, Elizabeth. *Wellington: Pillar of State* (1973)

Maccoby, Samuel. *English Radicalism* (1955)

Temperly, Harold W. V. *The Foreign Policy of Canning, 1822–1827* (1925)

Trevelyan, George M. *Lord Grey of the Reform Bill* (1929)

Woodward, E. L. *The Age of Reform* (1962)

Ziegler, Philip. *Melbourne* (1976)

18

Mid-Victorianism: 1841–1865

The mid-Victorian years were a time of remarkable prosperity. Although this prosperity was not evenly distributed across the nation, it was an improvement over the past. Thriving on free trade and not yet encountering any foreign competition, Britain had reason to enjoy its industrial leadership. The achievements of industry and the nation's unchallenged supremacy in world leadership bred a spirit of confidence in the present and faith in the idea of progress.

It was only natural that Prime Minister Peel would seek to identify the Tory party with the successful economic and political changes springing from the Industrial revolution and the legislation of the 1830s. This adjustment to the new middle-class ascendancy meant that both parties had largely accepted the idea of piecemeal reform, free trade, and an industrial, rather than an agrarian, society as the basis of Britain's prospering economy.

However, Peel's decision to repeal the Corn Laws and end agricultural protection also broke the unity of the Tory party and resulted in political instability and a confusion of party loyalties for the next twenty years. To many landowners and their tenant farmers the Corn Laws were the historic foundation of agricultural prosperity. In this period of party flux Lord Palmerston, an independent Whig, was virtually the indispensable political figure. His policy of conservatism at home and jingoistic liberalism abroad was popular with the mid-Victorian populace, if not with foreign chanceries. Throughout the Palmerstonian era foreign affairs dominated British politics more than any single domestic issue.

PEEL'S POLICIES

Robert Peel's sure administrative grasp provided able leadership for the Tories, and they responded by supporting his financial and factory reforms. The Irish potato famine only reinforced the political and economic logic in his mind to repeal the Corn Laws. This decision to become a free trader and to end agricultural protection for Tory landlords made economic sense, but ruined Peel politically and divided his party. It brought forth Benjamin Disraeli as the leader of the country squires, and the ensuing splinter permitted two decades of Whig-Liberal rule.

Peel and the Tory Party

Peel had already reformed criminal law and established the metropolitan police force in his capacity as Home Secretary. In 1841 he became Prime Minister. Although lacking in imaginative ideas or in the ability to anticipate the future, Peel was a skilled administrator and a pragmatist whose integrity and parliamentary performance had won him the admiration of many loyal followers, among them Gladstone. The country squires backed him, often grudgingly, as he met the immediate needs of tariff reform and industrial legislation, until he jeopardized their pocketbooks and their political traditions by supporting the arguments of the Anti-Corn Law League which he was politically obligated to oppose.

Factory Legislation

No provisions had been included in earlier legislation to limit directly the hours of adult workers or to insist on greater safety or better working conditions. Lord Ashley continued to press for such reforms. The investigations of a royal commission revealed some of the frightful conditions in the mines and resulted in Parliament passing the Mines Act in 1842. This act prohibited the employment in mines of boys under ten and of women and girls. The provisions for inspectors of mines were deleted from Ashley's bill by the House of Lords, but were established in another act in 1850. The Factory Act of 1844 restricted the working day of women to twelve hours and for children to six and a half hours. For the first time safety provisions were included to make the fencing of machinery for safety purposes compulsory. Ashley's Factory Act of 1847 reduced the working day to ten hours for thirteen- to eighteen-year-olds and for women. These acts signaled the transition to better treatment of workers after the unregulated conditions that existed earlier.

Free Trade

Robert Peel who had seen the benefits of Huskisson's tariff reductions in the 1820s in promoting commercial and industrial expansion and in increasing profits. He immediately began to pursue a similar policy as Prime Minister. To Peel, tariff reform was experimental and utilitarian and not part of any doctrinaire position. To others, such as Richard Cobden and John Bright, free trade had become an article of faith which was considered indispensable for a free and competitive society. In the 1840s the propaganda of the Anti-Corn Law League, the depression, and wretched weather conditions combined to convert the public and Peel to free trade.

TARIFF AND FINANCIAL REFORMS

In his budget of 1842, Peel succeeded in ending the fiscal confusion which he had inherited from the Whigs. He introduced an income tax of seven pence on the pound sterling on all annual incomes of £150. Never before had such a form of taxation been levied in time of peace; it has never since disappeared from British budgets. Peel then proceeded to reduce the tariff on some 250 articles. When this action increased, rather than diminished, state revenues, he accelerated further reductions so that by 1846 all duties were removed on exports, almost all raw materials were admitted free, and the tariffs on other imports were slashed. The Bank Charter Act of 1844, which limited the issue of banknotes, stimulated trade and public confidence and reduced inflationary forces.

The Anti-Corn Law League

In 1839 an Anti–Corn Law League was organized in Manchester with the financial backing and political support of the manufacturers. The League wished to rouse public opinion against the Corn Law which protected agricultural interests by keeping high the price of food and forbidding the import of lower-priced corn. Under the leadership of Richard Cobden and John Bright, two manufacturers of extraordinary energy and oratorical ability, the League sent out persuasive workers who preached the gospel of free trade at mass meetings in the most intensive campaign of popular agitation in the first half of the century. Presented with remarkable lucidity and reams of statistics, free trade became a slogan which promised to guarantee international trade and peace, to lower food prices for the workers and, incidentally, to provide higher profits for the factory owners.

Aided by the introduction of the penny post in 1840, which required only a penny postage, the League showered anti–Corn Law pamphlets (nine million tracts in 1843 alone) on the towns of England, while public meetings focused popular attention on the issue. Cobden and Bright, now members of Parliament, introduced motions in the Commons for free trade, but without success. Not until disastrous weather conditions ruined the harvests was Peel convinced that he must repeal the law which his party insisted that he protect.

POTATO FAMINE IN IRELAND

The incessant rains in 1845 ruined the wheat crop in England and rotted the potatoes, the peasants' staple, in Ireland. Over one million Irish emigrated as famine stalked the land. After deciding that only an abundance of cheap foreign corn could ease the distress, Peel temporarily suspended the Corn Laws. When his cabinet divided on the issue, Peel resigned but returned to office after the Whigs under Lord John Russell refused to put together an alternative ministry. Peel was now completely converted to free trade, and once convinced, he had the political courage to face the charge of betrayal by his party.

REPEAL OF THE CORN LAWS

The protectionist landlords of the Tory party, under the leadership of Lord George Bentinck and Benjamin Disraeli, bitterly assailed Peel for his "treason." Undeterred, Peel introduced his bill in June, 1846, to abolish the Corn Laws over the next three years. The motion passed the House of Commons with the support of the Whigs, Irish, and free traders of the Tory party and passed the House of Lords because of the loyalty of the Duke of Wellington to Peel's government. But on the night of final passage the vengeful Tories united with the Whigs and Irish to defeat Peel on an Irish coercion bill and to force his resignation. Four years later Peel died.

SIGNIFICANCE OF REPEAL

Politically, the repeal of the Corn Laws ruined Peel and elevated Disraeli to prominence in the Tory party. The ensuing splintering of the Tories into two factions permitted almost two decades of Whig-Liberal rule. Repeal, however, did not produce all the momentous changes predicted. Corn prices remained relatively unchanged until the 1870s when Canadian and American wheat entered England at such low prices that the English farmer could not possibly compete. Nevertheless, repeal was a significant victory for laissez-faire liberalism over protectionism and marked the final triumph of an industrial over an agricultural economy.

Free trade soon became a basic principle of Victorian England. In 1849 the Navigation Acts were abolished. In 1852 Disraeli and the Tory party accepted the inevitability of free trade, and Gladstone, Peel's devoted follower, completed the change to free trade in a series of brilliant budget presentations. Moreover, the Anti–Corn Law League demonstrated the effectiveness of popular agitation and organized pressure on an increasingly middle-class government.

The Chartist Movement

The meager political gains from the Great Reform Bill, the collapse of Owen's trade union movement, and the hardships of an economic depression produced agitation among the lower-middle and working classes for a voice in government. In 1838 William Lovett and Francis Place drafted the People's Charter. Its six points called for universal male suffrage, the secret ballot, equal electoral districts, payment of members of Parliament, no property qualifications for members of Parliament, and annual general elections.

The Chartists organized large meetings across the country. At their convention in London in 1839 a giant petition with over a million signatures was prepared and presented to Parliament. However, following the defeat of the People's Charter, the Chartists became divided. Most members refused to use violent methods and drifted into other organizations, such as the Anti–Corn Law League. Led by Feargus O'Connor, the physical-force party of the Chartists engineered riots in 1841. In the following year various factions combined to present a second petition to the House of Commons, which was defeated 287 to 59.

Chartism subsided until 1847–1848 when economic distress in the country and revolution on the Continent revived the movement. A third giant petition was prepared, and a march on Parliament to accompany the petition was planned. Instead, because of rain, the petition of two million signatures was carried quietly by cab to Parliament, and shortly afterward the Chartist movement faded into oblivion. Although Chartism was killed by ridicule and reviving prosperity, it drew attention to the political consciousness of the working class and the cause of parliamentary democracy. By 1918 all of the radical proposals of the Chartists, except the annual election of Parliament, were enacted into legislation.

DOMESTIC POLITICS, 1846–1865

The breakup of the Tory party in 1846 resulted in an unstable Liberal political dominance for the next two decades, except for two Derby-Disraeli stopgap ministries which lasted less than three years. Palmerston, Russell, and Gladstone led the loosely knit Whig-Liberal and Peelite factions during these years. Palmerston was strongly opposed to any significant extension of political or social democracy in England. By midcentury, a growing level of material prosperity, along with world leadership in industrial production and foreign trade, made the nation self-confident and comfortably complacent. The absence of any general European war strengthened this feeling of security and progress.

The Position of Britain in 1846

Thirty years of peace permitted Britain to enjoy the benefits of growing national prosperity and prestige abroad. Throughout the nineteenth century the British navy, unchallenged since Trafalgar, provided effective and silent security for Great Britain and its maritime empire. England's parliamentary institutions and the relative sensitivity of its governing classes to popular pressures gave the nation a unique immunity to the violent revolutions which wracked the Continent in 1848.

The middle classes respected the governing institutions which encouraged them to seek wealth through industrial expansion and competition. The laborers, for the most part, accepted the idea that political reforms preceded economic and social improvements; therefore, their agitation was constitutional, urging remedies within the existing framework of things rather than revolution. If the pressures were too great, or if patience was too short, emigration to Canada, Australia, New Zealand, Cape Colony, or Natal served as a safety valve. The annual exodus from Britain for the three years 1847–1849 was over a quarter of a million. The population remaining in Britain also increased, doubling between 1801 and 1851 to 27 million. The rapid industrial changes produced social and individual problems which were not solved by a laissez-faire market economy. Yet, in the prosperous period of 1846–1865 England lacked the party unity and extra-parliamentary pressures necessary to push through domestic reforms.

PARTY ALIGNMENT

Peel's resignation resulted in the splinter of the Tory party into a protectionist wing dominated by Disraeli and a smaller, but influential, faction loyal to its fallen leader and known as Peelites. Because the factions reciprocated open hostility for each other, the Whigs became the dominant group, even though their supporters were by no means united. The conservative Whigs under Russell and Palmerston, the ex-Tory and Canningite, saw little need for further reform. But the Radicals, led by Cobden and Bright, continued to push for "peace, retrenchment and reform." Since party loyalties were loose, members of Parliament frequently changed sides without discredit. Cabinets usually included more than one faction and changed their personnel frequently to obtain a majority. Furthermore, cabinets had to straddle issues to hold their divergent factions together. As a result little controversial legislation passed in these years as compared to the preceding or the succeeding decades.

Russell's First Administration, 1846–1852

Lord John Russell, leader of the Whigs in the House of Commons and highly respected for his moral and political integrity, formed the new government, but with no program and with limited success. Since the Peelites refused to enter and the Radicals were not invited, Russell's cabinet remained purely Whig in composition. Cabinet policy was constructed to win either Peelite or Radical votes because the cabinet's continuation in office was dependent upon their votes.

The immediate problem was Ireland, where the potato famine of 1845–1846 produced distress and disorders. A coercion Act passed by Russell's government and the distribution of free food did not end the disturbances or the feelings of bitterness against the British. Dissatisfied with O'Connell's moderate leadership and influenced by the wave of liberal and nationalistic revolts sweeping Europe in 1848, leaders of a Young Ireland movement plotted an uprising. The rebellion was prevented by the arrest of the leaders, but no solutions were found for Ireland's grievances. Peel and his followers supported the Whig government in order to save free trade and to repeal the Navigation Acts in 1849. Factory and public health legislation extended the reform measures argued and initiated a decade earlier.

In 1851 the uninspired Whig cabinet was defeated on a measure proposing parliamentary reform. When the Tories could not muster sufficient support for their party, Lord Russell returned, hoping for a coalition with the Peelites. The cabinet finally fell in 1852 over the ousting of the irrepressible foreign minister, Lord Palmerston, who was the only popular figure in the cabinet. His style of high-handed and independent diplomacy had long annoyed the Prime Minister and the Queen. When Palmerston approved Louis Napoleon's coup d'état of 1851 in France in spite of the cabinet's position of strict neutrality, Russell dismissed him. Palmerston retaliated by helping to defeat the cabinet before the end of the year.

The First Derby-Disraeli Government, 1852

The Earl of Derby (formerly Lord Stanley) became Prime Minister, with Disraeli as Chancellor of the Exchequer and leader of the House of Commons. The rest of the cabinet consisted of unknown protectionists. By this time Disraeli, with his parliamentary strategy and brilliant oratory, had begun to mold his band of landlords into a compact and disciplined body.

Derby held an election on the issue of free trade only to discover that the voters' preference for free trade left his party in a minority. Disraeli thereupon won the acceptance of his party for the free-trade principle, hoping to win the allegiance of the Peelites. Gladstone, leader of this faction after Peel's death, rejected the overtures and helped defeat Disraeli's budget, thereby terminating Derby's ten-month ministry.

Aberdeen's Coalition, 1852–1855

Lord Aberdeen, a Peelite, brought together a Whig-Peelite coalition of great individual talents which he was unable to manage. Aberdeen opposed Palmerston and Russell in foreign policy, and Palmerston objected to Russell's plan for parliamentary reform. Such dissensions within the cabinet demanded a strong prime minister, which the gentle, learned Aberdeen was not. Gladstone, as Chancellor of the Exchequer, followed in the tradition of Peel. His budgets under Aberdeen and later under Palmerston (1859–1865) set up several principles which became the orthodox Liberal theories of national finance: income taxes were to be used for emergencies rather than as a basic source of revenue; taxes were to be reduced by installment; there would be steady retrenchment in government expenses; and virtually all duties would be abolished. Lord Aberdeen's leadership was sufficient for peacetime, but not for the Crimean War, which he opposed and for which the nation's armed forces were sadly unprepared. The resulting military confusion aroused a public outcry against the war office and the government. In January 1855, Aberdeen resigned.

Prime Minister Palmerston, 1855–1858

The stalemate in Crimea made the public clamor for "Pam's" aggressive and patriotic brand of leadership. When Queen Victoria was unable to find an alternative, Palmerston became Prime Minister and infused new vigor into the war effort. The public believed that his leadership helped win the war the next year. By this time the Peelites had left the cabinet, leaving Palmerston with a precarious Whig majority. In 1857 Palmerston called an election, and the voters demonstrated their confidence in him by giving his supporters a clear majority. But since party lines were still in flux, his majority disappeared the following year when controversy with France developed over the Italian revolutionist Felice Orsini, who had procured bombs during his stay in England with which to assassinate Emperor Napoleon III. The result was the defeat of Palmerston's government over his Conspiracy to Murder Bill.

The Second Derby-Disraeli Government, 1858–1859

Once again the Peelites refused to unite with the Conservatives, leaving the new ministry with only minority support. A bill proposing parliamentary reform was introduced, and the ministry called an election in 1859 with the hope of having found a popular issue. The Conservatives increased their strength, but not sufficiently to win a majority. Derby's cabinet thereupon resigned, and Queen Victoria returned the seals of office to Palmerston.

Palmerston's Second Ministry, 1859–1865

Palmerston's second cabinet remained in office until his death in 1865. Its comparatively long tenure was due to the continued weakness of the Tories and the fusion, finally, of the Peelites, Whigs, and Radicals into the Liberal party. Palmerston's old Whig and aristocratic convictions tolerated no expansion of political democracy in the country, so that the more liberal members, led by Gladstone, had to wait until the Prime Minister's death to introduce further reform legislation. However, both Palmerston and Russell supported the unification of Italy by Cavour and helped to preserve the unity of the United States by an official position of neutrality.

The Age of Machinery

The midcentury was a period when England basked in the economic benefits of its claim to the title of "workshop of the world." In the years 1850 to 1870 an industrialized, urbanized, and mechanized Britain increased exports from £71 million to nearly £200 million. Next to agriculture—still the nation's largest single industry—were textiles, employing over one and a half million in 1851 and becoming the most valuable single article of export. Half a million were employed in mines and quarries and over one hundred thousand in the making of machinery. The commercial development of Henry Bessemer's steel process in 1856 enabled Britain to take a commanding lead in iron and steel exports. This rapid development of industry and population meant that the island could supply neither sufficient foodstuff for its cities nor raw materials for its factories. The full impact of this fact, however, was not felt until later decades.

Mid-Victorianism

To many observers the opening of the Crystal Palace—Britain's Great Exhibition and first world's fair in history—on May 1, 1851, was the high noon of Victorianism, with its firm confidence in the rightness of things English and its faith in the future. The buoyant mood created by the nation's wealth, industrial supremacy, and invincible Royal Navy prompted a public confidence based upon the unquestioned conviction that the most scientific law of the century was the Law of Progress. No statesman embodied the character and self-assertiveness of the industrial middle class better than Palmerston; perhaps that was why he was so immensely popular. Yet with this self-satisfaction was a willingness to accept criticism. With critics like Charles Dickens, Matthew Arnold, and Thomas Carlyle, the nation was prodded to improve its social condition.

MORAL CONSCIENCE

The typical mid-Victorian was religious as well as materialistic. Christian virtues and the Bible were as important as success in business, and not infrequently linked together. Evangelicalism and the Nonconformist conscience pervaded the entire fabric of life and resulted in strict observance of Sunday, worldwide missionary work, family devotions, and propriety of dress and manners in public. Coupled with liberal humanitarianism, the public conscience of the British people was pricked into improving the condition of the poor, rehabilitating criminals and social outcasts, and extending democratic and religious values and institutions to poorer classes.

MATERIAL PROGRESS

Economic prosperity, more than any other single feature, best defined mid-Victorian Britain. By any measure Britain's trade and industrial production outranked that of its competitors. In 1850 Britain produced two-thirds of the world's coal, half of its cotton manufacture, and 40 percent of its hardware. By 1870 Britain produced half the world's steel, and its foreign trade was greater than that of France, Germany, and Italy combined, and four times that of the United States. London, with a population of over three million, became the banker of the world, and sterling, pegged to the gold standard by Peel's Bank Act (1844), became the currency of international banking. Although the burgeoning middle class claimed the largest share of the benefits from this prosperity, the laborers also had better working conditions than a generation earlier and a higher standard of living.

PALMERSTON'S FOREIGN POLICY

Lord Palmerston was the third outstanding British foreign minister of the century (following Castlereagh and Canning). For thirty years he personified the attitudes of early Victorian England and acquired a personal ascendancy seldom equaled in English politics. His arrogant patriotism and practice of brinkmanship, backed by the Royal Navy, delighted the masses even as it unsettled his colleagues, the Queen, and foreign rulers. Yet, paradoxically, Palmerston's noisy meddling in European politics based on an astute understanding of the need for a balance of power did not involve Britain in any major hostilities; whereas the Crimean War broke out during the ministry of the genteel and conciliatory Aberdeen.

Basic Principles of Nineteenth-Century Foreign Policy

Although Palmerston frequently appeared impulsive and improvised policies on the moment, claiming that Britain had no eternal enemies, certain national interests were paramount. The more important interests included a balance of power in Europe, maintaining naval and commercial supremacy, preserving Turkey against encroachment by Russia, and protecting the sea routes to India. Like Canning, Palmerston also reflected public sentiment. During these years English liberalism, evangelicalism, and humanitarianism favored the support of liberal and nationalist movements abroad and shared a hatred of autocracy. To these sentiments Palmerston gave energetic support.

GREAT BRITAIN AND BELGIUM

When Palmerston became foreign minister in 1830, he immediately faced the problem of revolution on the Continent, sparked by the Paris uprising in July. The most serious disturbance threatening Britain's security was the Belgian revolt against the Congress of Vienna settlement, which had united the Netherlands and Belgium under the Dutch monarchy. Belgian nationalism never accepted this alien overlordship, and French sympathy was with the Belgian cause. Palmerston called a conference of five powers— the Congress system—to arrange a suitable settlement. When the Dutch and the French renewed the war, Palmerston, by masterful diplomacy that combined flexibility with firmness, secured another armistice and an independent Belgium. In 1839 a treaty was signed by the five powers (Britain, France, Austria, Prussia, and Russia) guaranteeing Belgium's independence and perpetual neutrality. Palmerston had kept Belgium free from the control of a major power and maintained a balance of power to preserve peace.

THE NEAR EAST

Palmerston's concern was that the dissolution of the crumbling Turkish empire would make Russia dominant in the Near East. He suspected that Russia had designs on Turkey when it made a defensive alliance with the Sultan of Turkey in 1833 to contain the Pasha of Egypt, Mehemet Ali, and his son's conquest of Syria. In 1839 a second crisis arose between the Sultan and Mehemet Ali. This time France intruded and backed the Pasha's claim to Syria, convinced that neither Britain nor Russia would cooperate to oppose French interference. Palmerston sent in the British fleet to prevent French domination and made an alliance with all the major powers, except France, to force Mehemet Ali to relinquish Syria. Palmerston's diplomatic victory kept Turkey from becoming a satellite of Russia and kept French influence out of Egypt. However, Britain became tied to the defense of an oppressive and corrupt Turkish empire in the process.

THE FAR EAST

Palmerston's government forced the Chinese to abandon their traditional policy of diplomatic isolation and limited trading privileges for foreigners. He sent gunboats to China when the Chinese government refused to receive British officials who were serving as trade officials for Britain and the East India Company. In 1839 the Chinese, in an effort to end the importation of opium, forced the British commission in Canton to confiscate all opium in the possession of British merchants. This act led to the Opium

War in 1840 which the British won with their superior naval and firepower. The Treaty of Nanking (1842) gave diplomatic recognition to Britain, opened five additional ports to trade, required China to pay an indemnity for the confiscated opium, and ceded the island of Hong Kong to Britain.

PEEL'S FOREIGN POLICY

Only during Peel's five-year ministry (1841–1846) did Palmerston relinquish control of foreign affairs for any length of time. The conciliatory Lord Aberdeen directed the Foreign Office in a much less belligerent fashion. Strained relations with the United States were mended by two treaties: the Webster-Ashburton Treaty of 1842 resolved a territorial dispute on the Maine–New Brunswick border; and the Oregon settlement of 1846 averted the possibility of war by extending the forty-ninth parallel to the Pacific as the boundary between Canada and the United States but left Britain all of Vancouver Island.

PALMERSTON IN CONTROVERSY, 1846–1852

Palmerston's practice of acting independently of both the cabinet and the monarchy disturbed Prime Minister Russell and angered Queen Victoria. However, Palmerston's prejudices and patriotism, and even his insolent manner in rebuking foreign governments, won the applause of a chauvinist Parliament, press, and populace. "Sending in the fleet and defending Britain's trade and honor" were the trademark of Palmerston's policy. Diplomatically, he had great success in using the conference system of foreign ministers to settle issues.

Continental Revolts, 1848. Palmerston offered vocal encouragement to the chain of liberal and nationalist uprisings which took place on the Continent that year. He condemned the repressive measures of the old regimes in restoring their authority and was an advocate of Italian liberty and unification. These views won him the admiration of British and Continental liberals, and made England a haven for political exiles, such as Lajos Kossuth and Guisippe Mazzini.

Don Pacifico. In 1850 Don Pacifico, a Portuguese Jew who had been born in British Gibraltar, appealed directly to Palmerston in supporting his claim against the Greek government for damages to his property by a mob in Athens. When diplomatic channels did not bring immediate action, the impatient Palmerston ordered the British fleet to seize Greek ships. Immediately the Greek government recognized the claim, but such high-handed action brought a censure from the House of Lords and a vote of confidence in the House of Commons. Palmerston won the vote by emotionally arguing that a British subject could count on British protection throughout the world, just as could a Roman subject in the days of the Apostle Paul by claiming *"civis Romanus sum"* (I am a citizen of Rome). To the person in the street such arrogant patriotism, British honor, and universal justice were seen as synonyms in this case.

Louis Napoleon. Palmerston unofficially approved Louis Napoleon's overthrow of the French Republic in 1851. Since the cabinet was taking a position of strict neutrality, Lord Russell used the incident to dismiss his controversial Foreign Minister in 1852. Without the powerful Palmerston the cabinet was defeated in the Commons before the end of the year.

The Crimean War, 1854–1856

Britain blundered into, and through, an unnecessary war with Russia which only the press and public opinion had wanted. This enthusiasm for the war changed to criticism when the press revealed the bungling of the military commanders and the high mortality rate among the sick and wounded British soldiers. The war forced the resignation of Lord Aberdeen and gave the popular Palmerston his first prime ministership.

CAUSES

Russia once again became impatient to control the Straits and win access to the Mediterranean. In 1853 Czar Nicholas I renewed the Russian proposal to divide Turkey among Britain, France, and Russia. Britain feared the expansion of Russia southward would lead to Russian designs against the British in India. The precipitating cause of the war was a controversy in Palestine in which priests of the Roman Catholic and the Orthodox churches clashed over control of the Church of the Nativity in Bethlehem. France and Russia immediately claimed the right of protector. The Czar then extended his demands to include the protection of Greek Catholics in Turkey, believing, mistakenly, that the conciliatory Aberdeen would not offer military support to the Sultan. Turkey declared war on Russia, whereupon Russia promptly sank the Turkish Black Sea fleet. Led on by uncontrollably bellicose public opinion, Britain came to the rescue of Turkey, along with France and Austria.

COURSE OF THE WAR

After the Russians were driven out of the Turkish provinces, the war revolved around the allied siege of the Russian naval base at Sevastopol. The conspicuous shortcomings of the allied military organization, the breakdown of the commissariat in the bitter cold of winter, and the lack of medicine and hospital care for the ill—seven soldiers died of fever for every one killed in action—were duly reported by the *Times*, causing a public outcry in Britain. One of the most foolhardy cavalry charges in history, that of the Earl of Cardigan's light brigade against heavily fortified Russian positions, occurred at Balaklava and was immortalized by the poet Tennyson. When Sevastopol was finally taken (1855), Palmerston wished to continue the war, but Napoleon III of France had other projects in mind and wanted peace.

THE TREATY OF PARIS, 1856

According to the terms of the treaty, the independence of Turkey was maintained, all Russian and Turkish conquests were restored, the Black Sea and the Dardanelles were closed to warships, Serbia gained internal autonomy, and the Sultan promised protection for his Christian subjects. The peace settlement halted the expansion of Russia, but did little more. In Britain, two important results of the war were the founding of the Red Cross, an outcome of Florence Nightingale's heroic nursing efforts in the field hospitals, and the reform of the British army.

The Indian Mutiny, 1856

Disaffected Sepoys—Indian soldiers in British employ—revolted against alien rule and the westernization of their culture. Although the revolt was crushed without too much difficulty, the uprising prepared the way for Indian nationalism, ended Pitt's system of dual control in India, and widened the breach in British-Indian relations.

BACKGROUND

Between Pitt's India Act (1784) and the zenith of power of the British East India Company under the governor-generalship of Lord Dalhousie (1848–1856), British officials had rapidly expanded and consolidated their rule in India. Intervention in native wars and the frequent disorder in Indian states lured empire builders, such as Richard Wellesley, the marquis of Hastings, and Lord Dalhousie, to take over the whole of India and administer it either directly as part of British India, or indirectly, through treaties with native princes. By 1856 the rapid pace of westernization through education, industrialization, and attacks on Indian customs made the Indian soldiers fear that the Hindu culture would be supplanted.

Dalhousie's vast annexations and the imposition of the doctrine of lapse (all princely states reverted to Britain when a prince died without heir) seemed to jeopardize the future of India. Morale in the Bengal army was low. Soldiers were incensed over the introduction of a new cartridge lubricated with the fat of cows and hogs. The greased cartridge appeared to be a deliberate insult to the Hindu, to whom the cow was sacred, and to the Moslem, who was forbidden to eat pork. In May, 1857, the Bengal army mutinied and marched on Delhi.

REBELLION

The Sepoy mutiny was largely confined to the upper Ganges Valley and was not supported by the native armies of the other regions. At Cawnpore all Europeans were massacred, and only two successive relief columns saved Lucknow. Within a year the revolt was stamped out but its consequences were significant. The political power of the East India Company ended when the India Act of 1858 placed full responsibility for the government of the Indian empire under a cabinet minister responsible to Parliament. Indians were allowed to compete for positions in the prestigious Indian Civil Service in a belated attempt to remove some of the grievances which had provoked the mutiny. More significant was the change in the British position in India: the mutiny increased the isolation of the colonial ruler from the native, whereas the rebellion made efforts to justify the British presence in India much more difficult. To the Indian people the uprising became a rallying point for later nationalist movements.

Italian Unification

The government won broad consensus of support for Palmerston's adroit handling of diplomatic relations with the Italian states. Here Palmerston, Russell, and Gladstone rallied British opinion in support of Count Cavour's efforts to transform the separate Italian states into a united, liberal nation. Emperor Napoleon III of France helped Cavour oust the hated Austrians from northern Italy but withdrew his aid when the separate Italian states sought to unite. At this point Britain stepped in to prevent hostile Austrian or French interference and to permit a popular plebiscite which resulted in unification. British power was still sufficient for Palmerston to assert moral sanctions and threats without actual military intervention.

The American Civil War

Palmerston and Russell announced no clear-cut public policy, but steered a cautious, neutral course in the controversy over recognition of the Confederate States; their bias, if any, was in favor of the South. The upper classes and the press generally sympathized with the South. The great cotton factories were hurt by the loss of southern American cotton, but workers accepted the ensuing unemployment in a demonstration of loyalty to the slave-free North.

Two incidents endangered Britain's official neutrality. Sailors from a United States cruiser stopped and boarded a British ship, the *Trent*, and arrested two Confederate envoys en route to England. This violation of neutral rights caused the cabinet to draft a belligerent note which made the North disavow its actions in order to ensure British neutrality. In turn, the North accused the British government of deliberate negligence in allowing a Confederate raider, the *Alabama*, to be launched from a British shipyard to prey on northern shipping. After the war Britain paid substantial damages in compensation. The decisive victories of the Union armies in 1863, coupled with Lincoln's declaration of emancipation, prevented any further thought of British intervention in the American Civil War.

Denmark and Prussia

As a final venture in personal diplomacy Palmerston supported Denmark in its dispute with autocratic Prussia over the duchies of Schleswig and Holstein. In the past the threat of British intervention had been sufficient; this time Otto von Bismarck forced Palmerston's hand by allying with Austria and invading Denmark in 1864. However, British public opinion would not support land forces on the Continent and the Royal Navy was not intimidating in a land war. Palmerston had to back down on his promise of aid to Denmark. The Prime Minister died the following year, before the aggrandizement of Prussia under Bismarck completely upset the balance of power in Europe.

By 1865 Palmerston's influence in the diplomatic world of personal politics and liberal nationalism abroad was already waning. It was being replaced in Europe by the Realpolitik *(power politics) of Bismarck. Britain continued to fear France and Russia far more than an emergent Germany.*

Palmerston was the last of the statesmen-aristocrats to lead Britain before modern party politics emerged under his successor, Gladstone. By 1865 pent-up reform measures were released which had stalled while Palmerston was Prime Minister, mainly because of his eighteenth-century Whig ideas on the franchise and on the limited function of government.

During these years—the "high noon" of nineteenth-century peace and prosperity—Britain was clearly the dominant industrial and naval power in the world. At home increasing prosperity and expansion of markets—and the reticence of Whig leadership to change the status quo—caused a temporary reprieve in the push for further reforms. With Palmerston's death the pace again quickened.

Selected Readings

Best, Geoffrey. *Mid-Victorian Britain, 1851–1875* (1971)

Briggs, Asa. *Victorian People: A Reassessment of Persons and Themes, 1851–1867* (1963)

Burns, William L. *The Age of Equipoise: A Study of the Mid-Victorian Generation* (1964)

Cecil, Algernon. *Queen Victoria and Her Prime Ministers* (1953)

Checkland, S. G. *The Rise of Industrial Society in England, 1815–1885* (1964)

Dodds, John W. *The Age of Paradox: A Biography of England, 1841–1851* (1952)

Gash, Norman. *Politics in the Age of Peel* (1977)

Greville, Charles C. F. *The Greville Memoirs, 1827–1860* (1963)

Hammond, J. L., and Barbara Hammond. *Lord Shaftesbury* (1969)

Houghton, Walter. *The Victorian Frame of Mind, 1830–1870* (1957)

McCord, Norman. *The Anti–Corn Law League, 1838–1846* (1958)

Smith, F. B. *Florence Nightingale: Reputation and Power* (1982)

Southgate, Donald. *The Passing of the Whigs, 1832–1886* (1962)

Southgate, Douglas. *The Most English Minister: The Policies and Politics of Lord Palmerston* (1966)

Vincent, John. *The Formation of the British Liberal Party, 1857–1868* (1977)

Young, George M. (ed.) *Early Victorian England, 1830–1865* (1934)

Woodham-Smith, Cecil. *The Great Hunger* (1963)

19

Victorian Politics: Gladstone and Disraeli, 1865–1886

1867	Second Reform Bill passed
1868–1874	First of four Gladstone ministries
1870	Passage of first National Education Act
1872	Ballot Act passes, providing for the secret ballot
1874–1880	Ministry of Benjamin Disraeli
1875	Passage of Public Health Act
1878	Congress of Berlin
1880	Gladstone's second ministry begins
1884	Passage of Third Reform Bill
1885	General Gordon killed at Khartoum
1886	Gladstone's first Irish Home Rule Bill defeated in the House of Commons

The mid-Victorian interlude, when political alignments were confused and fluid, and reform was secondary to foreign affairs, drew to a close around 1865. Under the leadership of Gladstone and Disraeli, Britain moved into a new age of transition and reform. The Liberal party became the dominant political force during these twenty years.

The Victorian compromise of the Palmerstonian era which was based on the alliance of the aristocracy with the middle class was now expanded to permit the extension of political democracy. The clashing personalities of Gladstone and Disraeli, statesmen of outstanding, but widely different, abilities, dramatized the political and social issues of these years.

A new admiration for imperialism became evident, although it would not peak in popularity until the 1890s. By the time of Gladstone's second ministry the overriding issue of the day was the Irish Question; it would dominate the political agenda.

GLADSTONE AND REFORM

Gladstone's political position slowly evolved over the decades from high Toryism to the very embodiment of British Liberalism with its theme of "peace, retrenchment, and reform." His moral earnestness, his faith in the political sense of the ordinary citizen, and his extraordinary financial talents appealed to the nation and helped complete the metamorphosis of the Whigs into the Liberal party. The legislation of his first ministry brought about institutional reforms long overdue.

Gladstone and Disraeli

Two statesmen, entirely different in background and in style, dominated political affairs for the twenty years after the death of Palmerston. William E. Gladstone's background was one of middle-class wealth, privilege, and upper-class education. After wavering between politics and the Anglican ministry, Gladstone entered Parliament as a member for the ultra-Tory seat of Oxford and became a follower of Sir Robert Peel. In public life he was determined to put a religious imprint on politics as surely as his personal life expressed religious convictions; his appeal to morality fit the temper of the times. During his half-century in the House of Commons (including serving as Prime Minister four times), Gladstone became increasingly liberal on religious and political issues. His superb skills in oratory and in drafting legislation made him one of the great parliamentarians of all time. For nearly thirty years he was the "conscience of England" and leader of the Liberals.

In contrast, Benjamin Disraeli was a most unlikely person to achieve the leadership of the Tory party. A London Jew, a romantic novelist lacking in wealth or political connections, Disraeli was educated privately, and had a flamboyant style and dress. A master of sarcasm and debate, Disraeli became the leader of the protectionist Tories after he attacked Peel for abandoning the Corn Laws. He had a gift for managing people and he showed both audacity and ability in his management of Parliament. Once in power he took a vital interest in social legislation and renovated the party's aristocratic traditions to changing times. His pride in England's national institutions and his unabashed imperialism caught the admiration of his colleagues and of Queen Victoria.

The Second Reform Bill, 1867, and the Third Derby-Disraeli Government, 1866–1868

Upon the death of Palmerston in 1865, Lord Russell became Prime Minister. His cabinet colleague, Gladstone, introduced a long overdue bill for the extension of the vote to urban workers. A group of Whigs under Robert Lowe opposed their party's bill and united with the Tories to defeat it. Thereupon, Derby and Disraeli organized a third minority government. By now the earlier apathy about the franchise bill disappeared as trade unions and new organizations of workingmen arranged mass demonstrations and mobs rioted in London. Disraeli persuaded his party to back reform, thereby robbing the Liberals of their program and winning the gratitude of the urban workers. Gladstone was enraged over Disraeli's tactic, but the bill passed with the assistance of the radical wing of the Liberal party in 1867.

A small redistribution of seats occurred with the Second Reform Bill, but the major change was in the extension of the franchise to every male householder in a borough who paid poor rates (taxes). In the towns the low level at which property qualifications were set made male suffrage nearly universal and satisfied most of the groups pressing for reform. In the counties the franchise was enlarged by reducing from £10 to £5 the annual value of property ownership required for voter qualification. The bill nearly doubled the number of voters.

That year Lord Derby resigned because of ill health. For the next eighteen months Liberal votes and popular satisfaction with the Reform Bill permitted Disraeli to serve as Prime Minister. Parliament proceeded to pass the British North America Act (1867) which created a federal government and constitution for Canada. The act marked another peaceful step to colonial self-government and helped to unify the divisive colonies of Canada and protect the new nation from possible American expansion northward at the end of the Civil War.

Gladstone's First Ministry, 1868–1874

Gladstone reunited the dissident wings of the Liberal party by his efforts to redress Irish grievances. Rebellion had broken out in Ireland in a violent attempt to relieve distress and end British rule. The uprising which was planned by the Fenians (a secret organization established in 1858 by Irish Americans) became another abortive effort to win Irish independence. Instead of more coercive acts, Gladstone proposed that the government pacify the Irish by disestablishing the Anglican Church in Ireland. Prime Minister Disraeli opposed the proposal and lost his Liberal allies, forcing his resignation. The election of 1868 endorsed Gladstone and gave the

Liberals a majority of over one hundred. Gladstone began the first of his four administrations with an ambitious program of reform.

DISESTABLISHMENT OF THE CHURCH IN IRELAND, 1869

As the first of his remedial measures for Ireland, Gladstone introduced a bill to disestablish and disendow the Anglican Church in Ireland. Although a devout Anglican himself, he opposed the injustice of a Catholic populace supporting an alien church attended almost exclusively by their landlords. The bill placed the Anglican Church on a voluntary basis and permitted approximately £9 million of its assets to remain within the Church; another £7 million was appropriated for charity and education in Ireland.

IRISH LAND REFORM, 1870

A second grievance of long standing was the exploitative custom of landlords leasing land on a year-by-year basis. If peasants improved their tenements, the landlord could either eject the tenant or raise the rent without compensation for improvements. There was no redress in the courts. In spite of landowner opposition, Gladstone pushed through Parliament an Irish Land Act which copied the tenant custom in Ulster and made illegal the eviction of tenants without compensation for their improvements. The practical results of the bill were disappointing because no provisions were included to prevent unscrupulous landlords from raising rents exorbitantly and ousting tenants for inability to pay. Nevertheless, for the first time the rights of the tenant were recognized by law.

THE EDUCATION ACT, 1870

The great extension of the franchise in 1867 added another argument for establishing a system of public education, since only one half of the children of elementary school age were in attendance in 1869. The laissez-faire attitude of the Palmerstonian era and the heated controversy over religious instruction in state schools—insisted upon by Anglicans, objected to by Dissenters—had prevented any effective action. W. E. Forster's education bill survived the controversy and passed both Houses. It authorized the local government, in any locality where existing voluntary schools were inadequate, to permit popularly elected school boards to establish public schools. These schools were to be funded by national and local taxes, and by fees which could be remitted in the case of poor children. Attendance between the ages of five and thirteen could be made compulsory by the local school board. State aid to the voluntary schools was increased and religious instruction was left unrestricted. In the new public schools such instruction was to be non-sectarian and non-compulsory. In 1880 attendance at elementary school was made compulsory, and in 1891 all fees were abolished.

BALLOT ACT, 1872

The aim of the Ballot Act was to establish the Australian (or secret) ballot, recommended thirty years earlier in the People's Charter, in order to protect the newly enfranchised voter from intimidation at the polls. Especially in Ireland the landlord or shop owner lost his political influence over his workers. The law was a further step toward remedying corrupt political practices.

JUDICATURE ACT, 1873

The judicial machinery created in the Middle Ages continued in operation but with increasing confusion and with glaring abuses as three rival courts wrangled over jurisdiction. Simple cases were often involved in legal complexities that delayed justice and raised costs. The Judicature Act coordinated this legal machinery into one supreme court of judicature, consisting of a court of appeal and a high court of justice. The latter was divided into (1) the king's bench; (2) the chancery; and (3) the probate, divorce, and admiralty. Certain civil suits could still be appealed to the House of Lords, which continued as the highest court of the land. A system of life peerages was introduced so that lords with legal training could deal with the judicial duties of the House of Lords.

ARMY REFORMS

Secretary of War Edward Cardwell proposed a series of army reforms that were sorely needed, especially after the Crimean War. When the House of Lords prepared to kill sections of the bill, Gladstone put through the measures by royal ordinance (similar to an executive order in the United States), thereby avoiding the need for a parliamentary statute. The reforms reduced the size of the standing army, organized an effective reserve, provided for short-term enlistments, and abolished the purchase of army commissions. The abolition of the old custom of "purchase" stirred angry protests from the upper classes, which provided most of the officers.

ADDITIONAL REFORMS

Gladstone ended the monopoly of the Church of England in higher education by abolishing all religious tests at the universities. In 1870 open competitive exams were inaugurated for positions in the civil service. This reform provided a higher level of competence and more continuity in administration—two significant improvements, since the civil service became increasingly important as the state enlarged its activities. In 1871 a Local Government Board was formed to coordinate the numerous state supervisory agencies which had been established over several decades. Working conditions were improved by the Factory Act Extension Act (1867) and the Coal Mines Act (1872).

Foreign Policy   Less popular with voters was the foreign policy of Gladstone. He appeared disinterested in the extension of empire, preferring for England a moral to an imperial prestige. Critics claimed that his financial economies provided budgetary surpluses at the expense of military influence. Britain remained neutral in the Franco-Prussian War, during which Prussia became the most powerful state in Europe. Russia took advantage of the war to denounce the restrictive clauses of the Treaty of Paris. Britain protested but participated with the treaty's signatory powers in a conference which agreed to most of Russia's demands. This decision was regarded by the populace as a British surrender. In dealing with the United States, Gladstone set a wise precedent in submitting the issue of the *Alabama* claims to an international tribunal of arbitration in 1872. The tribunal dismissed the exorbitant, indirect claims but awarded the United States $15,500,000 in gold for direct damages. Once again popular opinion felt that Gladstone was not asserting Britain's position as a great power.

Liberal Defeat   By 1873 the government's foreign policy was generally condemned as too pacifist for a major power. Furthermore, the government had carried through so much reform legislation that the electorate seemed satiated. Each bill had alienated certain groups, and members of Parliament resented Gladstone's habit of equating his reforms with moral righteousness. Meanwhile, Disraeli had built up an attractive program and an effective party organization, the National Union, which won the loyalty of many urban workers. In the election of 1874 the Conservatives won a clear majority for the first time since 1841.

DISRAELI AND THE NEW TORYISM

The use of the regulative powers of the state to improve the quality of British life was accepted by Disraeli in the 1870s. As Prime Minister he educated the Conservative party to the social obligations of "Tory democracy," especially since the "have nots" outnumbered the "haves" in voting numbers after 1867. In foreign and imperial policy his ideas were more dramatic, popular, and also more dangerous than those of Gladstone. Disraeli identified the Conservative party with the patriotic imperialism of the day and provided Britain with a new concept of empire. Sooner than his contemporaries, Disraeli sensed that the two most powerful and popular forces of the immediate future would be social reform and imperialism.

**State
Intervention**

The reforms of Gladstone's ministry laid the foundation for a modern State in which the old institutions, such as the House of Lords and the monarchy, were accommodated to new political and social philosophies. By 1875 the earlier liberal philosophy, with its accent on competitive individualism, self-improvement through private initiative, and minimal government regulation of trade and industry, had given way to a majority viewpoint favoring regulative legislation that could improve society where private initiative was inadequate or indifferent.

How to reconcile individualism and collectivism in a free society became a dilemma which plagued political philosophers and politicians throughout the late nineteenth and twentieth centuries. John Stuart Mill published his *Principles* in 1848; for forty years this treatise served as a guide to social and political reformers (often termed radicals) in their efforts to achieve a more equitable distribution of wealth and the participation of all classes in the benefits of an industrial society. The failure of laissez-faire policies to protect society from exploitation and private greed encouraged the gradual growth of municipal ownership—"gas and water socialism." Both political parties continued to give lip service to their old doctrines and slogans, but each was eager to woo the new mass electorate with attractive programs. As a result Marxism had only modest interest for British workers since there was little interest in class warfare and political changes were possible without a revolution. Until the Syndicalist strikes in 1910 a social consensus in Britain was evident that reflected considerable agreement on basic values, such as self-reliance and item-by-item reform. General prosperity and the emerging welfare state contributed to a rather quiescent working class in these decades.

TORY DEMOCRACY

Besides protecting the established institutions of Britain from undue change, Disraeli saw the political advantage and the human benefits which would accrue from improving the economic and social conditions of the working class. He convinced his party that the economic and political position of the upper classes would be jeopardized more by an embittered working class than by a contented one. An intelligent aristocracy, argued Disraeli, devoted itself to the social welfare of all classes. From this time onward Disraeli's emphasis on "Tory democracy" became an important plank in the Tory political program.

DOMESTIC LEGISLATION

In 1875 a Public Health Act, systematizing sanitary laws, an Artisans' Dwellings Act, permitting municipalities to clear slums and erect new dwellings, and a Rivers Pollution Act were evidence of Conservative interest in the physical welfare of the workingman. In the same year, the Conservatives reversed the laws restricting picketing and limiting the bargaining position of trade unions. Measures were passed which made peaceful picketing legal and put employer and employee on the same legal footing. In 1876 trade unions were included within the scope of the Friendly Societies Acts, and collective bargaining was now legally possible. Two acts halted the historic enclosure of public lands and commons and reversed the process by restoring some lands for use as public parks. In 1878 the Factory and Workshop Act replaced previous legislation on hours and conditions of labor with a completely revised code.

The Changing Economy

Since the international market and export trade had become the arbiter of the British economy, Britain became dependent upon international trade for prosperity. Already, the first signs of future economic trouble were in evidence. Cobden's prophecy of world peace and prosperity through world trade remained a fiction. Instead, Britain was losing its midcentury position of unchallenged industrial leadership as Germany, France, Italy, and the United States became vigorous competitors and set high tariffs to keep out foreign produce.

More conspicuous was the collapse of British agriculture. By 1870 the revolution in transportation brought into Britain cheaper foreign wool and grain than local farmers could offer. Even the perishable market was threatened when commercial refrigeration in the early 1880s permitted Australian, New Zealand, and South American produce to flood England. The politically sacred catchword "free trade" halted any effective move to protect agriculture, and a rapid decline set in.

During this period, the most successful working-class movement was the growth of the cooperative societies. Founded in 1844 and tracing its ideas to Robert Owen's philosophy of self-help, the movement expanded from retail stores to wholesale trading, and eventually to production and distribution. By 1889 the societies had a membership of 805,000.

Disraeli and Victoria

In 1872 Disraeli made his famous Crystal Palace speech in which he exalted the Crown as the fountain of the new imperialism. Four years later, and over the opposition of his party, he had Parliament confer the title of Empress of India upon Queen Victoria. In turn, the Queen responded to and confided in Disraeli as she had done with no other Prime Minister since Melbourne. Her open dislike for Palmerston and Gladstone was now contrasted to her unconcealed partiality for Disraeli and the Conservatives. She appeared to believe that Disraeli was the only Englishman who had really appreciated Prince Albert; only Disraeli was able to persuade the Queen to relinquish her seclusion and mourning after Albert's death and return to public life. The harmony of their relationship became an intolerable insult to Disraeli's rival, Gladstone. In 1876 the Queen elevated Disraeli to the peerage as Earl of Beaconsfield, and the Prime Minister moved to the House of Lords, leaving the House of Commons to the uninspired leadership of Sir Stafford Northcote.

Foreign and Imperial Policy

Disraeli, as well as the Queen, was intrigued with the idea of a great eastern empire that would contain further Russian expansion in that area. His policy was vigorous, risky, and generally successful. In contrast to Gladstone, Disraeli actively supported a colonial empire and believed in Britain's imperial destiny.

SUEZ CANAL

In 1875 Disraeli secretly bought for the British government the 177,000 shares of Suez Canal stock previously owned by the Khedive of Egypt. The Khedive was chronically bankrupt and had offered his shares for sale in France. To forestall a French monopoly and to give England a voice in the management of the strategic canal route to India, Disraeli borrowed £4 million from the House of Rothschild and beat the French in purchasing the shares. This audacious act delighted the Queen and the nation. The purchase was to lead to British interest in, and eventual occupation of, the Nile Valley.

THE EASTERN QUESTION

The combination of Turkish misrule and persecution of Christian subjects, the Russian support of pan-Slav unrest and interest in annexing the Straits, and the emergent nationalism among the Balkan states that threatened both Austria and Turkey led to an international crisis. In 1875 Bosnia and Herzegovina, two Balkan provinces, revolted against Turkey. Russia, Austria, and Germany wished to put pressure on Turkey to reform, but Disraeli feared Russian influence in the area more than he resented Turkish misrule. The next year the Bulgarians revolted against the Turks, but were crushed after enduring terrible atrocities at the hands of the Sultan's troops.

Eventually, the revolt spread, and Serbia and Montenegro joined the Bulgars in fighting their Turkish overlord. Britain, thereupon, joined the three other great powers in a conference at Constantinople to force reforms on the new Sultan, Abdul Hamid II. The Sultan, who refused all demands, was convinced that Britain feared Russia too much to permit force to be used against him. Russia, therefore, acted alone and invaded the Balkans in 1877. By the following year Russian troops were besieging Constantinople. Disraeli threatened British intervention, but the Turks surrendered, and peace was made at San Stephano.

The treaty provided for an enlarged and autonomous Bulgaria under Turkish suzerainty and an independent Serbia, Montenegro, and Romania. Turkish rule in Europe almost disappeared. The settlement disturbed Disraeli because it gave Russia access to the Mediterranean through a satellite, Bulgaria. Therefore, he held that the treaty was unacceptable and that an international conference must reconsider the entire matter. His ultimatum to Russia was backed up by dispatching the fleet to Constantinople and troops to Malta. Russia gave way to Disraeli's diplomacy, and a pleased British populace could not help but recall similar triumphs in foreign affairs under Palmerston.

Congress of Berlin, 1878. Bismarck presided at the conference, but Disraeli was the dominant figure and secured most of his demands. Macedonia was returned to Turkey, and Bulgaria was cut in half, thus keeping Russia away from Constantinople. Bosnia and Herzegovina were placed under Austrian administration. Britain secured the island of Cyprus as a naval base and promised to protect Turkey's Asiatic possessions. Because Disraeli had rebuffed Russia without war and had won a "peace with honor," the settlement was considered a diplomatic triumph. Later events revised this judgment as Russia became less of a threat in the Near East and the suppression of Slav nationalism in the Balkans created incessant friction and precipitated World War I.

IMPERIAL WARS

The locale of the next clash between British and Russian spheres of interest was in Afghanistan. Here Britain demanded that the local ruler accept a British envoy to deter Russian influence in the country. When the order was refused, a British military expedition was sent to Afghanistan. The Second Afghan War (1878–1880) required two British invasions. This open aggression proved unpopular in Britain.

In 1877 the British annexed the Transvaal, a Boer republic in South Africa, in order to promote federation and avert an impending Zulu war. Although the anarchic and bankrupt conditions in the republic improved, neither federation nor peace followed. Many in Britain regarded the annexation as undisguised imperialism; furthermore, the annihilation of a British regiment at the outset of the Zulu War in 1879 brought dismay and doubts about Disraeli's imperial policies.

The Election of 1880

In 1876 Gladstone came out of semi-retirement to denounce Disraeli's support of the Turks in spite of their cruel misrule in the Balkans. In the campaign of 1880, Gladstone lumped together all the imperialistic ventures of Disraeli as examples of the immorality of imperialism. Sweeping through northern England and Scotland like an itinerant evangelist, he impressed the electors in provincial halls with his lofty principles and his magnetic oratory. Since the depression and the costly imperial wars had drained the Treasury, Gladstone did not fail to contrast this fact with the budgetary surpluses of his last Liberal administration. The election was a clean sweep for the

Liberals. Disraeli retired from politics in poor health and died the next year. Queen Victoria reluctantly asked Gladstone, who was seventy-one, to become Prime Minister when Lord Hartington, the titular head of the Liberal party, informed her that a cabinet could not be formed without him.

IMPERIAL AND IRISH DEVELOPMENTS

In contrast to his effective first administration, Gladstone's second was bedeviled at every turn by imperial complications abroad and parliamentary obstruction at home. Thus very little significant legislation was passed, except for an Irish land act and a third parliamentary reform bill. The primary reason for this inattention to other issues was Gladstone's preoccupation with Irish home rule. From 1880 to World War I, the Irish question dominated the British political scene and jeopardized the very foundations of constitutional parliamentary government. When Gladstone became convinced that Irish home rule was the only solution, he steadfastly fought for it, but was unable to carry his entire party with him. The splintered Liberal party made possible a Conservative ascendancy for the next two decades.

The Rise of the New Imperialism

During the three decades following 1870, a conscious expansion of empire took place among European nations, brought on by an emotional and militant form of nationalism, and by the ramifications of the Industrial Revolution. The triumph of nationalism in Germany, Italy, Japan and the United States was of an explosive and expansive variety, substantially different from the liberal nationalism of the 1840s. Since physical enlargement was limited in Europe, imperialism took the form of an expansion overseas, with a scramble for colonies beginning in earnest.

At the same time, imperialism gained momentum by the renewed interest in colonies as a source of raw materials and as a market for manufactures. Britain began to be threatened by the industrial and military rivalry of Continental powers. When these powers placed their flag and protective tariffs over new territories, such militant and economic nationalism jeopardized Britain's security and her policy of free trade. By 1880 the revolution in transportation—the steamship, the railway, the Suez Canal—made imperialism feasible and profitable as never before and opened up new areas of the world to western penetration. It also made practical for the first time the federation of England's self-governing colonies. Joseph Chamberlain became the indefatigable champion of imperial federation after J. R. Seeley's *Expansion of England* (1883), a best seller, put forth the arguments for the founding of the Imperial Federal League in 1884.

The new imperialism caught the popular imagination in England and was reflected not only in the public heroes of the period, but also in the literary output. In the writings of Joseph Conrad, Robert Louis Stevenson, H. Ryder Haggard, and Rudyard Kipling the excitement, pride, and glory of empire were vividly portrayed; the press became sensational and jingoistic, exploiting the popular taste for imperial glory. The admiration given to such heroes as Charles "Chinese" Gordon, Cecil Rhodes, Lord Kitchener, Sir Alfred Milner, Lord Cromer, and Sir Frederick Lugard was in recognition of their extraordinary imperial ventures rather than any domestic accomplishments. Justifying imperialism on a higher plane was the old humanitarian impulse of a sense of moral mission—Kipling's "white man's burden"—which would bring the benefits of English administration and of Christianity to other people. This conscious effort to equate British self-interest with moral purpose was sincerely accepted by large segments of the English people at the same time that it was condemned by foreign observers as an exercise in hypocrisy.

GLADSTONE AND IMPERIALISM

Gladstone's campaign promises to retreat gracefully from the imperial ventures inaugurated by Disraeli were impossible to fulfill. In the scramble for colonies in the 1880s no major European power could remain unaffected. It is perhaps ironic that the "anti-imperialist" Gladstone was drawn into imperial commitments more extensive than Disraeli had ever entertained. Gladstone, on principle, hesitated to use force on a lesser power and, therefore, usually used force too late and even more fully, because his initial vacillation had frequently increased the disorder. Consequently, the idealism of his policies was blurred by the ambivalence of his actions.

South Africa. The Boers in the Transvaal, descendants of Dutch and French Calvinists who had emigrated to South Africa in the seventeenth century, renewed their anti-British sentiments after the Zulu War had relieved them of their fears from that quarter. They confidently expected Gladstone to repudiate the annexation of the Transvaal which he had denounced so fervently when out of power. When, instead, he claimed that British sovereignty was essential to law and order and to the protection of the native tribes, the Boers rebelled in 1880 and defeated a British detachment at Majuba Hill in 1881. Although the British populace demanded retaliation, Gladstone concluded peace negotiations which guaranteed the Transvaal independence subject to British suzerainty. In 1884 the Convention of London deleted the suzerainty clause. The British retreat in the Transvaal was unpopular at home and only encouraged Boer nationalism. The Boers, who already despised the power and the indecisive policies of Britain, were less inclined than ever to come to terms with British colonies in South Africa.

Egypt. In 1876 Britain and France intervened in Egypt to ensure payment of the Egyptian debt when the Khedive defaulted on his financial obligations. An ensuing Egyptian uprising against the Khedive and foreign intervention resulted in pillage, anarchy, and the murder of Europeans. A joint French-British fleet was planned, but the French backed out. Gladstone reluctantly permitted British forces to enter alone and put down the rebellion and announced that the occupation was only temporary. Sir Evelyn Baring, the British consul-general, became the real power in Egypt under the nominal sovereignty of the Khedive. Baring modernized and reformed the Egyptian government, backed by a British army of occupation that remained in the country.

The Sudan. A Muslim fanatic proclaimed himself the Mahdi, or Messiah, and rallied the Sudanese tribesmen against the chronic misrule of their Egyptian overlords. When an Egyptian army under British generals was overwhelmed trying to subdue the Mahdi in 1883, Baring and Gladstone decided to abandon the Sudan as soon as they had extricated all Egyptian personnel from the country. General Charles Gordon was commissioned to handle the evacuation. Once in Khartoum, he sent out only the women and children and delayed the military evacuation in the hope of controling the situation and maintaining a British presence; within a month he was cut off. Gladstone's next problem was how to rescue Gordon and the garrison. The cabinet delayed in committing itself to major intervention but eventually dispatched a relief expedition which arrived two days after Gordon and his troops had been slaughtered by the Sudanese. The political repercussions were violent. The Queen and the nation blamed Gladstone for Gordon's death, and the government barely survived a vote of censure in the House of Commons.

Colonial Competition. British interest in the interior of Africa had been stimulated by the exciting adventures (1857–1873) of Richard Burton, John Speke, Samuel Baker, David Livingstone, and Henry Stanley, who were searching for the source of the Nile and exploring the Congo basin. Their arguments in favor of commerce and Christianity, along with the attempt of rival powers to secure colonies, prompted Britain to make territorial claims, usually by granting charters to commercial companies. Gradually Britain extended control over the interior of the Gold Coast colony; in 1850 a British naval squadron captured Lagos, and ten years later it was annexed to the Crown. In 1885 a protectorate over the Niger Delta—the "Oil Rivers"—was proclaimed. In East Africa Germany's sudden interest in a colonial empire challenged long-time British activity in the area. During the 1880s British North Guinea, North Borneo, and Upper Burma were added to the empire in the east. The ground rules for establishing colonial claims to African territory were laid at the Berlin conference of 1884–1885, where fourteen powers gathered to decide the destiny of the Congo (granted to Leopold II of Belgium) and to determine the manner in which Africa could be partitioned among European powers with a minimum of friction. No Africans were invited to the conference on the destiny of their continent.

The Penjdeh Crisis. On taking office, Gladstone ordered the evacuation of British forces from Afghanistan, leaving the country independent. Abd-er-Rahman Kahn, the new Amir, accepted British friendship and money in return for British recognition of his country's independence. In 1885 Russian troops occupied Penjdeh on the Afghanistan border and defeated the Afghans in battle. The way was now open for a Russian advance on India, and the British cabinet and European powers considered war imminent. The crisis was resolved by Russian acceptance of arbitration, but Afghanistan continued to be one of the areas where Anglo-Russian spheres of interest clashed.

Domestic Politics

The cohesion of Gladstone's first ministry was conspicuously absent in his second. The Whig leaders, Granville and Hartington, were restive over Gladstone's interest in political democracy and in Irish home rule and feared the socialist ideas of such Radicals as Joseph Chamberlain and Charles Dilke. Gladstone, who was described as "half-Tory and half-Radical," had no intense interest in the social legislation of the Radicals or in making the Liberals a labor party. Besides the conflicting ideologies within his cabinet, Gladstone was plagued by the sustained obstructionism of the Irish Nationalist party and the attacks of the Tory democrats—the Fourth party— led by Lord Randolph Churchill. The Tory democrats made a deliberate effort to clog Liberal legislation and create a progressive image of the Conservatives which would win votes at the next election.

PARTY ORGANIZATION

Before 1861 local party supporters had seen to the registration of voters. Then the Liberals set up a national Liberal Registration Association in London under the control of the parliamentary whips. The enlarged electorate after 1867 and the tightening of the election laws demanded major changes in political organization. Constituency associations became part of national organizations, and political clubs were opened for workingmen by both parties. Disraeli organized the National Union of Conservatives in 1867 and a Conservative Central Office in 1870. Meanwhile Joseph Chamberlain, a manufacturer and Liberal, had established a powerful municipal political machine, the Birmingham Caucus, which won every municipal election in Birmingham and elected only Liberals to Parliament. Its success prompted the establishment of the National Liberal Federation in 1877.

Gradually, the foundations of the modern party system were being established. Gladstone was the first major political figure to stump the country in a campaign. Elections were being decided more by the appeal of the party leader and the party's platform than by the qualities of rival candidates in the voters' constituency. This development enhanced the positions and powers of the prime minister and of the leader of the opposition; it also reduced the chances of an independent, or a critic, winning party backing or sufficient votes at election time. With the transition from oligarchy to democracy, the parties became powerful organizations, whereas the independent member of Parliament with a free vote became one of the casualties of the change.

REFORM LEGISLATION

Imperial and Irish problems, along with sharply divergent views within the Liberal party, combined to hinder the passage of reform proposals. Gladstone's special interests were not in social reform, but in the pacification of Ireland and in political liberalism. In order to remedy the loopholes of his first land act, Gladstone's Irish Land Act of 1881 guaranteed the "three F's" demanded by Irish tenants: fair rent, fixity of tenure, and free sale of their tenancies. A land commission with adjudication rights was appointed. This remedial legislation satisfied the tenants' grievance over high rents, but it arrived too late. By this date nothing short of home rule would satisfy Irish nationalists.

In 1884–1885 Gladstone introduced and Parliament passed the Third Reform Bill. The bill extended the franchise to all householders in the county as the 1867 bill had done for the towns. With this act, four out of five adult males became eligible to vote. The second part of the act (1885) redistributed parliamentary seats and made Britain a parliamentary democracy. It abandoned the ancient principle of representation by counties and boroughs, where the aristocracy and landlord could often determine the representation; instead it established largely single-member constituencies with representation based on population. The membership in the House of Commons was increased to 670.

IRISH NATIONALISM

Dormant Irish nationalism was revived in the 1870s by Isaac Butt and Charles Parnell. The latter, a Protestant landlord with a violent hatred of the English, was willing to use any means to achieve independence from English rule. He became president of the Land League in Ireland in 1879 and succeeded Butt as leader of the Home Rule Association. Parnell determined to win home rule by inciting agrarian violence and by wresting land from the landlords in Ireland. Correspondingly, the Irish parliamentary bloc carried on a deliberate policy of obstructionism and filibustering at Westminster in order to make parliamentary procedure impossible so long as Irish independence was denied.

The tactics were successful and the Irish question overshadowed all other issues in British politics. Acts of agrarian violence against landlords and their property numbered over 2,500 in 1880. Peasants boycotted anyone taking a farm from which a tenant had been evicted, and new rules of Parliamentary closure were adopted to permit Parliament to function. Parnell sabotaged Gladstone's Land Act of 1881 in order to keep up the agitation. Gladstone finally had Parnell arrested and applied coercive acts to Ireland until Parnell agreed to curb the outrages. However, Irish extremists murdered the Irish secretary of state and undersecretary in a Dublin park, and public opinion forced Gladstone to resume coercion and make no more concessions to Parnell. Under these circumstances the Prime Minister privately came to the conviction that only home rule could solve the Irish question.

FALL OF GLADSTONE, 1885

The death of General Gordon and the Penjdeh crisis produced strong popular protests over Liberal foreign policy. In Parliament, the defections among Gladstone's followers over his Irish policy permitted Parnell to ally with the Conservatives and defeat Gladstone's ministry in June 1885. Lord Salisbury formed a caretaker government until the act redistributing parliamentary seats could be implemented and an election held. In the interim, Salisbury rewarded Parnell by passing the Ashbourne Act which provided a fund from which Irish peasants could get loans at low interest to buy their land from the landlord.

GLADSTONE'S THIRD MINISTRY

Chamberlain's "unauthorized program" of social legislation helped the Liberals in the counties, but Parnell's support for the Tories in England increased their borough seats. The 1885 election results made Parnell and his eighty-six Irish members the decisive balance of power. When Gladstone's conversion to home rule became known, Lord Hartington immediately left the Liberals and joined the Tories. Salisbury gave up all ideas of concessions to the Irish, and Parnell, of course, threw his support to the Liberals. Salisbury's government was defeated in the opening week of Parliament, and Gladstone began his third administration with a promise to provide home rule for Ireland.

THE FIRST HOME RULE BILL, 1886

For sixteen days Gladstone defended his bill which would provide an Irish legislature with responsible government, except for specific reserved areas. The plan, which was attacked by the Tories, aroused strong protests in the Liberal party from Whigs, old Radicals like John Bright, and Gladstone's chief colleague, Chamberlain. The latter left the cabinet and voted against the bill. Protestant Ulster (Northern Ireland) promised to fight rather than submit to a Catholic majority in the south. Religious and nationalist emotions in England were aroused as opponents predicted the dire consequences which would follow Irish independence. In the vote on the bill, ninety-three Liberals defected to defeat the measure, and Gladstone immediately called an election on the issue.

SPLIT OF THE LIBERAL PARTY

The Whig section of the party, led by Hartington, had already deserted Gladstone on the issue of home rule for Ireland; now Chamberlain, the Radical leader, opposed the purpose of the bill. In the election of July 1886, the Liberal Radicals refused to back home rule and, instead, campaigned as a separate Liberal Unionist party committed to maintaining union with Ireland. The coalition of Conservatives and Liberal Unionists won an easy victory over Gladstonian Liberals and Irish Nationalists. Gladstone split the Liberal party over Ireland, just as Peel had splintered the Conservatives forty years earlier over the Corn Laws and agricultural protection. Nevertheless, the Irish question was not solved simply by the electoral defeat of home rule.

Under two outstanding parliamentary and political leaders, Gladstone and Disraeli, the extension of political and social democracy was accelerated, following a passive interlude under Palmerston. Britain's movement toward democracy was evolutionary, rather than revolutionary, with utilitarian arguments far more successful than doctrinaire theories.

Party organization and the extension of the vote largely ended the historic influence of the aristocracy and landed interests in dominating political life. Both Liberals and Conservatives catered to the new mass electorate.

The growth of the British empire and the intractable problem of Ireland were the dominant issues of these two decades. Neither would recede in importance as the Tories began twenty years of political dominance.

Selected Readings

Blake, Robert. *Disraeli* (1966)
Clark, G. Kitson. *The Making of Victorian England* (1962)
Cruise, O'Brien Connor. *Parnell and His Party, 1809–1890* (1957)
Eldridge, C. C. *England's Mission: The Imperial Idea in the Age of Gladstone and Disraeli, 1868–1880* (1973)
Hammond, John. *Gladstone and the Irish Nation* (1964)
Longford, Elizabeth. *Queen Victoria, Born to Succeed. (1965)*
Magnus, Philip. *Gladstone* (1954)
Mill, John Stuart. *Autobiography* (1873)
Winks, Robin W. (ed.) *British Imperialism: Gold, God, Glory* (1963)

20

The Late Victorian Years: Democracy at Home, Empire Abroad

British interest in the expansion of empire quickened in the last quarter of the nineteenth century. Imperialism became a dominant theme in British thought and policy, as it was among other major powers—France, Germany, Russia, and the United States—in these years. The earlier ascendancy of the Pax Britannica based on naval and industrial supremacy no longer guaranteed security against Continental competition or militarism.

In this era, with its self-conscious restlessness and indirection, the march of social democracy and the extension of empire were the most consistent features of British history. The twentieth century ushered in an era of political deterioration and violence in Britain. Nineteenth-century assumptions and practices—from the belief in evolutionary reform to respect for parliamentary rules—were disregarded by those demanding revolutionary changes in society.

By 1914 the crises over Irish home rule, the violence of strikers and suffragettes, and political warfare over reform of the House of Lords had almost paralyzed British political life. Only the outbreak of a greater menace—war in Europe—shelved these problems for the time being.

POLITICAL REALIGNMENT

In 1885 the political Radicals were not far from their goal of universal suffrage; the objectives of full democracy and a welfare state were the logical extension of their utilitarian convictions and won the support of the masses. The county councils, the "People's Budget," unemployment and old-age legislation marked this political trend. In the process the traditional two-party, two-House parliamentary arrangement which sheltered fluid and multiple-interest groups began to fragment, as the House of Lords became almost solidly Conservative, and as politics became increasingly identified with either single issues or with economic interests. First the Irish and then the trade unions left the traditional parties to form organizations that would advance their particular interests or class.

Conservative Growth

Reliance on the country squires and the clergy had left the Conservative party on the defensive and in the minority until Disraeli expanded the base of this support by his attention to social reform and imperial expansion. In 1886 the Conservatives began two decades of power by keeping their rural constituencies and by gradually winning from the Liberals the urban middle class and the manufacturers. In their opposition to Gladstone's Irish program almost the entire Whig aristocracy in the Lords deserted the Liberal party and gave the Conservatives a permanent and irremovable majority in the House of Lords. The English middle class was largely opposed to Irish home rule and supported the Tories on this matter. So did Joseph Chamberlain who led the Liberal Unionists in bolting from the Liberal party in 1886. He allied with the Conservatives, and he and Lord Randolph Churchill pressed for economic and social reforms in the Tory platform. Thus Disraeli's emphasis on Tory democracy was revived in the Conservative party by Chamberlain's influence. For most of two decades (1886-1905) Lord Salisbury and his nephew, Arthur Balfour, gave the country what it seemed to want: good, efficient government at home, imperialism abroad, and opposition to Irish home rule.

Liberal Confusion

Only once after 1886—in 1906—did the Liberal party again win a majority of seats in England. The party lost its domination of the urban seats and remained strong only in the Celtic fringes of Wales and Scotland, and with Nonconformists. Their old slogan of "peace, retrenchment, and reform" was no longer appealing to an age which wanted more empire and governmental services, not less, and which had already won most of the earlier political objectives that the Liberals favored. The party was reduced to promoting reforms, such as disestablishment of the Church in Wales or liquor licensing, to hold its Celtic and Nonconformist supporters; but to win urban votes it would have to drop home rule, support imperialism, and lure labor votes by the promise of social legislation.

The Liberal commitment to home rule, however, limited its attention to social welfare and lost its most vigorous promoter, Chamberlain. The Liberals were also plagued by the problem of leadership. Gladstone had put such an indelible image on the party that no one of equal stature could be found to replace him. The two most eminent heirs, Charles Dilke and Joseph Chamberlain, were eliminated, one by his divorce, the other by his opposition to home rule. Consequently, the party remained divided and dispirited until 1905.

The Birth of the Labor Party

Trade unionism and non-Marxist socialist societies joined ranks in 1900 to elect labor representatives to Parliament. After receiving full legal rights in 1875, the nonpolitical and conservative Trades Union Congress was at first content to promote industrial legislation through the Liberal party. But the unskilled laborers organized unions and favored strikes and more active political participation. In 1886 a special electoral committee of the Trades Union Congress endorsed and helped elect eleven working-class members to Parliament. They sat as Liberals, and this "Lib-Lab" alliance continued until 1900. By that date the trade unions had two million members.

Meanwhile English socialism—insular, nonviolent, and evolutionary—had appeared. English socialists were largely non-Marxist intellectuals critical of the existing economic and social structure. The Fabian Society (1883), which attracted such intellectuals as George Bernard Shaw, Graham

Wallas, Sidney and Beatrice Webb, and H. G. Wells, promoted gradual social reform through the extensive intervention of the state and were particularly active in the London County Council. Labor churches, preaching social welfare, helped spread Fabian ideas to the workers, as did Keir Hardie, who broke with the Liberals, entered Parliament in 1892 as a labor candidate, and established an Independent Labor Party (ILP) in 1893. The ILP shortly won the approval of the Trades Union Congress for independent political action.

In 1900 a conference of socialist societies, cooperative societies, and trade unions met in London and set up the Labor Representation Committee to establish a distinct Labor group in Parliament. J. Ramsay MacDonald was elected secretary of the committee, and in the general election of that year two seats were won out of fifteen contested. In 1906 the Labor party won fifty-three seats.

The Great Debate

As the virtues of mid-Victorianism were refuted and superseded by a diversity of creeds, latter-day Victorianism probed its conscience and looked for a new set of values. Political and economic freedom were not enough, unless citizens were equipped to improve the quality of life with the new freedom. Should the state preserve freedom of action, or should it "improve" society directly by collective action? Before the government could wage war on poverty, unemployment, or on slums, a revolution in finance had to take place. Disappearing with the old individualism was the tendency to fashion legislative programs with the taxpayer in mind. After 1885 and the extension of the vote to city workers, the majority of voters favored larger national budgets because the burden of increased taxation would fall on others. By the end of the century the Victorian sense of political compromise and of agreement on the efficacy of representative government were no longer taken for granted. World problems were more complex than imagined, and the democratic state had bred emotionalism and political violence as well as freedom and liberty.

TWO TORY DECADES

Under two prime ministers from the Cecil family, the Marquess of Salisbury and his nephew and successor, Arthur Balfour (whose ancestors, William and Robert Cecil, had managed the royal government under Queen Elizabeth and King James I), the Conservative party, in alliance with Chamberlain's Liberal Unionists, governed Britain from 1886 to 1905, except for one brief Liberal ministry. With the Liberals in disarray, the time was ripe for Conservatives to extend Disraeli's formula of imperialism and social reforms. Lord Salisbury directed his attention to foreign affairs and permitted Chamberlain to nudge the Tories toward several items of social welfare. The Irish agitation for home rule was temporarily contained by the death of Parnell, and by the government's policy of "killing home rule with kindness." When the Cecils left office after twenty years, neither the Irish question nor England's social problems had been solved, only postponed. Salisbury's foreign policy of splendid isolation appeared far less appealing after the Boer War emphasized the diplomatic loneliness of such a position.

Lord Salisbury and His Colleagues

Salisbury formed his second administration (1886–1892) from Conservatives when the Liberal Unionists declined to join. He appointed his nephew, Arthur Balfour, as Irish Secretary, and under Balfour's steady administration Ireland achieved two decades of relative peace and prosperity. Salisbury's chief interest was foreign diplomacy, and he successfully kept England out of war while sanctioning the advance of imperialism. The Prime Minister, although no reactionary, was too aloof from the people to concern himself about social legislation. Lord Randolph Churchill, who became Chancellor of the exchequer and leader of the House of Commons, tried to commit his party to a strong labor program by offering to resign if his budget estimates were not accepted. To his surprise he found that he was not indispensable, and the Liberal Unionist G. C. Goschen replaced him in the cabinet. The reform measures that were passed, therefore, were largely the efforts of Joseph Chamberlain who continued to be as radical a Unionist as he had been a Liberal.

CONSERVATIVE ADMINISTRATION, 1886–1892

Except for occasional disturbances in Ireland, Salisbury's second administration was rather quiet. The aristocratic Prime Minister was respected for his administrative talents, but he never caught the popular imagination as had Gladstone or Disraeli. To ensure Liberal Unionist support several domestic reform measures favored by Chamberlain were passed. The County Councils Act of 1888 recast the political structure of local government by transferring administrative authority from the justices of the peace to popularly elected councils. The Technical Education Act of 1889 authorized school boards to offer technical as well as elementary education.

IRISH DEVELOPMENTS

Arthur Balfour, Secretary for Ireland, maintained order through an even-handed enforcement of a permanent coercion act, and at the same time he worked vigorously to alleviate the economic and social grievances of the Irish. A series of acts—the Ashbourne Act of 1885, the Balfour Act of 1891, and the Syndham Act of 1903—partly relieved the squalor of the peasants' living conditions by encouraging them to purchase their farms. The Wyndham Act went so far as to force the landlords to sell to their tenants. The program was quite successful, and Balfour's efforts were aided by the internal wrangling of the Irish Nationalist party. In 1890 Parnell was named as co-respondent in a divorce case. Irish clergy and Nonconformist Liberals alike publicly censured him, and the controversy split his party in two. Parnell died in 1891, but the division between his supporters and his critics continued for a decade until John Redmond reunited the two factions.

GLADSTONE'S FOURTH MINISTRY

The election of 1892 left the Conservatives in a minority, and within weeks Salisbury's government was brought down by the combined votes of the Liberals and the Irish Nationalists. Thus at the age of eighty-three Gladstone began his fourth ministry (1892–1894). The Liberal platform, known as the Newcastle Program, promised an amazing variety of reform proposals. However, few bills were even debated because Gladstone insisted on pushing through an Irish home rule bill first. The new bill of 1893 survived all amendments and passed the House of Commons, but was overwhelmingly defeated by the Conservative House of Lords. Rather than force an election on the issue, Gladstone retired the following year, after serving sixty-two years in Parliament. Failing in vision and in hearing, and out of touch with the Liberal party of the 1890s that wanted bigger military expenditures and more radical social legislation, the Grand Old Man had outlived his age; four years later he was dead and was accorded a state funeral.

Prime Minister Rosebery. Queen Victoria selected the Earl of Rosebery, a personable, unpredictable aristocrat, to succeed Gladstone as Prime Minister. Although a statesman of promise, Rosebery's talents were conspicuously hidden in office, and his administration was lacking in achievement. His chief rival for party leadership was the able Sir William Harcourt, Chancellor of the Exchequer, whose budgets heavily taxed landed inheritances and anticipated the "socialist" Liberal budgets of the next decade.

SALISBURY'S THIRD MINISTRY

The election of 1895 returned 340 Conservatives and 71 Liberal Unionists, who joined the Conservatives against the outnumbered Liberals (177) and Irish Nationalists (82). Rosebery's aggressive imperial policies had alienated the Liberal rank and file, and Irish home rule and liquor licensing had antagonized even more voters. Lord Salisbury took the post of Prime Minister, the last peer to hold that office. Arthur Balfour served as leader of the House of Commons, and Joseph Chamberlain chose the Colonial Office where his passions for imperial growth and consolidation were soon demonstrated. One social reform, the Workmen's Compensation Act of 1897, was passed. This measure made the employer liable for compensation to injured workers according to rates set by law. Other social schemes were set aside because of the Boer War.

ELECTION OF 1900

The Boer War almost ruined the floundering Liberal party which had failed since 1894 to find either an appealing party position or a leader who could update its Gladstonian image. Sir William Harcourt succeeded Rosebery as party leader, but fared no better. Two years later Harcourt was replaced by Sir Henry Campbell-Bannerman, who had served in the cabinet under Gladstone and whose generous and affable nature seemed to make conciliation possible among the divided Liberals. The outbreak of the Boer War, however, only sharpened the breach. One wing of the party, the Liberal Imperialists led by Herbert Asquith, Edward Grey, and Richard Haldane, backed the war without reservation; the other wing under David Lloyd George, John Morley, and Robert Reid condemned the imperialist venture and were nicknamed the "pro-Boers." Caught in the crossfire of both wings was Henry Campbell-Bannerman who had misgivings about the war, but agreed that the war must end in the annexation of the Boer republics. The Salisbury government exploited this division by holding a general election in 1900 (commonly termed the khaki election because it was an obvious attempt to translate wartime patriotism into votes for the party in power). The war was the only real issue, and the Conservative-Unionist coalition campaigned on the slogan "A seat lost to the Government is a seat gained by the Boers." The Unionists won the election but with a reduced majority, much to their surprise.

DEATH OF VICTORIA

Queen Victoria died in 1901 after the longest reign—sixty-four years—in English history. In her later years, she had regained the esteem of the nation which respected her as the symbol of Victorian progress and of the British empire. Her sense of duty, pride in empire, and conventional morality refurbished the idea of monarchy which had been tarnished by the preceding Hanoverian monarchs. She was succeeded by her eldest son, Edward VII, who was nearly sixty. Edward became a much loved and sociable monarch who relished the many public functions demanded of a king. Although he never understood the rapid changes which the twentieth century was introducing into British society, his charm and goodwill tours abroad made him the most popular monarch since Charles II.

Economic Conditions

The wonderful prosperity of mid-Victorianism, which peaked about 1870, was followed by what the business world termed the "Great Depression" for the years between 1873 and 1898. In absolute terms Britain's wealth and real wages continued to improve, but agricultural depression and working-class unemployment ended the buoyant optimism of the earlier years. No longer did Britain have an absolute lead in trade and industrial output. Germany and the United States were now growing at a much faster pace. More than ever Britain's entire economy depended on world trade. As other nations imposed tariff barriers to protect their trade, Britain saw more value in the expansion of a colonial empire as a market for manufactured goods.

Urban studies in 1900 indicated that about 30 percent of Britain's population lived in a state of chronic poverty. Wealth was still very unevenly distributed. As the problems of slum housing, poverty, and health increasingly became public issues for debate, the old complacency disappeared. Sensitivity to social problems became more pronounced as writers, economists, and politicians sought a more desirable accommodation between capitalism and socialism.

Conservatism in Decline, 1901–1906

Following the Boer War a rapid reversal of party fortunes took place as the Liberals patched up their wartime divisions and turned to the defense of public education and free trade. The Conservatives, sharply divided over postwar policy, faced attacks from Nonconformists, free traders, and critics of the government's South African policies.

TAFF VALE DECISION

The House of Lords, in its capacity as the highest court of appeals, decided in favor of the Taff Vale Railway's suit for £32,000 in damages against the Amalgamated Society of Railway Servants. This decision made trade unions financially liable for the actions of their members and drastically handicapped all strike activity. When the Conservatives made no effort to curb by statute the effects of this decision, the trade unions for the first time actively supported working-class candidates for Parliament. These trade unionists campaigned under the label of the Labor Representation Committee (LRC). In 1906 the LRC changed its name to the Labor party.

PRIME MINISTER BALFOUR

In July 1902 Arthur Balfour succeeded his uncle, Lord Salisbury, as Prime Minister. Balfour, aloof, urbane, and efficient, proved to be an adept parliamentary leader, but was constantly harried by adverse circumstances. His first extensive reform in education (the Education Act of 1902) replaced 20,000 local school boards with the authority of the local government and made county and borough councils responsible for all types of schools. The state assumed full responsibility for education and brought the voluntary schools under its authority, although religious instruction in schools was retained with optional attendance. The act equalized standards at the local level and permitted a systematic expansion of secondary education. The bill turned out to be a political liability, however, because it aroused vigorous opposition from Nonconformists who opposed the intrusion of the state into education and tax money for schools where Anglican doctrine would be taught.

THE LICENSING ACT, 1904

The influential temperance movement agitated for a reduction in the number of outlets licensed to sell liquor. Balfour's bill supported local licensing authorities in their refusal to renew the expired licenses of some public houses (taverns) but provided compensation from funds distributed by the liquor industry to owners who lost their licenses. Immediately critics claimed such compensation would endow the liquor trade. The bill passed, but Balfour lost the large temperance vote.

THE TARIFF CONTROVERSY

Free trade was a nineteenth-century article of faith in Britain. In 1902 Joseph Chamberlain challenged its continued merits as an economic policy and embarrassed his cabinet colleagues by coming out publicly for an imperial preference tariff and for import duties on food. A year later he resigned from the cabinet to stump the country as an advocate of tariffs and protectionism. By this time the Conservative party was splintered three ways on the tariff issue: the Free Traders, the Tariff Reform League, and those such as the Prime Minister who stood in the middle. Balfour opposed a food tax and imperial preference, but agreed to a retaliatory tariff to diminish foreign tariffs. By the end of 1903 Balfour had lost both wings of his cabinet, and only his consummate skill prevented a dissolution. The dissension among the Conservatives handed the Liberal party the one issue, free trade, around which its divided factions could rally.

IMPERIAL AND FOREIGN AFFAIRS

In the second half of Queen Victoria's reign British imperialism became a popular movement, and empire builders won a level of support from home authorities not found earlier. The British habit of emigrating continued unabated during the century. Twenty million Britons emigrated between 1815 and 1914. They populated Canada, Australia, New Zealand, and scores of other regions from Singapore to the West Indies. By 1900 the British empire included a quarter of the people in the world and nearly a quarter of its lands.

These empire builders were, of course, often interested in gold and glory, but they were also inspired by a sense of duty, often instilled in them in their public-school training, to extend overseas the blessings of English institutions. This ideal was twofold and somewhat paradoxical: to conquer and govern the new empire, and to grant self-government and independence to the old. By 1900 this world empire sharpened a growing hostility between Britain and a militant Germany hungry for world-power status. German diplomacy failed to realize that its military posturing frightened Britain, France and Russia into submerging their traditional antipathy to one another to the point of allying themselves together against the threat of a powerful Germany.

Self-Government in the Settlement Colonies

Between 1867 and 1907 three of Britain's overseas settlement areas became self-governing nations, bound to Britain only by loyalty, common institutions, and a common allegiance to the throne. The evolution from colony to Commonwealth of Nations was in process. This transition came peacefully with no efforts to halt the process in the white settlement communities because England had profited from experience in the American Revolution.

CANADA

In 1867 the British North America Act created a federal union of four provinces. The first of the dominions blended the British cabinet system with a federal-provincial structure necessitated by its large size. Under the vigorous leadership of Prime Minister Sir John A. MacDonald, Canada expanded and consolidated its territories by absorbing the west and northwest through the purchase of the landholding rights of the Hudson Bay Company, and by the building of a transcontinental railway—the Canadian Pacific. By 1905 Canada's nine provinces were no longer fearful of annexation by the United States and had become prosperous primary producers.

AUSTRALIA

The six separate colonies in Australia had won responsible government between 1852 and 1870. This development was prompted by the discovery of gold in 1851 which multiplied the population and led to a democratization of government. However, federal union was delayed until 1901 because of the rivalries among the colonies. Finally, an Australian constitution was accepted which provided a federal system resembling the American prototype except for its cabinet form of government. The practical values of ending separate tariffs and railway gauges, coupled with the fear of Japanese, German, and American expansion in the South Pacific, finally triumphed over separatist loyalties.

NEW ZEALAND

Britain annexed New Zealand in 1840, and in 1853 the settlement obtained a large measure of self-government. After two wars with the native Maoris, the white settlers dominated the country. Since New Zealand was small in size, no federal system was necessary, and dominion status came easily in 1907. By that date planned and systematic immigration and public works had resulted in a society that was responsive to political and social experiments.

Imperial Federation

Between 1887 and 1922 seven imperial conferences were convened in an effort to promote centralization among the self-governing members of the empire. Proponents of centralization argued for it on three levels: political (imperial federation), economic (imperial preference), and military (imperial defense). Joseph Chamberlain, the Colonial Secretary (1895–1903), provided the momentum for these conferences, claiming that imperial union made economic and political sense just as federal unions in Canada and Australia were obvious advantages over separate colonies. At these imperial conferences Chamberlain proposed the establishment of a council which could make agreements binding on the member countries, thereby making the self-governing members share in the responsibility and expense of the empire. His "Weary Titan" speech of 1901 pointed out that the dominions were enjoying the privileges of naval protection without making any significant contribution to the British navy. Prime Minister Laurier of Canada led the opposition to centralization on the grounds that it was reversing the trend to autonomy, because Britain, by its population, power, and prestige, would inevitably dominate any federal union. By 1911 the centralizers had been defeated on every issue.

Popularity of Empire

Popular support for British imperialism was at its patriotic and emotional peak between Queen Victoria's Golden Jubilee and the Boer War. In 1887, and again in 1897 at the Diamond Jubilee of the Queen, the British seized the opportunity to celebrate their successful imperial expansion with magnificent spectacles. Troops and dignitaries from every colony came to London. "Drunk with the sight of power," the populace scarcely heeded the penitential admonition of Rudyard Kipling the poet laureate, whose verse and prose reflected imperialism at its best.

In contrast to Kipling, the jingoistic and grasping type of imperialism was supported in theory by social Darwinism, a misapplication of the Darwinian hypothesis to human races, and in print by a yellow press. Alfred Harmsworth (later Lord Northcliffe) reduced the price of his newspaper, the *Daily Mail*, to a halfpenny, and introduced a tabloid-style of sensational journalism to glorify imperial heroes and British power. Circulation boomed and other papers copied the format. This type of imperial fever reached its climax in the admiration of the exploits of Lord Kitchener on the Nile and Lord Roberts in South Africa. As the empire grew, so did criticism of imperialism. Free traders and middle-class radicals denounced colonies as expensive, useless, and the cause of needless rivalry with other powers. Yet nothing halted the acquisition of new possessions. By 1900 the *Pax Britannica* represented the largest, most populous, and wealthiest empire yet seen.

Indian Policy

The title of Empress of India that Parliament conferred upon Queen Victoria in 1876 did not shift political control of India any more than the India Act of 1858, which placed India directly under parliamentary control. The effective administration of India depended on the three thousand district officers and specialists who served in the Indian civil service. This efficient and effective bureaucracy was open to Indians, but the nature of the exam virtually restricted competition to graduates of Britain's public schools and universities. The successes of the civil service were striking: public health, transportation, and the administration of justice were improved, famine decreased, and literacy and population increased. However, Indian nationalists desired to be rid of the English; good government was no substitute, in their minds, for self-government.

Indian intellectuals, inspired by the Western literature of revolt and freedom, stirred the national consciousness and revived native literature and history. The All-India Congress was founded in 1885 to promote Indian self-government. The British made a token response to this growing nationalism by the Council Acts of 1894 which placed a minority of elected Indians on the legislative councils, and by the Morley-Minto reforms of 1909 which introduced elective Indian participation in government. Communal representation—separate electoral roles—was also granted as a concession to Muslims. However, the Hindu-Muslim animosity complicated the introduction of responsible government because the Muslim minority feared that their rights would be jeopardized by a Hindu government.

During these years British frontier policy for India contained Russian expansion in Afghanistan and checkmated French, German, and Russian ambitions in Persia. After the Penjdah crisis of 1885, the subsequent frontier history was generally peaceful. Lord Curzon's viceroyalty (1899–1906) produced a treaty with Tibet and the new Northwest Frontier provinces as buffers against rival powers. If Curzon's reforming zeal brought about great educational, technical, and economic advances, his unwitting haughtiness in bearing and attitude, nevertheless, alienated him from the Hindus and occasioned his recall in 1905 by the new Liberal government. He was succeeded by Lord Minto.

Imperialism in China

The ease with which recently industrialized Japan defeated China in the Sino-Japanese war (1895) revealed two things: the rise of Japan as an imperial power in the Far East, and the tempting weakness of China. There was an immediate scramble for China's wealth and trade. Russia, France, and Germany forced Japan to restore its conquests on the mainland and claimed economic spheres of influence for themselves. Britain's favorable position in China since 1840 was jeopardized. The partition of China was opposed, but European rivals gave no heed to British protests. Britain and the United States favored an "open door" policy for China which would give all nations equal rights in economic exploitation, but which would forbid the formal partition of China. As a result, British and American support prevented the political dismembering of China, such as occurred in Africa, but the economy and wealth of China soon became controlled by a consortium of major powers.

African Expansion

The partition of Africa by European powers was completed by 1914. Only France with 4,200,000 square miles of empire exceeded the British holdings of 3,300,000 square miles. Germany followed with 1,100,000 square miles and Belgium with 900,000 square miles. The explanations heard in Britain most frequently for this expansion were the obligation to carry out a "civilizing mission" and bring commerce and Christianity to these underdeveloped areas, the moral obligation to bring order where there was strife and disorder, or the need to claim certain territory to save it from being annexed by their European rivals.

EAST AFRICA

The treaties that Carl Peters and the Society for German Colonization secured from African chiefs reactivated British interest in East Africa, a territory nominally under the Sultan of Zanzibar. Sir William Mackinnon acquired a charter for the British East Africa Company after an Anglo-German agreement in 1886 recognized German suzerainty in Tanganyika and British influence in Kenya. Meanwhile, a religious war had erupted in Uganda, and Captain Frederick Lugard was sent by the British East India Company to restore order. However he discovered that Peters had already persuaded the King of Buganda to sign a treaty with Germany. In 1890 Lord Salisbury won German recognition of British control over Kenya, Uganda, and the Sudan, in return for ceding to Germany the island of Heligoland in the North Sea. In 1895 the British government purchased Mackinnon's chartered company and began construction of a railroad from the coast through Kenya to Uganda. White settlement followed.

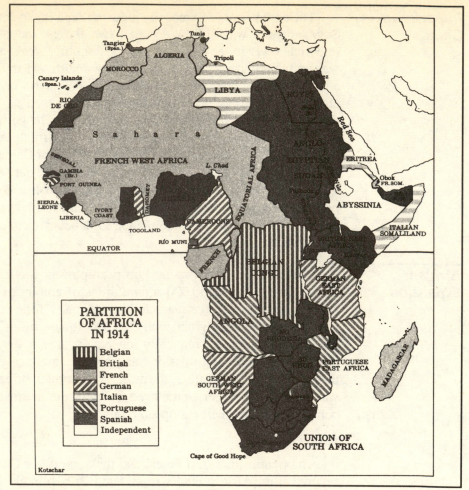

Fig. 20.1 Partition of Africa in 1914

WEST AFRICA

In 1884 the German annexation of Togoland, Cameroons, and Southwest Africa stirred the British to action. The Royal Niger Company (formerly the United African Company) under Sir George Goldie received a charter in 1886 to administer the Niger delta and the interior. In return, the company would attempt to suppress the slave trade. Sir Frederick Lugard was hired by the company. He made treaties with native rulers and subdued the independent north. By 1914 northern and southern Nigeria were united under the governorship of Lugard, who became the most successful exponent of indirect rule—Britain claiming paramount power with local government operating through native chiefs.

In 1871 the British purchased Danish and Dutch interests in the Gold Coast, but the small coastal colony was constantly threatened by the fierce Ashanti in the interior. When punitive expeditions and wars did not break

Ashanti power, Chamberlain declared a British protectorate over the interior in 1901. The introduction of cocoa soon made the Gold Coast the world's leading producer of cocoa products. Unlike East and South Africa with their temperate climates, there was virtually no white settlement in West Africa.

SUDAN

Following Charles Gordon's death the Sudan experienced a decade of frightful anarchy. The disorders were such a constant threat to neighboring Egypt that finally the British determined to restore order. Lord Kitchener led a British army southward and annihilated the Dervishes at the decisive Battle of Omdurman in 1898. When Kitchener continued up the Nile to Fashoda, he encountered Captain Marchand and a French expedition which had arrived from the French Congo. This clash of rival imperial ambitions produced a diplomatic crisis and a war spirit in London and Paris. France finally backed down when its one ally, Russia, refused support. Kitchener completed the annexation of the Sudan, and until 1953 the country was a British protectorate jointly administered by Britain and Egypt.

The Boer War

In the last decades of the nineteenth century relations between Boers and Britons worsened. The deteriorating relationship was brought about by internal circumstances, such as the conflicting personalities of Cecil Rhodes and Paul Kruger, and the discovery of gold, and by such external events as German intervention in southern Africa and the popular sentiment in Britain in favor of imperialism. In 1899 the differences led to war.

BACKGROUND

The discovery of diamonds in 1870 and gold in the Transvaal in 1885 resulted in a great influx of foreigners into South Africa. The Boers feared that their political autonomy and separatist society were jeopardized by this invasion. Under Paul Kruger, president of the Transvaal, the Boers discriminated against foreigners in the country, excluding them from the vote, and taxing them heavily. The English immigrants protested and demanded their political rights. Their cause was supported by Cecil Rhodes who, besides making a vast fortune in gold, had organized the greatest of the chartered companies—the British South Africa Company—and had incorporated Rhodesia into the empire in 1888. The following year Rhodes became Premier of the Cape Colony and pursued his dream of federating the British and Boer colonies in South Africa and of establishing a Cape to Cairo railway. When the Kruger regime halted these aspirations, Rhodes agreed to a private uprising to bring the Transvaal under British rule.

The resulting Jameson Raid of 1895 was a fiasco and only increased the suspicions of the Boers about British intentions. Kaiser Wilhelm acerbated the friction by publicly supporting Kruger. Between 1895 and 1899 Chamberlain, as Colonial Secretary, and Lord Alfred Milner, as British High Commissioner, negotiated with Kruger over the grievances of English residents in the Transvaal; however, Boer nationalism was unbending, and the negotiations failed. German arms were transported to the Transvaal and the two Boer republics began to mobilize. The British dispatched troops, and in October 1899, the Boers attacked the British colony of Natal.

WAR AND PEACE

At first mounted Boer commandos swept through Natal and besieged the larger part of the British forces at Ladysmith and at Mafeking to the west of the Orange Free State. An alarmed and humiliated Britain rushed her two most famous generals, Lords Roberts and Kitchener, and the largest British army ever assembled to the relief of the beleaguered cities. Before the end of 1900 the Boer states were invaded and their armies defeated. However, the Boers refused to surrender and for eighteen months mobile commando units waged guerrilla war. By the use of such stringent measures as block-houses and concentration camps, Boer resistance was gradually overcome. By 1901 both their leading generals, Louis Botha and Jan Christian Smuts, agreed to negotiations.

The terms of the Peace of Vereeniging (1902) were generous. The two Boer republics were added to the empire but were promised self-government in the near future. The Dutch and English languages were equally recognized in schools and courts, and Britain offered £3 million for economic reconstruction. When the Liberals won the election of 1906, Prime Minister Campbell-Bannerman immediately honored the pledge of self-government to the Transvaal and the Orange Free State. This unusual magnanimity captured the respect and support of Botha and Smuts and permitted Rhodes's dream of a federal union of the four colonies (Cape, Natal, Transvaal, and Orange Free State) to be realized in 1910.

IMPACT OF THE WAR ON BRITAIN

Although most of the populace rallied behind the government and 30,000 troops joined the British army from the dominions, the Boer War divided the Liberal party and isolated the country diplomatically. The foreign reaction was almost uniformly hostile, and the revelations to Britain that its isolation was anything but splendid (with a powerful Germany rearming) made its leaders eager to find allies.

Relations with the United States

In 1895 President Cleveland threatened force when Britain rejected an American offer to arbitrate a border dispute between Venezuela and British Guiana. Prime Minister Salisbury refused to respond in kind to this martial spirit and consented to arbitration. The outcome was a decision favorable to Britain and, equally important, more friendly relations between Britain and the United States. During the Spanish-American War only Britain among the European powers was sympathetic to the American position. This growing Anglo-American rapport was reflected in the Hay-Pauncefote Treaty (1901) which annulled the previous Clayton-Bulwer Treaty that had guaranteed joint control of any interoceanic canal. The new treaty provided that the United States alone could build and control the new canal. Britain was relinquishing its imperial power in the Caribbean to the United States.

From Isolation to Alliance

Moral sanctions and the Royal Navy had permitted the methods of Victorian liberalism to serve Britain well, until the Franco-Prussian War upset the balance of power on the Continent. Salisbury kept England free of alliances in spite of Germany's adventurous foreign policy. But by 1900 Britain found this position of "splendid isolation" no longer tenable and altered its foreign policy to one of limited commitments. The division of the Great Powers of Europe into two camps, the isolation of Britain during the Boer War, Germany's challenge to British sea power, and the increasing danger to Britain's exposed and scattered colonial and commercial empire made alliances seem worth the risk of Continental commitments.

TRIPLE ALLIANCE

In 1882 Bismarck concluded the Triple Alliance (Germany, Austria, and Italy) to strengthen Germany against any effort of France to seek revenge for its humiliating defeat in the Franco-Prussian War. He also arranged an alliance of the three emperors of Germany, Austria, and Russia as protection for Germany's eastern borders. In 1890 the clever and unstable Kaiser Wilhelm II let lapse the alliance with Russia, whereupon Russia and France formed an entente out of common fear of Germany; the entente became the Dual Alliance in 1894. Thus the great powers of Europe were again divided into two camps, and Britain found it increasingly difficult to win cooperation from any of their members on foreign or imperial matters.

ANGLO-GERMAN RELATIONS

Traditional enmity and current imperial rivalries in the Middle East and Africa continued to strain Anglo-Russian and Anglo-French relations, making Germany the logical partner for a British alliance. Under Bismarck relations with England were generally friendly, but they deteriorated after his ouster and the Kaiser's abandonment of Bismarck's "limited aims" in Europe. In spite of the belligerent manner of German diplomacy, Britain, through the overtures of Salisbury, Chamberlain, and Lansdowne, made three efforts to conclude a German alliance between 1895 and 1901. The negotiations failed because Germany was convinced that England could not come to terms with France or Russia. The negotiations also failed because the German Foreign Office was both resentful of Great Britain's colonial holdings and suspicious of its motives in seeking an alliance. In turn, German naval rearmament caused apprehension in Britain, and the German Emperor's provocative interference in the Boer dispute angered the British public. The failure of Germany to join Britain in opposing Russian encroachments in China and Korea drove Britain into a defensive alliance with Japan in 1902. The pact promised to provide military assistance if either country were attacked by more than one power. This alliance was the first formal step away from isolation.

THE ENTENTE CORDIALE, 1904

The next step achieved by Prime Minister Balfour was an agreement which settled the outstanding colonial issues dividing France and Britain. The entente promised French recognition of the British occupation of Egypt in return for British support of French interests in Morocco. Anglo-French relations had been cool ever since the Fashoda crisis in the Sudan in 1898. However, these feelings were dwarfed by France's need for Britain as an ally if war broke out between France and Germany and the desire of Britain for the friendship of a major European power.

THE TRIPLE ENTENTE, 1907

Sir Edward Grey, Foreign Secretary of the new Liberal government, concluded an agreement between Russia and Britain. Traditional hostilities between the two nations were reduced after the defeat of Russia by Japan and by their mutual fear of a militant Germany. British naval supremacy was being challenged by Germany following Wilhelm's crash program of ship building, while Russian influence in the Middle East was being challenged by Germany's friendship with Turkey. The entente settled imperial rivalries between the two powers in Persia and along the frontier of India. This agreement between old rivals surprised Germany. From the Kaiser's perspective, these alliances encircled Germany. In turn, Germany had made its own alliance, the Triple Alliance of Germany, Austria, and Italy. Each European camp viewed with increasing suspicion the activities of the other.

THE NEW LIBERALISM AND DOMESTIC ANARCHY

The years from 1906 to 1914 were a time of crisis and domestic violence in Britain. The rules of political warfare and parliamentary procedure were violated; the duel between the two Houses of Parliament resulted in a drastic reduction of the powers of the Upper House; workers, women, Ulsterites (residents of northern Ireland) and army officers disregarded the laws and constitutional customs of the land. As a result, nineteenth-century liberalism and the belief in the efficacy of evolutionary reform and moderation were no longer the prevailing political assumptions. They were replaced by a new generation of voters who pushed for radical social reform and the expectation that the state should remove the causes of poverty and unemployment. The expansion of political democracy during the nineteenth century produced an electorate that expected increasing economic and social democracy.

Election of 1906

The Liberal victory was of epic proportions, sweeping 377 seats to only 157 for the Conservatives and Liberal Unionists combined. In addition, the 53 members of the new Labor party and the 83 Irish Nationalists would support the government, rather than the Conservatives, on most measures. The Liberals interpreted their landslide as a mandate for social legislation, even if they failed to gauge fully the extent of unrest among the electorate. The Liberal government was willing to make concessions to the political pressures of the disaffected groups, whereas the Tories chose to use the Conservative House of Lords to prevent a drift toward socialism and a welfare state.

The Liberals and the Lords

Unlike the House of Commons, the House of Lords had not been reformed in the nineteenth century. Nor was it a nonpartisan body; since the desertion of the Liberal peers over Gladstone's Irish home rule issue, the Upper House had been turned into an overwhelmingly Conservative stronghold. Under the Salisbury-Balfour Conservative governments the House of Lords cooperated readily to pass partisan issues such as the Education Act (1902) which had not been an election issue. In contrast, the Conservatives now used their great majority in the House of Lords to block measures passed by the House of Commons and to frustrate the Liberal government. David Lloyd George, Chancellor of the Exchequer, and a brilliant and eloquent party spokesperson, claimed that the House of Lords was no longer a watchdog of the constitution, it was merely "Mr. Balfour's poodle."

Balfour, former Tory Prime Minister and now leader of the opposition, did not have the votes to block Liberal measures in the House of Commons, but the partisan attitude of the House of Lords was revealed by its rejection of two important measures passed by the Lower House in 1906—an Education bill, and a plural voting bill. The latter would limit a person having property qualifications in several districts to only one vote.

LIBERAL LEGISLATION

Some significant legislation, however, was passed by the Liberals under Prime Minister Campbell-Bannerman in 1905-1908. Responsible government was granted to the Transvaal and Orange Free State. A Workmen's

Compensation Act (1906) extended the liability of the employer for the payment of compensation to employees injured at work. The Trade Disputes Bill (1906) freed the trade unions from the legal restrictions and liabilities placed upon them in the Taff Vale decision.

Campbell-Bannerman resigned in 1908 and was succeeded by Asquith. Prime Minister Asquith was a Nonconformist lawyer, loyal to his colleagues and noted for his high personal standards and gentlemanly disposition. He was unpretentious and, above all, he was a moderate, believing in the essential rightness of conciliation and compromise. He appointed Lloyd George to the Exchequer and Churchill to the Board of Trade. These two colleagues, so different in background, helped push social legislation through Parliament. An Old Age Pension Bill (1908) provided for immediate noncontributory pensions for each citizen seventy years of age with an annual income of less than £31. To improve conditions of labor in the sweated industries, a Trade Boards Act of 1909 set up trade councils which fixed by law a minimum living wage and maximum hours of work. In 1911 the National Insurance Act became law and provided for insurance and protection against unemployment, sickness and disability. The government, employer, and employee all contributed to the scheme which brought fourteen million workers under its provisions.

THE PEOPLE'S BUDGET

The conflict between the Liberal government and the conservative House of Lords came to a head with the introduction of the budget by Lloyd George in April 1909. To pay for naval expansion and the old-age pension program, Lloyd George proposed new taxes: a super-tax on annual incomes over £5,000, increased death duties, land taxes, and income tax schedules. The tax increase bore most heavily on the wealthy, particularly the great landholders. The House of Commons passed the budget after long and tumultuous debate, but the House of Lords rejected it 350 to 75. Their repudiation of the budget plunged Britain into a constitutional crisis because an unwritten but established convention since 1671 denied the House of Lords the right to amend or veto a money bill. The peers replied that the proposed budget was not a legitimate money bill but a scheme to bring about a socialist revolution.

Decline of the House of Lords

The cry of 1832 by critics of the unreformed House of Commons, "mend it or end it," was now heard again as Parliament debated the proper jurisdiction of the Upper House. Checkmated by the House of Lords, the Liberal government took the volatile issue to the electorate in order to win approval for the budget and for a statutory reduction in the powers of the Lords.

In the election of 1910 Asquith failed to get the popular mandate that he anticipated. The election results gave the Liberals 275 seats, Conservatives 273, Irish Nationalists 82, and Labor 40. Asquith's government was now dependent upon the Irish, who held the balance of power. The Irish supported the Liberal government's budget which this time passed in both houses, but the condition for Irish support was that the Upper House would be reformed to prevent the Lords from vetoing Irish home rule as they had done previously. Asquith introduced legislation which would permit the House of Lords to delay a money bill no longer than one month and other bills no longer than two years before becoming law irrespective of the consent of the peers.

SUCCESSION OF GEORGE V

At this juncture Edward VII died, and a political truce was declared. King George V, conventional in outlook but with a high sense of duty and good judgment, called a conference of the leaders of the two parties to work out a compromise. The five-month conference failed to bring agreement. The reform bill, backed by Liberals and Irish Nationalists, passed the House of Commons but was rejected by the House of Lords. Therefore Asquith asked for a dissolution of Parliament and for the King to promise to create sufficient peers to pass the Parliament bill if the Liberals were restored to power in the forthcoming election. The assurance was reluctantly given. The ensuing election (December 1910), fought on the issue of the House of Lords, gave the Liberals and the Conservatives 272 seats each; once again, Irish and Labor votes returned the Liberal government to power.

PARLIAMENT ACT, 1911

Again the Liberal bill passed the House of Commons and went to the House of Lords. Aware of the royal guarantee to create new peers, the Tory leadership advised acceptance of defeat, but a "last ditch" movement among adamant peers almost forced the King to make good his promise. The bill finally passed 131 to 114. The Parliament Act (1) authorized the speaker of the House of Commons to define a money bill; (2) permitted the House of Lords to delay such a bill for only one month if the House of Commons had given its consent; (3) declared that all other bills would become law if passed by the House of Commons in three consecutive sessions; and (4) reduced the legal life of Parliament from seven to five years. The act regulated by statute the relationship between the two houses and made it impossible for the peers to challenge again the supremacy of the House of Commons.

Years of Crisis, 1911–1914

During these years the traditional values and institutions of Britain were undermined. The sense of fair play and genius for compromise which so often characterized nineteenth-century Britain was buried in unparliamentary diatribes of His Majesty's Loyal Opposition. There was open defiance by suffragettes, industrial workers, Protestant Ireland, the Tory leadership, and the army. Prime Minister Asquith and his government seemed helpless to halt this breakdown of tradition and order. By 1914 the Liberals had lost the confidence of middle-class Nonconformists, labor, and Ireland—the blocs which provided the Liberal party with its mandate for social reform in 1906.

THE SUFFRAGETTES

Since no party would support women's suffrage, and since conventional efforts to promote their cause had been unsuccessful, direct and violent steps were initiated. Mrs. Emmeline Pankhurst, founder of the Women's Social and Political Union (WSPU), and her daughter, Christabel, led the demonstrations. Their militant tactics included burning down 107 buildings, bombings, smashing shop windows, interruption of public meetings, and hunger strikes when imprisoned. Violence was a form of self-expression as well as emancipation from the roles expected of Victorian women. The suffragette violence created both impetus for and a backlash against votes for women. The harassment of parliamentary leaders by suffragettes finally forced Asquith to offer a nonparty vote on women's suffrage. However, the government did not promote the measure and the war intervened before any bill was passed.

INDUSTRIAL STRIFE

When the Liberals passed only one major social measure (the National Insurance Act) after the 1910 election, the workers, like the suffragettes, took direct action to raise their wages and to force the country to hear their demands. The new political power of the workers and the trade unions was publicly flaunted. Their class consciousness was stirred and their dissatisfaction with slow change was increasingly in evidence. French syndicalism also affected the most militant of the union leaders. This doctrine, developed by the French philosopher George Sorel, urged workers to paralyze the nation by general strikes and to seize factories and shops. Its call for violence frightened both the governing class and many workers.

Major strikes among dock and railway workers and coal miners (1911–1912) forced the government to intervene and grant the miners' demand for a minimum wage guaranteed by an act of Parliament. In 1913 the three big unions of miners, railway workers, and transport employees agreed to act together and to make demands of their employers at the same time. By the summer of 1914 walkouts in these three industries were imminent, and a general strike, which suggested overtones of a class war, was predicted for autumn.

TORY AND ULSTER DEFIANCE

Asquith introduced an Irish home rule bill in 1911, as he had promised the Irish Nationalists in return for their support of his Liberal government. No longer able to rely on a veto in the House of Lords after passage of the Parliament Act, the Tories, with cynical zeal, challenged the Liberals to force home rule on Ulster. Andrew Bonar Law, the new leader of the Conservatives, led the attack on home rule, effectively assisted by Sir Edward Carson and F. E. Smith. Their reckless speeches counseled defiance of both law and constitutional process and the use of force to prevent home rule if necessary. The home rule bill that passed the House of Commons in 1912, supported by John Redmond and the Irish members of Parliament, would give Ireland autonomy in home affairs, but would reserve certain powers, such as defense and foreign affairs, for London.

The industrialized and Protestant northeast (Ulster) feared that home rule would reverse their favored position if the rural, Catholic south dominated an Irish Parliament; they clung to their self-conscious separateness. Under Sir Edward Carson's provocative leadership, Ulster declared that it would repudiate home rule, regardless of what Parliament might decree. A volunteer army was raised in Ulster and a covenant was signed by half a million pledging to defy home rule at all costs. Southern Ireland insisted that nothing short of a united Ireland would suffice. An Irish Nationalist volunteer army was recruited to counter the Ulster volunteers. The irresponsible talk of the Conservative leadership was matched by the indecision of Prime Minister Asquith who was unable to control the course of events. In March 1914 the home rule bill came up for its third and final reading in the House of Commons.

The issue now shifted to the army which was strongly unionist in sentiment. At the army barracks in Curragh, British officers announced their refusal to fight against the Ulster rebels, and there was no reprimand from their superiors for this mutiny. Civil war seemed imminent in Ireland. King George intervened to bring the party leaders to a conference, but an impasse was reached and reported to the House of Commons on July 14. Only the outbreak of World War I a week later prevented the domestic crisis from deepening. In September 1914 the Home Rule Act automatically became law, but its implementation was suspended for the duration of the war.

The constitutional processes and political institutions of Britain had been shaken by the actions of those who were impatient with slow change or no longer accepted the legislative process. The Liberal party was unable to absorb this new radicalism and became caught in the crossfire of the Tory right and the Labor left. Only the outbreak of war on the Continent halted the deterioration of domestic affairs within Britain and gave the Liberal party a temporary reprieve.

Although the transition to the twentieth century was accompanied by violence and impatience with British institutions, it is also important to note that Britain was a leader in political and social reforms in these decades. The influence of "things British" from lawn tennis to asphalt roads to the English language and missionary hospitals made an indelible imprint on the rest of the world in the nineteenth century, to a degree not matched before or since by Britain.

Selected Readings

Bebbington, D. W. *The Nonconformist Conscience: Chapel and Politics, 1870–1914* (1982)

Bernstein, George L. *Liberalism and Liberal Politics in Edwardian England* (1986)

Dangerfield, George. *The Strange Death of Liberal England, 1910–1914* (1961)

Jenkins, Roy. *Asquith* (1964)

Kennedy, A. L. *Salisbury* (1953)

Magnus, Philip. *King Edward the Seventh* (1964)

Manchester, William. *The Last Lion: Winston Spenser Churchill; Visions of Glory: 1874–1932* (1986)

McIntyre, W. David. *Colonies into Commonwealth* (1966)

Meacham, Standish. *A Life Apart: The English Working Class, 1890–1914* (1977)

Morris, James. *Pax Britannica: The Climax of Empire* (1968)

Nowell-Smith, Simon H. (ed.). *Edwardian England, 1901–1914* (1964)

Pelling, Henry. *The Origins of the Labour Party, 1880–1900* (1965)

Pugh, Martin. *The Tories and the People, 1880–1935* (1985)

Rover, Constance. *Women's Suffrage and Party Politics in Britain, 1886–1914* (1967)

Webb, Beatrice. *My Apprenticeship* (1926)

21

Nineteenth-Century Life and Thought

1798 Wordsworth and Coleridge jointly publish their *Lyrical Ballads*, ushering in Romanticism in literature

1819 First all-weather, macadamized (asphalt) roads

1830 Era of the modern railway opens with George Stephenson's railroad from Manchester to Liverpool

1832 Passage of Great Reform Bill

1837 Accession of Queen Victoria to the throne

1850 Poet laureate Alfred Lord Tennyson publishes *In Memoriam*

1859 Publication of Charles Darwin's *On the Origin of Species*

Charles Dickens publishes *A Tale of Two Cities*

John Stuart Mill, founder of Utilitarian Society, publishes essay *On Liberty*

1865 Birth of Rudyard Kipling, most popular writer of the century and storyteller of imperial expansion

1870 First National Education Act passed

1876 Dr. Joseph Lister introduces antiseptic techniques in surgery

1886 Gladstone's first Irish home rule bill defeated in Parliament

1887 Queen Victoria's Golden Jubilee and tribute to the British empire

1901 Death of Queen Victoria; accession of Edward VII

*T*he *nineteenth century was Britain's greatest age in power, material progress, and in political liberalism. Although great diversity characterized the various phases of Victorianism, several generalizations can be made about the century. It was a period largely free of the wars and revolutions that wracked the Continent. Protected by the Pax Britannica (naval supremacy) and motivated by its faith in progress, Britain attained pre-eminence in the world for its stable and constitutional government and for its liberal, reformist creed.*

Until the latter part of the century a certain unity of spirit was recognizable in the nation, brought about by national security, self-confidence, a common moral code based on religious duty, and a belief in the efficacy of utilitarianism and the superiority of British institutions. Real wages and the condition of the poor improved substantially.

The core of Victorianism contained a sense of moral seriousness, articulated brilliantly by such cultural critics as Matthew Arnold and John Henry Newman. The strident voices and propensity for violence exhibited by agitators demanding radical change at the end of the century unraveled this earlier harmony and demanded recognition and a new structure for society. Victorian liberalism gave way to liberal socialism.

THE AGE OF PROGRESS

The almost universal faith in man's progress, bulwarked by eighteenth-century rationalism, the triumphs of science, and by the persuasiveness of a religion of duty and of political liberalism, was everywhere in evidence; perhaps most of all in the rapid expansion of the economy. In almost every area, except architecture, the nineteenth century had geniuses.

Condition of the People

By every statistical index the population of Britain (16 million in 1801, 41 million in 1901) was more numerous, better fed, better housed, more healthy, more literate, and better governed in 1900 as compared to 1800. The rate of material progress which was made possible by British inventions and Britain's head start in the Industrial Revolution also helped to liberate the mind from ignorance and old fears. However, modern fears appeared in the guise of mass unemployment and the mass killings of scientific war. As a result of evangelical and utilitarian concern, the public conscience had been awakened, and a growing sense of public responsibility for social and economic misery was in evidence. Private charity was increasingly supplemented by massive state assistance, such as the Old Age Pension Act and the National Insurance Act. The death rate dropped sharply throughout the century as medicine became scientific and effective and as food became more plentiful and varied. Real wages in 1900 were almost double the figure for 1850 as the benefits of the Industrial Revolution were beginning to be more equitably shared.

THE LABORING CLASS

The urban laborers had borne the brunt of the miseries resulting from the dislocations and revolutionary changes of the Industrial Revolution. But in the nineteenth century conditions of the working class improved through factory and public health legislations, free elementary education after 1870, old-age pensions, more leisure time and open spaces, better entertainment, and the growth of trade unions. As the franchise was gradually expanded, workers sensed their political influence and used this power for practical legislative goals. Nevertheless, class differences remained substantial, and in 1900 one-third of the wage earners of Britain still lived in chronic poverty.

Industrial Expansion

The engineering industry and new markets sustained the rapid industrial expansion of the first part of the century. Britain's natural resources, superior industrial organizations, financial stability, and merchant navy prompted an enormous increase in trade. Between 1850 and 1870 exports of coal increased 500 percent, the exports of iron and steel goods 400 per- cent. In 1856 Henry Bessemer's invention which produced steel cheaply in large quantities gave Britain the lead in steel manufacture. This prosperity, in turn, permitted British companies to develop and invest in the economies of other countries. Not until the 1870s was Britain threatened by Germany and the United States as serious competitors. Thereafter, Britain gradually declined from a position of unchallenged industrial leadership.

TRANSPORTATION

The full effects of the Industrial Revolution could not be realized until cheaper and more rapid and reliable methods of transportation were available. The revolution in transportation, begun in the eighteenth century, was accelerated in the nineteenth.

Roads. All-weather macadamized roads (known today as asphalt roads) were introduced in 1819 by John Macadam, a Scottish engineer. These improved roads and the removal of tolls permitted rapid transportation of commodities and regular wagon and stagecoach services between manufacturing centers. Main roads came under the control of the county councils in 1888.

Railways. George Stephenson began the era of the modern railway with the opening of a line between Manchester and Liverpool in 1830, which became an immediate success. Between 1825 and 1837 ninety-three railway acts of all kinds were passed by Parliament. By 1848 some five thousand miles of railways were laid. Railways, with their cheapness of travel, investment possibilities, and encouragement of heavy industries, helped change the economic structure of the country.

Steamships. Marine freight was another source of wealth because Britain carried nearly two-thirds of its foreign commerce in its own ships. Regular transatlantic steam navigation dates from 1838, but steam tonnage did not catch up with sail until 1883. The introduction of iron, which the country had in large quantities, made Britain the world's leading shipbuilder. Construction of the Suez Canal (1869) shortened the voyage from England to India and made shipping even more profitable.

Agriculture

The rapid fall of the price of grain after 1815 and the setback suffered by the repeal of the Corn Laws created an agricultural slump. There followed twenty years of prosperity (1853–1873) as a result of new tools and machines, better fertilizers, and the opening up of distant markets through railway transportation. However, British farmers could not compete with the cheaper grain from North America or with the meat and dairy products shipped by refrigerated freighter from Australia and New Zealand. Lower food prices benefited the city dweller, but free trade hurt the farmer.

Scientific Achievements

The triumphs of science in the century were astonishing. Ordinary citizens exulted in the impressive scientific advances because they fit in so properly with their idea of progress and material well-being. Charles Darwin's *On the Origin of Species* (1859) revolutionized mankind's conception of the processes of evolutionary development with its emphasis on "natural selection."

PHYSICS AND CHEMISTRY

In 1808 John Dalton introduced a scientific theory concerning atoms which between 1857 and 1879 was elaborated upon by James Clerk Maxwell and J. P. Joule. Clerk Maxwell developed the kinetic theory of gases and established the existence of atoms as real substances. Electromagnetic waves were established theoretically by Michael Faraday, mathematically by Clerk Maxwell; most electric machinery depends upon Faraday's principles. Joule concluded from experiments that heat was a form of energy and recorded the amount of energy necessary to produce a given amount of heat.

MEDICINE AND SANITATION

Medicine became scientific and medical advances were readily adopted by the medical profession. James Simpson, a professor of medicine, was the first to use chloroform. In 1876 Dr. Joseph Lister established antiseptic surgery after his success in the antiseptic treatment of open wounds. Edward Jenner had introduced vaccination against smallpox in the eighteenth century, and vaccination was standard practice by the mid-Victorian years. An improved diet along with improved housing and working conditions also made people more resistant to tuberculosis and other infectious diseases. A significant drop in the death rate took place between 1800 and 1870.

Victorian insistence on cleanliness as an outward sign of respectability encouraged both personal hygiene and sanitary regulations for towns and factories. Baths, indoor plumbing, and hot water became available to large numbers. Continental observers declared that "the English think soap is civilization." Effective sewage systems, purified running water, and health legislation were introduced in most municipalities. Disraeli's Factory Act of 1878 included detailed provisions for maintaining cleanliness and proper ventilation in shops and factories.

GEOLOGY AND BIOLOGY

In 1830 Charles Lyell offered a comprehensive explanation of the history of the earth as traced by the record of rocks and fossils. His theory, published in *Principles of Geology*, emphasized the natural and evolutionary development of the earth. In biology Charles Darwin's theory of organic revolution changed a static Newtonian world into a universe of constant change and growth. His advancement of the theory of evolution affected not only the sciences, but many other fields of thought as well. Darwin's hypothesis can be observed in the philosophy of Herbert Spencer, the ethics of Thomas Huxley, the poetry of Tennyson, and in the prose of George Meredith and Matthew Arnold.

NINETEENTH-CENTURY LIFE AND THOUGHT

There was no single Victorian theme in literature or in thought because the century encompassed figures as diverse as John Henry Newman and William Morris, or William Wordsworth and John Stuart Mill. However, Victorian life and thought was influenced by the implications of the Industrial Revolution and the Newtonian and Darwinian conceptions of the universe. Literature, art, religion, and philosophy kept struggling with the questions of mechanism and freedom, empiricism and idealism, creationism and change.

Three Phases of Victorianism

Peace, progress, and political liberalism characterized most of the century bounded by the Napoleonic Wars and the First World War. However, the age can be described more accurately in smaller units since Queen Victoria's long reign put an illusory uniformity on a period of time in which ideas, manners, and values changed profoundly.

EARLY VICTORIANISM, 1815–1850

Britain accepted the gradual democratization of government and society after the public conscience had been stirred by the ideas of the American and French revolutions and by the convictions of English utilitarians and Evangelicals. National institutions made adjustments to absorb this democratic radicalism and to make Britain a leader in world opinion at the same time that its industrialization and inventiveness made it preeminent in the production of manufactured goods. By mid-century Britain was near the peak of its power and prestige, confident in the belief that economic prosperity based on free trade and parliamentary institutions could bring happiness and peace.

MID-VICTORIANISM, 1850–1870

This era was the apex of Victorian self-confidence, devotion to duty, and faith in the efficacy of political liberalism. Generally, British industrial and naval power was used to advance liberalism abroad; in England the accent was on freedom for the individual citizen. Although contemporary critics attacked the easy supremacy and the middle class and capitalist values of the period, the prevailing belief remained firm in the inevitability of progress to solve the nation's problems and to keep Britain great.

LATE VICTORIANISM, 1870–1914

Britain's industrial and commercial supremacy no longer went unchallenged, and militarism and industrial rivalry jeopardized the Pax Britannica. The rest of the world had not been converted to either free trade or to parliamentary democracy. Liberalism, free trade, political compromise, and mid-Victorian moral values were undermined by their failure to guarantee security to the English citizen in a world of aggressive nationalism and impersonal economic forces. In the search for new goals, ancient values and institutions were no longer revered or even respected. Twentieth-century political, economic, and social forces, such as trade unionism and women's suffrage, demanded recognition.

Victorian Morality

Victorianism was a reaction against the loose morality of the Regency period. Along with the smugness and philistinism which critics such as Matthew Arnold exposed, the period exhibited the prevailing virtues and moral values of a society molded by business interests, Evangelicalism and humanitarianism. Industriousness, self-help, religious duty, Sabbath observance, propriety of moral conduct, liberality of mind, and the stability of family life were the conventional standards of the times. Nevertheless, the exceptions to these standards, as seen in the nonconformity of William Thackeray, Oscar Wilde, or George Meredith, were so numerous that the stereotype of the age may be more limiting than illuminating, because

Victorians were equally engaged in shedding the cant and maudlin sentimentality inherited from the late eighteenth century. The moral fiber and the continuity of national institutions provided the cohesiveness and the astonishing readjustment to change which really marked the century.

Victorian Women

The nineteenth century was still very much a male-dominated world. There were, of course, notable exceptions, such as Florence Nightingale, the founder of nursing, and authors such as Mary Ann Evans (George Elliot) and the Brontë sisters. However, only late in the century was there any willingness to allow women to have a public role and be treated legally as equals of men. The right to vote did not come until the twentieth century. Queen Victoria herself gave no support to female emancipation, calling women's rights nothing but "wicked folly."

Perhaps nothing did more for the emancipation of middle-class women than the reduction in the size of the family. The average woman in 1860 had six children; in 1900 only three. Women could now spend their time on more than childbearing and childrearing. In 1857 the Divorce Act was passed. The Married Women's Property Acts of 1870 and 1882 and the opening of civil service posts to women provided a few business and professional opportunities.

In 1869 women won the right to vote in municipal elections, and the following year they could vote for school boards and be elected as school board members. In the 1870s both Oxford and Cambridge added women's colleges, and the four Scottish universities began to admit women in 1892. The new popularity of bicycling and other sports helped bring about an emancipation in female clothing.

Religion

Probably in no other century, except the seventeenth and perhaps the twelfth, did religion, or public figures such as Gladstone or Charles Kingsley speaking in the name of religion, exercise so much influence. Evangelical convictions, shared by Nonconformists and Anglicans alike, placed high value on Bible reading, upright conduct, moral discipline, and seriousness of purpose. This sense of duty and the satisfaction of such stewardship explains, in part, the Victorian admiration for missionaries, statesmen, and writers, such as Livingstone, Gladstone, and Tennyson. By the latter part of the nineteenth century the universality of this religious code disappeared as scientific knowledge increased, Biblical criticism arose, and conventional Christianity was put on the defensive by the attacks of Darwin's followers. Within the church the issue of fundamentalism (a belief in the literal truth of the Bible) versus liberalism was dividing theologians and laity.

The Universities

Thomas Arnold (1795–1842), headmaster of Rugby, incorporated a sense of service and idealism into the public schools of England by overhauling the curriculum and placing greater emphasis on character training and the obligations of Christian citizenship. The need for reform of institutional life and curricula at the universities was equally evident, but the changes were less striking than those in secondary education. Some modest internal reforms occurred before Parliament forced reform in the government of the universities by acts in 1854 and 1856. By 1871 all religious restrictions were abolished. In 1836 the University of London was founded, and in 1848 it granted admission to women students.

Literature

Nineteenth-century literature was remarkable for its diversity of style and content. Wit, drollery, social satire, elegant essays, novels, serious criticism, and tales of adventure appealed strongly to an increasingly literate nation. In no other century did literature have such a popular impact.

ROMANTICISM, 1798–1832

The major Romantic poets in this period were William Wordsworth (1770–1850), Samuel Coleridge (1772–1834), Lord Byron (1788–1824), Percy Shelley (1792–1822), John Keats (1795–1821), and the poet-novelist Sir Walter Scott (1771–1832). In reaction to the neoclassicism of Pope and Johnson with its emphasis on order and classical forms, the Romanticists consciously broke away from these conventions. They featured ordinary people and simple language, a revival of medievalism, and an appreciation of nature. Their faith in the individual often prompted support of democracy and revolution. Byron and Shelley rebelled against the old social order and literary forms and stirred not only a literary revolution with their passionate idealism and novel imagery, but also affected political and social attitudes of the time. Wordsworth and Coleridge were eloquent advocates of liberty and sympathized with the French Revolution. In 1798 they published jointly their *Lyrical Ballads* which introduced simple rustic themes written in a style of language "really used by readers." Jane Austen (1775–1817) wrote six novels during this period. Her popular heroines, such as Elizabeth Bennet in *Pride and Prejudice*, were lively, human, and interesting.

VICTORIAN POETRY

Alfred, Lord Tennyson (1809–1892), sentimental and romantic in inclination, was the most popular of the Victorian poets and became poet laureate in 1850. His *In Memoriam* (1850) is one of the great elegies in English poetry. Robert Browning's (1812–1889) poetry was more erudite and original than Tennyson's but was never fully understood by the public and therefore not as popular. Among his finest poems were *The Bishop Orders His Tomb* and *The Ring and the Book*. Elizabeth Barrett Browning's (1806–1861) intense feelings and poetical fluency were reflected in her *Sonnets from the Portuguese*. Her *Cry of the Children* gave poetic support to social reform. Dante Gabriel Rossetti (1828–1882) and his sister, Christina, were founders, with others, of the Pre-Raphaelite Brotherhood, a group of poets and painters who turned to the themes of the Middle Ages for inspiration. William Morris (1834–1896), artist, designer, and poet, revealed his love for the romantic past and for beauty for its own sake in *The Earthly Paradise* and *The Defense of Guenevere and Other Poems*. His socialistic convictions were expressed in *News from Nowhere* and *A Dream of John Ball*. Algernon Swinburne (1837–1909) defied the conventional Victorian mores by writing sensual and pagan lyrics. His metrical skill was not only flawless but also fascinatingly complex in execution.

VICTORIAN NOVELISTS

The novel attained preeminence in the nineteenth century. Charles Dickens (1812–1870) caricatured and sentimentalized Victorian Londoners in such moving stories as *David Copperfield, Oliver Twist*, and *A Tale of Two Cities*. William Thackeray, a contemporary of Dickens, was a master character-painter and satirist of the English upper classes. Avoiding sentimentality, he used subtle wit to expose the sham and hypocrisy of society in such novels as *Vanity Fair, Pendennis*, and *Henry Esmond*. Mary Ann Evans (1819–1880), writing under the pseudonym of George Eliot, revealed effective character analysis amid stern moralizing in *Silas Marner* and *Mill on the Floss*. The Brontë sisters, Anne and Charlotte, portrayed much of their ill-starred lives in *Agnes Grey* and *Jane Eyre*. Emily's novel *Wuthering Heights* (1847) is a tale of madness on the moors that has retained its haunting and mystical appeal to the present. Charles Kingsley (1819–1875) was a Christian socialist who sympathized with the working classes in *Yeast*, attacked evolution in *Water Babies*, and dramatized Elizabethan adventure in *Westward Ho*. Benjamin Disraeli's brilliant and cynical novels *Vivian Gray* and *Coningsby* examined the different social classes of England. Anthony Trollope (1815–1882) modeled his writing after Thackeray and described the respectable people of a cathedral town in *Barchester Towers*. George Meredith (1828–1909) was an intellectual poet and novelist. In novels such as *The Egoist* he was primarily concerned with a psychological study of his characters. Lewis Carroll (1832–1898) lectured in mathematics at Oxford, but became far better known as the author of *Alice's Adventures in Wonderland* and *Through the Looking Glass*; both are nursery classics.

PERIODICAL LITERATURE

Magazines and literary reviews in nineteenth-century England became famous for the high caliber of their editors and contributors, and for the instruction of their reading audience. The *Edinburgh Review*, a Whig quarterly, was founded in 1802. Its rivals were the Tory *Quarterly Review* (1809) and *Blackwood's Edinburgh Magazine* (1817). In 1841 *Punch* began publication as a humorous weekly; its contributors took great delight in lampooning opponents of social reform. The first issue of the *Cornhill Magazine*, edited by William M. Thackeray, appeared in 1860.

LITERARY CROSSCURRENTS

By the end of the nineteenth century the comfortable supremacy, the unity, and the liberal creed of individualism and freedom found in Victorian England were in retreat. The apprehension and confusion of these years in which social and political forces produced such rapid change were apparent in the literature. A variety of themes and trends resulted which defy classification as writers searched for new values. Influenced by Continental writers, the aesthetic school of the 1890s emphasized the symbolic, the sensual, and the worship of ideal beauty. William Butler Yeats (1865–1939) and Oscar Wilde (1854–1900) were the most significant aesthetes. Wilde won fame for his witty comedies, Yeats for his lyrical expressions of Irish nationalism. The novelists of these years were superior to the poets in both the quality and volume of their writing. Samuel Butler's (1835–1902) novel *The Way of All Flesh* followed the tradition of the French naturalists, but focused on the author's spiteful comments on Victorian values and against his own family.

Other writers also challenged the "art for art's sake" school by their accent on rugged action and the romance of adventure. Robert Louis Stevenson (1850–1894) became popular with such blood-and-thunder adventure tales as *Treasure Island* and *Kidnapped*. Rudyard Kipling (1865–1936) voiced in verse and prose the imperial glories of the empire, with special attention to the British "mission" in India. Joseph Conrad (1857–1924) was perhaps the most original of these novelists. The color, rhythm, and psychological probings of his characters were well portrayed in *Lord Jim* and *Heart of Darkness*. Thomas Hardy (1840–1928) wrote beautiful short lyrics and increasingly pessimistic novels, such as *Tess of the D'Urbervilles* and *Jude the Obscure*, that were superb in their intimate knowledge of character and of the English countryside. Sir Arthur Conan Doyle (1859–1928) created the brilliant fictional detective hero Sherlock Holmes. Turn-of-the-century writers and Fabian reformers were H. G. Wells (1848–1946), who wrote about prewar England with humor and understanding, and George Bernard Shaw (1856–1950), Britain's outstanding dramatist of the early twentieth century.

Victorian Thought

The industrial revolution wrought such startling changes in the economic, political, and social organization of society that it spawned an intellectual revolution which embraced the world of science. At the same time critics resisted its dehumanizing effects. For many, evolution, material determinism, utilitarianism, and political liberalism were admired as hallmarks of progress. Others feared that individuality of character, beauty, and spiritual values were sacrificed for a bourgeois and mechanistic culture.

DARWIN AND HIS SCHOOL

The publication of *On the Origin of Species* in 1859 which set forth the hypothesis of natural selection not only unsettled many Victorians who believed in the instantaneous creation of the universe, but also upset those who claimed there was some purpose or desirable end in progress. Darwin's evolutionary theory implied only blind, mechanical chance. Undisturbed by the limitations placed by Darwin on this theory, his followers applied the Darwinian hypothesis to society. The philosopher Herbert Spencer (1820–1903) coined the phrase "survival of the fittest," and applied Darwin's theory of natural selection to social institutions and to the study of humanity; Thomas Huxley (1825–1895) popularized Darwin's writings and equated ethics with a scientific understanding of life; and Matthew Arnold (1822–1888) applied Darwin's theory of evolution to Christianity.

CRITICS

For all its buoyant self-confidence Victorian England was saved from complacency by self-criticism. The crass public taste and the worship of material success were judged by masters of social criticism. Thomas Carlyle (1795–1881) was a Puritan moralist who lashed out at the mechanization and loss of spirituality in Victorian England. *Past and Present* and *The French Revolution* revealed his explosive and eccentric style and his doctrine of hero worship. John Ruskin (1819–1900) aroused public consciousness to the ugliness of the machine age in art and architecture. Ruskin later turned from aesthetics to ethics and economics and wrote on behalf of industrial and social reform. Matthew Arnold, who was celebrated as a literary and cultural critic, was also a serious Biblical scholar who repudiated literal interpretation of the Bible. His *Culture and Anarchy* was the most devastating critique of the three social classes of mid-Victorianism. John Henry Newman (1801–1890), a leader in the Oxford movement, retained independent views on religion and education even after his conversion to Roman Catholicism. Newman's intellectual achievement and spiritual integrity were compassionately exhibited in the *Apologia pro Vita Sua*. His keen analysis of the value of classical education was presented in the polished prose of *The Idea of a University*.

HISTORIANS

Robert Southey (1774–1843), poet laureate and historian, wrote important biographies of Nelson and Wesley. Thomas Carlyle provided fiery and moralizing works, such as *Oliver Cromwell's Letters and Speeches*, *The French Revolution*, and the *History of Frederick the Great*. Whig interpretations of English history, glorifying Parliament, progress, and Protestantism, dominated the nineteenth century, especially in the works of Thomas Babington Macaulay, George O. Trevelyan, and John Richard Green.

JOHN STUART MILL AND DEMOCRATIC LIBERALISM (1807–1873)

Utilitarianism had been used to liberate people from restrictions on trade and from discrimination against religious or political minorities; it was less effective in solving economic problems relating to the industrial economy. Personal freedom had failed to bridge the gap between the wealthy employer and the impoverished worker. Classical economists in Britain, such as Adam Smith, Thomas Malthus, and David Ricardo, said nothing could be done about it in a free society; the randomness of the law of supply and demand was simply a fact of life. At first Mill accepted their economic doctrines until he viewed the wretched conditions of the factory towns. Then he shifted his views to urge major reforms that included (1) distribution of wealth by means of a progressive income tax, (2) universal education, (3) trade unions to improve the bargaining position of the worker, and (4) community factories to permit workers to share in the profits of their place of employment.

Mill addressed the same problems as Marx and the socialists, but supported neither, fearing that Marxian violence and rapid change could introduce greater ills than what they were seeking to cure, and that the socialists' demand for government controls of production would tyrannize a free society. Mill is thus a transitional figure between the eighteenth-century concept of English liberalism, which attempted to free the individual from restrictions, and the twentieth century which put more emphasis on the obligation of society to provide economic and social security and freedom from exploitation, even at the expense of freedom of action. In many ways Mill was a foil to Marx. His nonviolent proposals appealed to more workers than the more violent course urged by Continental Marxism or syndicalism.

VICTORIAN GOVERNMENT

The prestige and influence of nineteenth-century Britain was derived as much from its political inventiveness as from its industrial supremacy. Without repudiating the traditional forms of institutions, the Victorians adapted their political system to reconcile the demands of a mass electorate with the traditional governing classes within Parliament. Such devices as the party and cabinet systems, civil service examinations, and the extension of the franchise permitted democratic change without destroying the continuity of political institutions.

State Intervention

Benthamism, with its principle of "the greatest happiness for the greatest number," along with Evangelical and Nonconformist convictions were incorporated into laissez-faire arguments to buttress the opinion that less law would provide more liberty. This doctrine helped abolish political and religious disabilities and the Corn Laws in the first half of the century. But its negative side meant that the state could do little to relieve the glaring economic and social inadequacies of industrial Britain which could not be changed by individual effort. Edwin Chadwick, John Stuart Mill, and the Fabians transformed Bentham's principle into a positive doctrine which urged massive state intervention to relieve economic misery and to bring about social reform. Government regulation of industry, municipal ownership of utilities, a national education act, and the reorganization of local government were the results.

INSTITUTIONAL CHANGE

Unlike France in the nineteenth century with its numerous constitutional arrangements that included emperors, republics, and monarchies, institutional change in Britain did not occur through sudden shifts in the form of government. Rather, it took place by modification and adaptations of the functions and relationships of existing institutions. Essentially, the political history of one generation became the constitutional practices of the next. Britain remained a constitutional monarchy, but political power moved from Parliament to the people as represented in the House of Commons.

The Status of the Crown

The monarch remained the most prominent symbol in the political system. Under Queen Victoria, what Walter Bagehot (in his *English Constitution*) termed "the dignified role of the monarchy" was enhanced. The Hanoverian rulers who had preceded her were neither loved nor admired by their subjects. Respect for the institution of the monarchy saved them from losing their throne. Beginning with Queen Victoria, the institution of monarchy was saved by the nation's respect for the high caliber of the rulers. Admired and, at the end of her reign, venerated, she became the embodiment of the English character and the focal point of the British empire. The symbolic and emotional significance of the monarchy now outstripped its political functions, although Victoria took an active interest in affairs of state and was outspoken in her opinions on ministerial choices. But the fact remains that after 1839 ministries were formed which the electoral or parliamentary situation demanded despite the Queen's preferences. Her rejection of Peel in favor of Melbourne in 1839 was the last time that the monarch selected a prime minister who did not have the support of a parliamentary majority.

The Cabinet

The British cabinet system was essentially the growth of conventions. The transformation of the cabinet from a group of ministers, responsible to and chosen by the king, to an executive body governing in the king's name and responsible to the majority in the House of Commons, was a gradual process. Whereas the American cabinet system accents the separation of powers, the British arrangement emphasizes the close union of the executive and legislative powers. A cabinet minister must be a member of Parliament. Under Queen Victoria cabinet government and agreement of the ministry on cabinet policy became a constitutional convention and political practice. Ministers who differed on policy left the cabinet. As the franchise was expanded and as sovereignty shifted to the people, it became necessary for the cabinet to become responsible to the House of Commons in order to justify staying in office. In the nineteenth century the cabinet usually consisted of some sixteen to twenty members.

Parliament

The nineteenth century was the golden age of the private member of Parliament because rigid party discipline had not yet demanded an automatic party vote. Before the century was over Parliament had achieved effective control of the executive and made it responsible to the elected House of Commons. In turn, the House of Commons became more representative of the people as the removal of religious and property restrictions for membership made it possible for Dissenters, Roman Catholics, Jews, atheists, and the laboring classes to sit in Parliament; women were admitted in 1918.

Beginning with Robert Peel and his Tamworth Manifesto, candidates published their views on public questions. This foreshadowed the political platform (the Newcastle Program of 1892) and the practice of "going to the people" to settle a controversial question, such as home rule for Ireland. Parliamentary procedure became more elaborate as closures on debate were introduced and standing committees established. The Speaker of the House of Commons became nonpartisan. The power and prestige of the Upper House diminished as the political system became democratized, although the membership of the House of Lords more than doubled during the century to over four hundred. The Parliament Act of 1911 formally asserted the secondary role of the House of Lords.

Party Organization

In earlier centuries political parties were often deplored as factions conspiring to divide the nation. During the nineteenth century parties acquired their organizational form, first on a local basis and later nationally. By 1900 parties were not only tolerated but also had become an essential mechanism of the parliamentary system. The growth of party organization was a direct result of the expansion of the electorate. Its purpose was to get out the vote and help get the candidate elected. Parties provided a mandate for some sort of cabinet government and permitted the growth of an "alternative government." The duty of Her Majesty's Loyal Opposition was to oppose and to keep the government honest and responsible.

Party whips date from 1714 when the office of Patronage Secretary to the Treasury was created. Party organization grew out of the requirements for voter registration in the Great Reform Bill. A political committee, closely associated with the whip, emerged in each party and maintained contacts with local party agents. In 1861 the Liberals set up the first National Liberal Registration Association. In Birmingham Joseph Chamberlain had organized such an effective municipal machine, controlled by a central committee (caucus), that it was expanded to a national party organization in 1877. With its establishment and success the independent candidate and the minor party became victims of the two-party system.

The Civil Service

The vast expansion of the civil service was one index of the increased functions of the state. In 1832 civil servants numbered 21,300. By 1914 some 280,000 were employed. The increasing scope of parliamentary business and the technical nature of much legislation resulted in much wider discretionary powers (called delegated legislation) being granted to government departments. Patronage was replaced by competitive civil service examinations in 1855 in which the caliber of the candidate's education played an important part. After 1870 all administrative grades were filled by university-level exams.

Local Government

In 1835 municipal councils, elected by ratepayers, were set up in the towns. The Local Government Acts of 1888 and 1894 abolished the numerous appointed and elective local boards and councils in the counties by setting up two new elective units of local government, the county councils and county boroughs. These councils managed administrative business and social services formerly handled in an erratic manner by the dozen overlapping local councils. Social services were improved and expanded under municipal ownership.

Reform of the Judiciary

Complaints over the complicated and competing forms of pleading in various courts led to legislation to correct such abuses as the absence of trial by jury in the court of chancery. The whole judicial system, however, was restructured by the Judicature Acts of 1873 and 1875. A high court of justice took over the jurisdiction of the king's bench, common pleas, and exchequer courts, as well as the probate and divorce divisions. The jurisdiction of this new high court of justice was divided into three divisions: (1) chancery, (2) king's bench, and (3) probate, admiralty, and divorce. The act also established a court of appeal to hear pleas from these three divisions.

*T*he 1906 election marked the high tide of the nineteenth-century reform movement. By that time most of the objectives of earlier Victorian liberalism were won. Britain was a parliamentary democracy, and religious and political restrictions on the individual had been removed.

The Victorian Age was clearly one of Britain's greatest eras. Certainly it was its greatest in world influence, in material progress, political liberalism, and in industrial innovation and leadership. What was remarkable was that the Pax Britannica lasted so long, not that it finally came to an end.

By the eve of World War I the moral and social liberalism of the Liberal party was still recognizable, but the idealist, reformist, and rational doctrines of the old liberal tradition were no longer sufficient. Evangelicalism and upper-middle-class rule were being replaced by the new political platforms and doctrines of trade unionism and socialism. Women's suffrage, industrial strikes, and Irish home rule unraveled the domestic tranquility at home; in Europe the Pax Britannica was jeopardized by mounting international tensions and threats. Victorian liberalism was simply unable to control or cope with the demands of this new age of violence.

Selected Readings

Arnold, Matthew. *Culture and Anarchy* (1932)

Bailey, Peter. *Leisure and Class in Victorian England* (1978)

Briggs, Asa. *Victorian People* (1965)

Brinton, Crane. *English Political Thought in the Nineteenth Century* (1962)

Chadwick, Owen. *The Victorian Church*. 2 vols. (1966, 1970)

Checkland, S. G. *The Rise of Industrial Society in England, 1815–1885* (1964)

Crow, Duncan. *The Victorian Woman* (1972)

Himmelfarb, Gertrude. *Victorian Minds* (1972)

_____*Marriage and Morals Among the Victorians* (1986)

Hunt, E. H. *British Labour History, 1815–1914* (1981)

Mansergh, Nicholas. *The Irish Question 1840–1921* (1975)

Rostow, Walt W. *The British Economy of the Nineteenth Century* (1948)

Schultz, Harold J. *English Liberalism and the State: Individualism or Collectivism?* (1972)

Strachey, Lytton. *Eminent Victorians* (1963)

Willey, Basil. *Nineteenth Century Studies* (1949)

Young, George M. *Victorian England: Portrait of an Age* (1953)

Vicinus, Martha (ed.). *Suffer and Be Still: Women in the Victorian Age* (1980)

22

Britain and World War I

1914 Britain declares war on Germany, August 4, following the German invasion of Belgium

Germany's Schlieffen Plan and armies fail to capture Paris; trench warfare ensues on the Western front

1915 Prime Minister Asquith creates a coalition cabinet to prosecute the war more vigorously

1916 The Verdun and the Somme offensives on the Western front fail with overwhelming casualties

Britain adopts compulsory military service for the first time

Lloyd George replaces Asquith as Prime Minister

Easter Rebellion in Ireland fails in its effort to establish an independent Irish republic

1917 Revolution in Russia overthrows the Czar

United States enters the war

1918 German High Command surrenders on November 11

Parliament passes act giving women the vote for the first time

"Coupon Election"; Lloyd George and coalition candidates are victorious

1919 Treaty of Versailles signed; League of Nations established

The effects of four years of total war, beginning with such abruptness and lasting seemingly forever, shattered the lives of a whole generation in Britain. No other four years of British history produced such an overwhelming sense of the futility of war or produced a greater cleavage between prewar and postwar generations as did World War I.

The immediate effect of the war was disillusionment. Progress and reason were no longer self-evident truths. The war also accelerated the tempo of changes already taking place in Britain; especially the loss of old beliefs and values, a shift of wealth to new classes, the emancipation of women, the introduction of conscription, and the expansion of state planning and controls under such far-reaching measures as the Defense of the Realm Act.

The war did not intrude on a Britain basking in internal peace and tranquility. In truth, the outbreak of hostilities diverted the disruptive domestic forces that were threatening to engulf Britain in a civil and class war over Ireland and in a general strike. International violence replaced the threat of domestic discord. Out of the war came a new view of the power of the state to bring about victory in war and social change in the postwar years.

THE WAR EFFORT

The German invasion of Belgium unleashed an emotional wave of patriotism that, at least for the first two years, gave Britain and the empire almost complete unanimity of purpose in waging war against Germany. No one, however, expected that a general European war could last more than a few months. When the war of attrition dragged on, and the casualties mounted, the cautious Asquith was ousted in favor of the dynamic Lloyd George as Prime Minister. He immediately organized a war cabinet which provided the first highly centralized control of the war effort. The war was finally won in the West, where it began, when the Allies built up a preponderance of manpower and resources and seized the offensive after American reinforcements arrived.

Background of the War

Between 1870 and 1914 there was an extended interval of armed peace as national rivalries and a series of diplomatic crises increased tension among European states until the breaking point was reached. Many explanations of the war's origin have been given. No one cause or country was solely responsible, although from Britain's perspective the fear that Germany was aspiring to a hegemony in Europe provoked Britain's entente with France and Russia as a defensive alliance. Nationalism, sharpened by imperial rivalries and jingoistic propaganda, was probably the most fundamental cause of the war. When war broke out in 1914, the alliance system worked against the localization of the conflict; instead, it drew treaty partners into it.

Prior confrontations that escalated tensions included: (1) The First Moroccan Crisis, 1905. German statesmen tested the strength of the recent Anglo-French Entente (1904) by challenging French domination of Morocco. Germany insisted on an international conference (Algeciras, 1906) and suffered a diplomatic defeat as its uncompromising attitude drew Britain, France, and Russia closer together. (2) The Bosnian Crisis. In 1908 Austria annexed Bosnia and Herzegovina in violation of the settlements made at the Congress of Berlin. The Kaiser backed his Austrian ally, and war was only averted when Russia withdrew its backing from the Balkan states. (3) The Second Moroccan Crisis, 1911. Germany sent a gunboat to Agadir to oppose French expansion in Morocco and to win concessions from France. Britain insisted on being consulted and took an active hand in the diplomacy. The crisis was relaxed when France ceded part of the French Congo to Germany in return for German recognition of French interests in Morocco. (4) The Balkan Wars, 1912–1913. The Balkan states of Serbia, Bulgaria, Montenegro, and Greece joined to defeat their former overlord, Turkey. At London a peace settlement was reached (1913) when Britain restrained Russian and Serbian demands, and Germany made Austria conciliatory. After a bitter quarrel among the Balkan allies, Greece and Serbia conquered and partitioned Bulgaria. This development weakened Austria's prestige and threatened its multi-ethnic empire. By 1914 the entire Balkan region was simmering over disputed territories and yearning for self-determination.

Declaration of War

The final diplomatic crisis that precipitated World War I was the assassination of Archduke Francis Ferdinand, heir to the Austrian throne, on June 28, 1914, by Bosnians who were Serbian sympathizers. The Austrian government used this incident as an excuse to end the Serbian menace to its restless empire. With German approval, Austria sent Serbia an ultimatum so calculated as to be impossible to accept. On July 25 Serbia met all but one of the demands. Still unsatisfied, Austria declared war on Serbia, despite the efforts of Britain's foreign secretary, Sir Edward Grey, to arrange an international conference.

This time Russia did not back down as protector of the Slavic nations, but began to mobilize its troops. Since the German war plan counted on a decisive victory in the West before Russia could effectively fight a war in the East, Germany demanded Russian demobilization and French neutrality. When the ultimatums were rejected Germany declared war on Russia on August 1 and on France two days later. The majority of the British cabinet and nation were opposed to entering the war until Germany violated a joint treaty obligation of 1839 to respect the neutrality of Belgium. The German invasion of Belgium quickly shifted British opinion since it had long been a cardinal policy in Britain that no hostile power should dominate the Low Countries. Britain sent an ultimatum to Germany to withdraw. When no reply was received, on August 4 Britain and the British empire declared war on Germany.

The War Effort

Both sides expected a short war like the Franco-Prussian War of 1870 and planned accordingly. Germany pinned everything on the success of its Schlieffen plan—a blueprint which carefully anticipated the swift defeat of France in the West to avoid the traditional fear of a major war on two fronts. The plan failed and trench warfare, with its immobility and attrition, became the pattern on the Western front. Thus the decisive factor in the long run was economic or logistic, rather than tactical. At the outbreak of the war, the Central Powers (the coalition of Austria-Hungary, Germany, Bulgaria, and the Ottoman empire) had the superior position for a defensive war, better communications and better equipped armies, and a more centralized command. On the other hand, the Allies had control of the seas and greater reserves of manpower and war materials from overseas areas. These advantages became decisive as the war progressed. Total warfare was introduced as the entire economy, human resources, and willpower of the nation became absorbed in the struggle.

CAMPAIGNS IN 1914

The prospects of a speedy and conclusive victory in France disappeared as Belgian resistance and the arrival of the British Expeditionary Force assisted the French in stopping the German advance at the First Battle of the Marne. The Germans also failed to capture the Channel ports which would have cut Anglo-French communications. By December the battle line consisted of a series of trenches extending from Switzerland to the coast. On the Eastern front large Russian armies moved quickly into East Prussia where they met two disastrous defeats at Tannenburg and the Masurian Lakes. By the end of 1914 the Eastern front had become stabilized; the Russians could defeat the Austrians, but the Germans with superior artillery, supplies, and organization systematically pushed back the Russians. Inferior communications, a shortage of munitions, and an utterly incompetent government crippled the Russian war effort. Before the end of the year Turkey joined the Central Powers.

CAMPAIGNS IN 1915

Heavy casualties occurred on the Western front as machine-gun emplacements and barbed wire entanglements made obsolete the persistent infantry charges. By the end of the year Russia had lost Poland as well as a million troops on the Eastern front. Bulgaria joined the Central Powers and helped to overwhelm Serbia, whereas Japan entered on the side of the Allies. Italy deserted the Triple Alliance and joined the Entente Powers after being enticed with promises of postwar spoils. To open the Straits and provide vital supplies to Russia, the British and Australians began the Gallipoli campaign in February. Blunders in planning and execution forced the British to withdraw in 1916 after heavy casualties. Winston Churchill, sponsor of the plan, became the scapegoat and lost his Admiralty post.

CAMPAIGNS IN 1916

The Russians recovered from their costly defeats of 1915 and inflicted heavy losses on the Austrians. Romania joined the Allies but suffered swift defeat by the Central Powers. On the Western front the Germans at Verdun-sur-Meuse and the Allies at the Somme failed in their attempts at a major breakthrough. The losses were immense. The Somme offensive alone cost the British 400,000 casualties, the French 200,000, and the Germans 500,000. The result of such mindless human destruction was to advance the Allied lines two or three miles. To rebuild her depleted ranks, Britain adopted compulsory military service for the first time. The only major encounter of the British and German navies occurred at the indecisive battle of Jutland. British losses were heavier, but the German fleet never again ventured out to challenge British control of the seas.

CAMPAIGNS IN 1917

To end the stalemate and force Britain into a negotiated peace, Germany resorted to unrestricted submarine warfare in the hope of starving the island kingdom into submission. The German government announced that all shipping, enemy or neutral, approaching Great Britain would be sunk on sight. In April alone 875,000 tons of shipping was torpedoed. The ruthlessness of these sinkings helped bring the United States into the war that same month. Offsetting this gain was the military collapse of Russia and the Bolshevik revolution in November which led to a separate and severe peace treaty dictated by Germany. German armies were now free to concentrate their entire resources on the Western front. Here French morale cracked when their offensive collapsed, and the British and Canadians had to hold off the Germans in Flanders. The Allied position worsened when the Italian front was breached and the Italian army was routed at Caporetto. British victories in Mesopotamia and in Palestine, along with the entry of Greece into the war, brought about the defeat of Turkey.

CAMPAIGNS IN 1918

In March the Germans began their last great offensive on the Western front before United States troops could provide the Allies with the balance of strength. Although the Germans made three successful drives they could not sustain the attack. With the Allies finally in agreement on a united command under Marshal Foch, and with huge American forces assisting, the counteroffensive broke through the Hindenburg line in August. The four Central Powers were forced out of the war, one by one. On November 11 the German High Command surrendered before Allied armies reached German soil.

OTHER FRONTS

Although the two main theaters were the Eastern and Western fronts, the war was fought around the world. Except in East Africa, German colonies were easy conquests for Japanese, British, South African, and Australian forces. In the Near East the British, assisted by the fabled exploits of T. E. Lawrence (Lawrence of Arabia), dismantled the Turkish empire in 1917–1918. Aerial warfare played a spectacular but comparatively minor part in the war.

The Home Front

Domestic controversy was sidetracked for the duration of the war as the conflict became a moral crusade that engulfed the emotions and the economy of the entire nation. Parliament dropped all controversial legislation, and opposition to the government, within or without Parliament, was virtually nonexistent. What little dissent there was, was condemned as unpatriotic. For nine months normal party lines were observed. But when the prospects of a short war disappeared, the Conservatives insisted on sharing in the execution of the war effort. Prime Minister Asquith, pressured by Bonar Law and Lloyd George, brought eight leading Conservatives and one Labor member into a coalition cabinet in May 1915. He muted the criticism of the munitions shortage by moving Lloyd George to the newly created Ministry of Munitions. However, the coalition government of twenty-two members was too unwieldy an instrument with which to execute the quick and critical decisions necessary in a war of such magnitude. Nor was Asquith, by temperament or experience, able to offer decisive leadership to the cabinet or rally the country to face the consequences of a long war.

EASTER REBELLION, 1916

The militant Sinn Fein extremists in Ireland exploited England's critical condition to stage a general uprising with the assistance of German arms. But the plans for Easter Sunday miscarried as British security blocked the landing of munitions, and Irish public opinion failed to support the Sinn Fein insurgents in Dublin. The rebels surrendered after a week of fierce fighting. Fifteen of their leaders were executed. Asquith shrank back from Lloyd George's imaginative proposal, supported by Unionist leaders, for home rule at once for the twenty-six southern counties. English failure to act completed the ruin of the Irish constitutional party. The discredited extremists became martyrs and heroes. Sinn Fein, instead of dying, replaced the Irish Nationalists as the vital political force in Ireland, committed to violence, if necessary, to achieve independence from Britain.

Lloyd George

Asquith had already sacrificed two of his ablest colleagues, Richard Haldane and Winston Churchill, limited the authority of Lord Kitchener, Secretary of War, and agreed to a coalition government in order to satisfy his critics. But when the year 1916 brought increasing war weariness, heavy casualties, and no prospects of ending the war of attrition in France, public and press criticism of Asquith's leadership became strong. The nation wanted a leader who could offer and demand the supreme effort necessary to win the war. Asquith had hesitated to exploit the emergency powers granted the government, and his cabinet was conspicuously lacking in coordination.

A small war council with full cabinet power to administer the war effort was demanded by Lloyd George, Bonar Law, and William Maxwell Aitken, the powerful press lord (and later Lord Beaverbrook). Asquith retreated and agreed to the proposal until he realized that in such an arrangement he would only be a figurehead under Lloyd George. In the maneuvering that followed, Asquith resigned and refused to serve in the new coalition. Lloyd George, the fiery Liberal orator known as "The Wizard of Wales," became Prime Minister in December 1916, backed by the Labor party and Liberal and Tory backbenchers (ordinary members of Parliament with no ministerial rank)—a revolt of the press and the people against the magnates of both old parties.

THE WAR CABINET

Lloyd George reorganized the central machinery of government in order to conduct the war with more vigor and efficiency. Lloyd George, like Pitt the Elder in the Seven Years' War and Winston Churchill in World War II, had the charisma and unshakable resolution to galvanize the war effort of the nation. A war cabinet of five members (Lloyd George, Bonar Law, Lord Curzon, Lord Milner, and Arthur Henderson) was small enough to meet frequently to exercise supreme command of the war effort. Other cabinet ministers were summoned only to discuss questions affecting their departments. This important constitutional change, like the creation of the two wartime coalition governments, was accomplished without any formal electoral or parliamentary approval.

A Nation at War

Under Lloyd George government control of the economy was greatly accelerated. Permission for this extension was granted by parliamentary action under three Defense of the Realm Acts (known as DORA). Government agencies managed shipbuilding, food production and distribution, and the supply of wool and cotton. War socialism had already placed munitions, coal, iron, steel, and railroads under state control. Conscription of manpower for military service was decreed in 1916 to fill the ranks decimated by trench warfare. Food rationing began in 1918. The nation became accustomed to vastly increased governmental intervention in the economy and in society. Extensive state planning and centralization of power was a byproduct of the war years. If such state planning and authority was useful in running the war, a growing number of citizens began to ask why such state socialism could not also be equally effective after the war.

PEACE AND POLITICS

Lloyd George took advantage of the gratitude of the nation to hold an election in 1918 which perpetuated the coalition government into the postwar period. The Coalition candidates swept the election, but at the cost of splitting the Liberal party. The Prime Minister was a leading negotiator at the Paris Peace Conference which attempted to obtain mutual security and a lasting peace. A compromise, but stern, peace treaty was finally agreed upon which failed to approach the idealism that President Wilson had anticipated in his Fourteen Points. The fundamental problem was that Allied cooperation collapsed at the moment of victory. The alliance against the Central Powers, like all coalitions, was formed against someone, not for something. With the enemy defeated, old rivalries and national self-interests were reasserted. The peace settlement was further complicated by impulsive promises, such as those made to Italy in the midst of the war, and feelings of vindictiveness toward Germany.

Cost of the War
Over ten million troops were killed and at least twenty million wounded: 760,000 British soldiers died and another 1,700,000 were wounded. Although other major belligerents (except the United States) suffered larger numbers, British losses were highly selective, because many of the casualties (before conscription was introduced) came from the families and public schools that had traditionally provided leadership in public life. The absence of this generation of young men was keenly felt by England twenty years later. Material destruction was slight in comparison to the invaded countries. The greatest loss was in the sinking of 40 percent of the merchant fleet. More serious was the financial damage. Inter-Allied debts were staggering, and New York replaced London as the world's banking center. The war cost Britain £9 billion, most of which was raised by borrowing so that the national debt was fourteen times greater in 1918 than in 1914. In the long run, the chief economic cost of the war was the ruin of foreign trade; Britain never regained the markets lost to Japan and the United States. More intangible,

but equally real, was the moral bankruptcy which the war spawned. War psychology and hate propaganda encouraged a spirit of ruthlessness and insensitivity to nonconformity. After 1916 the savageness and senselessness of the war brought a feeling of disillusionment and futility.

Reforms of 1918

The war hastened the extension of political democracy. Women defense workers made such an important contribution that opposition to women's suffrage disappeared. The Representation of the Peoples Act gave the vote to women over thirty who occupied premises or land with a rental value of £5, or whose husbands did so. The statute also extended the male franchise by abolishing practically all property qualifications. The measure more than doubled the electorate and increased the membership of the House of Commons to 707. An Education Act improved the educational benefits of the working classes by making elementary schooling compulsory between the ages of five and fourteen. Furthermore, child labor was sharply limited; the act halted the large number of children discontinuing school at the age of twelve and becoming unemployed because of lack of skills.

The Coupon Election

With an electorate now swollen by the new franchise and eight years having passed since the last election, Lloyd George had a strong case for a general election. Besides, the Prime Minister was at the peak of his prestige as "the man who won the war." Labor decided to withdraw from the coalition, and Asquith and his wing of the Liberal party refused to support Lloyd George. The Conservatives and Lloyd George Liberals received a letter of support (the coupon) signed by Lloyd George and Bonar Law. At first, the coalition candidates campaigned on a note of reconstruction and idealism. But the national temper wanted revenge upon Germany, and by the end of the campaign Lloyd George was appealing to the vindictive mood of the voters. Coalition candidates, largely Conservative, won in a landslide with 478 seats. The Asquith Liberals returned only 28. Labor, with 59 seats, became the official opposition. The election introduced twenty-seven years of Conservative hegemony in British life, and postwar politics began in an atmosphere of bitter personal grievances among party leaders.

Peacemaking

By the end of the war the Hapsburg and the Ottoman empires had already disintegrated. The basic problem for the victors was the future of Germany. On this issue the diplomats were often the victims of such circumstances as the demand for a speedy settlement, the French obsession with security against another German invasion, the secret treaties made during the war, and the chauvinism of the victors.

The armistice of November 11, 1918, was reached on the basis of President Wilson's Fourteen Points which reflected the ideals of nineteenth-century liberalism in calling for open covenants (treaties), freedom of the seas, removal of tariff barriers, reduction of armaments, and self-determination for subject people. The fourteenth point was the creation of an international organization to keep the peace.

Paris Peace Conference, 1919

Twenty-seven Allied nations sent delegates to the peace conference, but the dominant figures were President Wilson, Georges Clemenceau (Premier of France and chairman of the conference), and Lloyd George. With Italy's Premier Orlando, they formed the Big Four. Lloyd George mediated the differences between Wilson's high idealism and Clemenceau's obsession with a powerful Germany. The 1918 election victory had added to Lloyd George's prestige. He favored reasonable terms with moderate reparations, but popular criticism of his leniency moved him closer to the position of Clemenceau. Early ideals, such as self-determination, were sacrificed to appease the demands of Japan and Italy for territorial gains. Wilson was forced to make concessions but stood firm in his insistence on a League of Nations. The Big Four agreed on German disarmament, but argued bitterly over reparations as the urgency of finishing the draft of the treaty aggravated the frenzied atmosphere of the conference.

Treaty of Versailles

Germany signed the treaty on June 28, 1919. Article I provided for a League of Nations. Another article placed the guilt for the war on Germany and its allies. Germany ceded Alsace-Lorraine to France; several border provinces to Belgium; portions of East Prussia, including a corridor to the Baltic Sea, to Poland; and Schleswig to Denmark. The industrial Saar Valley was placed under international control for fifteen years, and the Allies were to occupy the Rhineland for the same period. The Rhine's east bank was to be demilitarized. The German standing army was set at 100,000 men, an air force was forbidden, and only a token navy permitted. Furthermore, Germany lost its colonies and had to pay reparations.

MANDATES

The German colonies and large portions of the Ottoman empire were divided among the victors as mandates (trusteeships) under League auspices. Britain received Tanganyika and large parts of the Cameroons and Togoland in Africa. In the Near East Iraq, Palestine, and Transjordan came under British rule. The declaration by Arthur Balfour in 1917 supporting a Jewish homeland after the war was not acted upon by Britain. It was reluctant to pursue this goal at the expense of Arab goodwill. The Union of South Africa received German South-West Africa, and the German Pacific islands went to New Zealand and Australia.

REPARATIONS

Lloyd George's position shifted during the election campaign to a harsh stand on reparations, contrary to his earlier persuasion—and to the armistice agreement—that reparations should be demanded only for damages to the civilian population. At Versailles he supported the inclusion of war pensions. In 1921 a reparations commission set the final figure at $32 billion, an amount impossible for Germany to pay. Efforts to exact these reparations became one of the most explosive sources of friction among France, Britain, and Germany in the following years.

LEAGUE OF NATIONS

Wilson preferred an imperfect treaty with the League of Nations to a perfect one without it, because the League was to provide the processes that would promote peace and prevent, or punish, future aggression. He also hoped that this organization could prevent a recurrence of the international anarchy and tensions which had provoked the Great War. The main organs of the League were: (1) an assembly in which each member state had one vote, (2) a council of five permanent members (United States, Britain, France, Italy, Japan) and four elective, (3) a secretariat with limited executive functions, and (4) the World Court of Justice established at the Hague. Lloyd George had no trouble getting the treaty passed by Parliament. Only four members of the House of Commons opposed it. In contrast, the treaty was defeated in the United States Senate. Consequently, the United States retreated into isolationism and never joined the League.

Other Treaties. Within a year of Versailles four treaties were signed with Austria, Bulgaria, Hungary, and Turkey. The treaty with Austria formally broke up the crumbling Hapsburg empire which had already fragmented into such new states as Yugoslavia and Czechoslovakia on the general formula of self-determination. By 1920 there were eight new sovereign states in Europe.

Appraisal of the Peace

The Treaty of Versailles was soon attacked by John Maynard Keynes, the English economist, and by many other critics as a Carthagenian peace—utterly ruthless. It was true that nationalistic pressures undermined many of Wilson's Fourteen Points; however, to expect a just and moderate peace, given the dislocations and emotions of the time, was virtually impossible. The Treaty of Versailles was less severe than the treaty Germany imposed on Russia when it dictated the terms after Russia sued for peace in 1919. In retrospect, the peace turned out to be a halfway measure, neither harsh enough to keep Germany powerless, nor moderate enough to conciliate Germany in the postwar years. The cry to "vindicate Versailles" would be used by German Nazis to reassert German nationalism and power.

World War I was unlike any previous war. From rationing to conscription to war socialism, total war engulfed Britain for the first time and accelerated social change.

The war began with a mood of exaltation and idealism until the murderous reality and futility of trench warfare brought on a profound disillusionment. Deeply rooted convictions, such as the belief in the inevitability of progress, were shattered.

The war ended Britain's century of pre-eminence in world history; however, there would be a time lag before this fact was recognized either in Britain or in the world. The postwar years would become a time of difficult readjustment for Britain. The war was a catalyst in bringing about social and political change, such as in the emancipation of women, and the breakup of the United Kingdom of Great Britain and Ireland, as Ireland (excluding the northern six counties) finally won its efforts to secede from British rule.

Selected Readings

Fussel, Paul. *The Great War and Modern Memory* (1975)

Grey, Edward. *Twenty-Five Years* (1937)

Hart, Liddell, and Sir Basil Henry. *A History of the First World War* (1970)

Hurwitz, Samuel. *State Intervention in Great Britain, 1914–1919* (1949)

Jones, Thomas. *Lloyd George* (1951)

Remarque, Erich. *All Quiet on the Western Front* (1928)

Sassoon, Siegfried. *Memoirs of an Infantry Officer* (1930)

Steiner, Zara S. *Britain and the Origins of the First World War* (1977)

Taylor, A. J. P. *Politics in Wartime* (1965)

Tuchman, Barbara. *The Guns of August* (1962)

23

Depression and Decline: Britain Between the Wars

1919 Treaty of Versailles signed

1921 Establishment of the Irish Free State ends rule from London for Ireland; Ulster withdraws from the new Irish state

1922 T. S. Eliot publishes *The Waste Land*

1924 First Labor government formed under Prime Minister J. Ramsey MacDonald

1926 First general strike in Britain

1928 Alexander Fleming discovers penicillin

1929 Wall Street crashes; beginning of world economic slump

1931 Statute of Westminster establishes the British Commonwealth of Nations and the equal status of all dominions with Britain

A national coalition cabinet is formed, headed by MacDonald

1933 Hitler comes to power in Germany

1935 Invasion of Ethiopia by Mussolini

1936 George V dies; Edward VIII accedes to the throne

Edward VIII abdicates the throne; his brother, George VI, is proclaimed King

Civil War begins in Spain

1938 Hitler annexes Austria by force

Munich agreement is signed by Germany, Italy, France and Britain guaranteeing the integrity of the remainder of Czechoslovakia

1939   World War II begins with the German invasion of Poland on September 1

A period of very difficult readjustment for Britain followed the First World War. The disillusionment with the mass killings and futility of modern warfare touched all phases of British life. Britain's position as a world power was in question and its foreign trade was disrupted. The 1920s were haunted by memories of the last war's fearful costs; the 1930s were a time of anxiety that another European war was very possible.

After the war English politics were dominated by economics. Unemployment and a wildly fluctuating trade cycle forced an agonizing reappraisal of the British economy. One of the casualties was free trade—an article of faith in the prewar Liberal creed. Other casualties of the interwar years were British naval supremacy, the virtual disappearance of the Liberal party, and the failure of the League of Nations to provide collective security against aggression.

For the most part, the two decades preceding World War II were years of disappointment and drift for Britain, although the rise of the Labor party to power and respectability and the imaginative evolution of the empire-commonwealth were significant achievements.

AFTERMATH OF WAR, 1918–1924

The psychological exhaustion and the disenchantment resulting from World War I produced a desire for a return to normalcy as well as a mood of self-conscious frivolity and cynicism. However, the economic dislocation brought about by unemployment and the loss of foreign markets made reconstruction difficult. When the economy failed to recover satisfactorily, a new political alignment based upon economic class interests began to emerge. The cabinet under Lloyd George achieved a workable solution to the Irish problem, but could not save itself. The fall of Lloyd George introduced a shifting alignment of minority and coalition governments which became a political hallmark of the next two decades.

Economic Developments   The rapid demobilization of over four million troops within a year was facilitated by the boom of 1919–1920 which absorbed most veterans into the economy. Wartime controls were also rapidly removed in an effort to return to the economic practices of prewar years. Reconstruction proceeded on the basis of laissez-faire capitalism which had made England wealthy before the war. Unfortunately, world conditions had changed drastically, and Britain could no longer produce as efficiently as many of its competitors; nor were world markets found to replace those either lost to its competitors or curtailed by the economic nationalism stimulated by the war.

Inflation, strikes, and wage increases marked the boom until it broke suddenly in late 1921. The recession was brought on by the government's slashing of expenditures, increased taxes, overproduction of primary products, and the illusion of an insatiable world market. Prices and wages fell. From 1922 to 1929 unemployment jumped to two million and averaged 12 percent of the labor force—double the prewar figure. The trade unions threatened a general strike in 1920, and the specter of an economic class war loomed near. The government passed the Emergency Powers Act (1920), restoring its wartime emergency authority to meet the threat. Otherwise the decontrol of industry was accelerated.

In 1921 Lloyd George lost working-class support when the striking miners were defeated in their effort to prevent the mineowners from cutting wages. The government helped the working class by subsidizing the building of more than 200,000 houses and making housing another social service of the government. The Unemployment Insurance Acts of 1920 and 1922 extended the original insurance scheme of 1911 to the entire working class. This assistance relieved worker discontent by making unemployment bearable—and another obligation of the state. However, little effort was made to attack the fundamental causes of unemployment and low production.

The Irish Settlement

The Irish problem was the most explosive political issue facing the coalition. Lloyd George achieved a settlement that for the time being kept both Catholic and Protestant Ireland within the British empire and avoided a major civil war in Ireland. However, no Irish settlement could satisfy all parties involved, and the issue once again sapped British political stability. By 1922 a settlement was reached that was acceptable to most parties. The settlement was Lloyd George's last great achievement before he was ousted as Prime Minister.

UNDECLARED WAR, 1919–1920, AND PARTITION

In the general election of 1918 candidates of the Sinn Fein ("We Ourselves" party, demanding an independent Irish republic) captured 73 of the 105 Irish seats. They refused to take their seats at Westminster; instead, they went to Dublin and declared Ireland independent. An unofficial civil war followed as the Irish Republican Army and a special British occupation army, called the Black and Tans, engaged in guerrilla tactics and terrorism.

The prewar effort to coerce Protestant Ulster (the six northern counties) into a united and independent Ireland was dropped. Ulster had contributed so many soldiers for the war that their wishes could not be dismissed to appease a rebellious southern Ireland that opposed participation in World War I. Therefore, the fourth Home Rule Bill (1920) provided for the partition of Ireland and a single-chamber Parliament in each region. This Parliament would legislate for its own region except for a few reserved areas which remained under the control of the British Parliament. Ulster accepted the Government of Ireland Act, but the south ignored it, and fighting continued.

THE IRISH FREE STATE

King George V appealed for a truce, and Lloyd George offered the Irish leader, Eamon de Valera, dominion status for Ireland. In October 1921, the Irish delegates, led by Arthur Griffith and Michael Collins, were persuaded to sign an agreement in London which set up the Irish Free State with the right of Ulster to withdraw—a right which it immediately exercised. The moderates among the Irish Republicans accepted independence and dominion status within the British empire. De Valera led the intransigent faction in repudiating the treaty ratified by the Irish Dail (Parliament). In 1922 open warfare began in southern Ireland, this time between the pro-treaty party of Collins, which won the election, and de Valera's extremists who did not accept the results of the election. By December of 1922 the Irish Free State came into existence with William T. Cosgrove as president of the executive council.

Fall of Lloyd George

The Tory backbenchers (those holding no ministerial posts), prompted by Stanley Baldwin, President of the Board of Trade, defied the coalition leadership and determined to contest the next election along party lines. They argued that Lloyd George would ruin the Conservative party in time, just as he had divided the Liberals. Bonar Law's support of the backbenchers doomed the coalition government. On October 19, 1922, Lloyd George resigned and Bonar Law became Prime Minister. Contributing to Lloyd George's fall were (1) the Conservatives' suspicions of his dynamic and opportunist leadership and his indifference to party politics; (2) his militant pro-Greek policy in the Chanak crisis between Turkey and Greece which angered many Conservatives and frightened a war-weary public; (3) the loss of working-class support in the postwar years; and (4) the political repercussions of the Irish settlement.

THREE-PARTY POLITICS

No political leader with Lloyd George's capacity or dynamism replaced him, partly because the mood of the populace preferred tranquility to controversy and crisis. Labor emerged as the dominant party of the left, but the Liberal party refused to disappear. A parliamentary majority became difficult to achieve in the ensuing three-party contests. The Conservative domination of these interwar years was assisted by the division among the Liberals, and by the withdrawal of the large Irish—and usually Liberal-Radical—bloc from Westminster after Irish home rule.

Bonar Law's Government, 1922–1923

Law formed a cabinet largely from political unknowns because thirteen Conservative ministers of the coalition refused to serve under him for betraying the coalition government. He immediately called an election and campaigned on the platform of tranquility and stability—a platform appropriate for the times and for the Prime Minister's conventional nature. The Conservatives won a clear majority of seats, but only 5½ million out of the 14 million votes cast. Six months later Law left office because of serious illness.

Stanley Baldwin's First Government, 1923–1924

King George V chose Stanley Baldwin rather than Lord Curzon (deputy Prime Minister and Foreign Secretary) to succeed Law largely on the consideration that the Prime Minister should be in the House of Commons. The stolid conservatism and homely virtues of Baldwin appealed to the nation as he eulogized the old virtues of faith, hope, love, and work as the salvation of the country. Within six months he called a surprise election to win a mandate for a protective tariff. The move restored party unity by encouraging Austen Chamberlain, Arthur Balfour, and Lord Birkenhead to rejoin the Conservative party. The election also unified the Asquith and Lloyd George factions on the one issue—free trade—that could bring the Liberals together. The Conservatives lost 90 seats, whereas Labor added 50. The Liberals with 158 seats became the balance of power.

The First Labor Government, 1924

Asquith refused to form a coalition with the Conservatives, and in January 1924, Baldwin resigned after losing a vote of confidence in Parliament. J. Ramsey MacDonald became Prime Minister of Britain's first Labor government. The inexperienced cabinet showed no more inventiveness than the Conservative cabinet in dealing with unemployment and other domestic issues. Only the Housing Act (1924), which followed the pattern of the Conservative housing program, was successful. No doctrinaire socialist program was possible under the circumstances because the government depended upon Liberal votes for its majority. In foreign affairs MacDonald persuaded France to accept a moderate reparations settlement, but Labor's efforts to restore normal relations with Soviet Russia brought Conservative and mounting Liberal opposition. In October MacDonald's government fell in the controversy over recognition of Russia, forcing MacDonald to call a general election—the third in three years.

Foreign Affairs

After the Paris Peace Conference in 1919, Lloyd George took the lead in calling international conferences to promote the economic and financial reconstruction of Europe, but was unable to solve many problems. The British economist John Maynard Keynes indicted the Treaty of Versailles in his *Economic Consequences of the Peace* (1919) as being too harsh on Germany. His argument helped Britain to modify its position on German reparations. But an Anglo-French rift developed when France took a hard line on reparations and demanded full measure. In 1923 efforts to exact reparations led to French occupation of the German Ruhr and the collapse of German currency. The victimized German middle class saw France and the treaty as the causes of their misfortune. Prime Minister MacDonald persuaded the French to accept a plan proposed by Charles Dawes of the United States for stabilizing the German mark and systematizing the payment of reparations. France, with its obsession for security, made bilateral alliances with Belgium, Poland, and Czechoslovakia instead of relying on collective security as Britain had urged.

At the Washington Disarmament Conference of 1922 Britain abandoned its traditional naval supremacy in order to halt the expensive shipbuilding rivalry with the United States and Japan. A ten-year holiday on new naval construction was adopted, and the ratio of 5:5:3:1.75: 1.75 in battleships was established respectively for Britain, the United States, Japan, France, and Italy. However, general disarmament did not follow.

Postwar Society

A political realignment, intimated in the election of 1906, became a fact after the war. No longer did the political leaders come from the same class or schools or share the same fundamental views of society. Even the term "middle class" had lost its magic. Political identity became increasingly associated with economic interests. The Right was united by opposition to socialism, fear of Communist Russia, admiration for traditional British institutions and values, and advocacy of protection (tariffs) and limited government intervention in the economy. They also favored a political democracy led by the traditional governing class.

The Left drew its mass support from labor and its leadership from the trade unions, socialist societies, and dissident Liberals. They favored nationalization of major industries, opposed the gold standard, supported collective security abroad, and friendship with Russia, and the extension of social services. They believed that the expansion of the franchise ("one man, one vote") demanded greater equalization of goods and services.

The immediate postwar years reflected an inevitable reaction against war, especially a war as dehumanizing as the Great War had been. The illusion of a better world failed to materialize for the soldiers who were fortunate enough to return home. Instead, the old order and the older generation of leadership continued to prevail. A lowering of standards occurred at all levels of public life. Indifference to world developments—a psychological isolationism—and the urge for self-indulgence and distraction introduced rapid changes in manners and social customs. The emancipated woman, the flapper, the birth of jazz, the popularity of commercialized sports and movies, and the increase of sexual freedom were indices of this change. The war hastened the decline of religion and of Nonconformist (non-Anglican Protestant) influence. The Nonconformists had been one of the major voting blocs of the Liberal party.

Educational Inequality. A basic fact of British society was its inequality. In 1929, 2.5 percent of the people owned two-thirds of the country's wealth. The English educational system sustained this inequality. The upper classes sent their children to the expensive and excellent "public schools" such as Rugby and Eton and then to Oxford and Cambridge. Many of the middle classes paid costly fees to send their children to grammar schools, while most of the working classes received a quite mediocre elementary education until the school-leaving age of 14. These different educational tracks shaped three different worlds: that of the governing classes, that of business and professionals, and that of the wage earners.

NATIONAL AFFAIRS, 1924–1939

The overriding spirit of these fifteen years was one of inertia and drift. Opinions and warnings were offered and consciences prodded but little in incisive action or positive programs was encouraged by the three prime ministers (Baldwin, MacDonald, Chamberlain) of the period. This timid conservatism, one that hesitated to offer a vigorous program of any sort, mirrored a nation seeking stability, normalcy and escape. Baldwin weathered a general strike but failed to deal with the fundamental economic problems causing it. The economic crisis brought on by a world-wide depression resulted in a national government of all the parties. The broad political base of this national government gave it great stability but no concerted program and left only an impotent opposition that could not provide a serious alternative choice in the elections.

Prime Minister Baldwin

In 1924 the Conservatives won an easy victory with 411 seats. They benefited from the collapse of the Liberals, who returned only 42 members, and from the Red scare introduced by the "Zinoviev letter" which had the effect of linking the Labor party with Russian Communism. Conciliatory and patient, Baldwin led a united party and a strong cabinet into a period of prosperous normalcy. In 1925 the postwar economic crisis ended, Germany was stabilized, and British production, profits, and wages began to rise.

Winston Churchill, Chancellor of the Exchequer and now a Tory, returned Britain to the prewar gold standard. In 1928 a new Representation of the Peoples Act gave women the vote on equal terms with men. But a conspicuous lack of leadership was evident in fiscal, educational, and unemployment policies.

SOCIAL WELFARE

The most vigorous action of Baldwin's second government was in social legislation. Neville Chamberlain, Minister of Health, pushed through twenty-one bills. By 1929 400,000 new dwellings had been built with government assistance. The Widows, Orphans, and Old Age Pensions Act of 1925 extended the provisions of 1911. Relief benefits were reduced but extended indefinitely to all who were in need. The Local Government Act of 1929 reorganized county councils and reformed the ancient poor law structure by transferring the care of the poor to the county.

THE GENERAL STRIKE, 1926

The mining industry had been chronically ill since the war, and four government commissions had studied its problems. Wages in coal mines had lagged far behind the cost of living, yet the government was preparing to end its subsidy; in addition, the mineowners wanted to slash wages. Neither management nor labor would accept the Simon Report on reorganization of the industry. The Trades Union Congress called a general strike, and for nine days in May some three million union members stopped working. The strike was neither violent nor revolutionary and was soon broken by Baldwin's firm stand, divided union leadership over the purpose of the strike, and the lack of public support. The prestige of Baldwin was at its peak, but he failed to take any constructive action; actually, he did nothing except restrict the labor movement by the Trade Unions Act of 1927. The act declared all general strikes illegal and prohibited the use of trade union dues for political purposes unless so requested in writing by a member. As a result, union membership dropped almost 50 percent.

The Second Labor Government, 1929–1931

Baldwin fought the election of 1929 on the slogan of "Safety First." The Liberals under Lloyd George offered the most promising platform for increasing production and reducing unemployment. The election gave Labor 289 seats, the Conservatives 260, and the Liberals 58. For the first time, Labor was the leading party, crushing the center Liberals in spite of their spirited campaign. MacDonald began his second minority government and within five months encountered the Great Depression which had spread from Wall Street across the Atlantic. By 1932 the steep drop in prices reduced purchasing power and increased unemployment in Britain to a peak of over 3 million.

Britain was particularly susceptible to economic trends by reason of its reliance on world trade. Although the moderate Labor government introduced a modest program of public works, the austerely orthodox Philip Snowden at the Exchequer discouraged a major attack on unemployment, because current tax revenues alone could not finance any program of expansion. The government attempted to mitigate the situation by such steps as separating unemployment insurance from government relief payments and extending the latter, and by passing the Greenwood Housing Act (1930) to subsidize slum clearance. Such meager and traditional legislation was due, in part, to the obvious difficulties of a minority government confronting a world depression. But it was also due to MacDonald's ineffective leadership which looked for excuses for inaction. Unable to find any unity of purpose among his ministers or to control his own cabinet, much less the parliamentary Labor party, MacDonald seemed to have lost interest in the Labor program; he was on better terms with the Conservatives than with many of his own party. In July 1931, a parliamentary committee predicted a deficit of £120 million and warned of an approaching financial crisis. The May Report recommended increased taxes and retrenchment in government expenditures, including relief payments. On August 23 MacDonald resigned after the majority of his Labor cabinet and party opposed the proposed reduction of unemployment relief and pensions.

National Government, 1931–1935

MacDonald was persuaded by George V to head a national coalition cabinet of four Laborites, four Conservatives, and two Liberals. The Labor party repudiated the new coalition, but the Liberals and Conservatives backed it. The cabinet cut expenditures and abandoned the gold standard. In the general election of November, the national government won 554 of the 615 seats. Labor, in opposition, was bitter over the "betrayal" of MacDonald and charged that the crisis had been a bankers' plot to ruin the Labor government. MacDonald and Baldwin, in their unimaginative and unhurried manner, proposed the orthodox and traditional remedies of protection and frugality to counter the economic slump. The Keynesian theory of massive government interference in the economy to moderate the business cycle was incorporated in the American New Deal, but not in Britain.

END OF FREE TRADE

The election of 1931 was considered a mandate for protection. The following year a general tariff was established, and at Ottawa an imperial preference for British commonwealth trade and bilateral tariff bargains were negotiated. The world economic climate was for protection of home products at the expense of world trade. When the cabinet gave in to these protection sentiments the Liberal and Labor ranks were further splintered. Several Labor and Liberal ministers left the cabinet, leaving the government made up overwhelmingly of Conservatives under a Labor Prime Minister.

END OF REPARATIONS

President Hoover granted a year's moratorium on reparations and war debts before the Lausanne Conference of 1932 virtually canceled them. The United States, however, still insisted on the payment of war debts, although no reduction in the high American tariff was offered to facilitate payment. France quickly ceased payments and Britain paid reduced installments on its war debt until 1934; thereafter, it ceased payment altogether.

GOVERNMENT BY NEGATION

In 1933 economic recovery began, not from government action, but from a combination of rising productivity, wages and employment, a housing boom, and favorable terms of trade. By 1935 unemployment fell below two million, yet the recovery was erratic, and the concentration of mass unemployment in depressed areas accented the contrast between poverty and prosperity. The Unemployment Act, which consolidated the insurance and relief system, and the Special Areas Act of 1934, which attempted to move unemployed to more prosperous areas, were mild efforts to relieve unemployment. Nevertheless, the government made no major effort to intervene in an economy which could not find work for two million of its citizens. A balanced budget, not deficit financing, was the order of the day. In this period economic nationalism and high tariffs had so shrunk international trade that British industry was heavily handicapped. However, little was done to adapt the economy to more domestic trade.

ELECTION OF 1935

Because of his health MacDonald resigned in June 1935, and Baldwin, the real power in the cabinet, began his third ministry. The November election gave Baldwin's conservative coalition a vote of confidence with 428 supporters of the national government successful at the polls. The Labor opposition jumped from 59 to 154. Clement Atlee became leader of the Labor party after George Lansbury resigned in opposition to a Labor resolution supporting League sanctions against Italy, which had invaded Ethiopa. Atlee's mission was to heal the party which was sharply split over the question of defense. Foreign affairs increasingly occupied the attention of the government.

Abdication Crisis, 1936

George V, beloved and admired as the ideal constitutional monarch, died early in 1936. He was succeeded by Edward VIII, his eldest son, who was already popular at home and well-known throughout the empire. For almost a year a self-imposed press censorship prevented the British from knowing of Edward's affection for Wallis Warfield Simpson, a twice-divorced American woman. Baldwin advised the King of the popular disapproval of such a match, whereupon Edward requested a morganatic marriage that would not give his wife the usual titles or status of a Queen.

By this time the news had broken, and a constitutional crisis appeared imminent. A "King's Friends" party was urged by Winston Churchill and the Rothermere and Beaverbrook presses. But popular opinion, all three political parties, the Church of England, and the dominion Prime Ministers strongly opposed the marriage. Baldwin handled the situation in a masterful manner in clearing the Abdication Bill by 403 to 5 votes. Edward VIII chose to abdicate rather than abandon the woman he loved. On December 12 his brother, the Duke of York, was proclaimed King George VI. The new monarch, shy and with a halting manner of speech, never expected to be thrust into the public eye in such a fashion or to accede to the throne. Their rule was exemplary, however, and George and his wife, Elizabeth, made possible a return to the esteem and admiration that was his parents'. British and Commonwealth allegiance to the monarchical institution was not jeopardized by the abdication.

Neville Chamberlain

Baldwin retired in 1937 after having presided jointly with MacDonald over British national life for fourteen unheroic years. The resourceful and patient Baldwin had revealed his tactical skill in weathering domestic problems and avoiding strong or controversial action as he had shunned such stronger personalities as Lloyd George and Churchill. He was replaced by Neville Chamberlain, a Conservative who had been in five previous cabinets and had made his mark, in the tradition of his father, in the field of social legislation. Disraeli, Joseph Chamberlain, Lloyd George, and Neville Chamberlain were the architects of the welfare state that was erected by the Labor government after the Second World War.

Chamberlain had excellent training and ability in domestic affairs; however, he came to power, unfortunately, when foreign affairs were of critical importance. A man of rigid competence and integrity, Chamberlain deceived himself by insisting on handling foreign affairs as if they were commercial problems that could be negotiated by reasonable agreement and by rules of conduct that he considered fair and proper. The consequent disaster of his foreign policy dwarfed his earlier achievements as minister of housing and as chancellor of the Exchequer.

Literature

The writings of the interwar years revealed the disjointed spirit of the times. This is portrayed symbolically in T. S. Eliot's *The Waste Land* (1922). The disillusionment of the twenties and the moral hangover flowing from the Great War was witnessed as well in the plays of Noel Coward (*Private Lives, Cavalcade*), the novels of Aldous Huxley (*Antic Hay, Point*

Counter Point), and the stream-of-consciousness method of James Joyce (*Ulysses*) and Virginia Woolf (*Jacob's Room, To the Lighthouse*). D. H. Lawrence (1885–1930) introduced a stream-of-consciousness technique into many of his writings, such as *Sons and Lovers* and *Lady Chatterley's Lover*. He revealed an intense preoccupation with the mystic powers of sex and intimated that blood and flesh (instinct) was superior to conscious intelligence.

In the thirties escapist fads and cults helped Britons get away from the inertia of the government. Social concern revived. The condition of England became the theme of such critical authors as J. B. Priestley in *English Journey* and George Orwell in *The Road to Wigan Pier*. The public mood was also reflected in Aldous Huxley's utopian nightmare novel, *Brave New World* (1932). Since the Right controlled the great newspapers during these years, the Left voiced their opinions in the influential *New Statesman and Nation* and in the economic and political writings of G. D. H. Cole, Harold Laski, and Raymond Postgate.

The Sciences

John Maynard Keynes offered a new and revolutionary economic framework in his *General Theory of Employment, Interest and Money* (1936) that would actively involve the government in "jump starting" the economy, but his ideas could not shake the economic orthodoxy of the national government. In 1919 Sir Ernest Rutherford, director of the Cavendish Laboratory, published an account of his splitting of the nitrogen atom. This led to new fields of discovery in radio-physics and the development of radar in 1935 by Sir Robert Watson-Watt and Sir Henry Tizard. In 1928 Sir Alexander Fleming discovered penicillin. Most pioneer research was conducted at the universities so that during the interwar years Cambridge was recognized as the physics center of the world.

IMPERIAL AND FOREIGN AFFAIRS: LOCARNO TO MUNICH

Between the wars Britain was eminently more successful in imperial than in foreign affairs. The satisfactory evolution of the self-governing dominions into the British Commonwealth of Nations was a unique achievement unmatched by any former empire or colonial power. Only Ireland and India were restless with retaining ties to Britain. In foreign affairs the quest for security culminated in the Locarno Pact and the Kellogg-Briand Treaty. Thereafter, Japan, Italy, and Germany undertook belligerent foreign policies when they discerned that collective security meant, in practice, collective fear of strong action. Emboldened by the paralysis of League action and the failure of Britain and France to do anything more than protest, the dictators became increasingly aggressive.

The thirties were a period of drift and lost opportunities for Britain. The mood of the country and of its leaders was that the risk of another major war was more greatly to be feared than the growth of tyranny. By 1939 appeasement had permitted both tyranny and war in Europe.

Steps to Self-Government in India

World War I had greatly stimulated Indian nationalism, and as early as 1917 Britain had agreed to the eventual granting of dominion status to India. The Government of India Act (1919) took the first step in this direction by introducing limited responsible government on the provincial level, and a two-chamber central legislature nationally, but with real power reserved for the viceroy and his executive council. These concessions were too meager to satisfy Mahatma Gandhi and the Indian Congress party and prompted Gandhi to launch a campaign of nonviolent civil disobedience to speed up independence. During the twenties communal riots, marches, and increasing unrest resulted in a parliamentary commission under Sir John Simon which led to a round table conference in London in 1930–1931.

The wide differences in the proposals of the Hindus, Muslims, and the Indian princes brought about a constitutional impasse. Gandhi again resumed his civil disobedience campaign and was jailed by the British authorities. The second Government of India Act, which created a British-made constitution, set up a federal system in 1935 with virtually full, responsible government in the provinces and increased powers for the central legislature. The Conservatives in Britain felt that the act gave India too much autonomy. The Labor party and Indian leaders denounced it as short of the promised dominion status (comparable to Canada). World War II intervened before the act was fully implemented. Independence for India would be delayed until 1947.

Dominion Nationalism

The response of the self-governing dominions (Canada, Australia, New Zealand, and South Africa) in World War I had been the supreme test of Britain's liberal philosophy of empire based on free association instead of legal obligation or coercion. The contribution of the dominions to the war effort was remarkable. Together they sent over one and one-half million troops, and India sent an equal number. Imperial unity was so pronounced that the imperial federalists, led by Lionel Curtis and his Round Table, anticipated its postwar extension. In 1917 the Imperial War Conference proposed "continuous consultation and concerted action" after the war.

Instead, the war stimulated dominion nationalism more than interdependence. As a result decentralization, rather than centralization, was predominant after the war. Each dominion insisted on signing the peace treaty and joining the League of Nations as an individual state, not merely as part of the British empire delegation. The dominions, except for New Zealand, refused to rally to Britain's cause in the Chanak conflict between Greece and Turkey. Ireland set a precedent by exchanging its own ambassador with Washington. Other dominions followed. In 1925 a new cabinet office for dominion affairs separated the dominions from the rest of the British empire. By 1926 imperial unity was seen in common institutions and in allegiance to the Crown, but not in common policies or centralized organizations.

BALFOUR REPORT AND STATUTE OF WESTMINSTER

The Imperial Conference of 1926 attempted to define formally what had already taken place in fact. Lord Balfour presided over the committee that worked out the draft which, for the first time, defined the relations of the dominions and Britain. The committee wisely refrained from drawing up a formal constitution with an inflexible relationship that could not continue to evolve. Canada, Australia, New Zealand, South Africa, Newfoundland, and the Irish Free State were all satisfied with Lord Balfour's final draft which defined the Dominions as "autonomous communities within the British Empire, equal in status, in no way subordinate one to another . . . united by a common allegiance to the Crown, and freely associated as members of the British Commonwealth of Nations."

This acknowledgment of equality of status between the dominions and Britain was legally confirmed by the Statute of Westminster (1931), which forbade any act of the British Parliament to apply to a dominion without the consent of the dominions. The Balfour Report ranks along with the Durham Report of 1839 as a landmark in the evolution of the British colonies toward self-government. The lesson of the American Revolution had been well learned.

Irish Developments

In 1923 de Valera, the intransigent republican, finally dropped his violent opposition to the dominion status of the Irish Free State. Instead, he planned to win his objectives from within the Dail. In 1932 he succeeded the moderate Cosgrave as Prime Minister and immediately severed the remaining links with Britain by ignoring the Governor-General, abolishing the oath of allegiance to the Crown, and ending appeals to the Judicial Committee of the Privy Council. In 1936 the Irish lower chamber abolished the more moderate Senate, and the next year de Valera wrote his republican political philosophy into the constitution of the newly named Eire (replacing the Irish Free State). Ireland was a reluctant member of the commonwealth, having come into it against its will after a bitter civil war. De Valera was therefore obsessed with the goal of complete separation. World War II delayed this step, but in 1949 Ireland left the commonwealth to become an independent republic.

Foreign Affairs, 1924–1931

Baldwin's bland insularity did not prevent these years of the interwar period from being the most promising in foreign affairs. Under two able foreign ministers, Austen Chamberlain and Arthur Henderson, Britain took an active part in improving relations with Germany and France and in supporting collective security through the League of Nations.

HIGH TIDE OF SECURITY

Before its fall in 1924, the Labor government had recognized Russia and agreed to the Dawes Plan on German reparations; MacDonald had even helped draft the Geneva Protocol for the peaceful settlement of international disputes. Although Parliament never approved the Protocol, the mood of international conciliation it encouraged permitted Austen Chamberlain, the new Tory Foreign Secretary, to continue MacDonald's efforts of reconciliation among Britain, France, and Germany. This rapprochement produced the Locarno Pact (1925) whereby the Franco-German frontier was guaranteed by Britain, Italy, France, Germany, and Belgium. There were also provisions for the settlement of disputes by diplomacy, conciliation, or arbitration. The achievement of these treaties permitted Chamberlain to share the Nobel Peace Prize for 1925. The next year Germany entered the League, and both European security and economic stability seemed promising. But opportunities were wasted thereafter, not from opposition but from inertia. Lord Cecil finally resigned from Baldwin's cabinet because of Britain's hesitation to be committed either to international arbitration or to disarmament. Britain signed the Kellogg-Briand Pact (1928) renouncing war, but it was only a platitude and not a plan of action to keep the peace.

Foreign Affairs under Labor, 1929–1931

The Labor government under Ramsey MacDonald and his Foreign Secretary, Arthur Henderson, was more consistent than Baldwin's government in implementing the principles of arbitration, arms reduction, and security through the League of Nations. Diplomatic relations with Russia were restored in spite of the sustained opposition of the Conservatives. At The Hague Henderson presided over the Political Commission which achieved the evacuation of Allied troops from the Rhine; he also signed the optional clause of the Statute of the Permanent Court of International Justice which required referral of all international disputes to that court. MacDonald chaired the London naval conference (1930) during which partial success was achieved by Britain, the United States, and Japan in extending the 5: 5: 3: ratio on battleships agreed to in 1922 to other warships as well. By this action Britain agreed to share naval supremacy with the United States.

The Drift to War, 1931–1938

Fascists in Italy, Japan, Germany, and Spain were not deterred by collective security based largely on paper or moral sanctions. Force and the threat of force met no effective response from the major powers in the League or from the United States, largely because of the popularity of pacifism in Britain, memories of the horrors of World War I, and a preoccupation with domestic problems brought on by the depression. The thirties showed that Britain and the commonwealth would not fight for the enforcement of either League authority or for the sanctity of peace treaties. Hitler and Mussolini interpreted this attitude as a sign of political decadence and military weakness; however, Britain and the commonwealth would fight when they finally sensed that national survival was at stake. By that time options other than all-out war were lost.

JAPANESE AGGRESSION

Collective security collapsed first in Asia when Japanese troops invaded Manchuria in 1931. China appealed to the League of Nations and to the United States, but neither made any response sufficient to deter Japan. A League commission, under Lord Lytton of Britain, rebuked Japan but hesitated to recommend sanctions. Japan withdrew from the League in 1933 and launched a direct attack on China. In its first major test the League failed to take effective measures to keep the peace; and it was this shortcoming that invited aggression elsewhere.

FAILURE OF GENERAL DISARMAMENT

The World Disarmament Conference of sixty nations opened at Geneva in February 1932. The supporters of collective action anticipated that agreement here would be the capstone to European peace and security. Germany demanded equality with other powers and threatened to rearm if other nations did not disarm. France insisted on greater security before it would disarm. In Germany the Nazis and the Nationalists opposed the policy of pacification that Gustav Stresemann had promoted in the twenties. The British delegation, led by John Simon, offered no plan and no leadership in the impasse. British sympathies were with Germany more than with France. In January 1933, Adolph Hitler came to power. In October he withdrew the German delegates from both the disarmament conference and from the League of Nations. The following year the disarmament conference was adjourned indefinitely.

GERMAN REARMAMENT

Hitler substituted rearmament for conciliation as a better method to vindicate the "wrongs" of the Versailles Treaty. In 1935 he openly violated the treaty by denouncing its disarmament clauses and by introducing conscription. Although Britain, France, and Italy protested and had the League condemn this action, no further steps were taken to halt German rearmament. The British responded by arranging a naval pact with Germany in June of 1935. This move alienated France and implied British support of Germany's rearmament. France bolstered its security with a bilateral defensive pact with Russia.

BRITISH REARMAMENT AND PUBLIC OPINION

British public opinion opposed rearmament and military action against distant aggression. MacDonald and Baldwin deferred to this viewpoint which was dramatically revealed in the National Peace Ballot of 1934. Over eleven million voters favored international disarmament and collective security through the League. The Labor party, led by George Lansbury, urged reliance upon collective security while voting against the increased expenditure in armaments to provide it. The Conservatives supported half-hearted independent action by Britain outside the League, but their timid actions and meager success in increasing armaments neutralized the effectiveness of this approach. From 1936 to 1939 Baldwin asked annually for increased armament expenditures from a reluctant Parliament.

MUSSOLINI'S AGGRESSION

The Italian invasion of Ethiopia in 1935 took place in spite of an appeal from Emperor Haile Selassie for League protection against open aggression. The League invoked mild economic sanctions against Italy but excluded the one essential commodity, oil. Thus the sanctions only angered the Italians without impeding their conquests. In Paris in December, Foreign Secretary Samuel Hoare and Pierre Laval drafted a treaty designed to appease Italy and prevent a general European war by offering Benito Mussolini one-half of Ethiopia. British public opinion loudly denounced this betrayal of the League and of collective security which the national government had promised to support only a month earlier in the general election. Hoare resigned, and Baldwin appointed Anthony Eden as Foreign Secretary in an effort to placate public feeling.

Mussolini completed the conquest of Ethiopia and contemptuously withdrew from the League in 1937. The Ethiopian crisis divided Europe into two camps and encouraged Mussolini to ally with Hitler in the Rome-Berlin Axis of 1936. Because it had failed to take effective action against aggression, the League, for all practical purposes, became an anachronism after 1936. Furthermore, the Hoare-Laval scheme indicated that the big powers would sacrifice the small powers to avoid a general war. Thereafter, each country looked for new means of protection after the failure of collective security. Belgium became neutral; Poland exchanged an alliance with France for one with Germany.

HITLER IN THE RHINELAND

While the western powers were preoccupied with Italy's aggression, Hitler took the opportunity to unilaterally break the Versailles and the Locarno treaties by sending troops into the demilitarized Rhineland. Public and political opinion in Britain would not support sanctions, military or economic, against Germany for militarizing its own territory. France was unwilling to act without British support. The Council of the League denounced Germany's violation of international treaties but recommended no further action. Britain had no desire to risk war to support collective security under the League or to prevent the violation of international treaties.

SPANISH CIVIL WAR

The division of Europe into a Fascist and non-Fascist camp was sharpened by the civil war in Spain. To prevent the conflict from spreading into a general war, Baldwin's cabinet, supported by France, took the lead in setting up a committee of nonintervention in the war. As it turned out, nonintervention aided General Franco and the Fascist Nationalists because Britain, France and most other states honored the agreement. However, Italy and Germany showed continued contempt for international agreements and liberally aided General Franco and his troops. Only Russia gave formal assistance to the Loyalists and thereby helped to delay the Fascist victory in Spain until 1939. Winston Churchill warned of the consequences of the failure to rearm and sought to rally public opinion, but languor prevailed in the cabinet.

The hope continued that the dictators could be appeased short of war. For the first time significant opposition to the government's foreign policy was being heard. The ideological implications of the Spanish war split and embittered British politics. Pro-Republicans were charged with communist sympathies, while the government was condemned by its critics as a tool of class interests friendly to fascism. Nevertheless, to stop Hitler after 1936 would demand either full rearmament in peacetime or an alliance with Stalin, and neither option was politically palatable; that was the real problem.

Personal Diplomacy

Foreign policy became Neville Chamberlain's personal and primary concern from the day he became Prime Minister in May 1937. The Foreign Office was bypassed and parliamentary criticism was ignored. Surrounding himself with like-minded advisors, such as Lord Halifax, Neville Henderson, Samuel Hoare and John Simon, Chamberlain and this inner cabinet operated on the assumption that Hitler's objectives were limited and his appetite satiable. Thus Chamberlain believed that by reasonable agreement, rather than by force, he could win peace. This industrious, rigid man with confidence in his own abilities and in the purity and rightness of his policies would have provided forceful and efficient domestic leadership in the twenties. But he was tragically miscast for dealing with Hitler, who practiced diplomacy in a manner alien to Chamberlain's rules of conduct. By appeasement Chamberlain probably delayed war for one year. But the delay assisted German rearmament more than Germany's opponents. However, the year permitted Britain to build up an effective air force and to win commonwealth backing, both of which were lacking in 1938.

GERMAN STRATEGY

Chamberlain's plan was to find satisfactory terms whereby tensions with Germany over Central Europe, armaments, and colonies could be resolved amicably. Interviews with British diplomats convinced Hitler that Britain would not forcibly oppose his alteration of the map of Europe. Chamberlain knew nothing of Hitler's meeting with his armed forces in November 1937, during which he plotted the seizure of Austria and Czechoslovakia.

Italian Negotiations. Chamberlain's policy of appeasement produced an agreement with Italy on April 16, 1938, whereby each country promised not to extend their bases in the eastern Mediterranean. Britain would recommend to the League of Nations the recognition of Italian sovereignty over Ethiopia, and Italy would withdraw its troops from Spain. Chamberlain hoped to strengthen his hand in negotiations with Hitler by settling disputes peacefully with Hitler's ally, Mussolini.

Austria and Czechoslovakia. The Nazis had intimidated Austrian leadership since 1934. In March 1938, Hitler took the country by force. Chancellor Schusschnigg's appeal for help had brought no support from Italy, France, Britain, or Russia. The British Government made only a routine protest of the Nazi coup.

Immediately Hitler applied pressure on Czechoslovakia. In September 1938, Chamberlain met Hitler at Berchtesgaden and agreed to the cession of the Sudeten territory to Germany if its citizens voted for such on the basis of self-determination. Only a week later at Godesberg Hitler made new demands for Sudetenland in a meeting with Chamberlain. When the Godesberg Memorandum was rejected by Britain, France, and Czechoslovakia, Hitler demanded his terms by October 1 or threatened war. A general war now seemed imminent. Hitler suddenly turned conciliatory and promised to make the Sudeten his last territorial claim; he offered to meet with Chamberlain, Mussolini, and Edouard Daladier of France.

Munich. During the week of September 22, 1938, Hitler, Chamberlain, Daladier and Mussolini settled the fate of Czechoslovakia without even the presence of Czech representatives. Sudetenland was ceded to Germany, and the integrity of the rest of Czechoslovakia was guaranteed by the signatories. In France and Britain there was hysterical relief and praise for their leaders who had brought "peace in our time." Hitler had privately and publicly stated limits to his expansionist plans, and it was now up to him to demonstrate whether he wished to prevent or merely postpone war. In March 1939, he violated his guarantee and seized the rest of Czechoslovakia. Chamberlain had been deceived; appeasement had failed to halt aggression. British foreign policy now underwent a sudden about-face. Within six months Europe was again at war.

Economics and the search for collective security short of military intervention dominated the two decades between the wars. For eighteen of those years the Conservative party was the largest party in Parliament and for sixteen years had a clear majority of seats. In retrospect, the period has often been described as one of drift and lost opportunities.

The Fourth Home Rule Bill for Ireland finally resolved centuries of Irish-British hostility, although not completely; the ongoing conflict in Northern Ireland today testifies to the continuation of the political and religious issues that have tormented this country.

Significant progress in imperial affairs, especially with the self-governing dominions, marked these years. In contrast, the quest for collective security brought promise of a peaceful world only in the late twenties in the passage of the Locarno Pact and the Kellogg-Briand Treaty. The behavior of the new European dictators mocked the serious efforts to limit their appetites for expansion short of armed resistance. Appeasement allowed Hitler time to build a powerful military machine. The fear of another major war was greater than the fear of tyranny in European states. However, hostilities could not be avoided indefinitely. Twenty years after the end of World War I Britain and her allies were again at war with Germany.

Selected Readings

Beaverbrook, William M. A. *The Decline and Fall of Lloyd George* (1963)

Blake, Robert. *The Unknown Prime Minister: Bonar Law* (1955)

Blythe, Roland. *The Age of Illusion: England in the Twenties and Thirties* (1964)

Churchill, Winston A. *The Gathering Storm* (1948)

Feiling, Keith. *Life of Neville Chamberlain* (1946)

Gilbert, Martin. *The Roots of Appeasement* (1967)

Graves, Robert, and Hodge, Alan. *The Long Weekend: A Social History of Great Britain, 1918–1939* (1963)

Kee, Robert. *The Green Flag: A History of Irish Nationalism* (1972)

Manchester, William. *The Last Lion: Winston Spencer Churchill; Alone, 1932–1940* (1988)

Marquand, David. *Ramsey MacDonald* (1977)

Middlemas, Keith, and Barnes, John. *Baldwin: A Biography* (1969)

Mowat, Charles L. *Britain Between the Wars, 1918–1940* (1955)

Nicolson, Harold. *King George V: His Life and Reign* (1958)

Stevenson, John. *British Society, 1914–1945* (1984)

Taylor, A. J. P. *English History, 1914–1945* (1965)

Wilson, Trevor. *The Downfall of the Liberal Party: 1914–1935* (1966)

Ziegler, Philip. *King Edward VIII: A Biography* (1991)

24

The Age of Churchill and World War II

1939 Hitler violates Munich agreement and seizes all of Czechoslovakia in March

Nonaggression Pact signed between Stalin and Hitler, August 23

Germany's invasion of Poland on September 1 begins World War II

1940 Chamberlain resigns as Prime Minister on May 10; Winston Churchill succeeds him and forms a national government

France falls to German forces and surrenders, June 22; the Battle of Britain begins

1941 Hitler launches a surprise attack on Russia in June

Japanese bomb Pearl Harbor, December 7, bringing the United States into the war

1942 Allies achieve first victories on all three fronts: North Africa, Russia, and in the Pacific

Beveridge Report recommends a comprehensive social insurance scheme

1943 Critical battle of Stalingrad concludes with a Russian victory

1944 D-Day, the invasion of France on June 6, is launched by Allied troops

1945 Yalta Conference, at which the Big Three—Roosevelt, Churchill, and Stalin—agree on postwar division of Germany and other territorial arrangements

United Nations Charter is approved by fifty nations at San Francisco

British general election ousts Churchill and Conservatives; Labor party wins first clear-cut parliamentary majority

After the paralysis and drift of the interwar years, Britain became galvanized to heroic resistance in 1940 under Winston Churchill's forceful leadership. World War II became total, killing as many civilians as soldiers. Once again, as in World War I, the war was conducted by a coalition government whose powers were almost limitless.

Far more than in any previous conflict, the Second World War became a struggle for survival, because Hitler's aim was the mastery, not merely the hegemony, of Europe. Air warfare and bombing raids ended the safety of Britain's island security and naval supremacy which had protected Britain for the previous nine hundred years.

When Britain refused to yield, Hitler turned elsewhere. His fatal error was to overtax the German war machine by extending its commitments on three fronts. In time the world wide Allied coalition brought against the German war machine the implacable logic of geography, communications, transportation, and superior resources. This coalition of Allies turned the tide of war as the preponderance of power moved against the Axis powers (Germany, Italy, and Japan). The defeat of Germany became almost a Pyrrhic victory for Britain because the peace ended its status as a first-class power.

MOBILIZATION AND WAR

After Munich Britain reverted to its historic principle of allying with the weak and against the strong to prevent one-power domination of the Continent. A crash program of rearmament and civil defense commenced. Britain promised to protect Poland, but an eastern European security system without Russia was no deterrent. When Germany and Russia signed a nonaggression pact on August 23, 1939, Hitler's hand was free to strike against Poland. World War II began on September 1, 1939, when German armies invaded Poland.

Aftermath of Munich

Except for convincing the dominions and British public opinion that appeasement would not keep the peace in Europe and buying a year's time to triple the strength of the Royal Air Force, the strategic balance sheet agreed to at Munich was largely negative for Britain and Europe. A fortified Czech border, thirty-six Czech divisions, the vast Skoda munitions works, and a genuine democratic state were sacrificed to satisfy Hitler. The pact was also a moral and diplomatic loss. The support of Britain for the strongest European power, instead of the weakest, and the failure of France to honor its alliance with Czechoslovakia caused Britain and France to lose prestige and the respect of eastern Europe. Poland became isolated and an easy mark as Hitler's next victim. Russia, in particular, was suspicious of the Munich pact, because its terms seemed to encourage Hitler to expand eastward instead of westward.

Since Russia could not count on either Britain or France, it was willing to make a calculated and cynical nonaggression pact with Germany to buy time before facing a German threat itself. An Anglo-French mission to Russia made half-hearted efforts at an alliance, but instead of reconciling differences, Russia accepted on August 23 Germany's proposal of a ten-year Nonaggression Pact. Stalin gained more by buying time than by an uncertain alliance with Britain and France, and Hitler eliminated the threat of major war on two fronts. In May 1939, Hitler and Mussolini completed a military alliance with the Pact of Steel.

Mobilization

Prime Minister Chamberlain still had some illusions after Munich about persuading Hitler to keep the peace; therefore, he refused to bring into his cabinet vocally anti-Hitler critics, such as Winston Churchill, who might anger the dictator. Nevertheless, he accepted the inevitability of preparing for the worst. A substantial defense budget for 1939–1940 speeded up rearmament. In 1939 approximately eight thousand planes were produced as compared to under three thousand in the previous year. The navy was overhauled and was far superior to the German fleet when war broke out. The badly neglected British army of five divisions was to be raised to thirty-five divisions. To obtain such a force conscription was introduced. Civil defense preparations provided for air-raid shelters, the evacuation of children from large cities, and emergency fire and transport organizations. During the same year German military production increased at twice the pace of Britain's. Even so, British rearmament angered Hitler, while his persecution of the Jews alienated British public opinion against him. In some influential quarters of the nation, however, Hitler was regarded as the lesser evil, as the guardian of Western culture against godless communism.

War: First Stage

On September 1, 1939, the German invasion of Poland began. Britain and France honored their pledges to Poland and declared war on Germany two days later. The German *blitzkrieg* ("lightning war") by ground and air forces overwhelmed the valiant but smaller, old-fashioned Polish army that still relied on cavalry. On September 17, Russia attacked Poland from the east. Polish resistance ended on September 29. Neither Britain nor France was able to get troops into Poland. Germany and Russia partitioned Poland according to the terms of a secret protocol signed at the time of the Nonaggression Pact. Russia occupied Estonia, Latvia, and Lithuania and attacked Finland in November. Finland capitulated in March 1940, after a stout resistance in a winter war against the Russians. Hitler and others concluded that the Russian army was weak after its poor showing in Finland.

THE PHONY WAR

After the fall of Poland there was a six-month lull in land operations known as the "phony war." British and French forces took a defensive position behind the elaborately fortified Maginot Line on the French border facing the German Siegfried Line. Another long and immobile conflict like the First World War was anticipated by the French generals. No bombing occurred. Britain began a full-fledged naval blockade of German imports and exports, hoping to strangle Germany's economy and force it to terms. German shipping was swept from the seas, and on April 4 Chamberlain declared that Hitler had "missed the bus" by his inactivity. Five days later the German *blitzkrieg* in the West opened, directed against Denmark and Norway.

CHAMBERLAIN RESIGNS

The Prime Minister by temperament and conviction was conspicuously lacking in the qualities needed for war leadership. His hopes and everything he had worked so patiently to accomplish short of war had failed. His canon of fair play and the honoring of international agreements had been mocked by Hitler. Now faced with a world war, he made only token efforts to get Labor to join the national government. He did set up a war cabinet of nine, including in it his former critics, Churchill and Anthony Eden. The phony war gave Chamberlain some hope, but the German victory in Norway increased criticism of his war leadership, not only from the opposition, but from his own party as well. Labor agreed to join a coalition government, but not under Chamberlain's leadership. On May 10, 1940, Chamberlain resigned and advised King George to summon Winston Churchill, the only leading Conservative other than Harold Macmillan who was not identified in some way with the Baldwin-Chamberlain policies of the 1930s.

Churchill's War Leadership

At the age of sixty-five, Churchill was called to lead the nation in the crisis of war, whereas he had been shunned as too rash in judgment and too controversial in the prewar years by party leaders. Chamberlain agreed to serve in Churchill's cabinet, thereby avoiding a party split similar to the one which had occurred in World War I when Lloyd George succeeded Asquith as Prime Minister. A new coalition government of Conservatives, Liberals and Laborites was formed, directed by a small war cabinet of five (later nine) members.

In Winston Churchill Britain found the exceptional qualities needed for leadership in war. His brilliance and energy had been recognized since the Boer War, but he had never been fully trusted. He now became the forceful and eloquent spokesman of British defiance, mobilizing the English language as one of the tools to rally the nation to face the risks of total war. His stirring speeches sustained the firmness of purpose of an island people as they stood alone against Hitler's Third Reich. The coalition war cabinet which Churchill had set up was more truly national than any of its predecessors. From Labor he brought in Clement Attlee as deputy Prime Minister and Ernest Bevin as Minister of Labor and National Service. Churchill kept the post of Defense Minister himself and also took over many functions of the Foreign Office, preferring to deal directly with Roosevelt and Stalin. Churchill asserted British influence and power sufficiently for the term Big Three—Roosevelt, Stalin, and Churchill—to be fully justified during the war years.

TOTAL WAR

With the *blitzkrieg* in the West the power of the German war machine dispelled any illusions about the conflict settling down to static trench and economic warfare. The collapse of France left only Britain to face the full force of Nazi power. The ensuing Battle of Britain failed to break British morale or give Germany control of the air. Hitler therefore turned eastward against Russia in June, 1941. By the end of the year the United States and Japan were also major belligerents. Late in 1942 the tide of victory turned as the overextended commitments and theaters of combat placed an impossible burden on Axis power.

No part of British society nor the economy escaped the demands of total war. Old animosities were set aside in a common coalition against the Axis powers. Britain and Russia became allies, Labor ministers and the trade unions lent solid support to Churchill, and the emergency powers of the state became virtually unlimited.

The Fall of France

On May 10, 1940, Germany attacked France through Belgium and the Netherlands, thereby outflanking the Maginot Line. The Dutch and Belgian armies capitulated, and by May 23 the Germans had penetrated the line of the dispirited French armies at Sedan and reached the Channel, trapping the British Expeditionary Force and some French units to the north. The surrounded troops turned what could have become a major disaster into the incredible evacuation of Dunkirk. Fighting their way to the beaches, 338,000 soldiers were evacuated to Britain by 887 private and Royal Navy vessels. The army was saved, but all its equipment was lost. On June 10, Italy entered the war and attacked France from the south in order to share the spoils. Humiliating armistice terms were accepted by France on June 22, leaving Britain and the commonwealth to face Hitler alone for the next year.

Battle of Britain

The British turned down Hitler's peace overtures and braced themselves to resist the mightiest military force ever assembled up to that time. Hitler commenced preparations for a sea and airborne assault—Operation Sea Lion—and invasion barges were assembled in the Channel ports. But first the Nazis had to attain air superiority over England and the Channel. In July the Battle of Britain began as the German Luftwaffe tried to destroy the Royal Air Force and shatter British morale. Air warfare no longer allowed the island to escape the devastation of war. For three months up to one thousand bombers came every day, and every night thereafter for six months. The incendiary bombs were aimed at the cities instead of industries. The blitz took a heavy toll in civilian casualties and in property damage, but the will of the British to resist never faltered.

George VI and Queen Elizabeth symbolized the quiet strength of British endurance during the Battle of Britain. Their calm and steady encouragement of their subjects added to the will of the island kingdom to stand alone against Hitler. Three German planes were shot down for every plane lost by the small but superb Royal Air Force. Instead of winning air superiority, Hitler suffered the loss of more than half of his total first-line air strength. In October Hitler canceled his invasion plans and turned instead toward the Balkans and Russia. British morale was also lifted by the easy victory of General Wavell and his army, even though outnumbered five to one, over the Italians in Egypt and Libya.

Battle of the Atlantic

With the entire west coast of Europe in German hands, Hitler now concentrated his submarines and air force against British shipping in the North Atlantic and in the Mediterranean. By June 1941, over half a million tons a month of British shipping were being sunk—at a rate faster than could be replaced. Yet, as in 1917, food, oil, and other essentials had to reach England or the country would be forced to capitulate. To avoid this peril, President Roosevelt stretched the strict restrictions of the American neutrality legislation of 1935 and provided help to Britain. In September 1940, the United States gave Britain fifty overage destroyers in return for long-term leases of eight air and naval bases in the western Atlantic. In March 1941, the Lend-Lease Act authorized Roosevelt to put American resources at the disposal of any country whose defense was deemed vital to the security of the United States. This permitted a steady flow of supplies to Britain and other Allies amounting to $45 billion by July 1945. The United States merchant marine, often protected by escort vessels of the Canadian navy, carried these supplies to Great Britain.

United Nations

Britain finally gained two major allies when Germany invaded Russia and Japan attacked the United States in 1941. Immediately the war was transformed from a European to a global struggle. Although the initial momentum and careful preparations gave Germany and Japan important victories, the entry of Russia and the United States into the war ultimately provided the preponderance of power to bring about the Axis defeat. It was the fatal tendency of Germany and Japan to overextend the theaters of war, and in the long run their strategic blunders outweighed their tactical gains. On January 1, 1942, twenty-six nations, henceforth called the United Nations, signed a massive military alliance pledging total cooperation against their common enemy.

Invasion of Russia

In April 1941, the Germans successfully invaded the Balkan peninsula and rescued the Italians in Albania from defeat by the Greeks. With the southern flank of the German army protected, Hitler launched his surprise attack on Russia on June 22, 1941, which was aimed at annihilating the Russian armies before winter. Since success depended on immediate and decisive victory, one hundred and fifty German divisions attacked along a 1,600-mile front, but were met with unprecedented resistance. By the end of the year, the key objectives of Moscow and Leningrad were still in Russian hands. The German armies were ill prepared for the coldest winter in living memory and for the appalling problem of supplying such a distant and extended front. German brutality and contempt for the Russians only stiffened Russian resistance, whereas, at the beginning, many Russian civilians and troops were not particularly opposed to the threat to Stalin's regime.

Japanese Aggression

Britain and the dominions declared war on Japan after the Japanese attack on the United States naval base at Pearl Harbor, December 7, 1941. Britain and the United States were now formal allies. In the next six months Japan rapidly created a new empire in the southeast Pacific. Japanese armies seized the British possessions of Hong Kong, Malaya, Singapore, and Burma, thereby threatening India and sealing off the Burma Road and supplies to China. The Philippines and the Dutch East Indies were also occupied, and the invasion of Australia was expected since the Japanese were already in New Guinea.

The Year of Disasters

Until late 1942 the Allies were on the defensive and suffered successive defeats on every front. The German spring offensive in Russia was carried to Stalingrad, gateway to the Caucasian oil fields and to control of the Middle East. In North Africa General Rommel and his Afrika Korps had pushed the British back almost to Cairo. Japan could not be checked in the Pacific. During this time Churchill and Roosevelt agreed to give the war in Europe priority and unify their military and economic operations. Machinery for integrating the war effort was established; in each theater of war one person was given command of the land, sea, and air forces of the United States and the British commonwealth.[*]

The Tide Turns

The summer of 1942 marked the high tide of Axis fortunes in North Africa, Russia, and in the Pacific. Victory in Egypt and at Stalingrad could have linked the two German drives, forced the British out of the Middle East, and brought the German armies to India to join the Japanese advancing from the east. But on all three fronts the Axis thrusts were halted, and successful counteroffensives were undertaken. Thereafter, the United Nations mounted an all-front offensive, and Britain's role in the war, in contrast to the first three years, was overshadowed by the might of Russia and the United States.

NORTH AFRICA

In October 1942, the British Eighth Army under General Montgomery won the first decisive battle of the desert war at El Alamein. Rommel's Afrika Korps retreated across North Africa. While the retreat was in progress, a large Anglo-American amphibious force landed in northwest Africa and hemmed in the German forces. After heavy resistance in Tunisia the Germans surrendered in May 1943. More than 250,000 German and Italian troops were captured, including seventeen Axis generals. The "soft underbelly" of Europe—Italy and the Balkans—was now exposed to Allied attack.

THE RUSSIAN FRONT

The critical battle of Stalingrad was the turning point of the war in Russia. By January 1943, the crack German Sixth Army was destroyed, and Stalingrad remained in Russian hands. The Russians began a continuous offensive along the vast front until the last of two hundred German divisions were driven out of Russia in 1944.

THE PACIFIC

British reinforcements to India finally halted and then routed the Japanese in north Burma. The Battle of the Coral Sea on May 7 and the Battle of Midway on June 4–7, 1942, caused heavy damage to the Japanese fleet and frustrated planned attacks on Australia and Hawaii. Later in the summer American and commonwealth forces landed on Guadalcanal and

---

[*] The Pacific area was commanded by Admiral Nimitz; the southwest Pacific by General Douglas MacArthur; southeast Asia by Lord Louis Mountbatten; the Middle East by Sir Harold Alexander; and the European front by General Dwight D. Eisenhower.

other Pacific islands. These operations were limited because the Allies were giving priority to the European theater.

NAVAL AND AIR SUPERIORITY

In 1943 the Allies won the Battle of the Atlantic after suffering over four million gross tons of shipping losses in the preceding year. Unprecedented shipbuilding by the United States allowed new tonnage to exceed losses by late 1943. Radar, depth charges, fast escort vessels, and the use of aircraft cover helped break the U-boat menace. Allied air supremacy was also won in 1943. Day and night British and American bombers reduced many German cities to rubble; however, the massive strategic bombing had little effect on either German morale or production. Its primary outcome was massive destruction: the killing of civilians and the destruction of historic cities.

INVASION OF ITALY

Since 1942 Stalin had insisted on a second front in Europe to take German pressure off the Russian front. Unprepared for a major offensive against Hitler's European fortress, British and American forces instead invaded Sicily in July 1943, and the Italian mainland two months later. Mussolini resigned and Italy surrendered. Nevertheless, strong German resistance continued, and the Allied advance up the peninsula was slow and arduous. Not until April 1945, did Allied troops finally reach the Po Valley.

Second Front   On D-Day, June 6, 1944, the long-awaited Allied invasion army, transported from British ports in 4,000 ships, landed in force on five Normandy beaches. The greatest air, land, and sea operation in military history was successfully launched. Within twenty days a million Allied troops were in France. Britain had become an arsenal in the gigantic buildup for Operation Overlord. General Dwight D. Eisenhower was Supreme Allied Commander in western Europe with Air Chief Marshal Sir Arthur Tedder as deputy. The German armies were unable to contain the invaders, and the Allied forces rapidly liberated Paris and western France. On August 15, American and French armies executed an amphibious landing in southern France and pursued the Germans up the Rhine Valley. By the end of 1944 France was almost entirely liberated. A furious German counteroffensive in Belgium—the Battle of the Bulge—only temporarily slowed down the Allied advance. The Germans made their last stand behind the Siegfried Line along the Rhine.

The Final Assault   By January 1945, Russian troops were deep in eastern Germany; on April 19, they entered Berlin. The western Allied armies crossed the Rhine and reached the industrial Ruhr in April. That same month Russian and American armies met at the Elbe. Germany was split in two, but Hitler insisted on resisting to the bitter end. During the final year of the war Germany launched its new weapon, the "vengeance bomb" (V-1) against British cities. These pilotless jet planes, or "buzzbombs," caused civilian casualties and distress but served no specific military objective. In September the V-2, a rocket-propelled bomb, replaced the V-1 as a more destructive instrument of scientific war.

VICTORY IN EUROPE

On May 7, 1945, the Germans made an unconditional surrender to General Eisenhower at Reims, and the war in Europe officially ended the following day. Hitler reportedly committed suicide in Berlin while the city was under siege by the Russians, and Mussolini was shot by Italians in Milan.

The War Economy

World War II proved to be a great leveler socially and economically. All classes shared the air raid shelters and suffered the same stringent rationing controls. The tax burden was heaviest on the upper- and middle-income brackets, the increase in taxes being most obvious on the previously favored middle-income families. Ironically, only the war ended unemployment and sharply raised the wage scales. By 1944 out of every nine members of the total labor force, two were in the armed forces, and three in war production. As in World War I, the powers of the central government again became virtually limitless, although more tolerance was shown toward individual rights and nonconformity than in World War I. The Emergency Powers Acts of 1939 and 1940 conferred on the government wide-ranging control over public safety and the conduct of the war. The concern over excessive power being delegated to ministries resulted in the House of Commons setting up a Scrutiny Committee in 1944 to serve as a watchdog over every new order sent out by ministries and to bring any order considered objectionable to the attention of Parliament.

Wartime Conferences

Numerous allied conferences took place during the war, first to plot the strategy for defeating Hitler, then to arrange a political settlement for the defeated or conquered countries. Agreement on the former came easier than on the latter. As the tide of war turned in favor of the United Nations, national and ideological differences divided the victors. The postwar objectives of Stalin were in direct conflict with the principles of the democracies.

ATLANTIC CHARTER, 1941

Churchill and Roosevelt conferred on board the battleship *Prince of Wales* in August 1941. Although the United States was not a belligerent, the conversations dealt with military strategy and produced a joint statement on war and peace aims. The Atlantic Charter was a declaration of common ideals which echoed Woodrow Wilson's Fourteen Points. The democracies would seek no territorial gains and would support self-determination of nations and the Four Freedoms. On January 1, 1942, representatives of the twenty-six nations endorsed the Atlantic Charter and agreed not to make a separate peace with the enemy.

CASABLANCA AND QUEBEC, 1943

At the Casablanca Conference in January Churchill accepted Roosevelt's insistence on unconditional surrender as the only basis for peace; however, the Prime Minister and the President could not agree on military strategy. Churchill favored a Mediterranean operation through the Balkans in order to limit Russia's penetration, whereas Roosevelt's military advisors argued for a cross-Channel invasion of France. The only agreement reached was on the invasion of Sicily.

TEHERAN, 1943

After Churchill and Roosevelt met with Chiang Kai-shek in Cairo in November and agreed to the restoration of Japan's seizures in Asia, the first Big Three meeting took place in Teheran. Stalin strongly supported the American position on a French invasion and repeated his promise that Russia would attack Japan after Germany's defeat.

YALTA, 1945

Stalin was in an excellent bargaining position in February 1945. Russia already controlled eastern Europe and its armies were approaching Berlin, whereas the Anglo-American armies had not yet crossed the Rhine. Furthermore, western advisors considered Russian assistance essential to the defeat of Japan—a task estimated to last at least eighteen more months after the fall of Germany. The Big Three agreed to divide Germany into occupation zones, to try German war criminals, and to turn over the problem of reparations, so vital to Stalin, to a commission. A decision on the future of Germany was postponed. Concessions in the Far East were guaranteed Stalin in return for declaring war on Japan. The boundaries of Poland were changed. Ukrainian Poland was ceded to Russia, and part of eastern Germany came under Polish control; in turn, Stalin agreed to free elections in independent Poland—a promise he never kept.

POTSDAM, 1945

The Grand Alliance visibly crumbled at Potsdam. Hitler, the common enemy of the coalition, was dead. Roosevelt had died in April, and, because of his defeat in the British general election, Churchill had to relinquish his place to Clement Attlee in the middle of the conference. Of the former Big Three only Stalin was left. The conference confirmed the proposals made at Yalta regarding Poland and Germany. Stalin would not relinquish the control that the Red army had won in central and eastern Europe. After Potsdam

Britain had few illusions over Russia's intention to exploit the political vacuum left by the destruction of Germany.

The United Nations Organization

Before the war ended, the Allies took steps to establish a new international organization to replace the discredited League of Nations. In 1943 the United Nations Relief and Rehabilitation Administration (UNRRA) was organized to help victims of Axis aggression. At Dumbarton Oaks (1944) British, American, Russian, and Chinese delegates drafted a charter for the United Nations which was approved at an international conference of more than fifty nations in San Francisco (April to June 1945). The United Nations consisted of a General Assembly of all member states, and a Security Council of eleven members, with five major powers—the United States, Russia, Britain, France, and China—having permanent seats. The United States and Russia insisted that the permanent members of the council have veto power over virtually all substantive actions.

Japanese Surrender

The Allied high command gave full attention to Japan following the defeat of Germany. Already the Fourteenth British Army had freed Burma, and American forces had taken Iwo Jima and invaded Okinawa. Vast preparations were under way for the final assault on the Japanese mainland. Instead, the end of the war came suddenly when the United States dropped an atomic bomb on Hiroshima on August 6, 1945, and another on Nagasaki three days later. The awesome destruction produced by these nuclear weapons prodded the Japanese government to accept terms of unconditional surrender on August 14. The use of such a weapon of destruction on civilians also mocked any superior moral standard claimed by the Allies during the war. The formal surrender occurred September 2 on board the battleship *Missouri* in Tokyo Bay. In the interval between the dropping of the two bombs, Russia declared war on Japan in keeping with its promise made at Yalta and in order to be assured of playing a role in the postwar settlement in Asia.

VICTORY IN EUROPE—SOCIALISM IN BRITAIN

Complete military victory came to the United Nations in 1945 as the Axis powers were forced into unconditional surrender. The destruction of World War II greatly exceeded that of World War I. Twenty-two million human deaths resulted from the war, more than half of them civilians. Material damages exceeded $2,000 billion. During the war Allied leaders had held a series of conferences to work out military strategy and postwar settlements. The Allies were united in their opposition to Hitler but not by any common postwar goals. In Britain there was little interest in a return to the 1939 social climate with its unemployment and its timid, traditional economic policies. The war had produced a revolution in the thinking of the British people, and they now wished the state would continue to intervene to raise the standard of living. Therefore, the voters gave the Labor party an opportunity to introduce the welfare state. With the war over in Europe, the dismal record of the Conservatives before the war was a deterrent to voting Churchill's party a mandate for dealing with postwar social and economic problems.

Social and Economic Planning

Since the war had ended unemployment and provided a sense of collective sacrifice and service, it became evident that this national purpose might also be transferred to the goal of a better society by postwar state planning. Before the war was over, social and economic reconstruction became acceptable to the nation, and Keynesian economics had become respectable and orthodox. A White Paper on Employment Policy (1942) pledged the government to the subsidizing of full employment. R. A. Butler's Education Act of 1944 raised the school-leaving age to fifteen and made the Ministry of Education the central authority for education in England and Wales. The Beveridge Report of 1942 attracted an enthusiastic response, except in certain Conservative party circles, to its proposals for extending social security to ensure comprehensive protection against poverty, sickness, unemployment, and ignorance, for all individuals "from the cradle to the grave." The report became the charter for the welfare state and foreshadowed the direction of postwar social reform.

Defeat of Churchill

By 1945 the nation was more than willing to transfer the systematic planning used in the war to achieve military victory to serve the goals of reconstruction and social justice in peacetime. Few wanted to relapse to prewar conditions even if this meant replacing their popular war leader, Winston Churchill, in the process. This national mood was decisively revealed in the repudiation of the Conservatives and Churchill and in the overwhelming endorsement of the Labor party.

GENERAL ELECTION, 1945

Churchill preferred to continue a coalition government, but Labor decided to withdraw from the coalition now that the war was over in Europe. Although Labor gave unstinting support to Churchill's wartime government, the party had misgivings about his unique abilities serving equally well in implementing their postwar reconstruction program. Therefore Churchill resigned on May 29 after the withdrawal of Labor, but agreed to head a caretaker government until an election could be held.

The Conservatives were confident that they could "Win with Winnie." Just as in 1918 a grateful nation had voted their approval of Lloyd George, Conservatives believed the voters would do the same for the architect of victory in World War II. In the campaign Churchill turned his eloquent oratorical powers against the Labor colleagues in his recent cabinet and warned the nation that socialism was inseparable from police-state totalitarianism. The voters paid more attention to the Labor manifesto, *Let Us Face the Future*, which offered attractive proposals for housing, full employment, and social security. On these matters the Conservatives spoke only vaguely. Many voters remembered the sorry Conservative record of the thirties, even though Churchill was not identified with the cabinets of those years. The electorate was more attracted to a program of social reconstruction than to a great war Prime Minister who was now only a party leader seeking a mandate to govern in a postwar era.

Labor Landslide. Only in 1832 and in 1906 had there been a comparable electoral landslide. In the election of July 5, the Labor party won 393 seats to only 189 for the Conservatives; the Liberals held on to only 11 seats. The magnitude of the change surprised everyone, not least of all Winston Churchill, who was meeting with Stalin and Truman at the Potsdam Conference. Clement Attlee, hardworking, conciliatory and modest, was confirmed by his party as their new leader and became Prime Minister on July 26. For the first time the Labor party had a clear-cut majority with a mandate for major change.

World War II lasted two years longer than World War I. Both wars were fought by Britain against the same enemy, Germany and its allies. The wars were similar in several respects. In both conflicts, Britain, France, Russia, and the United States fought together against Germany. In both conflicts Germany and its allies had initial military superiority. In each Britain and its allies held command of the seas, and resources outside of Europe—mainly the United States and the dominions—were required to build up the preponderance of power to defeat its enemies. In both wars forceful, eloquent war leaders—Prime Ministers Lloyd George and Churchill—replaced political leaders temperamentally unsuited for total war.

The war was also vastly different from World War I for Britain: 324,000, not 750,000 of its soldiers and civilians, were killed. It was also much more of a mobile, global conflict, compared to the trench warfare and stalemate of World War I. Although casualties were small compared to Russia, Germany, or Japan, economic losses were great. Britain lost its nineteenth-century stature but continued as a superpower after World War I. In contrast, after the Second World War Britain faced a diminished future. The United States had become the dominant world power.

Selected Readings

Beveridge, William. *Power and Influence* (1953)

Calder, Angus. *The People's War: Britain, 1939–1945* (1969)

Churchill, Winston S. *The Second World War* (1948–1953)

Feis, Herbert. *Churchill, Roosevelt, Stalin* (1967)

Hancock, W. Keith, and Margaret M. Gowing. *The British War Economy* (1949)

Payne, Robert. *A Portrait of Winston Churchill* (1974)

Taylor, A. J. P. *The Origins of the Second World War* (1961)

Waugh, Evelyn. *Men at Arms* (1952)

Woodward, Ernest L. *British Foreign Policy in the Second World War* (1962)

25

Postwar Reconstruction and the Decline from Greatness: 1945–1969

1964   Harold Wilson and Labor party achieve narrow victory, ending thirteen years of Conservative government

1967   British pound devalued again because of economic difficulties

1969   Voting age reduced to 18 by Parliament

De Gaulle again vetoes Britain's application for membership in the European Common Market

*W*orld War II reduced Britain to a secondary power. The emergence of two new superpowers, the United States and Russia, meant that, for the first time in five centuries, Western Europe was no longer the axis of political and military power. Britain's ability to accommodate itself to this decline from greatness and to transform an empire of 600 million subjects into a self-governing and voluntary commonwealth of nations, predominantly nonwhite, demonstrated the flexibility and the continuity of its institutions.

Within Britain the welfare state became part of the institutional and social structure of the nation. The Labor party used its electoral victory of 1945 to introduce it; the Conservatives dared not dismantle it. In these postwar years rapid social changes occurred in an attempt to equalize the rights and benefits of all citizens regardless of class. The maturity of Britain's political system withstood the strain of these rapid postwar changes. Britain's stature in world affairs, especially with the United States, was such that the nation's decline in strength was not followed by a corresponding decline in influence until a generation later.

During these years Britain's weakening position in world trade, along with wage, price, and inflationary pressures at home, made economic problems and policy, rather than foreign or commonwealth relations, the dominating issue of virtually every British government, except for a short period of prosperity in the fifties.

SOCIALISM AND POSTWAR RECONSTRUCTION, 1945–1951

"Imperial greatness was on the way out; the welfare state was on the way in."* Since the highly centralized management of World War II had convinced the British people of the merits of planning, the Labor govern-

---

* A. J. P. Taylor, *English History, 1914–1945* (New York: 1965), p. 600.

ment promptly attempted to implement a planned economy with a major program of nationalization and extensive social services. During these first years of peace Britain survived the critical economic crisis brought on by the war and its aftermath. To restore the war-ravaged economy, rationing and stringent controls were continued for nine years. When the Conservatives returned to power in 1951, further nationalization was halted, but the successful Labor policies of full employment and social services were sustained.

Reconstruction

The economic situation in 1945 was desperate for a nation which depended for survival on world trade. To win the war Britain had sacrificed its export market which provided the nation with food and work in time of peace. The invisible income from capital invested abroad and from shipping was lost, one-half of the merchant navy had been destroyed, and industrial equipment needed replacement and conversion to peacetime needs. The national debt had tripled to £23 billion, and for the first time reserves in gold and dollars were dangerously low. Bolstering the currency and keeping international payments in balance became the immediate problem. Expanded production to satisfy domestic needs and to provide a surplus for exports was essential; but industrial transition took time, planning, and money. The abrupt cessation of Lend Lease by the United States in August 1945, forced Britain to seek additional loans in order to purchase food and machinery from the United States. In this crisis Britain remained solvent and bought time with a $3.75 billion loan from the United States and a $1.125 billion credit from Canada. From 1948 to 1951 there were over $2 billion in further grants and loans from the United States under the European Recovery (Marshall) Plan.

CONTROLS AND RATIONING

Wartime restrictions and industrial controls were retained in an effort to discipline the nation to increase exports and prevent an adverse balance of payments. The Labor government assumed complete control of foreign exchange. Under Hugh Dalton, Chancellor of the exchequer, and later (1947) under Sir Stafford Cripps, licenses were required for exports and imports, production controls were decreed for industry, limitations were placed on foreign travel, and exorbitant taxes were attached to luxury goods in an effort to promote exports. Instead of better times, the deprivations of wartime continued in the postwar years without the incentives of wartime sacrifice. Rationing of meat, sugar, gasoline, tobacco, and clothing remained and was actually extended in the austerity budget of 1947. Waiting in queues, a scant and monotonous diet, and drab and inadequate housing were the order of the day.

Under Cripps's persuasion, compulsory arbitration was required to reduce the loss of production because of strikes. Trade union leaders reluctantly agreed to a wage freeze in 1949 which deterred salary boosts until 1951. Late in 1949 the pound was devalued from $4.05 to $2.80 in an effort to help the balance of payments with the dollar countries; however, devaluation only increased inflationary pressures within Britain. Export industries were encouraged but the controls and steep taxes often inhibited growth. Nevertheless, the public responded to the spirit of national solidarity and sacrifice invoked by Prime Minister Attlee, Foreign Secretary Bevin, and Cripps. The economy slowly improved as exports increased and employment remained high.

NATIONALIZATION

During 1946–1947 the Labor government fulfilled its campaign promises: the Bank of England, the coal, electrical power, and gas companies, and internal and external air and transport services came under public ownership by legislative act. The opposition of the House of Lords to the nationalization of iron and steel prompted Labor to amend the Parliament Act of 1911, limiting to one year instead of two the power of the Lords to veto legislation. In 1949 the Iron and Steel Act was passed. Such measures produced little resistance since the nation had grown accustomed to public control of industry and centralized planning during wartime, and considered this program of public ownership and planning for peace a logical postwar pattern.

The sharpest debates in Parliament were not over the direction of national policy so much as over the undue and "un-English" haste in putting through such major legislation. Nationalization, however, proved to be no panacea for the ills of industry. The coal industry remained chronically sick. Employees experienced little sense of partnership or of ownership in the nationalized industries because management remained largely under the same people. Conditions of employment improved, but the exaggerated hopes of raising production and efficiency through nationalization never materialized. No further nationalization occurred until the 1970s.

THE WELFARE STATE

More successful and permanent was the evolution of the welfare state. This postwar policy was anticipated by reports and commissions before the Second World War and by the Beveridge Report during the war (1942). In fact, the Labor party claimed its social and economic policies were based on the prescriptions for modernizing the economic system and providing fuller social justice than were the recommendations of the Beveridge Report produced by Churchill's coalition government during the war.

Prime Minister Attlee did a remarkable job of introducing these welfare services that provided "cradle to the grave" security. "Attlee achieved in peace what Churchill had magnificently achieved in war: a spirit of national solidarity and sense of community, able to transcend the strong fissiparous forces of modern life."* Unemployment virtually disappeared. Between 1938 and 1950 public expenditures for social service nearly doubled as the state accepted substantial responsibility for the economic and physical well-being of its citizens. A shift in the distribution of national income accompanied the taxation policy of the socialist government. Earned income tax rates reached 88% for the highest brackets. Critics argued that maximum welfare services came at the expense of maximum productivity and greater national income. Yet despite food and fuel crises, the British economy grew 4 percent annually between 1945 and 1951.

In contrast to its housing and health programs that favored the working classes, Labor's educational policies did little to end the class-ridden educational system that selected the well-qualified students at age eleven by means of the "eleven plus" exams and sent them on to grammar schools. Secondary modern schools and a few comprehensive schools were established for those less successful on the exams to continue their education.

Social Insurance. The National Insurance Act (1946), by incorporating many of the principles envisaged in the Beveridge Report, consolidated previous legislation dealing with unemployment, old age, and sickness. The act increased benefits and expanded coverage in each category. Every employee from age sixteen to retirement was required to contribute weekly, as was the employer. The Industrial Injuries Insurance Act (1946) replaced employer compensation with a comprehensive contributory scheme in which the government assumed financial responsibility for all industrial accidents. The National Assistance Act of 1948 ended the long-famous Poor Laws introduced in Queen Elizabeth's reign. Hereafter the government assumed the care of the poor.

The National Health Service. The National Health Service Act of 1946 provided free medical services in an effort to guarantee more uniform standards of health care. The need for a more comprehensive health service was agreed upon during the war not only by the three political parties, but also by the British Medical Association and the public. However, doctors were soon antagonized by the details of Aneurin Bevan's bill and by the controversial Minister of Health himself. After the bill was passed, hospitalization, drugs, medical treatment and office visits, spectacles, and dentures were provided free. The plan was not an insurance scheme with insurance premiums; the government paid the bill out of general taxation.

---

* David Thomson, *England in the Twentieth Century* (Baltimore: 1965), p. 229.

Patients chose their own physicians, and doctors were allowed to practice within or without the program. Within five years, 98 percent of all general practitioners entered the program on either a full-time or part-time basis. Doctors received both a minimum salary and fees per patient call.

Housing. Aneurin Bevan also initiated a crash program of government-subsidized housing construction. Strong measures were required since nearly one million of England's homes had been damaged or destroyed by bombing raids. The Housing Acts of 1946 and 1949 permitted the construction of 806,000 permanent homes and apartments by 1950 and the repair of an additional 330,000. Priority was given to public, low-cost rental units at the expense of private construction. Comprehensive town planning by county authorities, including the building of entire new towns in less congested areas of the country, was provided by the Town and Country Planning Act of 1947.

THE ELECTION OF 1950

In the election of February 1950, the Labor party campaigned on its five-year record and cautiously recommended further nationalization. Since 1945 Lord Woolten had greatly strengthened the Conservative party organization, and this new efficiency was readily apparent. The Conservatives promised to give priority to housing, reduce government controls, halt nationalization, and maintain full employment. They assured the electorate they would not dismantle the welfare state. The results of the election left Labor with a majority of only six in Parliament and without a mandate for strong action.

Attlee's Second Ministry. Labor's second term of office was plagued with difficulties, relieved only by an improvement in the foreign exchange in 1950 and the successful Festival of Britain, commemorating the centennial of the Great Exhibition of 1851. The outbreak of the Korean War demanded rearmament expenditures which, in turn, brought about increased taxes and prices. The choice between rearmament or expanded social services (the "guns or butter" dilemma) further split the Labor ranks which were already weakened by the retirement of Sir Stafford Cripps, through illness, and the death of the much-admired Foreign Secretary, Ernest Bevin. In April 1951, Aneurin Bevan and Harold Wilson, the leaders of the Socialist Left, resigned from the cabinet in protest over foreign policy. The Prime Minister was aging and ill and other ministers were feeling the strain of opposition tactics and all-night parliamentary sittings. The earlier vitality and unity of the Labor party were conspicuously lacking when Attlee called for a general election in October 1951.

AFFLUENCE AND TORY RULE, 1951–1964

The thirteen years of Tory rule that followed their 1951 election victory, and succeeding victories in the general elections of 1955 and 1959, solidified the postwar commitment to a welfare state. The Conservatives assured the electorate that they would not dismantle social welfare programs. By 1959 the Tories were spending 16 percent of personal income on welfare, compared to Labor's expenditures of only 14 percent in their last year in office (1951). The Tories expanded maternity benefits and child allowances, and built more subsidized new houses each year than the Socialists when they were in power. The Tories, however, did put a stop to nationalization and denationalized iron, steel and trucking. After years of postwar austerity, economic prosperity came to Britain in the fifties. The rapid growth of the world economy abroad and expanding production and consumption at home contributed to this prosperity.

The Return of Churchill

The Conservatives emerged from the 1951 election with 321 seats, Labor with 295, and the Liberals with 6 seats. During the campaign the Conservatives attacked Labor's austerity program and had emphasized their commitment to preserving the welfare state and to full employment. They also claimed they had greater talent in conducting foreign affairs than Labor.

At age seventy-seven, Winston Churchill formed his second government which included Rab Butler as Chancellor of the Exchequer and Anthony Eden as Foreign Secretary. He had eloquently praised private enterprise in his campaign oratory. Once in power his government denationalized iron and steel, ended rationing and food subsidies gradually over the next three years, and sharply reduced government regulations and controls. Economic planning continued, however, and socialized medicine was left intact.

In February 1952, King George VI died. Few monarchs had served their subjects with such devotion and self-effacing dignity. The much-loved King was succeeded by his daughter, Elizabeth II.

YEARS OF AFFLUENCE

The general improvement in the world economy reduced the price of raw materials and this, combined with greater freedom from government controls, raised production and the standard of living. The fifties were a period of economic prosperity for Britain. The real wages of workers rose 50 percent during the thirteen-year Tory rule. Britain entered the age of consumption, and both sales and production grew steadily. The years of austere economics under the Labor government had contributed to this postwar economic achievement since Britain learned to live within its means and the economy grew at an annual rate of 4 percent from 1945–1951.

The fifties were noteworthy since economic growth occurred without unemployment or undue inflation. At the same time Britain's industrial output grew 40 percent during this decade. British ingenuity and scientists assisted in this industrial recovery. British scientists won thirty-five Nobel prizes after 1945. Britain was the first nation to put into commercial use the turboprop and the jet airplane, and led the world in the fifties in the use of nuclear power. The prosperity was not permanent. Following the fifties Britain faced chronic balance of payments and inflationary pressures.

The Interlude of Eden

In April 1955, the still grandly eloquent Churchill, now eighty-one years of age, retired and was succeeded by his long-time heir apparent, Anthony Eden. The Churchillian team continued with only a reshuffling of cabinet posts. Eden called an election in May 1955, and his slogan of "peace and plenty" appealed to an increasingly affluent society. The election budget of 1955 reduced the income tax rate and ended the purchase tax on textiles. Meanwhile, Labor's intraparty debate continued to divide moderates and left-wingers; their party platform emphasized controls and nationalization—neither of which were attractive to a full-employment and cash-in-hand electorate. The Conservatives raised their parliamentary majority to 60 in the election and embarked on a program to promote partnership industry and to extend property ownership among the well-to-do working class and the lower middle class—the economic and political center of the electorate. Increasingly, the role of the Chancellor of the Exchequer, now held by Harold Macmillan, was becoming critical in an effort to cope with the problems of balance of payments, productivity, and inflation.

However, these domestic developments under Eden were overshadowed by colonial tensions in Cyprus and Kenya and by the debacle of Anglo-French intervention in the Suez Crisis (1956). In ill health Eden resigned on January 9, 1957, with his party divided over the Suez operation and the public confidence shaken.

New Leadership: Macmillan and Gaitskill

The Tories elected Harold Macmillan to replace Eden as Prime Minister. He presided over Britain's most prosperous postwar years, instead of over the bankruptcy of his party, as many predicted in 1957. His shrewdness, optimism, and genuine concern for the welfare of the people—he was the only leading Tory dissenter to break with the right-wing Baldwin-Chamberlain leadership before the war on both domestic and foreign policy—restored the confidence of the nation and salvaged Britain's relationship with Washington after the Anglo-American dispute over the Suez crisis in 1956 (see next section).

In the beginning Macmillan directed a noninflationary expansion of a mixed economy with great success. His unflappable Edwardian style and astute political touch blended happily with favorable economic conditions in the Western world to provide Britain with its consumer boon. The electorate responded to the Prime Minister's claim that they "never had it so good" by doubling the Conservative majority in Parliament to 100 in the election of October 1959.

Meanwhile, the Labor party was searching for unity and a new sense of direction after having implemented its earlier goals of social security, full employment, and full legal status for unionism. The death of Cripps and Ernest Bevin, and the retirement of Herbert Morrison and former Prime Minister Attlee left a bitter power struggle between Aneurin (Nye) Bevan and Hugh Gaitskill. Gaitskill was elected party leader in 1955 following Attlee's resignation. He favored a close alliance with America, a modest rearmament, and had no plans for more nationalization. His moderate position was attacked by the brilliant and eloquent Bevan and his supporters, who demanded unilateral disarmament, more socialism and public ownership, and less dependence on America. In party conferences the quarrel was bitter until the two leaders worked out an accommodation in 1959. A year later Bevan died; his death was an acute loss to both the party and Parliament since he had been one of the architects of Britain's postwar economy and society.

BRITAIN IN WORLD AFFAIRS: THE DECLINE FROM GREATNESS

The decline of Britain as a world power dates from 1918, not 1945. But only after the Second World War did the weakened position of the nation and the British empire become evident. Until 1961 there was a tendency to maintain the illusion (if not the substance) of former power by overextending military commitments around the world, invoking the majestic prose of Churchill, claiming a special relationship with the United States, and by remaining aloof from European economic and political integration.

The most remarkable achievement of the quarter century following World War II was the freedom and nationhood Britain granted to over 600 million of its subjects, in contrast to the annexation by Russia of over 100 million into the Communist bloc. Britain found that its role in foreign affairs was severely limited by circumstances resulting from World War II, such as economic bankruptcy and dependence for security upon the United States.

Britain's postwar foreign policy was based on the assumption that its unique position in world affairs rested on three overlapping circles of influence: a special relationship with America, the headship of the British commonwealth, and a continuing role as a major power in Europe.

The Cold War

The special relationship between Britain and the United States shaped their response to Russia's expansionist designs at the end of the war. It was Churchill at Yalta who first viewed Communist Russia as a threat to European political independence. British and American statesmen began to act in concert to counter Russia's expansion after they saw Stalin impose totalitarian regimes on Eastern Europe and place his armies on the Elbe River.

At first Foreign Minister Ernest Bevin made serious efforts to prolong wartime cooperation with Russia, but Russia's blatant manifestations of hostility and expansion in Eastern Europe frustrated any such hopes. The utter failure of the Conference of Foreign Ministers (London 1947) to agree on the future of Germany signaled the onset of the Cold War and a redirection of foreign policy by the West to contain Russian expansion. Britain immediately provided assistance to prevent a Communist takeover in Greece until President Harry Truman intervened with the promise of American aid (the Truman Doctrine) to Greece and Turkey. In March 1948, Britain declared its involvement in the defense of Europe, along with France, Belgium, Holland and Luxembourg, by signing the Brussels Pact, which promised mutual aid to any attacked member.

The four-power rule of Germany collapsed in 1947 and was followed by a Soviet blockade of Berlin in 1948. Instead of bowing to Russian pressure, the United States and Great Britain organized a massive airlift which supplied the western sector of Berlin with food and necessities during the 323-day blockade. In 1949 Britain took a leading role in forming the North Atlantic Treaty Organization (NATO) which consisted of Britain, the United States, France, Canada, Italy, Belgium, Holland, Luxembourg, Norway, Denmark, Iceland, and Portugal. Later, Western Germany, Greece and Turkey joined this defensive alliance. Britain's military cooperation with countries of Western Europe did not extend to economic or political union. Britain refused to join the supranational European Coal and Steel Community (known as the Schumann Plan) established in 1951. But that same year the Labor government showed the importance of its American relationship by tripling the budget for armaments and sending troops to Korea.

Britain and the United Nations

British statesmen played an active role in the development of the Charter for the United Nations and in the organization's later operations. The Assembly of the United Nations, with fifty-one states represented, first met in London in January 1946. The members elected a president and a secretary, and selected New York as the site of the permanent headquarters. The United Nations, like the League of Nations, was handicapped by lack of cooperation among the great powers. In 1946 Russia used its veto to prevent the creation of a United Nations military force and the international control of atomic energy. The UN Security Council was able to take immediate and strong action against Communist aggression in Korea (1950) only because Russia was boycotting the Council and, therefore, could not veto the proposals for action.

More successful, although less spectacular, were the specialized agencies affiliated with the United Nations, such as the World Health Organization, the International Monetary Fund, and the United Nations Education, Scientific and Cultural Organization (UNESCO). These organizations provided food, medical supplies, personnel, and loans to governments in an effort to relieve human misery and hunger and encourage economic growth and stability.

Anglo-American Cooperation

In contrast to the period following World War I, the United States became involved after World War II in aiding free nations against aggression, first in Europe and then around the globe. The European Recovery Program, proposed by George Marshall and approved by Congress, rehabilitated the floundering postwar economies of sixteen countries. In the first year of the program's operation (1948) Britain's economic crisis was eased by $980 million in Marshall aid. President Truman's Point Four Program (1950) was another economic weapon designed to combat Communism by sending capital, technical aid, and equipment to underdeveloped areas of the world.

Anglo-American cooperation was especially evident in ending the Berlin blockade and in setting up a federal German government at Bonn (1949) to govern the three Western zones of occupation. The British government supported the action of the United States in the Korean War and raised the defense budget over £1 billion to accelerate rearmament. In 1951 Ernest Bevin, the postwar architect of Anglo-American accord, died, but the close Anglo-American relationship continued under Churchill and Eisenhower. The first four-nation (United States, Britain, France and Russia) summit meeting, proposed by Britain, took place at Geneva in 1955. Not until the presidency of John F. Kennedy was Britain relegated to a conspicuously junior partnership in the Atlantic alliance.

Less Empire and More Commonwealth

The rapid liquidation of the British empire was another consequence of World War II. The war stimulated nationalist and independence movements in the non-Western world and left the European colonial powers too weak to counter the process successfully. In 1947 Britain still ruled nearly one-quarter of the world's people; twenty-one years later Britain brought home the last of its imperial forces from overseas. By that time Britain was no longer a world power in comparison with the massive armies, navies, and number of intercontinental missiles of the United States and Russia.

Britain's retreat from empire was achieved, in most cases, with dignity and with a minimum of conflict, so that after becoming independent the former colonies elected to stay in the commonwealth as alumni members of a free association of sovereign independent nations. The flexibility of the commonwealth was revealed in the decision of the conference of commonwealth prime ministers in 1949 to accept India's continuing membership even though the country was becoming a republic. The remodeling of the commonwealth ended the "common allegiance to the Crown" specified in the Balfour Report of 1926. In its place the British Monarch is accepted as the symbol of "the free association of its independent member nations and as such the Head of the Commonwealth." Between 1945 and 1969 Commonwealth membership rose from 6 to 26 sovereign states and changed to a predominantly nonwhite membership. Although the former colonies retained their membership and British investments were predominantly in commonwealth countries, the hope that Britain might lead a unified and powerful commonwealth never materialized.

PALESTINE

Palestine was a most complicated imperial problem. Britain had administered this territory as a mandate of the League of Nations since World war I but had never fulfilled its promise (the Balfour Declaration of 1917) to assure the Jews a national homeland. The 125 million Muslims in the British empire insisted that the flow of Jewish refugees into Palestine after World War II be stopped at once. Britain attempted to establish a compromise quota system, but this only brought violent clashes among Zionists, Arabs, and British. There were irreconcilable differences between the demands for a Jewish homeland and counter demands for an independent Arab state. Britain gave up its efforts at a solution and announced it would withdraw from Palestine on May 15, 1948. The United Nations followed this action by voting to partition Palestine into Jewish and Arab sections. Discord between Jews and Arabs provoked violence throughout the country as Britain tried in vain to maintain order during the final months of its mandate. The four neighboring Arab states refused to accept the new sovereign state of Israel in its midst in 1948 after the United Nations voted for its creation. An Arab-Jewish war broke out in April 1948. Israel defeated the Arab armies and expanded its boundaries beyond those established by the United Nations. The rest of Palestine was combined with Transjordan to form the new kingdom of Jordan.

THE MIDDLE EAST

Pan-Arab nationalism was also in opposition to British imperial interests elsewhere in the Arab world. The seven-state Arab League supported the evacuation of British and French troops from Lebanon and Syria in 1946. Rising nationalism caused Egypt to demand a revision of the Anglo-Egyptian Treaty (1936) which would guarantee the withdrawal of British troops from the Suez Canal base. In 1952 the corrupt regime of King Farouk was overthrown by a military junta, and Gamel Abdel Nasser, one of the leaders, became Premier and later President. Under Nasser's leadership an Anglo-Egyptian treaty was signed which planned for the final evacuation by 1956 of the British from the Suez Canal. The following year saw the creation of the Middle East Treaty Organization, a Cold War alliance against Russia, whose membership included Britain, Pakistan, Turkey, Iran, and Iraq.

SOUTHEAST ASIA

The British Labor party, after its election victory of 1945, honored its promise of independence for India; but the complex negotiations for withdrawal were bedeviled by the bitter communal dissensions between Hindu and Muslim and the adamant demands of the Muslim leader, Mohammed Ali Jinnah, for a separate state. Only the great respect the Indians had for Mohatma Gandhi, their inspirational leader who preached and practiced nonviolence, saved the Indian subcontinent from greater turmoil. Lord Louis Mountbatten, the new and able British Viceroy, presided over the final transfer of power. He succeeded in persuading Gandhi, Jawaharlal Nehru, leader of the Indian Congress Party, and Mohammed Ali Jinnah to work out a mutually acceptable transfer of power. Much to Gandhi's disappointment, only partition was acceptable to Jinnah. On August 15, 1947, the dominions of India and Pakistan came into existence. Nevertheless, large-scale violence marked the division of the country, and more than one million people were killed in the turmoil generated by communal and religious differences, among them Gandhi, who was assassinated in 1948.

In the same year Ceylon gained its independence. Conferences in London set up a new Federation of Malaya in 1957 (later expanded into Malaysia), after large British forces had finally crushed Communist guerrilla activities in the countryside. As the Cold War intensified in Asia, the United States and Britain attempted to check Communist expansion by the Southeast Asia Treaty Organization (SEATO) of 1954, whose membership included the United States, Britain, Pakistan, Australia, New Zealand, France, Thailand, and the Philippines.

AFRICAN INDEPENDENCE

Independence and freedom became the passwords of African nationalists after World War II. Self-government was granted readily in most British colonies by a gradual transfer of power. A fund of goodwill was thereby retained toward the former colonial power. The exceptions were in the colonies of Kenya and Southern Rhodesia where white settlers were unwilling to relinquish their dominant position to Africans on the basis of "one man, one vote." In 1956 the Sudan became an independent republic outside of the Commonwealth. The next year the Gold Coast became (as Ghana) the first sub-Saharan British colony to achieve independence. Nigeria, Uganda, Tanganyika, Zanzibar, British Somaliland, Kenya, and Sierra Leone achieved independence between 1960 and 1963. Under Churchill and Eden, British support for African independence was reluctant and passive; under Macmillan and his successors the transfer of power was greatly accelerated, and the colonial secretaries readily negotiated the constitutional arrangements necessary for separation.

CENTRAL AFRICAN FEDERATION

In 1953 the Central African Federation was formed by the union of Southern Rhodesia and the two protectorates of Nyasaland and Northern Rhodesia. The Federation was an experiment in multiracial partnership, but was established too late and offered too limited a franchise to the eight million blacks (vis-à-vis 300,000 whites) to have any hope of success. In 1963 the ten-year experiment under federal Prime Minister Roy Welensky collapsed when Britain reluctantly gave Northern Rhodesia the right to secede from the Federation. The next year Northern Rhodesia became the Republic of Zambia, and Nyasaland took the name of Malawi. Both countries became sovereign members of the commonwealth.

The ruling white minority in Southern Rhodesia was determined that no African majority would replace their privileged position. Britain, in turn, refused to grant their request for independence until a constitution was provided that would guarantee the gradual enfranchisement of the whole populace. The white-supremist Rhodesian Front government under Ian Smith defied Britain by proclaiming a unilateral declaration of independence in 1965. The British government promptly declared the action illegal and arranged for an economic boycott of Rhodesia through the United Nations. The country was isolated by the crumbling of the Portuguese empire on two sides of it and by world opinion. Its situation rapidly deteriorated into warfare between whites and black guerrillas. In 1977—too late for a peaceful transition—Smith reluctantly conceded the necessity for black majority rule.

SOUTH AFRICAN DEVELOPMENTS

The United party of Jan Christian Smuts was defeated in 1948, and the Afrikaner Nationalist party under Dr. Daniel F. Malan came to power. It extended and stiffened the policy of apartheid (physical separation of the races) in a determined effort to maintain the doctrine of white supremacy and racial segregation in a land where whites were outnumbered four to one by nonwhites. The government passed a series of acts to tighten control over all opposition to its policies. In 1960 the government proposed making the state a republic; however, the other commonwealth members condemned the country's racist policies and opposed its request to remain in the commonwealth as a republic. As a result South Africa left the commonwealth in March 1961.

The Suez Crisis   The withdrawal of Western colonial powers from the Middle East and the ensuing Arab-Israeli conflict fostered unstable conditions that invited intervention and competition by Communist and Western powers for Arab support. In 1955 the United States and Britain outbid Russia's offer of assistance to build the Aswan High Dam in Egypt but withdrew the offer the following year. Nasser responded to this rebuff by nationalizing the Suez Canal Company—an act which violated international agreements. When a proposal for a conference in London of twenty-two maritime powers was rejected by Nasser, and recourse to the United Nations Security Council was blocked by a Russian veto, Prime Minister Eden and Foreign Secretary Selwyn Lloyd met privately with Premier Mollet in Paris. The conferees apparently endorsed the Israeli attack on Egypt that was launched thirteen days later, on October 29. When Nasser rejected the Anglo-French ultimatum to withdraw his forces ten miles from the canal, the two countries attacked Egypt on October 31 and captured Port Said and a strip of the canal.

The policy of armed intervention found few supporters either in Britain or in the commonwealth. The press and the Labor party condemned the action as an assault upon three of the basic principles of postwar British foreign policy: solidarity with the commonwealth, the Anglo-American alliance, and adherence to the Charter of the United Nations. The United States, which had not been consulted, denounced the attack, and called for a cease-fire. Canada helped to arrange a United Nations task force to police the Ghaza Strip.

The British gained nothing by their military venture: the canal became unusable for shipping; Britain's oil pipeline in Syria was cut; British gold and dollar reserves fell sharply; and Nasser's military defeat by Israel was overshadowed by his diplomatic victory over Britain and France. The Suez remained in Egyptian hands. The only benefits to accrue from the Suez crisis were the submission of two major powers to the will of the United Nations and the establishment of an international police force. Politically, however, the Suez fiasco was a disaster for Eden, splitting his cabinet and contributing to his resignation in January 1957.

Defense Policies

Britain did not seek to avoid involvement in worldwide trouble spots in the postwar world as it had done in the period between the world wars. But its active participation in the security of the free world came at a time when it no longer had the power to enforce its will. British spheres of influence were no longer recognized. Realizing that in Europe and in the Far East it could no longer command respect as an independent power, Britain made the critical decision to join NATO and SEATO—permanent military associations for collective security. In 1954 Britain eased French fears and helped terminate Allied occupation of the German Federal Republic by maintaining military contingents on the European mainland. British dependence on the United States for missiles and atomic weapons made the Anglo-American alliance a cornerstone of postwar foreign policy. The support of the fast-growing commonwealth also became more important as Britain's ability to speak and act with independent authority declined.

In the Middle East the Labor and the Conservative governments tried to maintain British influence and a favorable power structure to keep the approaches to African from falling to hostile powers and assure a steady flow of oil from Iraq and Kuwait. The Anglo-Libyan Treaty (1953), the air bases in Malta, Cyprus, and Aden, the treaty with Kuwait, and the Baghdad Pact were attempts to implement this policy. However, after the Suez crisis British control of the political arrangement in the Middle East was no longer possible, and in 1957 the Eisenhower Doctrine guaranteed American support to this area. In 1973–1974 the oil embargo and quadrupling of oil prices by Arab states clearly demonstrated the diminution of British power in this former sphere of influence.

BRITAIN IN THE SIXTIES

The confidence that had characterized the fifties and the Conservative political dominance waned in the sixties. By 1964 it was the Labor party's turn to be united and on the offensive, with the result that Labor won the elections of 1964 and 1966. Economic issues and recurring balance of payment crises dominated successive governments during these years and accounted for the rapid turnover in the post of Chancellor of the Exchequer. Greater spending on social services in the affluent society and the single-minded pursuit of self-interest in the marketplace by trade unions made the wage-price escalation virtually impossible to control. Britain's international stature diminished during the sixties as the country became an auxiliary, rather than an ally, of the United States in nuclear and foreign policy. The United States and Russia made momentous decisions without consulting Britain, notably in the Cuban missile crisis of 1962. After making a candid appraisal of Britain's diminishing role outside Europe, Britain twice made application for entry into the European Economic Community in the sixties, only to have Charles de Gaulle, the President of France, veto its entry.

Political Changes

By 1959 the two party programs were not far apart. A new political equilibrium had been achieved slightly left of center, as compared to the political alignment in prewar Britain. Nationalization and doctrinaire socialism no longer stirred as much Labor interest, and the trade unions were losing their political consciousness. The Conservatives endorsed the welfare state and accepted the necessity of educational change and economic planning. The sudden death of Gaitskell and the Profumo scandal prompted a change in leadership of the Labor and the Conservative parties.

THE LABOR PARTY

The third defeat in succession for Labor at the general election of 1959 left the party disappointed and divided. Gaitskell vigorously opposed the Labor doctrine of earlier years, which demanded public ownership of the means of production, and fought the doctrinaire Labor members who advocated unilateral renunciation of nuclear weapons. By 1961 his views prevailed and a fresh program was issued urging careful planning for capital expansion and reorganization of education. Before he could lead the party in another election campaign, Gaitskell died suddenly in January 1963. Labor members of Parliament chose Harold Wilson as Gaitskell's successor. Wilson was a former lecturer in economics at Oxford before entering the House of Commons in 1945. He had opposed Gaitskell's election and views and became associated with the left wing of the party. However, upon his election to Labor leadership, Wilson achieved harmony by appointing most of his opponents to the shadow cabinet (cabinet counterparts held by the party out of power).

THE CONSERVATIVES

Prime Minister Macmillan's fortune changed after his election victory of 1959. By 1960 the economic upswing was spent and the balance of international payments was again adverse. In an effort to get the economy moving, Macmillan changed chancellors of the exchequer three times (D. Heathcoat Amery, Selwyn Lloyd, and Reginald Maulding) between 1960 and 1963, raised the bank rate to 7 percent, and called for a voluntary pay pause in all wages and salaries. By-elections in 1962 reflected the declining stock of the Conservatives. The failure at Brussels to gain entry into the European Common Market and the scandal of John Profumo, Secretary of

War, further damaged the government. Mr. Profumo's association with a call girl in private life not only resulted in his lying to the House of Commons, but also raised the question of a breach of national security.

Macmillan resigned in October 1963. Four candidates sought the party leadership but no candidate could win a majority among the Conservative members of Parliament. Macmillan therefore became the political broker and advised the Queen to invite Lord Home, the Foreign Secretary, to become Prime Minister. Once again the quiet, able R.A. Butler, who had held almost every major cabinet office, was bypassed for the prime ministership.

ELECTION OF 1964

Lord Home renounced his peerage so that he could lead the government from the House of Commons (and became Sir Alec Douglas-Home). He formed an able ministry and put off an election as long as possible to establish himself and reverse the opinion polls which gave Labor a decisive lead. By September 1964, the Labor lead had disappeared.

In the campaign, foreign affairs had little interest for the electorate: the important issues were cost of living, education, and housing. The pragmatic Wilson skirted most doctrinaire issues and promised "a white-hot technological revolution" and "genuine" economic planning. Assisting Labor's prospects was the feeling among the electorate that it was time for a change after thirteen years of Conservative government. The results of the October election gave Labor a thin majority of 4 seats over 304 Conservative and 9 Liberal seats.

ELECTION OF 1966

By March 1966, Wilson had shown resourcefulness and skill in governing for seventeen months with the smallest majority in British parliamentary history. His pragmatic policy in office was in striking contrast to his earlier vocal support for the doctrinaire left wing of the Labor party. With such a narrow majority Wilson avoided most controversial issues or campaign promises. On foreign affairs the Labor government backed American policy in Vietnam and resisted party efforts to reduce defense spending.

His budget of 1965 was one of the most unpalatable in years as it sought to curb inflation, reduce consumer spending, and promote exports. Encouraged by his success in halving Britain's trade deficit, Wilson called an election to seek a more secure majority in Parliament. In the campaign he promised long-term economic planning to modernize industry and raise productivity—which in 1965 remained virtually static in contrast to the rise in wages and prices.

The Conservatives went into the campaign with a new party leader. In January 1965, Sir Winston Churchill, the legendary symbol of British eloquence and defiance, died and was accorded a state funeral. Six months later,

Douglas-Home resigned in favor of a younger party leader. Edward Heath, Chancellor of the Exchequer in the last Conservative ministry, defeated Reginald Maulding for the post. Heath was unpretentious, a bachelor who was solemn and dogged, but no match for the nimble wit and persuasive oratory of Wilson during the campaign. In the election of March 31, 1966, the Prime Minister's prestige abroad and popularity at home, coupled with a sense of economic well-being in the nation, raised the Labor majority in the House of Commons from 3 to 97.

The Wilson Years

During Wilson's first term of office he had promised a technological revolution and superior economic planning. After two years he was scarcely more successful than Douglas-Home had been in solving the country's chronic economic problems of industrial inefficiency and economic growth without inflation. By the 1966 election the earlier "Kennedy style" had been replaced by the "family doctor" image, as the Prime Minister used television as his most effective medium to "inspire trust by his appearance as well as by his soothing words." During Wilson's eight years as Prime Minister he moved toward a centrist position in the party and did not hesitate to impose severe economic controls in an effort to curb inflation and to save the pound.

WINDS OF CHANGE

Wilson's rhetoric promising a "great crusade" of technological efficiency and planning was scarcely matched by his performance in office. The traditional compromising pressures of office, coupled with declining public appetite for new programs after the feverish cultural and political excitement of the first part of the decade, combined to produce only modest political controversy.

Nevertheless, the Labor government encouraged certain domestic changes at home just as Macmillan had accelerated the pace of change abroad from empire to commonwealth. Under Wilson the first major overhaul of the policies governing welfare services since the Beveridge Report of 1942 was made. The central proposal in the new program was to relate pensions to earnings to provide a pension of 50 percent of earnings averaged over a lifetime of work. Reflecting its growing orientation toward Europe, the government passed legislation ending the quaint, but irrational, British currency and replacing it with a decimal system. At the same time it introduced the metric system of weights and measures.

Considerable attention was given by Parliament to the younger generation. Imaginative efforts to cope with the growing drug problem were attempted, and in 1969 the voting age was reduced to 18 by the Representation of the Peoples Act. The age-old controversy over the dual school system (grammar versus secondary modern) was revived and resulted in the Government's Education Act of 1976 (during Wilson's third term of office), which required local authorities to reorganize secondary schools into a single comprehensive system. More controversial were changes in economic policy.

ECONOMY ON TRIAL

Low productivity, unofficial strikes, and an international crisis of confidence in British sterling plagued Prime Minister Wilson, as they had plagued most of his postwar predecessors. Until July 1966, the government continued its stop-go economic policies in a desperate effort to stabilize the inflationary wage-price spiral of the previous decade. Like previous ministries, Labor was determined to maintain the illusion of being a world power, avoiding deflation and unemployment at home, and saving the British pound from devaluation. The government was finally forced to admit defeat on all three. The July 1966, voluntary wage-price freeze was changed to a mandatory system with fines and prison sentences for violators. This restriction by a Labor government on the British workers' cherished right of collective bargaining surprised and stunned the unions. It was necessary because workers' wages had risen more than twice as rapidly as productivity between 1964 and 1966, and exports were being priced out of the world market.

Even these sacrifices were insufficient to weather the international run on Britain's slim financial reserves. In November 1967, the government was forced to devalue the pound from $2.80 to $2.40, raise the Bank of England's lending rate to 8 percent, and impose severe restrictions on installment buying. This action staved off the threat of bankruptcy and reassured the international financial community; it also signaled the end of an era. Without the former wealth from invisible trade, and the resources to maintain the illusion of a world power, Britain's diminished postimperial status became painfully apparent. The drastic budget measures of the Chancellor of the Exchequer Roy Jenkins between 1967 and 1970 succeeded in curbing consumer spending and stimulating exports. By 1970 Britain enjoyed a strong balance of payments position with a surplus of $1.5 billion.

IMMIGRATION

In 1962 the Conservatives passed the first Commonwealth Immigrants Act to restrict entry of commonwealth citizens who were without prospects of employment or means of self-support. The great influx of commonwealth immigration after 1958, especially from the West Indies and Pakistan (reaching a million by 1968) created social and racial tensions due to their concentration in congested areas of the industrial cities. In 1968 the Wilson government feared a heavy influx of Kenyan Asians and imposed further restrictions on commonwealth immigrants, in spite of protests from several commonwealth countries. At the same time the second Race Relations Act strengthened the 1965 act by banning all racial discrimination in housing and employment within the country. But racial relations deteriorated as the black immigrant population gave birth to large urban ghettos. The immigration issue helped spawn the racist National Front party, and in the seventies racial violence erupted in several cities. In 1978 Conservative party leader Margaret Thatcher called for "a clear end to immigration."

Britain and Europe

Britain had firmly committed itself through the Brussels treaty and NATO to a full military association with Western Europe, but had remained outside of the European Economic Community set up by the Treaty of Rome in 1957. Britain feared that the projected economic and political unification of the Common Market countries would conflict with its sovereignty and agricultural interests as well as with its Commonwealth connections. Instead, Britain proposed a looser association and in 1960 joined Norway, Denmark, Sweden, Austria, Switzerland, and Portugal in forming the European Free Trade Association. However, the "outer seven" failed to match the economic dynamism of the "inner six" of France, West Germany, Italy, Holland, Belgium, and Luxembourg. After making a candid reappraisal of Britain's diminishing role outside Europe, Macmillan's government made application for entry into the European Economic Community. The Labor party opposed the application. Early in 1963 the negotiations for entry came to a halt, not on account of Labor or commonwealth persuasion, but because of the veto of President de Gaulle, who resented Britain's attachment to the Atlantic Alliance with the United States.

In 1967 Wilson's Labor government, now a reluctant convert to Common Market membership, made a second application. Again de Gaulle prevented entry. De Gaulle's resignation in 1969 and the Tory election victory of 1970 provided the opportunity for a third, and this time successful, bid.

British Society

The fifties was seen as the decade of middle-class affluence and a rising gross national product. It was a period of relative contentment and prosperity after a decade of war and austerity. Many believed Prime Minister Macmillan's campaign oratory that "they never had it so good." The mood of the fifties was scientific and materialistic, not idealistic. In contrast, the "swinging sixties" became an angry, generational revolt against the staid contentment the fifties.

John Osborne's play *Look Back in Anger*, the radical *New Left Review*, and John Braine's *Room at the Top* typified the decade's rejection of the seemingly sterile and smug values of the previous generation. Its popular idols expressed anger, noise and revolt against their parents and cultural tradition. The sixties was the decade of the Beatles, the Rolling Stones, leather-jacketed rockers, long-haired mods, and rock-and-roll music. Student riots at universities and hooliganism at football matches also expressed the restlessness and discontent of society.

At the same time higher education flowered. Both Tory and Labor governments helped create and finance Britain's forty-two universities. Never before had so many working-class youth attended university. Throughout the nation class inequalities shriveled, but did not disappear. More than any other people, the British love to read. In the 1950s they read more newspapers per person than any other country. They were first among the six leading democracies in book-reading. The most historical minded of nations, the British learned much more about their past through the highly acclaimed historical investigation and writings of G. R. Elton, Sir John Neale, and Sir Lewis Namier. British philosophy dominated the postwar era with the works of Ludwig Wittgenstein, John Austin, and John Wisdom. The school of linguistic analysis became the dominant viewpoint in Britain and America.

Defense, Disarmament, and National Priorities

The rearmament of Britain following the Korean War, along with its worldwide commitments, raised again the old dilemma of "guns or butter" in an economy which could not afford both. Ban-the-Bomb marchers, the Committee on Nuclear Disarmament, and neutralists in the Labor party urged a policy of unilateral disarmament and isolationism. By 1961 the intensity of these sentiments had passed and Gaitskell reversed the Scarborough resolution of 1960 calling for unilateral disarmament. In 1963 Macmillan, "the champion of summit conferences," achieved a bipartisan objective with the nuclear test-ban treaty signed in Moscow by Britain, the United States, and the U.S.S.R. No comparable success was achieved in the general disarmament discussions which were begun at Geneva.

An independent nuclear deterrent was considered essential to Britain's defense and international stature, but the economy could scarcely sustain the massive expenditures required for such a program. In 1960 research on a British-designed "Blue Streak" missile was abandoned in favor of an American-made "Skybolt." The United States preferred that Britain support a multilateral NATO nuclear force rather than continue with its independent or Anglo-American deterrent.

By 1967 the Wilson government accepted the fact that Britain was no longer a world power and began to reduce its military obligations east of Suez. This planned withdrawal from Asia underlined the new priority of Europe over commonwealth and worldwide commitments. Through streamlining and economizing, the defense budget was cut to less than six percent of the gross national product by 1970. That year, for the first time, Britain spent more on education than on national defense; expenditures for social security had surpassed defense in 1963. The budget figures reflected realistic national priorities as well as the rise of the welfare state at home and the decline of British power abroad.

*B*ritain sustained its stature as a major power long past the time when it actually had the military or economic clout to enforce its will. The decline from greatness took place with dignity and with worldwide respect. The commonwealth of nations continued as a valued legacy even after the independence of its former colonies. In 1964 58 percent of British investments were still found in commonwealth countries.

The Labor and Conservative parties both moved toward the political center in the 1960s. Each party benefited from exceptionally able leaders in the generation after the war, in contrast to the interwar years. Within a decade of the end of World War II the welfare state had become part of British institutional life.

Britain made noteworthy strides in education, in a fairer distribution of wealth, in the expansion of social services, and in scientific achievements. These contributions, along with their creativity in contemporary culture, from London playwrights to the Beatles, now became the new British exports to America and other nations, rather than its earlier expansion of empire and the transplanting of political institutions.

Selected Readings

Bruce, Maurice. *The Coming of the Welfare State* (1968)

Bullock, Alan. *Ernest Bevin* (1960–1983)

Charlton, David. *Anthony Eden: A Biography*. 1982

Cox, C. B. and Dyson, A. E. *The Twentieth Century Mind: History, Ideas, and Literature in Britain*. vol. 3, 1945–1964 (1969)

Dalton, Hugh. *High Tide and After: Memoirs 1946–1960* (1962)

Harris, Kenneth. *Attlee* (1982)

Lindsey, Almont. *Socialized Medicine in England and Wales: The National Health Service, 1948–1961* (1962)

Lloyd, T. O. *Empire to Welfare State: English History, 1906–1985* (1986)

Marwick, Arthur. *British Society Since 1945* (1982)

Norman, Philip. *Shout! The Beatles in Their Generation* (1981)

Northedge, F. S. *Descent from Power: British Foreign Policy, 1945–1973* (1974)

Pelling, Henry. *Winston Churchill* (1974)

Sampson, Anthony *The New Anatomy of Britain Today* (1973)

_____*Macmillan: A Study in Ambiguity* (1967)

Titmuss, Richard. *Essays on "The Welfare State"* (1958)

Woodhouse, C. M. *British Foreign Policy Since the Second World War* (1962)

26

Contemporary Britain: 1970 to the Present

1969 Political terrorism and sectarian strife erupt in Ulster (Northern Ireland)

1970 Edward Heath and Conservatives defeat Wilson and Labor in general election

Equal Pay Act gives women equal pay with men for the same job

1973 Britain officially admitted as member of the European Economic Community

1974 Labor wins general election; Harold Wilson begins his third ministry

1975 Commercial oil production begins from North Sea wells

1979 Conservatives defeat Labor in general election; Margaret Thatcher becomes first female Prime Minister of Britain

1981 Wedding of Charles, Prince of Wales, to Lady Diana Spencer

Social Democratic Party (SDP) created; led by four former Labor cabinet ministers: Roy Jenkins, David Owen, William Rodgers, and Shirley Williams

1982 Britain defeats Argentina in war over control of Falkland Islands

1983 Thatcher and Tories win greatest electoral victory since 1906

1986 Britain and France sign treaty to build a rail tunnel under the English Channel

1987 Thatcher wins third successive general election

1990 Thatcher resigns; John Major elected party leader (and Prime Minister) by Conservatives

1991 Population of Britain is 57.4 million people compared to 38.2 million in 1901

These two decades (1970 to 1990) saw a Conservative party ascendancy with the two Tory prime ministers of these years, Edward Heath and Margaret Thatcher, holding office for fifteen of the twenty years. Thatcher was the first woman to serve as Prime Minister. She was also the only Prime Minster in the twentieth century to win three consecutive elections.

The move into the European Common Market in 1973 was visible evidence of Britain finally giving higher priority to the continent of Europe than to its American or commonwealth ties. Britain's future would be with Europe, not in worldwide economic or military influence. This new attachment to Europe was symbolized by the building of the Eurotunnel between England and France, ending Britain's insular separation.

Contemporary Britain no longer dominated the world economy as it did in its high tide of empire in Victorian England. But this small island, seventy-fifth in size among today's nations, continues its worldwide influence as one of the financial, publishing, theatrical, and musical capitals of the world. Its ancient institutions, such as the monarchy, have adapted to change. Its larger legacy, such as English law, language, and literature, continues to spread to every continent.

POLITICS IN THE SEVENTIES

As all three political parties changed leadership in the seventies, their political postures slowly tilted to the right, although the decade also revealed that the trade unions matched the government in power. For this decade, at least, no cabinet could govern effectively without the goodwill, or at least the neutrality, of the unions. The intractability of the centuries-old sectarian problem in Northern Ireland plagued each party in power. Even more complex a problem was the deteriorating British economy that by 1976 made national economic survival a serious question. The next year saw signs of economic recovery, resulting from efforts at self-denial and austerity not matched since the early postwar years when Cripps was at the Exchequer.

Edward Heath's Ministry

Prime Minister Wilson made a concerted effort to increase industrial efficiency. The critical problem was inflation which reached 8 percent by 1970. From 1966 to 1970 the Labor government tried to impose a wage and price freeze and restraints on unofficial strikes. In 1967 the Government took the long-postponed step to devalue the pound with some modest improvements in exports. In March 1970 Wilson called for a general election when the polls showed Labor with a comfortable 12 percent lead over the Tories. He assured the electorate that he could pilot the nation through the perilous times. Edward Heath charged Labor with responsibility for the country's inflation and strikes, and promised economic growth and a freer marketplace under a Tory government. Heath achieved a stunning upset in the election. Conservatives won 330 seats to 287 for Labor and only 6 for the Liberals.

Heath began his administration by making massive tax cuts in the hope of encouraging savings and stimulating economic activity. The government also cut its own spending. When strikes reached a high not known since 1926, the Tories countered with the Industrial Relations Act of 1971 which outlawed the closed union shop and made it illegal to compel a worker to join a union. Heath opposed government control of wages and prices and abolished Wilson's Prices and Incomes Board. The Prime Minister led the negotiations that led to entry into the European Common Market in 1973.

In spite of his mix of scientific management and laissez-faire economics he could not control inflation any better than Wilson. By 1973 it rose to 10 percent. Heath then made a complete about-face and pressed for wage and price restraints. The strategy broke down when the Arab oil embargo accelerated inflation following the Yom Kippur War in 1973.

Elections of 1974

By 1974 old ideological differences had resurfaced between the Conservatives and Labor parties. Prime Minister Heath emphasized the private sector and freedom for individual achievement, instead of reliance on the state, as the source of British economic vigor. Labor was more concerned with the distribution of wealth than its acquisition, in further nationalization, and in a more egalitarian society.

In late 1973 the British mineworkers sought a 30 to 40 percent wage increase, attempting to capitalize on the energy crisis produced by the OPEC oil embargo. Their claim was far in excess of Heath's anti-inflation guidelines. To conserve crucial energy supplies the government declared a state of emergency and put the nation on a three-day work week. In February 1974, the miners rejected the 16.5 percent raise offered and began a nationwide strike. Heath called a general election and campaigned on the issue of "Who Governs Britain?"—a single trade union or Parliament? The Labor party said they would rely on voluntary wage restraints by unions, promised further nationalization, and pledged to renegotiate more favorable terms for entry into the European Economic Community. The election results were indecisive. Conservatives won 296 seats, Labor 311, Liberals 14, and other parties 20.

Heath resigned after his efforts to form a Conservative-Liberal coalition failed, whereupon the Queen called upon Wilson, who formed the first minority government since MacDonald's in 1929. Wilson conceded to the coalminers' demands and also dismantled the controversial Industrial Relations Act, but shelved most of the campaign pledges to nationalize additional sectors of the economy. In October Wilson called a second election in a bid to win a majority in Parliament that would permit "policies for our national recovery." The results gave Wilson a narrow three-seat majority. Labor's campaign promised more nationalization of private industry and devolution of government to give local autonomy to Scotland and Wales.

NEW LEADERSHIP

Following Conservative defeats in the 1974 elections, Edward Heath lost out in balloting for party leader to Margaret Thatcher in February 1975. Mrs. Thatcher, daughter of a Lincolnshire storekeeper and former minister of education in Heath's cabinet, became the first woman to lead a major political party in Europe or North America.

In March 1976, Prime Minister Wilson suddenly resigned following the defeat in Parliament of his austerity plan to cut back public sector expenditures by £9.6 billion over a decade. Wilson had won four out of five elections as party leader and was the longest-serving Prime Minister since World War II. In the balloting among Labor members of the House of Commons for his successor, James Callaghan, a centrist in the party who had been secretary for foreign affairs in Wilson's cabinet, defeated left-winger Michael Foot to become Prime Minister. Three months later Liberal party leader Jeremy Thorpe, who had inspired a party renaissance in the 1974 elections by winning 19 percent of the popular vote, was forced to resign because of a homosexual scandal. David Steel was elected as his successor. In 1977 a "Lib-Lab" pact was worked out between Callaghan and Steel to sustain Callaghan's slim majority in the House of Commons and to prevent a no-confidence vote from succeeding and forcing an early general election.

National Affairs

The late seventies were difficult years for Britain. There seemed to be an indifference to improved productivity. Long vacations and fewer working hours were more important. Britain was compared to Italy, rather than to Germany or the United States, in per capita income and productivity. There was voter disillusionment with both major parties. Inflation seemed impossible to check, real incomes fell, and the balance of payments remained negative. The British and world press wrote about "the English disease" and an ungovernable nation. Trade unions demanded exorbitant wage increases and intimidated each government in turn with strikes and industrial paralysis.

Exasperation with the state of national affairs encouraged regionalism in the United Kingdom. In the 1974 election campaign the Labor party responded to intense regional pressures to grant limited home rule with a bill creating Scottish and Welsh assemblies that would have limited powers over many of their domestic affairs. Conservative leaders saw such devolution as a first step in legitimatizing the breakup of the United Kingdom. The Labor government delayed passage of its home rule bills until a referendum could be held in Scotland and Wales on the controversial issue. To the government's surprise the vote went against devolution in both Scotland and Wales.

A much more promising development was occurring in the North Sea. Before the 1970s Britain was almost wholly dependent on imports for its oil supplies. The first discovery of oil in the North Sea was made in 1969 and six years later commercial oil production began from the North Sea wells. By 1981 Britain was not only self-sufficient, but had become an oil exporter. In 1989 there were 44 offshore fields producing 1.18 million barrels a day. The oil revenue proved a mixed blessing. It made Britain virtually self-sufficient in energy, but at the same time it overvalued the exchange rate of the pound, creating difficulties for other British exporters.

Conflict in Northern Ireland

Submerged sectarian enmity in Ulster surfaced in 1969 when the reform-minded Prime Minister of Ulster, Terence O'Neill, tried to introduce a series of reforms to end religious and political discrimination suffered by the Roman Catholic minority. Violent clashes in Belfast and Londonderry prodded the Wilson government to call in British troops to assist in maintaining order. The tense situation was polarized further by Ian Paisley, a Presbyterian minister and militant spokesman of the Protestant extremists and by the provisional, and professedly Marxist, wing of the Irish Republican Army. It had supplanted the earlier Catholic civil rights movement and made its aim the reunification of the entire island, by violence if necessary. Its campaign of bombings and terrorism extended to British cities as well as to assassinations of English leaders, such as Earl Mountbatten of Burma and Airey Neave, Margaret Thatcher's parliamentary assistant.

Neither direct rule from Britain, begun in 1972, proportional Protestant and Catholic representation to a new Assembly in Northern Ireland in 1973, or proposals for Protestant-Catholic power-sharing could end the terror or bring civil peace to the area. In one year alone (1972) more than 10,000 shooting incidents occurred, with 312 deaths as a result. In the 1980s the overall level of violence diminished. Nevertheless, since 1969 over 2,800 people have been killed as a result of the IRA terrorist campaign and the Ulster Freedom Fighters. Both Protestants and Catholics in Northern Ireland refused to be intimidated by the terrorist tactics of the extremist wing of the Irish Republican Army. "Peace Women" Mairead Corrigan and Betty Williams won the Nobel Peace Prize in 1976 for their courageous efforts at reconciliation between Protestants and Catholics. Until an acceptable resolution could be found, both British political parties supported direct rule and the deployment of the army to maintain order.

In 1985 Prime Minister Thatcher and Prime Minister Garret FitzGerald of the Irish Republic concluded the Anglo-Irish Agreement to set up consultative intergovernment conferences to work on proposals for economic development and strengthening the influence of the Roman Catholic minority in Northern Ireland. By the agreement the Irish Republic formally recognized the sovereignty of Britain over Northern Ireland and pledged that no change in the status of Northern Ireland would be recognized unless approved by the majority of its people.

IMMIGRATION AND RACE

The social and racial tensions created by the great influx of Indian, Pakistani, Bangladesh and West Indies commonwealth immigration after 1958 erupted into racial and neighborhood violence from 1976 through 1981. From 1962 through 1981 restrictions were passed by Parliament, especially by the Tories, on immigration where no family member was in Britain or there was no assurance of gainful employment. Urban ghettos where second generation families suffered high unemployment bred the seeds of alienation and violence. The riots which involved white "skinheads" as well as immigrant neighborhoods, showed that Britain was not exempt from racial prejudice. The nation was a more violent society than it was in the 1950s as demonstrated in the hooliganism at football matches as much as in racial outbursts. Efforts to improve community relations and economic opportunity for immigrants increased stability and racial respect. In 1985 Britain elected its first Asian-born Lord Mayor of London and two years later its first four nonwhite Members of Parliament. In 1988 Britain's nonwhite population was 2.6 million.

The Welfare State and Industrial Efficiency

After World War II human welfare was fully accepted as a social responsibility of the state. In the early postwar years industrial productivity grew at a desirable pace (4 percent annually) as the welfare state was being implemented. The continuing challenge was how to achieve a satisfactory standard of living while placing restraints on public sector expenditures and competing successfully abroad. Finding a working balance between social benefits and industrial productivity was an issue for each postwar cabinet. Often proposals for maximizing social welfare were at the expense of maximum national production.

Britain's industrial inefficiency in the sixties and seventies resulted from a combination of circumstances and traditions. For two hundred years Britain has seldom had a favorable balance of visible trade. Britain prospered from its invisible trade—investments, shipping, banking, insurance—but lost this cushion when its investments were sharply diminished by two world wars and war debts, by the dollar replacing the pound as the staple of world currency, and by banking competition from New York and Zurich.

Low productivity in industry mirrored the values and habits of British management, education, and trade unions. The cult of the amateur and distrust of the specialist placed Britain at a distinct disadvantage in a highly specialized and competitive world. Indifference to efficiency reflected a lack of technical training due, in part, to the humanist tradition of the public schools and "Oxbridge," which produced well-educated graduates not likely to be attracted to the technological and vulgar world of business.

The trade unions, in turn, with a strong sense of class history, opposed and obstructed all attempts at technological innovation at the expense of manpower. Their restrictive practices and continual strikes frustrated efforts of both the government and forward-looking companies to compete internationally.

During the postwar years Britain experienced three social revolutions: one in education; another in the expansion of social services and the welfare state developed by Attlee's Labor government and its successors; and the third in a fifteen-year consumer spending spree introduced by Reginald Maulding's Tory budget of 1962, which substantially cut income taxes and tax rates on durable consumer goods. Each of these was inflationary in impact.

Britain and the European Common Market

After de Gaulle's veto of two previous bids for membership in the 1960s, Prime Minister Heath pressed hard for entry and negotiated with the European members amidst national and parliamentary debate in Britain over Britain's role on the Continent. The Conservatives generally supported entry; Labor members, including Wilson, largely opposed it. On the crucial parliamentary vote 69 Labor members defied party orders and voted for entry. The European Communities Bill passed and Britain officially became a member, along with Ireland and Denmark, on January 1, 1973.

After Labor won the 1974 election Wilson renegotiated more favorable terms of entry with the European Economic Community, and his cabinet now agreed to Britain's continued membership despite opposition from most Labor party members and trade union leaders. Wilson went over their heads to seek the first national referendum in Britain's history. After a lively public debate, the British electorate gave a resounding "Yes" vote to membership in June 1975, by a margin of 68 percent to 32 percent. Economic and political realism gradually won out over the history and identity of Britain being "in Europe but separate from it." The British had voted with their heads, not with their hearts.

THE THATCHER ERA

The election of 1979 is often compared to those of 1832, 1906, and 1945 because it set a new course for the nation, one reversing the drift toward government ownership, welfare services, and trade union power to an emphasis on less government and more individual initiative and enterprise. The election winner was Margaret Thatcher and the Tories. Her goal was to shift national priorities from a "wealth-redistributing" to a "wealth-producing" nation and to transform Britain from an outdated manufacturing economy into an efficient and competitive model.

Not only was she the first woman prime minister of Britain, she showed remarkable political leadership and talent by serving longer than any prime minister in the twentieth century and becoming the first prime minister since Lord Liverpool (1812–1827) to win three successive elections. Nicknamed "the Iron Lady," she was opinionated, direct in speech, strong in her conservative convictions, and fearless in implementing her program regardless of the political risks. Few thought that any prime minister could defy the powerful trade unions and win. Thatcher won the head-on encounter, and not only tamed the unions, but forced British socialism to change its own character and policies. For eleven years she set Britain's agenda and decided its priorities.

Election of 1979

Prime Minister Callaghan's steady and cheerful leadership through the worst years of Britain's discontent and economic paralysis (earning him the nickname "Sunny Jim") brought inflation under 10 percent for the first time in the decade and helped Britain become a net exporter. A social contract was worked out with the unions whereby they agreed to moderate their wage increases in return for the government's promise to keep inflation in check. Talk of the "English disease" and of the suicide of a nation halted. Then in the winter of 1979 Callaghan's successful three-year anti-inflation policy ended in a spasm of crippling strikes that approached the General Strike of 1926 in their paralysis of essential services and in the angry public backlash against the strikers. Garbage lay uncollected in the streets and hospital workers cut off the heat in their buildings. Only by yielding to 20 percent pay raises did the government get the strikers back to work. Labor popularity plummeted during the winter of discontent. The inability of Labor to control its own trade union supporters undermined public confidence in the government.

The failure of the government to win approval in regional plebiscites for its home rule, or devolution, bills for Scotland and Wales was the final event forcing an election. Disgruntled Scottish Nationalists withdrew their support of Callaghan's minority government. On March 28 a motion of no confidence in the government passed 311-310 in the House of Commons. Callaghan became the first prime minister ousted in a no-confidence vote since Britain's first Labor government, led by Ramsey MacDonald, was turned out 55 years earlier.

In the election campaign "Sunny Jim" Callaghan consistently outscored Thatcher in personal popularity polls. Thatcher campaigned for a freer economy and more individual accountability, as well as for less regulations in daily life and a promise to curb the powers of the unions. Labor attacked Thatcher as the "iron lady" who would be indifferent to Labor's "caring society." The election returns gave Europe its first woman prime minister and the Tories a 43-seat majority in Parliament. Trade union arrogance and a weariness by the electorate with Labor which had dominated British political life since 1964 were the major factors in Callaghan's defeat. In the Speech from the Throne the new government presented an ambitious program to reverse the tide of government intervention in British society and to emphasize the freedom of the individual instead of the responsibility of the state.

Domestic Politics

Margaret Thatcher, the daughter of a small-town grocer, had trained at Oxford as a research chemist and had served as a tax lawyer before being elected to Parliament in 1959. During Prime Minister Heath's ministry she had served as secretary of state for education and science. Her priorities as Prime Minister were clear: to provide incentives for private industry, to control inflation through monetarism (using government powers to try and keep the money supply in line with the supply of goods and services), and to reduce the number of government employees and the cost of social services and housing subsidies. Leading her cabinet of 22 members were Lord Carrington as Foreign Minister, William Whitelaw, Home Secretary, and Sir Geoffrey Howe, Chancellor of the Exchequer.

Her first act was to provide incentives for the private sector by reducing all income tax rates on wages (the highest rate went down from 83 to 60 percent) and to tame the power of the trade unions by the use of secret ballots to elect union officers and authorize strikes, banning secondary boycotts, and the dismissal of workers refusing to join closed union shops. In 1981 the government offered shares in British Aerospace as the first step in a massive privatization program.

The early years of "Thatcherism" brought decidedly mixed results. Britain became more divided socially, and the government's policies contributed to the riots that broke out in 1981 in London, Liverpool, and other cities. Inflation did decline to 8 percent by 1982 and living standards kept pace with inflation. However, efforts to combat inflation and hold down government services drove unemployment to over three million, a figure last seen during the Great Depression of the 1930s. Thatcher ruthlessly pruned underproductive nationalized industries and installed the most efficient technology, at the expense of manpower. By 1982 one in six in Britain was unemployed, but productivity per worker rose faster than in any country except Japan during these years (1980–1982). Growing resentment against the high social costs of the government's belt-tightening program and its freeze on social service expenditures, while increasing the budget for defense, caused an angry public backlash and almost open revolt in her own cabinet. Characteristically, Thatcher was unrepentant and uncompromising. By early 1982 she had become the most unpopular prime minister in the history of British opinion polls with only a 28 percent approval rating.

Labor Party Divisions

The Labor party was sharply divided after its defeat in 1979. Callaghan was replaced as party leader in 1980 by his deputy, Michael Foot, the leader of the party's left wing. Often viewed by the public as an eccentric British don more than a national leader, Foot was unable to quell the bitter power struggle between moderates and militant left-wingers in the party. Under the influence of Tony Benn, the left-wing radicals seized control of the union meetings and party conferences. The moderate policies of the Wilson and Callaghan years were repudiated when the Labor party came out in favor of unilateral disarmament, withdrawal from the European Common Market, the abolition of private schools, and the nationalization of banks and pension plans. The intraparty warfare helped Thatcher since the alternative to her right-wing government seemed even worse. The schism in the Labor party also fostered a new political party.

THE SOCIAL DEMOCRATIC PARTY

The left-wing domination of the Labor party and the Labor manifesto supporting neutralism and greater state powers caused four former Labor cabinet members—Roy Jenkins, David Owen, William Rodgers, and Shirley Williams—to resign from the party and form a new Social Democratic party (SDP). It sought to be a new center force between what Jenkins called "the ideological roller-coaster" that had characterized recent British politics. Other Labor members of Parliament joined the SDP and the new party won dramatic by-election victories in 1982. By then their parliamentary membership of 28 had allied with David Steel's Liberal party of 12 with the intent of contesting all seats in the next election.

The creation of a new party was a hazardous step since the British political system is hostile to third parties. As in the United States there is no proportional representation; only the top vote-getter in an election wins. The new party, more than anything, was a symptom of public frustration with both the Labor and Conservative parties and the desire for an alternative. The split in the Labor party weakened support for the Labor party throughout the 1980s, just as the Tory/Peelite split of 1846 and the Liberal/Liberal Unionist split of 1886 had weakened the Tories and Liberals respectively.

Foreign Policy

Lord Carrington, the Foreign Secretary, found a successful solution for Rhodesia whose white government had unilaterally declared its independence from Britain in 1965. Following a cease-fire and a constitutional conference a new charter for the colony was accepted by all parties. In 1980 Rhodesia became the independent state of Zimbabwe and elected to continue in the commonwealth.

THE FALKLAND ISLANDS WAR

In April 1982, the Argentinian military junta attacked the Falkland Islands, a British territory in the South Atlantic. Thatcher responded with a combination of diplomacy and force. At Britain's urging the EEC imposed trade restrictions and the UN Security Council demanded the withdrawal of the invading forces. Britain sent a naval task force that controlled the seas, as in Britain's glory days of old, and British troops forced the surrender of the Argentine troops on June 14. The short, successful war was highly popular in Britain and was seen as a moral victory, as much as a military one, since it stopped aggression and upheld international law. In the popular press it established Thatcher as the most resolute leader since Winston Churchill.

The Election of 1983

The "Falkland factor" contributed to Thatcher's landslide victory in this election. Her bold leadership won her great respect, even though her personality and her bossiness, seen even in lecturing senior cabinet ministers, did not produce affection. In the campaign she was assertive, aggressive, and purposeful in seeking another term to restore Britain to its rightful place of leadership and economic prosperity. She was helped greatly by Labor's inept campaign and unpopular platform that included abolishing the House of Lords, unilateral disarmament, and leaving the EEC. The Liberal-SDL alliance served to split the opposition vote, permitting Thatcher and the Conservatives to win the largest majority in parliamentary seats since Labor's victory in 1945. The outcome of the election gave Conservatives 397 seats, Labor 209, the SDP-Liberal alliance 23 (but with only 2 percent less total votes than Labor), Scottish and Welsh Nationalists 4 seats and Northern Ireland parties 17.

Thatcher reshuffled her cabinet, replacing the last remnants of the old guard that were not her brand of conservative Tory. In the new Parliament the government promised to democratize the trade unions and denationalize numerous industries. A deliberate effort was made to return to the private sector many of the industries which had been turned into public corporations by the Labor government since 1945. Between 1979 and 1989 the Thatcher government privatized 29 major businesses, including Jaguar automobiles, British Airways, and British Telecom. Employees received preferred rights to buy shares in these new companies. British shareholders jumped from 7 percent of the adult population in 1979 to 24 percent in 1990.

Banking and finance grew significantly as London maintained its role as one of the world's great banking centers. Dividends from overseas investments grew dramatically in the eighties. At the end of World War II Britain had become a debtor nation, but in the same decade that the United States under Reagan's policies became a debtor nation, Britain became the world's second largest creditor country, surpassed only by Japan. Much of this investment was poured into the American economy and into commonwealth countries. Contrary to popular opinion, British investment in the United States was greater than Japan's. In 1985, 24 percent of all new investment in the American economy was British compared to 10 percent from Japan.

THATCHER AND THE TRADE UNIONS

In Thatcher's second term a showdown with union power dominated domestic politics. The coal industry had been chronically ill since 1945. Between 1947 and 1982 the number of coal miners declined from 700,000 to 200,000. The National Union of Mineworkers, led by Arthur Scargill, its charismatic and militant Marxist president, had fought successfully to resist mine closings and to raise miners' wages. When the government sought to reduce tax subsidies to the nationalized coal industry, Scargill ordered a strike to stop further mine closings and to bring down Thatcher as the coal strike had brought down Prime Minister Heath in 1974. The strike lasted eleven months, but Scargill found Thatcher as resolute as she was in the Falkland war. Public sentiment turned strongly against Scargill. In March 1985 the strikers went back to work without a settlement. By facing down the militant core of miners, Thatcher encouraged moderate unionists and management to work out no-strike agreements and to choose consultation rather than confrontation.

The year 1986 saw the lowest number of working days lost to strikes since the 1950s. The Trade Union Act of 1984 had required the secret ballot for the first time in choosing union leadership and in voting on strikes. The decade of the eighties saw the decline in union membership and in their political power that could make or break a government in the sixties and seventies. In 1985 just 813 strikes were recorded, the fewest in 50 years. Trade union membership has fallen annually since 1979, with membership in 1989 at 10,158,000 compared to 13,289,000 a decade earlier. Forty-seven percent of Britain's workforce remained unionized in 1990 compared with 17 percent in the United States.

Other Developments in Thatcher's Second Term

Although stridently anti-Communist at times, Thatcher was also a pragmatist who adapted to changing times. She was the first of the Western leaders to declare publicly in a meeting with General Secretary Mikhail Gorbachev in 1984 that Britain could do business with the new Russia that *perestroika* and *glasnost* were creating. That same year she narrowly escaped assassination by the IRA terrorist bombing of her Brighton hotel; five Tory party associates near her were killed.

Shortly after the 1983 election Michael Foot resigned as leader of the Labor party. Neil Kinnock, an eloquent Welsh orator, in the tradition of David Lloyd George, was his replacement. Congenial and engaging on television, he devoted the years between elections to efforts to heal the split in Labor ranks between moderates and leftists. During these years (1983–1987) the SDP-Liberal alliance was headed by David Owen, the one-time Labor foreign secretary, and David Steel, the leader of the Liberals since 1976.

In 1984 Britain worked out arrangements with China on the severing of ties with one of the last of its important outposts of empire, the crown colony of Hong Kong. Britain's ninety-nine-year lease for the mainland portion of Hong Kong would end in 1997. In the 1984 treaty Britain agreed to turn over both the island and the mainland to China in 1997 in return for China's promise to maintain Hong Kong for at least fifty years as a separate "special administrative region of China," with its own "social and economic systems."

In 1986 Britain and France signed a treaty to build a Channel tunnel to provide rail transportation between the two countries. The project was the largest civil engineering project in Europe to be financed by the private sector. Service is scheduled to start in 1993 and greatly expedite the travel of passengers and freight between the Continent and the British Isles. Equally significant, the project, which had been proposed intermittently since the days of Napoleon, symbolized the linkage of Britain with the European Economic Community and the end of its historic separation from the Continent.

The Election of 1987

Following a diplomatic triumph in her five-day visit to Moscow in April 1987, Prime Minister Thatcher called for a general election for June. She campaigned on her eight-year record which had made Britain a more enterprising nation and which had cut regulations and tax rates. The majority of Britons were prospering, but at the expense of significant unemployment which had persisted at 11 percent of the workforce, totaling three million, for almost five years. The Labor leader, Neil Kinnock, waged an effective campaign and knew how to use television effectively, but the Labor platform had little new to offer except more social benefits and the return of trade-union privileges taken away by the Thatcher government. More than any single issue, Labor's "unilateral nuclear disarmament" plank turned off undecided voters in the campaign.

The outcome was a third Conservative victory in a row. Again, only a minority of the voters (42.3 percent) supported the Tories. Labor with 30.8 percent and the SDP-Liberal alliance with 22.6 percent split the opposition vote to give the Conservatives a majority of 105 in the new Parliament. Thatcher became the first prime minister in 160 years to triumph in three successive general elections.

The Third Thatcher Ministry

Although the divided political opposition permitted the Conservatives to win handily, the Thatcher government had substantial voter loyalty. Many were sympathetic with her taming of the trade unions. It was now clear that the government was sovereign and did not govern by the sufferance of the unions. There was also growing support for her policies that encouraged social mobility. She argued that society needed "a ladder of opportunity" as much as it needed "a safety net." But not even Thatcher dared to undo the fundamentals of the postwar welfare state such as the National Health Service or the long, paid summer vacations which averaged four or more weeks for manual workers by 1985. After the election she continued with the immensely popular plan of enabling renters living in public housing to purchase their own homes. In eight years the percentage of homeowners had grown from half to two-thirds. To build a property-holding democracy was one of her announced goals.

The most controversial new law was the Local Government Finance Act (1988) which established a time table to replace property taxes as the main source of revenue for local government with a new poll tax levied on every citizen between 18 and 65. Its political intent was to make the local councils, most of them dominated by Labor, accept responsibility for their spending. But the tax was clearly regressive, benefiting the wealthy and hurting the poor. When the tax went into effect, a "Boston tea party" of tax resisters that began as a decorous protest by 40,000 opponents ended up in serious violence and trashing of the city of London. The unrest drew attention to a new and more violent unemployed underclass. Thatcher's policies benefited some 70 percent of the population, but 20 percent lived below the poverty line and were worse off under the Tories who had cut spending on the public sector from 43 to 38 percent of national income.

The Education Reform Act of 1988 became law after 170 hours of parliamentary debate and 5,000 amendments. An earlier 1986 act reformed the composition of school governing bodies and required the appraisal of teaching performance. The 1988 Act provided for the establishment of a national curriculum (with three core subjects—English, Mathematics, and Science—and seven other foundation subjects) for children aged 5 to 16 in state schools and regular assessment of student performance. More parental choice in school selection was introduced with the authority for local school boards to opt out of the local education district and make their schools self-governing charitable trusts.

More technical and vocational education was offered and funded; city technology colleges were set up in urban areas, sponsored by industry and commerce. In higher education, the system of university funding was changed by the 1988 act. The long-standing University Grants Committee was replaced by the Universities Funding Council, with executive powers to allocate finances to individual universities. During a five-year span (1985–1990) the whole spectrum of elementary, secondary and higher education underwent the most far-reaching reform since the Second World War.

In foreign affairs Thatcher remained a steady ally of the United States. In the Gulf War of 1990 against Saddam Husein and Iraq, Britain provided more troops than any other allied nation except the United States.

Thatcher supported the recommendations proposed at the European Council at Milan in 1985 to move toward a single European Economic Community market with the free movement of goods, people, services and capital without passports or customs. The goal for completing this free market among the twelve member states was set for December 1992. When realized it will offer a greater tariff-free single market than the United States.

Although Thatcher supported this step without enthusiasm, her Anglocentric loyalties made her often abrasive in meetings with European leaders. She did not sense that other European leaders gave Britain its proper recognition and she had no interest in a future political union that would limit British sovereignty. In November 1990, at a summit meeting in Rome, Thatcher alone voted "no" to a timetable that would produce a single European currency by the year 2000. In protest Sir Geoffrey Howe, deputy Prime Minister, resigned, convinced that Britain must become a full-fledged player in the twelve-nation European Community. In Parliament he attacked her reflexive insularity on European issues and deplored her "nightmare image of a Continent . . . teeming with ill-intentioned people." A palace revolt against her leadership was in the making.

Prime Minister Thatcher faced a sudden challenge for the leadership of her party, and the country, in November 1990. Eleven years of political success was not sufficient to command ongoing party loyalty. Kinnock and the Labor party dropped their unpopular disarmament and nationalization proposals, and for the first time in many years public opinion polls favored Labor. The hated poll tax had created broad-based resistance across Britain. Michael Heseltine had resigned from Thatcher's cabinet in 1986 over disagreement on economic matters. Howe's resignation as deputy Prime Minister caused a sharp split among Tory members of Parliament. Resentment over her schoolteacher bossiness had alienated many of her colleagues. In the annual election for the leadership held before each new session of Parliament Thatcher faced serious opposition for the first time. Michael Heseltine, former defense minister, challenged her for the leadership. Thatcher won the most votes, but not the needed majority. Sensing she was vulnerable, Thatcher resigned to let her loyal cabinet supporters also compete for the leadership, preferring John Major, Chancellor of the Exchequer, or Foreign Secretary Douglas Hurd over Heseltine as her successor. On the second ballot on November 27 John Major came within two votes of a majority. Reading the results, Heseltine and Hurd withdrew their names and John Major, at age forty-seven, became party leader and Prime Minister.

THE THATCHER LEGACY

Thatcher lost for essentially two reasons: first were her views on Europe. As the EEC moved toward greater unity, she was increasingly at odds with European leaders and with the younger members of her own party who saw their destiny in a united Europe. The second reason was the cold political judgment of Tory members of Parliament that a new and younger leader would have a better chance to win the next general election against a rejuvenated Labor party.

The Thatcher legacy made an indelible imprint on British life. She tamed the unions and restored Parliament as the sovereign power in the nation. Her belief in market economics and the role of wealth creation rather than its distribution raised Britain's productivity and greatly expanded its citizens' ownership in their own homes and in purchasing shares in British industry. After the drift and permissive society of the sixties and seventies her aggressive, even if abrasive, leadership restored the nation's pride after being termed "the sick man of Europe" for two decades. Above all, she was fearless in adversity, even in her final weeks in office. At the same time a decade of Thatcherism had done little to diminish the gap between the rich and the poor. The growth of meritocracy in Thatcher's entrepreneurial world favored the successful, rather than the unsuccessful, in society.

Her successor's low-key amiability contrasted sharply with Thatcher's imperious style. Less ideological and combative than Thatcher, Major was also her protegé. He immediately reduced the hated poll tax that was so unpopular and announced that the poll would be scrapped by 1993. Major was clearly more conciliatory than Thatcher on Britain's relationship with the EEC. In a speech in June 1991 he made clear that Britain "cannot turn its back on the construction of a new Europe. That is where our history points, and our interest lies." His first budget showed little change of direction except in tone and taxation adjustments, which were more generous to the underprivileged and less so to the wealthy. Following the attempted coup in the Soviet Union in August 1991, Major was the first leader of the West to visit Gorbachev and Boris Yeltsin and to offer food and aid to the Russian people.

THE QUEEN'S GOVERNMENT

The Silver Jubilee festivities in 1977 to celebrate Queen Elizabeth II's twenty-fifth year as monarch dramatized for Great Britain and the commonwealth the dignity, ceremony, and continuity of British constitutional history. Again, in 1981, the worldwide interest in the wedding of Charles, Prince of Wales, to Lady Diana Spencer and the constant media coverage of the "royals" reveals the semimystical fascination of Britons and tourists for the institution of the monarchy. Despite recurring criticism, the monarchy is one of the few institutions that has not been damaged by the postimperial decline from greatness or seriously attacked in a technological and democratic world as an irrelevant institution.

The British system which separates power from glory helps to prevent political leaders from exploiting the mystique of the state and creating an imperial presidency or prime ministership as has occurred in other countries at times. The Queen is the head of state; the Prime Minister is the head of government. Voters show their displeasure with the government and its leaders without showing disrespect for the head of state. Prime ministers come and go, but the monarchy offers its subjects a sense of continuity and respect for a ruler who is above politics and is not partisan or campaigning to win an election. More than any other single tie, the Queen holds together the multiracial commonwealth and remains intensely interested in the welfare of its former territories. The use of the monarchy in state visits, with all its ceremonies and its separation from politics, has been a continuing asset in strengthening British diplomacy.

Role of the Monarchy

The Queen is not only the head of state, but also a symbol of the nation's history and unity as the most ancient secular institution in Britain with only one break in its continuity (1649–1660). The hereditary principle continues to be observed. The royal title in Britain is "Elizabeth the Second, by the Grace of God of the United Kingdom of Great Britain and Northern Ireland and of Her other Realms and Territories Queen, Head of the Commonwealth, Defender of the Faith." Over the centuries the title or claim to the Crown derives partly from statute and partly from British common law rules of descent. Any change from the current order of succession can only be altered by common consent of the commonwealth nations.

The Queen personifies the state, not the government. However, by law she is also head of the executive, head of the judiciary, a necessary part of the legislature, and the "supreme governor" of the established Church of England. The Queen can no longer act unilaterally on policy matters, but only on the advice of her ministers. In practice Britain is governed by Her Majesty's Government in the name of the Queen. Several important acts of government still require the Queen's participation. These include summoning, proroguing (discontinuing until the next session) and dissolving Parliament; giving royal assent to all bills passed by Parliament, and appointing the prime minister. The Queen appoints many officeholders, judges, and senior clergy, confers peerages and knighthood; and as head of state she has the power to declare war and to recognize foreign states. She gives audiences to her ministers, receives ambassadors, reads cabinet dispatches, and meets weekly with the prime minister.

Parliament

Parliament is the supreme legislative authority made up of the elected House of Commons, the largely hereditary House of Lords, and the Queen. There are no legal restraints, imposed by a written constitution, on the powers of Parliament. It can make, abolish, or change any law. The validity of any act of Parliament duly passed cannot be disputed in the law courts. The almost complete concentration of power in the prime minister and the cabinet in this century, and the decline in importance of the backbencher and of parliamentary debate, have provoked much discussion of the role and future of Parliament. The changes that have occurred, however, have been largely a result of the extension of popular sovereignty and the growth of party organization.

If the main function of the government is to govern effectively, it follows that any party in power will arrange the political and administrative machinery of the state in order to facilitate this function. No party would risk making arbitrary changes that were obviously against the will or best interests of the electorate or unannounced in the election campaign or they would risk voter alienation and repudiation at the next election. Parliament has tended to act in accordance with precedent. Change based on continuity has served as the axiom in British constitutional history.

THE HOUSE OF COMMONS

The House of Commons is elected by universal adult suffrage and consists of 650 members of Parliament (523 are from England, 38 from Wales, 72 from Scotland, and 17 represent Northern Ireland). The long-standing criticism that only people of means could afford to sit in the House of Commons because of the meager salary was muted in 1964 by the raising of the annual salary from £1,750 to £3,250, with a further increase to £5,750 in 1975. Thereafter salaries jumped dramatically. Since 1990 members of the House of Commons are paid £26,701. Cabinet members receive salaries ranging from £38,961 a year to £55,221, with the prime minister's salary set at £66,851. The chief officer of the House of Commons is the Speaker, elected by members of Parliament of all parties to preside over the House. The maximum sum a candidate can spend on a general election campaign is £3,648 plus 3 pence for each elector in a borough constituency or 4 pence for each elector in a county constituency.

THE HOUSE OF LORDS

In 1990 there were 1,189 members of the House of Lords, including the two archbishops and 24 bishops (the Lords Spiritual). The Lords Temporal consist of 764 hereditary peers who had succeeded to their titles, 20 hereditary peers who have had their titles conferred, such as the Prince of Wales, and 379 life peers. The House is presided over by the Lord Chancellor, who takes his place on the woolsack—a tradition dating from the Middle Ages, when wool was the chief source of the national wealth—and presides as ex-officio Speaker of the House. His salary exceeds the prime minister's by £25,000.

Recent changes in the Lords included the creation of life peers and peeresses as regular members in 1958, followed in 1963 by the Peerage Act which permitted hereditary peers to disclaim their titles and stand for election to the House of Commons. Viscount Stansgate (Anthony Wedgwood-Benn) and Viscount Hailsham (Quinton Hogg), both prominent politicians, were the first to relinquish the peerages they had inherited.

LOCAL GOVERNMENT

The late Victorian structure of local government which had served its function admirably when instituted in 1888 and 1894 had become inadequate by 1945 and lacked any structural arrangement for overall strategic planning between town and countryside. A royal commission on reform of local government under the chairmanship of Lord Redcliffe-Maud in 1969 resulted in the Local Government Act of 1972, which established a lower tier of borough councils. Greater efficiency and coordination in local government was the intent of this legislation.

Until 1986 Greater London and the metropolitan counties had their own councils, but these were abolished by the Local Government Act of 1985, which under Thatcher was designed to create a more economical and accountable system of government by removing yet another tier of local government. The bill was attacked for undue interference by the central government in local affairs and as a political move since the London and metropolitan counties were routinely controlled by Labor.

CONTEMPORARY BRITAIN

In 1991 the population of the United Kingdom of Great Britain and Northern Ireland was 57 million, of whom over 80 percent were urbanites. The most striking urban development since World War II was the growth of conurbation—the peripheral expansion of towns into a single, built-up area with common industrial interests. The human problems resulting from uncontrolled urban growth produced serious efforts at city and environmental planning. Imaginative new architecture dominates city skylines intermixed with historic buildings; new towns, such as Stevenage and Crawley, were established by statute as satellites of major cities. American-style "strip" cities along highways have been controlled by "green-belt" legislation that incorporated 12 percent of the land area. In 1969 the Civic Amenities Act gave additional powers to authorities to preserve or improve standards of environment in town and country. More recently the Control of Pollution Act (1974), the Environmental Protection Bill (1990) and two Clear Air acts have set out a wide range of powers and duties for local authorities, including control over waste, air pollution and noise.

A major postwar social revolution occurred quietly in education. The percentage of fifteen- to eighteen-year-old children attending secondary schools doubled between 1938 and 1956. The Labor party endorsed the comprehensive secondary school which offers all types of educational programs and makes no attempt to place students in particular curriculums based upon their performance in national exams. Under Thatcher a national curriculum with core subjects and individual students performance assessments was passed in the 1980s. Compared to other industrial nations, Britain was undereducated. The increase in enrollment and the belated effort to catch up in technical and vocational education, however, are signs of major change.

No longer was university education impervious to the social forces already permeating every other institution. University enrollment more than tripled between 1939 and 1980; and new postwar universities, such as the University of Sussex, were founded to accommodate the swelling student population. Full scholarship grants greatly increased access to university. By 1990 there were forty-seven universities in Great Britain and the Open University (University of the Air) established in 1969, made higher education available to another 80,000 by 1989 through extramural studies on television. In 1988 female students represented 46 percent of all full-time first-degree university enrollment.

Contemporary Britons were living longer—life expectation was seventy-two for men and seventy-nine for women in 1990, compared to forty-nine years and fifty-two years respectively at the beginning of the century. They were also more than twice as well off, in terms of material well-being, in 1990 as compared to 1951. According to the United Nations report of 1990, Britain ranked tenth out of 130 nations on an index based on social indicators such as life span, literacy, and purchasing power. Through most of the eighties the nation maintained a growth rate of over 3 percent, among the highest in the European Community. If religion suffered a continued decline in weekly communicants with only one in ten attending regularly, the British people religiously honored their loyalty to leisure and sports. By 1985, 95 percent of Britain's manual workers were entitled to more than a month of paid vacation. The popularity of the weekend for leisure and for sporting events continued to characterize the nation.

Britons were also healthier, enjoying cleaner air, and having more career choices than earlier generations. Although the nation continued to be a class-conscious society, social mobility, based on merit rather than inherited social rank or family position, has advanced noticeably in the past two decades.

Social factors, however, are hard to weigh in the balance sheet. Contemporary Britain also suffers an erosion of civility in public life and the emergence of an underclass, termed "yobs" or "lager louts" prone to violence. Reported crime has doubled in thirty years, although it is still very low by American standards. Families could take pride in their own home, in creature comforts like central heat and color television in 91 percent of all households. These same families were far more likely to be broken by divorce, and concerned about the breakdown of civility and moderation in flaunting the new wealth. An open affection for materialism and its trappings was increasingly lamented and the new affluence did not seem to translate into a sense of contentment or well-being in society.

This same nation that is so highly politicized and tolerated selfish special-interest power plays, such as in the trade union actions of the postwar years, could also, in an act of national restraint, face up to the internal economic threat to their survival in the seventies, even as they did so successfully in World War II against external threats to their survival. A remarkable resiliency and capacity for national renewal and renaissance of spirit continue to characterize the British people

British Culture

The mood of the fifties was materialistic, scientific and conformist, a time when Nevil Shute was Britain's best-selling novelist and the fascination of television made it the most popular pastime. The sixties saw a generational revolt that was both idealistic and angry, represented by the music of Mike Jagger and the writings of John Osborne. Discontent grew deeper and surfaced in students rioting at universities and rockers attacking mods at seaside resorts. Nevertheless, creativity and intellectual stimulation continue to do well in the British environment. London remains the publishing, musical, and theatrical capital of the world, and the British continue to win more Nobel prizes per capita than any other nation. In 1982 the Barbican Arts and Conference Center opened as perhaps the outstanding arts complex in Western Europe. Composers like Andrew Lloyd Weber (*Cats* and *Jesus Christ Superstar*) and Samuel Beckett (*Waiting for Godot*) retain the British tradition in the arts for inventiveness, wit, and imagination. In marked contrast to totalitarian societies, individualism and nonconformity are honored attributes and continue to be hallmarks of British society, as witnessed in the colorful careers of a Sir Winston Churchill or the Rolling Stones.

The British Achievement

Continuity and change, marked by a series of historic compromises, such as the Magna Charta and the Great Reform Bill, have been the hallmarks of the British achievement. Moderation and pragmatism in the pursuit of political and social goals are respected as virtues in British political life. As a result Britain in recent centuries has been spared much of the violence and rancor that accompany the clash of doctrinaire or dogmatic positions as is seen in so many countries and was dramatically observed in sixteenth-century England. In times of crisis, as in the Battle of Britain, the love of freedom and independence provided a unity and resiliency that was not evident to enemies who mistook mere dissent in public debate as a sign of debilitating division.

Parliamentary government, common law, a rich literary tradition, and the English language—and their expansion overseas—have been enduring tributes to Britain and its peoples. Since 1945 Britain's distinctive achievements have been its commitment to domestic social democracy, the successful restructuring of the commonwealth to encompass fifty largely non-white nations, and an industrial and economic renaissance in the eighties that once again made the originator of the Industrial Revolution a competitive force in the world economy.

Can British institutions and democratic forms continue to adapt to such rapidly changing conditions as the movement toward European unity and a scientific culture without sacrificing the distinctive qualities and traditions of the British way of life? In the eighties Britain proved that historical "structural" problems in education, industrial management, and union power were not so encrusted that they could not be adapted to the demands of the contemporary world. In one sense the old ideals of parliamentary democracy and the civilizing mission of the British empire have been either achieved or abandoned. The 1990s will determine what new ideals and vision, national or international, can provide meaning and purpose for this island nation. How the British people respond to these challenges will determine the shape and significance of their future achievements.

Contemporary Britain by 1990 was more than twice as prosperous materially as it had been when Elizabeth II began her reign in 1952. It was also a healthier and better-educated society, as well as a nation that had emerged from the voluntary divestment of the world's greatest empire with few scars and with remarkable dignity.

To "muddle through" the last three centuries of social and political changes without in its peculiarly British fashion revolution or radical institutional changes attests to the remarkable continuity and equilibrium of the British nation. No other nation today can match such a record of three hundred years of peaceful political and social change. Britain's constitutional legacy, and its cultural achievements continue to make their mark on other societies beyond its shores.

Selected Readings

Bedarida, Francois. *A Social History of England 1851–1975* (1979)

Blake, Robert. *The Conservative Party from Peel to Thatcher* (1985)

Butler, David, and Donald Stokes. *Political Change in Britain* (1974)

Central Office of Information, Foreign and Commonwealth Office. *Britain, 1991: An Official Handbook* (1991)

Central Statistical Office, Her Majesty's Government. *Social Trends 21* (1991)

Cole, John. *The Thatcher Years* (1987)

Colville, John. *The New Elizabethans, 1952–1977* (1977)

Cronin, James E. *Labour and Society in Britain, 1918–1979* (1984)

Gilbert, Alan D. *The Making of Post-Christian Britain* (1980)

Hey, John D. *Britain in Context* (1979)

Sampson, Anthony. *The Changing Anatomy of England* (1981)

Shrapnel, Norman. *The Seventies: Britain's Inward March* (1980)

Townshend, Charles. *Political Violence in Ireland: Government and Resistance Since 1948* (1983)

Appendix A

SELECTED READINGS

Blake, Robert. *The Conservative Party from Peel to Thatcher* (1985)

Briggs, Asa. *A Social History of England* (1983)

Bullock, Alan, and Maurice Shock. *The Liberal Tradition from Fox to Keynes* (1956)

Butterfield, Herbert. *The Origins of Modern Science, 1300 –1800* (1949)

Cam, Helen. *England Before Elizabeth* (1960)

Chicus, Philip. *England's Churches* (1984)

Churchill, Winston S. *A History of the English-Speaking Peoples*, 4 vols. (1956–1958)

Clark, George N. (ed.). *The Oxford History of England*, 15 vols. (1937–1965)

Cox, C. B., and A. E. Dyson. *The Twentieth Century Mind: History, Ideas and Literature* 3 vols. (1969)

Daiches, David. *A Critical History of English Literature* (1970)

Graham, Gerald S. *A Concise History of the British Empire* (1970)

Haskins, George L. *The Growth of English Representative Government* (1948)

Kanner, Barbara (ed.). *The Women of England from Anglo-Saxon Times to the Present: Interpretive Biographical Essays* (1979)

Lloyd, T. O. *The British Empire, 1558 –1983* (1984)

Mackenzie, Robert T. *British Political Parties* (1964)

McCaffrey, Lawrence. *Ireland: From Colony to Nation State* (1979)

Mitchison, Rosalind *A History of Scotland* (1982)

Roberts, Clayton, and David Roberts. *A History of England*, 2 vols. (1985)

Rowse, Alfred L. *The Heritage of Britain* (1977)

Sampson, Anthony. *The Changing Anatomy of England* (1981)

Smith, Goldwin. *A Constitutional and Legal History of England* (1955)
Strang, William. *Britain in World Affairs* (1961)
Trevelyan, George M. *History of England*, 3 vols. (1926)
Trevor-Roper, Hugh. *Essays in British History* (1965)
Williams, David. *History of Modern Wales* (1950)

Appendix B

SOVEREIGNS OF ENGLAND AND GREAT BRITAIN

Anglo-Saxons and Danes

KENT

Ethelbert, 560–616

NORTHUMBRIA

Ethelfrith, 593–617
Edwin, 617–633
Oswald, 635–642
Oswy, 642–670
Ecgfrith, 670–685

MERCIA

Penda, 626–655
Ethelbald, 716–757
Offa II, 757–796
Cenulf, 796–821

WESSEX

Ine, 688–726
Egbert, 802–839
Ethelwulf, 839–858
Ethelbald, 858–860
Ethelbert, 860–866
Ethelred I, 866–871
Alfred the Great, 871–899

Edward, 899–924
Ethelstan, 924–939
Edmund, 939–946
Edred, 946–955
Edwig, 955–959
Edgar, 959–975
Edward, 975–978
Ethelred II, 978–1016
Edmund, 1016
Canute, 1017–1035
Harold I, 1035–1040
Harthacanute, 1040–1042
Edward the Confessor, 1042–1066
Harold II, 1066

Normandy

William I, 1066–1087
William II, 1087–1100
Henry I, 1100–1135

Blois

Stephen, 1135–1154

Plantagenet (Anjou)

Henry II, 1154–1189

Richard I, 1189–1199
John, 1199–1216
Henry III, 1216–1272
Edward I, 1272–1307
Edward II, 1307–1327
Edward III, 1327–1377
Richard II, 1377–1399

Lancaster

Henry IV, 1399–1413
Henry V, 1413–1422
Henry VI, 1422–1461

York

Eward IV, 1461–1483
Edward V, 1483
Richard III, 1483–1485

Tudor

Henry VII, 1485–1509
Henry VIII, 1509–1547
Edward VI, 1547–1553
Mary, 1553–1558
Elizabeth I, 1558–1603

Stuart

James I, 1603–1625
Charles I, 1625–1649

Interregnum (Commonweath and Protectorate)

Council of State, 1649
Protectorate, 1653
Oliver Cromwell, 1653–1658
Richard Cromwell, 1658–1659

Stuart

Charles II, 1660–1685
James II, 1685–1688
William III and Mary, 1689–1702
Anne, 1702–1714

Hanover

George I, 1714–1727
George II, 1727–1760
George III, 1760–1820
George IV, 1820–1830
William IV, 1830–1837
Victoria, 1837–1901

Saxe-Coburg

Edward VII, 1901–1910

Windsor

George V, 1910–1936
Edward VIII, 1936
George VI, 1936–1952
Elizabeth II, 1952–

Appendix C

PRIME MINISTERS OF GREAT BRITAIN

Robert Walpole, 1721–1742
Lord Wilmington, 1742–1744
Henry Pelham, 1744–1754
Duke of Newcastle, 1754–1756
Duke of Devonshire, 1756–1757
Duke of Newcastle, 1757–1761
Duke of Newcastle, 1761–1762
Lord Bute, 1762–1763
George Grenville, 1763–1765
Lord Rockingham, 1765–1766
William Pitt, Earl of Chatham, 1766–1768
Duke of Grafton, 1768–1770
Lord North, 1770–1782
Lord Rockingham, 1782
Lord Shelburne, 1782–1783
Duke of Portland, 1783
William Pitt, the Younger, 1783–1801
Henry Addington, 1801–1804
William Pitt, the Younger, 1804–1806
Lord Grenville, 1806–1807
Duke of Portland, 1807–1809
Spencer Perceval, 1809–1812
Lord Liverpool, 1812–1827
George Canning, 1827
Lord Goderich, 1827–1828

Duke of Wellington, 1828–1830
Earl Grey, 1830–1834
Lord Melbourne, 1834
Sir Robert Peel, 1834–1835
Lord Melbourne, 1835–1841
Sir Robert Peel, 1841–1846
Lord John Russell, 1846–1852
Lord Derby, 1852
Lord Aberdeen, 1852–1855
Lord Palmerston, 1855–1858
Lord Derby, 1858–1859
Lord Palmerston, 1859–1865
Lord John Russell, 1865–1866
Lord Derby, 1866–1868
Benjamin Disraeli, 1868
William E. Gladstone, 1868–1874
Benjamin Disraeli, 1874–1880
William E. Gladstone, 1880–1885
Lord Salisbury, 1885–1886
William E. Gladstone, 1886
Lord Salisbury, 1886–1892
William E. Gladstone, 1892–1894
Lord Rosebery, 1894–1895
Lord Salisbury, 1895–1902
Arthur J. Balfour, 1902–1905

Henry Campbell-Bannerman, 1905–1908
Herbert H. Asquith, 1908–1916
David Lloyd George, 1916–1922
Andrew Bonar Law, 1922–1923
Stanley Baldwin, 1923–1924
James Ramsey MacDonald, 1924
Stanley Baldwin, 1924–1929
James Ramsay MacDonald, 1929–1931
James Ramsay MacDonald, 1931–1935
Stanley Baldwin, 1935–1937
Neville Chamberlain, 1937–1940
Winston Churchill, 1940–1945

Clement Attlee, 1945–1951
Sir Winston Churchill, 1951–1955
Sir Anthony Eden, 1955–1957
Harold Macmillan, 1957–1963
Sir Alec Douglas-Home, 1963–1964
Harold Wilson, 1964–1970
Edward Heath, 1970–1974
Harold Wilson, 1974–1976
James Callaghan, 1976–1979
Margaret Thatcher, 1979–1990
John Major, 1990–

Appendix D

THE COMMONWEATH OF NATIONS (with dates of independence)

*T*he commonwealth is a voluntary association of fifty independent states with a combined population of some 1,300,000,000, nearly a quarter of the world total. The Queen is recognized as head of the commonwealth by all fifty states; in addition she is also Head of State in seventeen of these countries. Their fully independent status in relation to Britain was legally formulated in the Statute of Westminster of 1931.

Queen Elizabeth II is head of state of:

United Kingdom of Great Britain and
    Northern Ireland
Antigua and Barbuda (1981
Australia (1901)
Bahama (1973)
Barbados (1966)
Belize (1981)
Canada (1867)
Fiji (1970)
Grenada (1974)
Jamaica (1962)
Mauritius (1968)
New Zealand (1907)
Papua New Guinea 1975)
Saint Lucia (1979)
Saint Vincent and the Grenadines (1979)

Solomon Islands (1978)
Tuvalu (1978)

Republics and National Monarchies in the Commonwealth

Bangladesh (1971)
Botswana (1966)
Brunei (1985)
Cyprus (1960)
Dominica (1978)
The Gambia (1965)
Ghana (1957)
Guyana (1966)
India (1947)
Kenya (1963)
Kiribati (1979)
Lesotho (1966)

Malawi (1964)

Malaysia (1957)

Maldives (1985)

Malta (1964)

Namibia (1990)

Nauru (1968)

Nigeria (1960)

Saint Kitts (1986)

Seychelles (1976)

Sierra Leone (1961)

Singapore (1963)

Sri Lanka (1948)

Swaziland (1968)

Tanzania (1961)

Tonga (1970)

Trinidad and Tobago (1962)

Uganda (1962)

Vanuatu (1980)

Western Samoa (1962)

Zambia (1964)

Zimbabwe (1980)

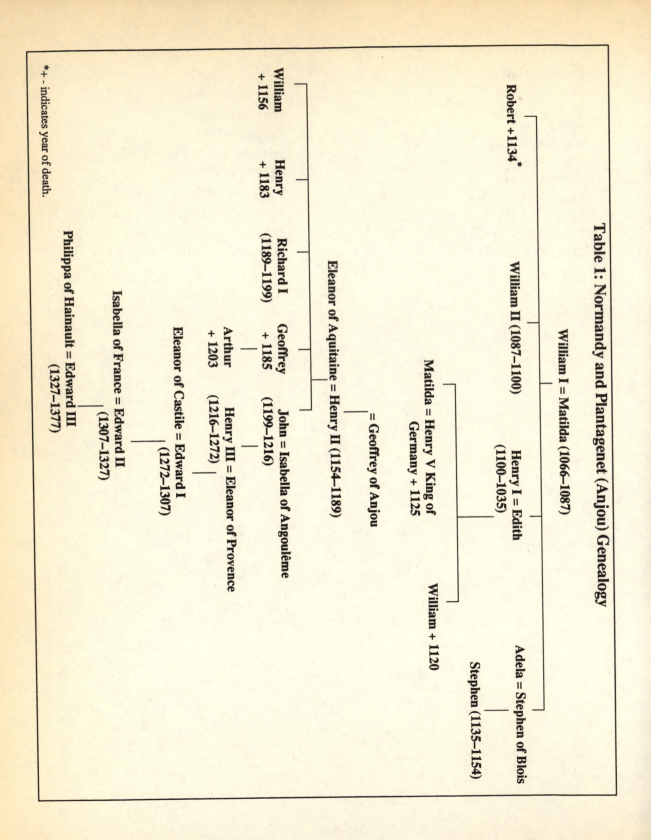

Table 1: Normandy and Plantagenet (Anjou) Genealogy

428

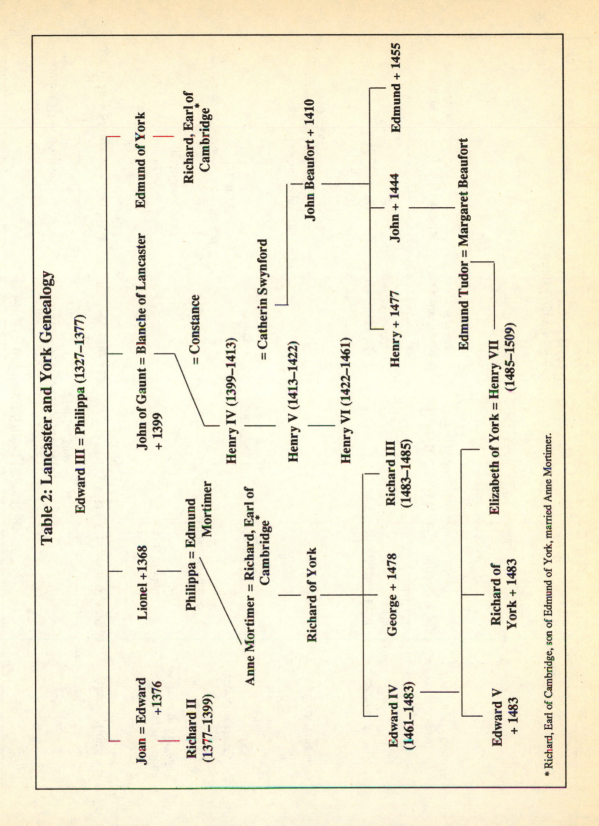

Table 2: Lancaster and York Genealogy

Edward III = Philippa (1327–1377)

Joan = Edward
+1376

Richard II
(1377–1399)

Lionel +1368

Philippa = Edmund
Mortimer

Anne Mortimer = Richard, Earl of
Cambridge*

Richard of York

George + 1478

Edward IV
(1461–1483)

Edward V
+ 1483

Richard of
York + 1483

John of Gaunt = Blanche of Lancaster
+ 1399

= Constance

Henry IV (1399–1413)

= Catherin Swynford

Henry V (1413–1422)

Henry VI (1422–1461)

Richard III
(1483–1485)

Elizabeth of York = Henry VII
(1485–1509)

Edmund of York

Richard, Earl of*
Cambridge

John Beaufort + 1410

Edmund + 1455

John + 1444

Henry + 1477

Edmund Tudor = Margaret Beaufort

* Richard, Earl of Cambridge, son of Edmund of York, married Anne Mortimer.

429

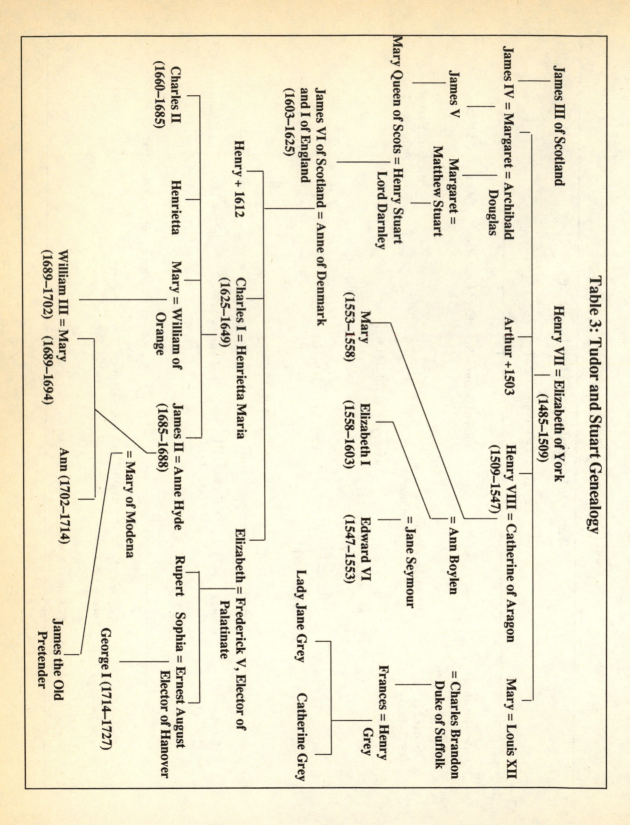

Table 3: Tudor and Stuart Genealogy

Table 4: Hanover, Saxe-Coburg, and Windsor Genealogy

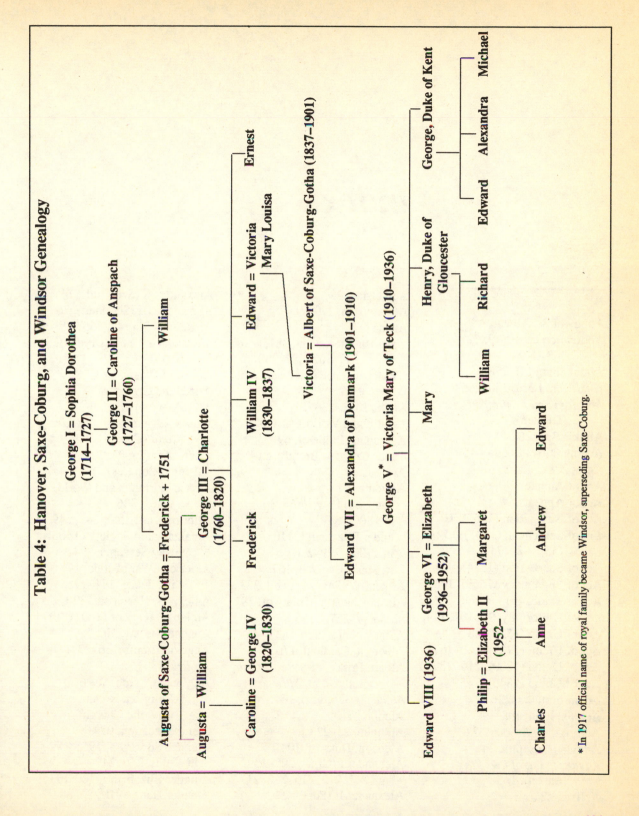

George I = Sophia Dorothea
(1714–1727)

George II = Caroline of Anspach
(1727–1760)

William

Augusta of Saxe-Coburg-Gotha = Frederick + 1751

George III = Charlotte
(1760–1820)

Augusta = William

Caroline = George IV
(1820–1830)

Frederick

William IV
(1830–1837)

Edward = Victoria
Mary Louisa

Ernest

Victoria = Albert of Saxe-Coburg-Gotha (1837–1901)

Edward VII = Alexandra of Denmark (1901–1910)

George V* = Victoria Mary of Teck (1910–1936)

Edward VIII (1936)

George VI = Elizabeth
(1936–1952)

Mary

Henry, Duke of
Gloucester

George, Duke of Kent

Philip = Elizabeth II
(1952–)

Margaret

William

Richard

Edward

Alexandra

Michael

Charles

Anne

Andrew

Edward

* In 1917 official name of royal family became Windsor, superseding Saxe-Coburg.

431

Index